# Interaction in Psychotherapy

The therapist–client relationship in psychotherapy is considered one of the most important factors in promoting well-being and facilitating change in clients. This pioneering book provides a novel perspective on relationships by focusing on how they are accomplished through client–therapist interactions. Drawing on the key concept of *affiliation* from conversation analysis, it provides new insights into how therapists and clients forge affiliations in the course of therapy and how therapists successfully re-establish affiliation with their clients following disagreement or opposition – or fail to do so. It is the first book of its kind to offer a systematic overview of the range of interactional practices found in a particular psychotherapeutic approach (Emotion Focused Psychotherapy, EFT). By forming linkages between psychotherapy concepts and conversation analysis, this timely study is of importance not only to scholars of linguistics and interaction, but also to clinicians and clinical researchers.

PETER MUNTIGL is currently Visiting Professor at Ghent University and Adjunct Professor at the Faculty of Education, Simon Fraser University. He is an Associate Editor for the journal *Frontiers in Psychology* (Psychology for Clinical Settings).

# Interaction in Psychotherapy

*Managing Relationships in Emotion-focused Treatments of Depression*

Peter Muntigl
*Ghent University and Simon Fraser University*

CAMBRIDGE
UNIVERSITY PRESS

CAMBRIDGE
UNIVERSITY PRESS

Shaftesbury Road, Cambridge CB2 8EA, United Kingdom

One Liberty Plaza, 20th Floor, New York, NY 10006, USA

477 Williamstown Road, Port Melbourne, VIC 3207, Australia

314–321, 3rd Floor, Plot 3, Splendor Forum, Jasola District Centre,
New Delhi – 110025, India

103 Penang Road, #05–06/07, Visioncrest Commercial, Singapore 238467

Cambridge University Press is part of Cambridge University Press & Assessment, a department of the University of Cambridge.

We share the University's mission to contribute to society through the pursuit of education, learning and research at the highest international levels of excellence.

www.cambridge.org
Information on this title: www.cambridge.org/9781107098428

DOI: 10.1017/9781316161739



First published 2024

*A catalogue record for this publication is available from the British Library.*

*A Cataloging-in-Publication data record for this book is available from the Library of Congress.*

ISBN 978-1-107-09842-8 Hardback

# Contents

# Tables

# Acknowledgements

The idea of using conversation analysis (CA) to explore the psychotherapy relationship arose during a "brainstorming session" between Adam Horvath and myself in a place called Kitsilano, while drinking an espresso or maybe two. That was over ten years ago. What soon followed was a research grant involving highly talented research assistants, presentations at conferences, collaborations, publications and more espresso, during which this idea began to take a more concrete shape. At one point, with the encouragement of Helen Barton from Cambridge University Press, the idea took the form of a book proposal and, some years later, developed into this book. That is the short story.

Many thanks are in order to different people. I begin with this project's main collaborators. Adam Horvath has contributed deeply at many levels. His intellectual input can be found in many pages of this monograph and, in practical terms, he has co-authored numerous of my past publications, not only related to the psychotherapy relationship but also to others. Adam's enthusiasm for wanting to explore how language and social interaction plays a central role in accomplishing the therapeutic relationship and the alliance has been, for me, a constant source of motivation. I thank Lynne Angus for her continued involvement in this project, her many contributions and her generosity in providing the research team with videotapes of the York I depression study. Without these tapes and the clients' willingness to participate in research projects, the findings presented in this book would not have been possible.

I have been fortunate in being able to work with several research assistants who have played an important role in helping me to develop many of the areas of this book: Lynda Chubak, Naomi Knight and Ashley Watkins. Their hard work and dedication have not only led to numerous publications, but also made this work very pleasurable. I am grateful to the *Social Sciences and Humanities Research Council* for having provided the financial means to do this research in such a stimulating team environment. We have benefitted greatly from the International Conference on Conversation Analysis and Psychotherapy (ICCAP) that has, over the years, offered an important venue in which we could discuss and develop our ideas with other scholars; notably, Anssi Peräkylä's extensive knowledge and experience of applying CA to psychotherapeutic contexts and Eva Bänninger-Huber's important work on displaying emotions. Thanks also to Helen Barton, editor at Cambridge, for her continued patience in waiting for the final book draft to be submitted.

Various chapters have benefited greatly from the careful reading and comments of the following people: Lynda Chubak, Alexa Hepburn, Adam Horvath, Anssi Peräkylä, Claudio Scarvaglieri and Olga Smoliak. Special thanks goes to Lynda Chubak for having proof-read all the chapters in the book. Three of the chapters in the book have been reworked from previous publications. Chapter 5 (Storytelling: Extended Accounts of Troubles) was rewritten from a previous publication: P. Muntigl, N. Knight & L. Angus (2014). Targeting emotional impact in storytelling: Working with client affect in Emotion-focused psychotherapy. *Discourse Studies 16*(6), 753–775. Chapter 6 (Chair Work) is a modified version of a *Journal of Pragmatics* article: P. Muntigl, L. Chubak & L. Angus (2017). Entering chair work in psychotherapy: An interactional structure for getting emotion-focused talk underway. *Journal of Pragmatics*, 117, 168–189. Chapter 7 (Repairing Disaffiliation in Therapy) is a reworked version of a previously published article on how emotion-focused therapists manage client disagreement: P. Muntigl, N. Knight, A. Watkins, A. O. Horvath & L. Angus (2013). Active retreating: Person-centered practices to repair disaffiliation in therapy. *Journal of Pragmatics*, 53, 1–20.

Lastly, thanks to my family – Stephi, Marie and Nicolas – for providing me with a nurturing environment that complements, and also provides a welcome distraction to, the academic world.

# Transcription Symbols

| **Symbol** | **Meaning** |
|---|---|
| [ | starting point of overlapping talk |
| ] | endpoint of overlapping talk |
| (1.5) | silence measured in seconds |
| (.) | silence less than 0.2-s |
| . | falling intonation at end of utterance |
| , | continuing intonation at end of utterance |
| ? | rising intonation at end of utterance |
| (word) | transcriber's guess |
| () | inaudible section |
| wor- | truncated, cut-off speech |
| wo:rd | prolongation of sound |
| word=word | latching (no audible break between words) |
| <word> | stretch of talk slower, drawn out |
| >word< | stretch of talk rushed, compressed |
| °word° | stretch of talk spoken quietly |
| word | emphasis |
| WORD | markedly loud |
| ↓word | markedly downward shift in pitch |
| ↑word | markedly upward shift in pitch |
| .hhh | audible inhalation, number of h's indicate length |
| hhh | audible exhalation, number of h's indicate length |
| heh/huh/hah/hih | laugh particles |
| wo(h)rd | laugh particle/outbreath inserted within a word |
| .hh hx | sigh |
| ~word~ | tremulous/wobbly voice through text |
| .snih | sniff |
| huhh.hhihHuyuh | sobbing |
| >hhuh< | sobbing – produced at a faster rate |
| ↑hhuh< | sobbing – if sharply inhaled or exhaled |
| ((cough)) | audible non-speech sounds |
| *italics (grey)* | non-verbal behaviour (actor indicated by initial) |

# 1 The Relationship in Psychotherapy

> Just as each little choice we make in communicative interaction can be assessed for its optimality for information exchange, it can equally be assessed for its optimality for maintaining (or forging) the current social relationship at an appropriate level of intensity or intimacy. (Enfield, 2006, p. 412)

## 1.1 Overview

Creating and maintaining a positive therapist–client relationship is considered to be essential in achieving therapeutic success. Damage to this relationship and the inability to repair disaffiliative episodes, on the other hand, are seen as detrimental to attaining good treatment outcomes. So far, research on the concept of the therapeutic relationship has focused almost exclusively on clients' and therapists' perceptions or observations on the quality of the relationship, but very little work has focused on how social relations between therapists and clients actually become negotiated through talk.

In this book, I aim to contribute to our understanding of the discursive and interactional processes used to manage social relations in psychotherapy conversations by providing answers to the following questions:

1. How do therapists and clients actually become affiliated in the course of therapy?
2. How do such affiliations become vulnerable and at risk?
3. How do therapists successfully re-establish affiliation with their clients – or fail to do so?
4. At which points in the interaction may disaffiliation, rather than affiliation, actually play a beneficial role for furthering psychotherapeutic aims?

This book draws from an extensive corpus of video- and audiotaped sessions involving interactions between emotion-focused or client-centred therapists and clients who suffer from major depressive disorder (MDD) (Greenberg & Watson, 1998). Using the methods of conversation analysis (CA) – an innovative approach to investigating the details of social interaction – I examine a range of psychotherapeutically relevant interactional sequences and activities in which the achievement or failure to become affiliated may deeply impact on therapist–client relations; for example, clients telling stories, therapists working with client emotions, therapists summarizing or interpreting client talk, therapists directing clients to engage in chair work, and clients displaying a reluctance to engage with the current therapeutic activity. This book thus provides detailed insight into the complexity of how a "talking cure" is practiced in person-centred therapies and also sheds more light on an area of mental health that has profound social consequences and that has so far received little attention in studies on interaction: depression.

In this introductory chapter, I begin with a brief overview of how the relationship – and an associated, more narrow, concept, the *therapeutic alliance* – has been conceptualized in psychotherapy research. I then turn to a description of emotion-focused therapy (EFT), which is given due consideration throughout the book, by discussing how it prioritizes the maintenance of a positive relationship. This is followed by some notes on clinical depression and how this illness has been characterized in the literature. I then proceed by situating the concept of 'relationships' within sociological studies on social networks and strong/weak ties and discussing how the therapist–client relationship can be located within these frameworks. Next, I briefly summarize some of the main studies that have made social relationships a topic of linguistic or interaction research. Finally, I provide an overview of the data and give an outline of each of the book's chapters.

## 1.2 Psychotherapeutic Views on the Relationship

The relationship – and especially its association with therapy process and outcome – is a topic that has been generating an abundance of interest and attention (e.g., Norcross, 2002, 2011; Norcross & Lambert, 2018; Wiseman & Tishby, 2015). Affect is often seen as comprising a central component of the relationship (Norcross & Lambert, 2018) and, in the most general terms, the relationship is formed through "the feelings and attitudes that counseling participants have toward one another, and the manner in which these are expressed" (Gelso & Carter, 1985, p. 159). This fairly general conceptualization is also matched with an effort from the psychotherapeutic research community to identify more specific relational elements that contribute to treatment effectiveness. Some of these elements include the alliance, goal consensus, empathy, positive regard and affirmation, congruence/genuineness and repairing alliance ruptures (see Norcross & Lambert, 2018 for the full list of elements).[1] Commenting on an

[1] In 2009, the American Psychological Association (APA) Divisions of Psychotherapy and of Clinical Psychology commissioned a task force to identify evidence-based elements of the psychotherapy relationship. An earlier task force was commissioned by the APA in 1999. The aims of this task force were to: "Identify elements of effective therapy relationships; Determine efficacious methods of customizing or tailoring therapy to the individual patient on the basis of his/her (nondiagnostic) characteristics" (Norcross, 2002, p. 6). The new list of elements from the 2009 task force has virtually remained the same, except for the exclusion of "self-disclosure" and "relational interpretation."

earlier, near identical list of elements from 2002, Horvath (2006) argues that there exists much overlap between various relationship elements and that, so far, no conceptual model has been put forward to explain how these elements may be linked into a cohesive framework.

Many of the relationship elements have been derived from two differing conceptualizations: Carl Rogers' client-centred approach and the therapeutic alliance. Each of these will be briefly reviewed.

### *1.2.1 Carl Rogers' Client-Centred Approach*

One of the most influential figures in psychotherapy that has deeply contributed to our understanding of the relationship is Carl Rogers. In 1957, Rogers proposed six necessary and sufficient conditions for promoting constructive personality change. These conditions are as follows (Rogers, 1957, p. 96):

1. Two persons are in psychological contact.
2. The first, whom we shall term the client, is in a state of incongruence, being vulnerable or anxious.
3. The second person, whom we shall term the therapist, is congruent or integrated in the relationship.
4. The therapist experiences unconditional positive regard for the client.
5. The therapist experiences an empathic understanding of the client's internal frame of reference and endeavors to communicate this experience to the client.
6. The communication to the client of the therapist's empathic understanding and unconditional positive regard is to a minimal degree achieved.

Elements 3–5 have received much attention in the literature and are presumed to be strongly interrelated. According to Kolden et al. (2011, p. 187), "neither empathy nor regard can be conveyed unless the therapist is perceived as genuine." In a similar vein, Elliott et al. (2011, p. 147) have argued that "because research has shown empathy to be inseparable from the other relational conditions, therapists should seek to offer empathy in the context of positive regard and genuineness. Empathy will not be effective unless it is grounded in authentic caring for the client." Further, each of these relational elements – empathy, positive regard, genuineness – have been shown to be associated with positive change (Elliott et al., 2011; Farber & Doolin, 2011; Kolden et al., 2011). Although Rogers' discussion of the relationship was based on his client-centred approach to therapy, he argued that these elements are necessary for virtually any type of client and any type of therapy (Rogers, 1957, p. 101). Thus, what he is proposing is a set of "common principles" that should guide therapists' responsiveness no matter which specific therapeutic technique is being used. The three elements that comprise some of the most fundamental aspects of the relationship – empathy, positive regard and genuineness – are briefly discussed in the following subsections.

*Empathy* Rogers (1951) argued that practicing empathy involves the ability to communicate one's understanding of another's experience by preserving the client's own personal frame of reference. What is important is: "to sense the client's private world as if it were your own, but without ever losing the 'as if' quality – this is empathy" (Rogers, 1957, p. 99). Roger's view of empathy and how it is to be used in counselling and therapy relates specifically to his client-centred approach; that is, the therapist's responses should not be directive by interpreting or assessing the client's experience. Instead, responses should give priority to the client's frame of reference and thus allow the client to maintain ownership of their own experience. The positive effects of empathy are reported to be extensive and far-reaching: Communicating empathy is considered to be especially important in fostering positive social bonds, improving the quality of care, promoting change and helping to achieve good treatment outcomes (Elliot et al., 2011, 2018; Greenberg et al., 1993; Suchman et al., 1997). The topic of empathy will be taken up as a main focus of investigation in Chapter 4.

*Positive Regard* This important relationship concept has been given a variety of labels such as "positive regard," "affirmation," "respect," "warmth," "support" and "prizing" (Farber & Doolin, 2011). Rogers (1957, p. 98) provides the following characterization: "To the extent that the therapist finds himself experiencing a warm acceptance of each aspect of the client's experience as being a part of the client, he is experiencing unconditional positive regard." With this form of therapist stance, the therapist refrains from passing judgement and promotes clients' ownership of their personal experiences. Thus, client experiences are not appraised as "good" or "bad" but are accepted in a warm and caring manner. Farber and Doolin (2011) also mention two important caveats with respect to positive regard. The first is that therapists may, for whatever reason, not always be able to "unconditionally" accept or praise what clients are telling them. The second is that positive regard is not conveyed in an absolute sense, but rather in degrees.

*Congruence/Genuineness* In relating with their clients, therapists should be congruent, genuine or "authentic." What this means in essence is that therapists should not hide behind their professional role or act in ways that are not consistent with how they "usually" present themselves to others. To quote Rogers, the congruent therapist "should be, within the confines of this relationship, a congruent, genuine, integrated person. It means that within the relationship he is freely and deeply himself, with his actual experience accurately represented by his awareness of himself. It is the opposite of presenting a façade, either knowingly or unknowingly" (Rogers, 1957, p. 97). In adopting this stance, therapists should not try to cover up their own present experiences even if they may appear at odds with doing productive therapeutic work. This would include "being afraid of the client" or "being unfocused due to the therapist's own current life circumstances." Thus, rather than pretend that they never have anything personal to contribute to the therapeutic encounter, therapists should be aware of what they are experiencing *in the moment* and offer the client some transparency by showing a willingness to communicate these experiences to the client (Greenberg & Watson, 2006). Another relationship principle, which some argue is an extension of the concept of congruence (Kolden et al., 2011), is termed *therapeutic presence* (Geller & Greenberg, 2002). Within this relational stance, therapists appear integrated and are open and receptive to what is happening in the moment (Greenberg, 2014).

### *1.2.2 The Therapeutic Alliance*

The therapeutic alliance – also referred to as the *working alliance, helping alliance* or simply the *alliance* – generally enters into discussions concerning the therapeutic relationship. Although there is not a clear consensus among researchers as to the definition of which constructs actually comprise the alliance (Horvath et al., 2011), many researchers draw from Bordin's (1979) conceptualization of the alliance as being composed of the following three features:

- agreement on goals;
- agreement and collaboration on performing tasks;
- the development of personal bonds.

Thus, the establishment of patient goals at the onset of therapy, the collaborative achievement of tasks closely tailored to the client's needs, expectations and capacities and the formation of mutual positive affect (i.e., liking each other) and trust are, taken together, important for forging a good alliance and for therapy success (Horvath & Bedi, 2002; Horvath & Symonds, 1991).

Although certain components of the alliance resemble aspects of the therapeutic relationship, it has been suggested that these two concepts are distinct. As Horvath et al. (2011, p. 56) have argued, "the alliance is not the same as the therapeutic relationship. The relationship is made of several interlocking elements (empathy, responsiveness, creating a safe secure environments, etc.). The alliance is one way of conceptualizing what has been achieved by the appropriate use of these elements." Seen at one level, the alliance references components of the therapy process that extend beyond, but are nonetheless relevant to, the construction of a therapeutic relationship. In fact, Bordin (1979, p. 254) makes this explicit when he states that "The goals set and collaboration specified appear intimately linked to the nature of the human relationship between therapist and patient." One can thus view the relationship as a much broader concept than the alliance, with the latter being a "subset" or in some sense an "achievement"; that is, having a positive relation develops an alliance between therapist and client and together they perform therapeutic work (e.g., alleviate the client's distress).[2] When discussing affiliation in this book – for consistency and to avoid confusion – I will mainly refer to the relationship rather than the alliance.

### *1.2.3 Alliance Ruptures*

The creation and maintenance of a productive therapeutic relationship – that is, through the provision of empathy, positive regard, authenticity and therapeutic presence – and a strong working alliance (i.e., through collaboration and agreement on goals and tasks and the formation of personal bonds) has been shown to be necessary for fostering change and achieving good therapeutic outcomes. A weakening of the therapist–client relationship, as for example through a rupture in the alliance, however, may instead act as a barrier to change and to achieving good outcomes. Recently, increasing attention has been devoted to alliance ruptures and to the resolution of these ruptures. Safran et al. (2011a, p. 224) define an alliance rupture as follows:

> A rupture in the therapeutic alliance can be defined as a tension or breakdown in the collaborative relationship between patient and therapist … Although the term *rupture* may imply to some a dramatic breakdown in collaboration, ruptures vary in intensity from relatively minor tensions, which one or both of the participants may be only vaguely aware of, to major breakdowns in collaboration, understanding, or communication.

There is a growing body of research supporting the claim that non-identified ruptures or ones that are not repaired likely lead to poor outcomes and even to premature termination of therapy and that the successful repair of ruptures tends to be associated with good therapy outcomes (Safran & Muran, 1996; Safran et al., 2001; Stiles et al., 2004). Some researchers suggest that the pattern of 'rupture + repair' may even be an essential aspect of the treatment process for some clients (Safran et al., 2001; Stiles et al., 2004). As Bordin (1994, p. 26) has argued, "the most important element in dealing with strains and ruptures in the working alliance is that they represent prime opportunities for change with persons whose psychological state creates the conditions most recalcitrant to alteration." Both the component model of the alliance and the rupture-repair aspects of Borden's model have received a great deal of empirical support (Horvath et al., 2011; Norcross, 2011; Safran & Muran, 2006; Stiles et al., 2004). Better treatment outcomes have been associated with the realization and development of a strong alliance (Horvath & Symonds, 1991;

[2] Adam Horvath (personal communication, June 6, 2021).

Horvath et al., 2011) and the repairing of alliance ruptures (Aspland et al., 2008; Safran et al., 2001).

Safran and Muran (1996) have identified two types of alliance ruptures: withdrawal and confrontation. In addition, they proposed a general model and a method in which the process of alliance rupture and its resolution may be documented. According to these authors, rupture and resolution moves through a set of generic stages and substages that involve attending to and exploring the rupture (cf. Aspland et al., 2008). A model of rupture resolution and an extensive list of the kinds of confrontational or withdrawing practices in which clients typically engage are documented in Eubanks et al.'s (2015) *Rupture Resolution Rating System (3RS): Manual.* Ruptures in the alliance have received some attention in the context of process experiential/EFT in terms of both therapist and client contributions (Greenberg & Watson, 2006). Therapists, on the one hand, may contribute to strains in the alliance when certain relationship conditions (e.g., empathy, acceptance, genuineness) are not adequately met. Further, especially when therapy does not appear to be unfolding in a straightforward manner, therapists may become frustrated, afraid or even anxious or may become too focused in trying to get their agenda underway (Greenberg & Watson, 2006, p. 132). From the clients' side, one of the main issues is that clients may have one or more problems in becoming engaged in the process of therapy that can lead to stress in the therapeutic relationship: 1) feeling ashamed; 2) being skeptical about the purpose and value of therapy; 3) being overly passive; 4) having diverging expectations from those of the therapist; 5) having difficulty constructing narratives and accessing memories; and 6) having difficulty exploring their feelings/difficulty *turning inward* (Greenberg & Watson, 2006, p. 133; Watson & Greenberg, 2000). It has also been suggested that, when clients show difficulties in accessing or representing their inner experiences, experiential therapists can enlist strategies to facilitate the development and maintenance of collaborative action by using metacommunication or implementing specific tasks to assist clients with turning their attention inward (Watson & Greenberg, 2000, p. 178). Episodes of relationship stresses and how they are interactionally managed will be examined in Chapters 7 and 8.

### *1.2.4 Relationship Principles in Emotion-Focused Therapy*

Most of the therapy conversations dealt with in this book involve emotion-focused interventions. EFT is a distinctive approach that combines elements of client-centred, gestalt and experiential therapies (Greenberg, 2002, 2010). It was originally termed process-experiential therapy (PET) in the early 1990s to distinguish it from other experiential approaches at the time, but has since come to be commonly referred to as EFT. Some of the main distinctive features of EFT include the recognition that emotions play a central role in organizing personal experience, implementing marker-guided responses strategies, the adoption of complementary relational styles of treatment (person-centred and process-guiding) and an adherence to humanistic values and principles (Elliott & Greenberg, 2007; Greenberg, 2010).

EFT practice is characterized by what is often termed the integration of "being" or "following" with "doing" or "guiding." In the former, the therapist is meant to adhere to client- or person-centred principles in which the client's experience is responded to in an empathic manner; thus, the therapist is said to follow and hence privilege the client's experience. This person-centred relational style is matched with a gestalt-oriented one (Perls et al., 1951), which has come to be referred to as *process-guiding*. This alternate form of relating constitutes a more directive or coaching therapy style in which clients are guided into various forms of therapeutic activities and experiences. Precedence is given to fostering a person-centred relationship. As Greenberg (2014, p. 351) argues, "When disjunction or disagreement occurs, the client is viewed as the expert on his or her own experience, and the therapist always defers to the client's experience." Further, when guidance is given, it should be performed in a non-imposing, tentative manner, in the form of a suggestion or an offer. For EFT, therapy works optimally when both treatment principles are in operation. For example, facilitating emotional work through guidance is best done in the presence of empathy. Further, episodes of "following the client" should at some point result in process-guiding through some form of task intervention, otherwise the therapy may not be progressing in the most productive way (Greenberg, 2014).

The provision of a beneficial therapeutic relationship is a central goal in EFT. The importance is placed on building a secure and validating relationship, based on the following three subprinciples from Greenberg (2014, p. 351):

1. *Empathic attunement*: being fully present, enter the client's frame of reference and track the client's immediate and evolving experiencing.
2. *Therapeutic bond*: genuinely communicate empathy, caring, and warmth to the client.
3. *Task collaboration*: facilitate involvement in goals and tasks of therapy.

In EFT practice, Rogerian relationship elements are taken on board – that is, empathy, genuineness and congruence – as are elements from the therapeutic alliance, such as collaboration on tasks, agreement on goals and development of bonds. Greenberg (2014) also specifies other important aspects of constituting an EFT relationship such as *therapeutic presence* and *coaching*. Therapeutic presence is a complex concept that draws heavily from Rogers' (1957) work, but moves beyond it in significant ways. It is predicated on therapists being with their client in the present moment at many different levels – not just relationally, but also cognitively, physically, emotionally and spiritually. Following Greenberg (2014, p. 353), coaching refers to the therapist's role as guiding the client through different tasks and activities and is argued to be a partnership, one that involves acceptance and change. In their role as coach, therapists are involved in two tasks: following and validating clients in their constructions of personal experience and guiding clients in a nondirective manner to explore emotion-focused goals.

## 1.3 Depression, Treatment and the Alliance

The clients that had participated in the conversations examined in this research are persons diagnosed with major depression disorder/ MDD. Depression is one of the most prevalent mental health illnesses affecting the human population. According to the World Health Organization (2017), over 300 million people suffer from depression worldwide, with a higher prevalence among females (5.1%) than among males (3.6%). Of the mental disorders, depression ranks as most debilitating; that is, responsible for more years lost (Smith, 2014). Definitions and diagnostic criteria of depression have undergone many changes through the different editions of the *Diagnostic and Statistical Manual of Mental Disorders*, which resulted in MDD becoming one of the most prevalent forms of mental health illnesses (Horwitz, 2011). In its most current conceptualization, MDD is associated with at least one of the two following symptoms that are present for extended durations: depressed mood or loss of interest or pleasure (DSM-5; American Psychiatric Association, 2013). To be classifiable as an MDD, for example, at least five of the following nine symptoms must be present (including at least one of the first two) during a two-week period, (nearly) daily and for nearly the whole day:

1. Depressed mood.
2. Markedly diminished interest or pleasure in activities.
3. Significant weight loss when not dieting or weight gain.
4. Insomnia or hypersomnia.
5. Psychomotor agitation or retardation.
6. Fatigue or loss of energy.
7. Feelings of worthlessness or excessive or inappropriate guilt.
8. Diminished ability to think or concentrate, or indecisiveness.
9. Recurrent thoughts of death (without a specific plan) or a suicide attempt or a specific plan for committing suicide.

Other attributes commonly associated with depression involve negative self-concepts, regressive and self-punitive wishes and changes in activity level (Beck & Alford, 2009). Conceptualizations of depression, however, tend to be increasingly viewed in more multifaceted terms, not simply as a mood disorder but as a complex syndrome that operates at a number of different levels: neuro-physiological, cognitive, emotion, behavioural and social (Greenberg & Watson, 2006).

Two general types of depression have been cited in the literature: one involving self-criticism (introjective) and the other involving dependency (anaclitic) (Blatt, 1974, 1995, 2004). Whereas a self-critical type depression can be linked to feelings of inferiority, guilt, worthlessness and failure, dependency type depression is associated with helplessness, fear of abandonment and need gratification. A qualitative study of clients undergoing EFT treatments for depression has identified two meta-themes that map onto Blatt's depression types (Greenberg & Watson, 2006): *self-oriented* and *other-oriented.* One of the most common self-oriented themes associated with depression has been found to be self-criticism (Greenberg & Watson, 2006, p. 51). This may involve feelings of inferiority when compared to others, being too sensitive or needy, having unacceptable feelings (i.e., internalizing "shoulds") and viewing oneself as unworthy or undesirable. Emotions have been found to play a central role in depression and, according to Greenberg and Watson (2006, pp. 56ff), depressed persons commonly feel trapped or try to avoid certain core emotions or "emotion clusters" such as shame and guilt, fear and anxiety, sadness and anger. Other-oriented themes were associated with dependency and included abandonment or rejection, isolation, loss and blame.

Depression has also received attention in an area of cognitive science research that places its focus on people's remembered past personal life events and how what has been termed *autobiographical memory* may shed light on a person's well-being. According to Conway and Pleydell-Pearce (2000, p. 261), such autobiographical memories are "of fundamental significance for the self, for emotions, and for the experience of personhood, that is, for the experience of enduring as an individual, in a culture, over time." Research suggests that people who suffer from depression have difficulty in recalling specific details of their life circumstances and there is a tendency to mainly access *over-general* autobiographical memories (Williams and Scott, 1988). These over-general memories have also been related to a range of deficits associated with reduced self-coherence, increased rumination and worry, impairment of social problem solving, a reduced capacity to imagine future events and delayed recovery from episodes of affective disorders (Conway & Pleydell-Pearce, 2000; Williams et al., 2007).

Other research, rather than focusing internally on the mind (i.e., memories), takes a more "outward," performative focus by studying how personal events are narrated in context. This approach takes a narrative-informed view of social life, suggesting that the stories we tell work to construct who we are, our feelings and how we make sense of the world around us (Angus & McLeod, 2004; De Fina & Georgakopoulou, 2012). According to Bruner (1986), narratives are a specific mode of thinking and acting in the world and reveal a "landscape of consciousness" that relates to our emotions (what we feel), intentions and moral accountability. Psychotherapy researchers have been exploring the interrelationship between emotion processes and narrative organization in depressed clients undergoing EFT or client-centred therapy (CCT) (Angus, 2012; Angus & Greenberg, 2011). They found that depressed clients tend to narrative personal life events as three different story types: *same old story*, *empty story* and *broken life story*. The most prevalent story type, "same old story," references maladaptive emotional-agentive themes that correspond with the following markers: a sense of stuckness and helplessness, a flat external voice, ramped-up (or down) adverbial expressions such as "always" or "never" and expressions of low agency (Angus & Greenberg, 2011, p. 60). Empty stories coincide with bare emotional content and focus instead on external details with minimal engagement from the narrator. Broken stories, by contrast, contain conflicting emotional plotlines and are marked by confusion, uncertainty and frustration, thus creating a narrative that lacks internal coherence. These stories seem to share the common features of low personal agency, helplessness and a "minimal" or depressed emotional content. Storytelling practices will be addressed further in Chapter 5.

There exists a range of empirically validated psychotherapeutic treatments for clinical depression. Some of the major forms of therapy include interpersonal therapy (IPT) and cognitive behavioural therapy (CBT) (Beck & Alford, 2009), CCT (Rogers, 1951) and EFT (Greenberg, 2010). EFT has been shown to be highly successful in treating depressed persons; for example, by reducing depressive symptoms and preventing relapse (Ellison et al., 2009; Goldman et al., 2006; Greenberg, 2010; Greenberg & Watson, 2006). Greenberg and Watson (2006) outline three phases of emotion-focused treatment for depression: 1) bonding and awareness; 2) evocation and exploration of emotionally laden experiences; and 3) transformation (e.g., of emotions, experience, self). In the first stage, emphasis is placed on forming bonds with the client (i.e., affirming client experiences, collaborating on therapeutic goals and tasks) and promoting the client's awareness of own internal experiences. The second phase is mainly concerned with evoking, supporting and accessing primary and/or maladaptive client emotions and with overcoming "blocks" or interruptions to emotional exploration. The third and final phase focuses on transformative processes that help clients in generating new emotional responses, encourage reflection to better understand clients' new experiences and narratives and support a new emerging sense of self.

During the middle phase, the client reveals or displays primary and maladaptive emotion schemes. These in-session problem states, seen as behavioral markers of emotional processing difficulties, prompt particular marker-guided task strategies (Elliott & Greenberg, 2007; Greenberg, 2010), as well as signal the client's in-the-moment readiness to work on a specific problem.

For example, following a behavioral marker revealing an emotional processing difficulty such as a sigh, shrug or expression of resignation, which may be conveying the client's experience of hopelessness, therapists may initiate a two-chair dialogue technique in which the client adopts two alternating roles that help to intensify the client's experience: one as the critic who points out the client's own sense of hopelessness and the other as that aspect of self who is experiencing the hopelessness (Greenberg & Watson, 2006, p. 108). These chair dialogues have the aim of heightening awareness of and forming contact between incongruent aspects of experience, which are considered necessary before being able to move into the final transformative stage of an integration and conflict resolution. As Greenberg and Watson (2006, pp. 108–109) state, "by actively saying to themselves 'You are worthless' or 'Nothing will ever change' and elaborating on these self-statements, clients begin to activate the feeling of hopelessness in the session. Once a client's emotional experience of hopelessness has been evoked, he or she is able to access the information that constitutes this experience in a 'hot' fashion." The sequential, interactional steps that therapists and clients generally follow to move into chair work will be discussed in Chapter 6.

As already discussed in section 1.2.3, clients may at times have difficulty in becoming engaged in the therapy process. Various blocks to engagement have been identified with depressed clients and include: feeling ashamed; being skeptical about the process; being overtly passive; having difficulty in constructing narratives and accessing memories; and having difficulty exploring one's feelings (Greenberg & Watson, 2006). In such circumstances, there may be difficulties in achieving empathic attunement (Greenberg, 2014), thus placing potential tension in the relationship. Yet it also may cause strains in the alliance, as there may be difficulty in achieving sufficient collaboration on tasks. In order to repair the relationship (and the alliance) in these contexts, Watson and Greenberg (2000) suggest possible strategies. One is that the focus in therapy should be momentarily placed on metacommunication; for example, clients could be encouraged to talk about their emotions, skepticism or reluctance to engage in therapeutic work. Alternatively, therapists may ask the client if there is anything about themselves (e.g., therapists' conduct) that the client is having difficulty with. Second, therapists could try to become more empathic or more appropriately responsive to the client's needs or situation. They could also slow down the pace of the intervention in progress or halt it altogether and instead switch to a different activity such as reflection. Third, therapists could display their own potential vulnerability by disclosing personal aspects of themselves. Fourth, therapists may work more assiduously at gaining client collaboration in tasks, by making the techniques and goals of therapy a topic of the conversation. Therapist interactional strategies to overcome client disengagement and withdrawal from chair work have been examined in Muntigl et al. (2020b).

## 1.4 Relationships and Social Connections

Sociological research has shown that close, empathic relationships maintained throughout social life are instrumental in promoting well-being, happiness and health (Dunbar, 2018). Persons enter into social networks of varying intensity, closeness and size, which may be separated into hierarchically differentiated structured types, based on degree of intensity, frequency of contact and number of possible members (Hill & Dunbar, 2003): *support network*; *sympathy group*; *active network*. Our support network generally consists of five members and would include a primary partner (e.g., spouse or "cohabitant"). These are members that a person tends to be in frequent contact with and would most likely turn to in times of crisis such as when emotional, social or economic support is required. The sympathy group, on the other hand, is somewhat larger, consisting of around fifteen members. These are "best friends" whom we contact at least once a month and whose sudden death would cause great distress (Hill & Dunbar, 2003). The active network is fairly large and is set at about 150 individuals. This group does not only supply an individual with a broad means of support but, perhaps most importantly, acts as an information exchange network. A person's contact with each of the members of this group is said to be much lower, around once per year. Frequency of contact, however, is not always a key factor in determining intimacy; what is important is rather the quality of information that is exchanged and the common ground that is established. For, as Enfield (2006, p. 413) argues, "this is why in one type of society I might have a more intensive, closer relationship with my best friend, even though I see very much less of him than my day-to-day professional colleagues."

It is probably correct to argue that the relationship between a client and therapist is of a different quality than the social network categories posited by Dunbar (2018). This may be because the psychotherapy relationship is not properly defined through "friendship" or "intimacy," but more as a (helping) professional relationship on par with doctor–patient, lawyer–client or even "priest–parish member." In this way, therapeutic relations are better defined as "serving a purpose" and as asymmetrical and, in this sense, does not constitute a *social* relationship per se but rather a *working* relationship in order to fulfill certain needs or goals. Nonetheless, by way of interaction, clients and therapists do form (and ongoingly negotiate) a relationship and so certain common relationship features will still apply and be relevant. For instance, contact and duration of visit between therapist and client is highly regulated, the nature of the social exchange is in many ways non-reciprocating (e.g., clients tell about their troubles but not the other way around) and the therapist's role is generally restricted to offering emotional support. As Goffman (1967, p. 41) has argued, "when a person begins a mediated or immediate encounter, he already stands in some kind of social relationship to the other concerned, and expects to stand in a given relationship to them after the particular encounter ends." It may be more instructive to consider the therapist–client relationship with respect to what Granovetter (1983) has termed *strong* vs. *weak* ties. Whereas strong tie relations generally consist of individuals who share a close personal relationship (e.g., family members, close friends; compare with Dunbar's *support* and *sympathy* networks), weak tie relations do not (e.g., acquaintances). Further, weak tie relationships are characterized as not interpersonally close and tend to be formed in more restrictive contexts that place constraints on our interactions, such as talk with neighbours, service providers and counsellors (Wright et al., 2010). Yet, it is generally assumed that relationships comprising *strong ties* are important in times of great need, when support is required for our security and welfare. Relationships that consist of weaker ties, however, have also been shown to play a relevant social role, especially in terms of providing others with access to diverse forms of information (Granovetter, 1983). In fact, research has suggested that people prefer to turn to weak-tie relationships when seeking advice because individuals from this network will often be less emotional and more objective than individuals (i.e., close friends and family) from strong-tie relationships (Adelman et al., 1987). Thus, psychotherapists' weaker ties with their clients may indeed be an advantage in these contexts of offering professional, emotional support and help. Wright et al. (2010) propose four dimensions of weak-tie support preference, which consists of aiding persons needing help to: 1) *access different viewpoints*; 2) *receive objective feedback from others*; 3) *have a reduced risk of being judged by others* (e.g., the therapist); and of providing professionals with 4) *reduced social obligations leading to discomfort, stress and conflict*. These dimensions, which seem to characterize most professional helping contexts and relationships, would seem to explain some of the benefits in seeking out therapists in times of trouble.

Whereas psychotherapy research has pointed to the importance of the therapist's posture or stance (e.g., being empathic, person-centred) in maintaining a good relationship with the client and sociology has drawn our attention to the value of looking at relationships in terms of networks and social ties, these research paradigms have not considered how relationships are achieved through language and interaction, and the give-and-take of conversations that are accomplished moment-by-moment. Enfield (2009) has taken significant steps to fill this gap and to provide a more comprehensive, pragmatic-oriented model of social relations by arguing that analysts should adopt a *relationship thinking approach*. I summarize just a few of his main points that are relevant to this book. First, relationships are built up and forged through interactions involving co-present participants. Second, living in the social world implies being part of a social system that is characterized through reciprocal role/identity (e.g., father–son; brother–sister) and polar (e.g., intimacy: close vs. distant) relations. Third, relationship grounded social behaviour emerges from competing interests, an interplay between positively and negatively valenced forces or propensities.[3] On the one hand, people may act with respect to positive pro-social tendencies (trust, compassion and affiliation) and, on the other hand, they may also be acting in accordance with what Enfield terms *Machiavellian tendencies*, which licence deception and competition. This view resonates strongly with Goffman's (1967, 1981) studies on *territories of self* and *face*. He argued that although people tend to cooperate by maintaining each other's *territorial preserves* (e.g., personal space, possessions, autobiographical information, rights to enter and exit conversations), persons may at times act in violation (territorial offences, threatening other's face) by encroaching or intruding on others' territorial preserves or face claims. Thus, persons are not always acting in accordance to pro-social interests, in order to save or reduce damage to face, affiliate or promote social bonding. Instead, they may behave in ways that may appear antagonistic or self-centred by creating boundaries, establishing difference, building coalitions and even hurting others (see also Goodwin, 1990). Therapeutic practices may also be, on a more global scale, guided by competing aims that involve both offering consistent support of the client's position and, at the same time, challenging the client's self-defeating, pathological perspective (Muntigl et al., 2020; Weiste, 2015). In fact, Bänninger-Huber and Widmer (1999) view these tendencies of (pro-social) support vs. challenge as necessary for performing therapeutic work and have characterized these competing tendencies in terms of what they call the *balance hypothesis* – see also Chapter 3.

## 1.5 Discursive Views of Relationships

In psychotherapy, relationship elements most often refer to some aspect of the "feelings" or "attitudes" between therapist and client. With Gelso and Carter's (1985, p. 159) definition of relationships (in psychotherapy), although some emphasis is placed on "the manner in which these are expressed," this does not generally seem to receive much attention. In fact, Norcross and Lambert (2018, p. 304) go so far as to caution that this part of their definition "potentially opens the relationship to include everything under the therapeutic sun." This reluctance to focus on "expression" may be because, as Strong and Smoliak (2018, p. 7) have claimed, "in today's era of evidence-based therapy … the focus has largely been on 'what works' and less on how what works (namely, interventions) can be shown to work through careful discursive analysis." Further, there has been a reliance on assessing relationship elements in terms of subjective measures, participant observations or

[3] Enfield actually uses the term *instincts*, which implies that they are innate, but I prefer to use the terms *propensities* or *tendencies* in order to leave this matter open to debate.

feedback questionnaires rather than in terms of its quality as a social construction between people (McNamee & Gergen, 1992; Shotter, 1993) or even as an accomplishment that is created and maintained (and transformed) through speakers' sequentially connected social actions (Buttny, 1993; Peräkylä, 2019). In this section, I discuss how relationships can be viewed as an ongoing interactional accomplishment; that is, by what interactional means are relationships displayed and oriented to? How, for instance, does a therapist display a "closer" or more "distant" relationship with the client and vice versa? Or, how do clients convey their understanding and approval (or disapproval) of how therapists have demonstrated their grasp and emotional support of the client's distress?

### *1.5.1 Language and Social Relationship Variables*

Alongside the content, representational or informational component, language and the contexts in which it is put to use also has a social dimension. This dimension has been referred to as *phatic* (Malinowski, 1923), the *relationship level* (Watzlawick et al., 1967), *interpersonal* (Halliday, 1994) and *stance* (Biber & Finegan, 1989), just to mention a few. Language is, of course, oriented toward a recipient and certain grammatical components, such as mood (e.g., choice of declarative or interrogative), modal expressions (epistemic or deontic), address terms (e.g., *tu* vs. *vous*) and affectual expressions (evaluations, emotions, judgements), among others, will work toward constructing interlocutors as close or distant, as equal or unequal (e.g., in terms of knowledge or "who gets whom to do what") or as symmetrical or asymmetrical (e.g., in terms of equality of access to discursive resources such as taking a turn at talk).

Within sociolinguistics and many discourse-based approaches, there has been much interest over the years in studying the connection between language use and the social relationship between persons. The concepts of *power* and *solidarity* were placed on centre stage in Brown and Gilman's (1960) influential paper to explain pronoun usage in European languages such as French and German that distinguish between *tu* and *vous*. Whereas power is said to constitute a non-reciprocating, asymmetrical relationship in which a degree of control may be exercised over another, solidarity is reciprocating and symmetrical and is largely determined by similarities in such areas as kinship (e.g., same parentage), education and vocation. A different and more comprehensive model was introduced in Brown and Levinson's (1987) classic book *Politeness*. This work drew from Goffman's (1967) concept of *facework* to explain how face threatening actions may be modulated in various ways depending on three sociological variables: *social distance* between speaker and hearer; relative *power* between speaker and hearer; and the culturally based, ranked *imposition* of the action. Interactions between persons were argued to be guided by two different kinds of so-called *face wants*: *negative face* or the desire to be unimpeded; and *positive face* or the need to be desired by others. People tend to abide by these general "face" principles in order to reduce threat to each other's face and, further, the way in which face threat is modulated will partly depend on the speaker's relationship in terms of power and social distance. Scholars have since been building on the power/solidarity and social distance relationship dimensions. For example, Tannen (1994) provides a list of concepts that lie in opposition to each other and form a continuum and that have been used to characterize varying aspects of social relationships: power/solidarity; asymmetry/symmetry; hierarchy/equality; distance/closeness.

Language use and relationship variables are often construed as working bi-directionally; that is, although power and distance may influence the language selections people make when interacting, these selections, in turn, will construct a certain kind of relationship between the speakers. This position of bi-directionality is especially salient in Halliday's (1985) sociolinguistic model – but see also Heritage's (1984) discussion of conversational sequences of which any social action is both *context dependent* (responsive of what came before) and *context renewing* (for the next action). From the angle of social context, speakers have available a range of linguistic choices to enact meaning and, from the angle of language, the linguistic choices selected from a given potential to make meaning will create a certain kind of social context and social relationship between the speakers. Thus, social contexts and relationships are never completely static in this view, but are nudged along different directions depending on the linguistic choices made.

### *1.5.2 A Conversation Analytic View of Social Relationships*

CA is the study of how cultural members organize their social conduct to perform actions or activities in the world and how conduct is sensibly and accountably produced from one moment to the next in interaction (Sacks, 1995a, 1995b; Sidnell & Stivers, 2013). One of the central concepts in CA is termed *sequence organization* (Schegloff, 2007). This is taken to mean that relevant aspects of social life involving some form of face-to-face encounter – be it opening and closing conversations, paying a bill at the counter, formulating a complaint, attending a medical consultation and so on – will be managed through cohesively connected actions in sequences that unfold over time. Further, the sequences used to build these social encounters will provide the basic scaffolding in which the interactants may achieve intersubjectivity and common ground and may forge social relationships. Thus, to the study of the constitution of relationships along CA lines, it becomes necessary to examine how the sequential ordering of conduct goes on to perform relationship work (see especially Peräkylä, 2019). Some of the most important conversational features of relationships, as seen through a CA lens, may be summarized as follows (see especially Mandelbaum, 2003):

1. Relationships are endogenous to interaction, created in and through talk.
2. Relationships are not static, but shift as interactions unfold.
3. Constituted as part of a focused activity, or as incidental to the main business of the conversation.

Just as features of context, such as pedagogic, counselling or medical activities, have been argued to be produced within the talk itself or *endogenously* produced (Heritage, 1984, p. 283), so will such relationship features such as intimacy and power. What is being stressed here is the point that relationship features are not considered as something outside of or separate from actual conversational features and are not to be taken as variables that merely explain or predict these features. Instead, this view stresses how conversational features may be accomplishing relationships. It should also be stressed, however, that relationships do not occur in a "social vacuum" but rather, in many cases at least, presuppose a history of shared life experiences. Thus, speakers will often leverage this ongoing history of associating to its full potential, producing social actions that may be properly fitted to the social statuses vis-à-vis their interlocutors. Stevanovic and Peräkylä (2014, p. 194), for example, illustrate this point with reference to teasing: whereas in intimate relationships, "teasing is often used to promote rapport and social closeness among the participants," it may be interpreted as harsh criticism when relations are more distant. This should not be taken to mean that teasing does not come with certain risks in close relationships. It is always possible for the person teased to take offence and treat the action as a violation of their territorial preserves or face wants (Goffman, 1981). Stevanovic and Peräkylä's (2014) work shows that actions can be inappropriate or appropriate depending on the relationship's degree of intimacy. Performing actions that index distance with potentially close persons can be as problematic as performing actions that index closeness with distant persons. The distance/closeness of actions is therefore linked with territorial boundaries involving personal information, ownership, conversational rights and so on.

Relationships are not fixed constructs, but may, from moment to moment, be challenged or altered through talk. Thus, Heritage's (1984) general point about the context-dependent and context-renewing features of talk most certainly applies to relationships as well. A prior speaker's action provides a new context through which the next speaker may ratify the social relations displayed (e.g., intimate or distant) or may work to modify the relation into, say, a more distant or intimate one. This dynamic account of relationship building, which is also extensively argued by Enfield (2006) in his discussion of affiliation, may also be viewed in terms of Heritage's (2012) distinction between epistemic *status* and *stance*: Whereas epistemic status refers to the relative "state of knowledge" between speakers for a given knowledge domain (e.g., as having more or less rights and access to certain information), epistemic stance refers to the interactional/linguistic means through which speakers index their state of knowledge (Heritage, 2012). Given this perspective, people enter into everyday and institutional encounters with epistemic statuses vis-à-vis each other, but they also maintain or work to change their status in these encounters by indexing a certain epistemic stance. Although status and stance are interrelated, status does not determine stance or vice versa.[4] With a view to relationships, persons entering an encounter with a certain relationship status (e.g., close or distant) may work to maintain or change their status through the linguistic-interactional selections made in their turns-at-talk.

Finally, although relationship work may be performed as part of a focused activity in which an aspect of the relationship between the speakers is made a central topic of talk, much of this work may instead be accomplished "behind the scenes," as accompanying but not visibly central to the main business of the interaction (Mandelbaum, 2003). Goffman (1971) referred to these forms of incidental conduct (e.g., seeking or evading others' hands, locking arms) as "tie signs." The more general point, however, is that irrespective of how overtly relationship work is being done or whether or not it is incidental or "intended," it is *always* being done and, as Enfield (2006) has argued, there is no time out from this interpersonal level during moments of interaction.

Relationships certainly are an extremely important component of social interactions and yet CA research has nonetheless generally adopted a cautionary stance in investigating social context more generally, and relationships more specifically. Part of the reason, as Mandelbaum (2003, p. 209) argues, is that, "like identity, although theorized to be omnirelevant, it can be hard to document the relevance of relationship to the way talk is done." In a series of papers, Schegloff (1987, 1992, 1997b) addresses some of the risks involved in bringing contextual or relationship categories into one's analysis. A brief summary of these risks are given in Schegloff (1987, p. 229):

> Efforts to relate levels of analysis via macro-relevant attributes of the participants in micro-level processes threaten underdevelopment of a full technical exploration of the micro-level processes. Efforts to bridge the levels by the use of vernacular conceptions of context are vulnerable to challenges to the adequacy of their warrant and to the directness of their linkage to details of the actual conduct of interaction.

[4] Other dimensions, such as deontics and emotions, have also been examined from this status/stance framework (see Stevanovic & Peräkylä, 2014).

Reframing Schegloff's caveats into a couple of basic guidelines that CA analysts may keep in mind when examining talk for its relationship implications may appear as follows:

1. Consider the range of interactional work a segment of talk may be doing, above and beyond what may be relevant regarding relationship construction.
2. Adequately demonstrate how a relationship category may be relevant for the interactants and consequential for how talk may proceed.

So for example, if there is an assumption that a power relationship may be relevant to the interaction, as may be assumed in doctor–patient or boss–employee role relationships, there is a risk that *other* work – or even the *main* discursive work – of the sequence may remain unnoticed and unanalyzed. To counteract this problem, a comprehensive account of how speakers are organizing their conduct and making sense of (and holding each other accountable for) each other's conduct needs to be given. In this way, it can be more convincingly shown whether power, some other relationship category or even something different altogether is important and relevant. Following this, a compelling warrant needs to be given, if it is to be assumed that relationship categories are playing a relevant role for the conversational participants. These caveats call upon the analyst to more deeply reflect on whether a feature of interaction, say *interruption*, is convincingly linked to gender or power or some other social category, or whether the interactional feature is produced in the service of interactional goals not directly related to these categories in *that moment* of the interaction.

*Activities and Sequences that Accomplish Relationship Work* Relationships are talked into being; that is, to have an intimate/strong or distant/weak tie people need to interact with each other. In developing a CA approach to studying relationship categories, Pomerantz and Mandelbaum (2005, p. 150) identify two areas of investigation by asking the following questions: 1) "How does invoking a relationship category operate with respect to accomplishing a locally relevant conversation action?" and 2) "How does performing certain conversational actions relate to enacting incumbency in specific relationship categories?" These questions draw from Sacks' (1995a) work on membership categorization. According to Sacks, categories are "inference-rich" and representative. For a given category term (e.g., stranger, friend, relative) there is an assumption that speakers will draw representative, category-appropriate inferences about the person in question. Further, activities can be "category-bound" and appropriately seen in terms of a given category of person or relationship:

> Interactants maintain incumbency in complementary relationship categories, such as friend-friend, intimate-intimate, or father-son, by engaging in conduct regarded as

appropriate for incumbents of the relationship category and by ratifying appropriate conduct when performed by the cointeractant. (Pomerantz & Mandelbaum, 2005, p. 160)

To be seen as visibly belonging to (or being an incumbent of) a certain relationship category, speakers must produce the sort of conduct that may be demonstrably and accountably linked to that category. Thus, constructing a specific relationship category between persons is a joint accomplishment in which a speaker displays relationship-appropriate conduct (for that category) followed by the other party's ratification of the conduct. Drawing from a range of prior studies in CA, Pomerantz and Mandelbaum (2005) list four sequence types that are highly relationship implicative. They are exemplary in showing how certain conversational actions relate to enacting incumbency in specific relationship categories pertaining to "intimacy," "involvement" and "closeness": 1) *inquiring about tracked events + providing more details on one's own activities*; 2) *discussing one's own problems + displaying interest in the other's problems*; 3) *making oblique references to shared experiences + forwarding the talk about shared experiences*; and 4) *using improprieties + taking up the other's improprieties by using additional improprieties and/or laughter*.

Pomerantz and Mandelbaum (2005) also claim that two of the activities rely on a history of shared experiences together and seem to be necessary for enacting enduring close relationships: updating each other concerning past events and creating contexts for displaying mutual shared knowledge and experiences. The other two activities – troubles telling and producing and taking up improprieties – rather, do not presuppose that the persons have a history of shared experiences and, thus, "are not limited to ongoing intimate relationships, yet constitute moments of intimacy and strong affiliation" (Pomerantz & Mandelbaum, 2005, p. 169).[5] For the psychotherapy context, it is important to note that therapists and clients, because they tend to meet at regular intervals, may also develop their relationship over time. Furthermore, the first session or encounter between therapist and client marks the setting in which their relationship begins to take form (see Scarvaglieri, 2020). The kinds of sequential patterns accomplished in this first encounter may, therefore, provide a critical context in which the relationship may continue to be shaped in a more or less productive way in subsequent encounters.

Although all these sequence types identified by Pomerantz and Mandelbaum have been shown to occur in some form that will be tailored to the therapeutic context, troubles telling sequences will be, for most therapies, by far the most common. This sequence type provides a powerful means for therapists to provide empathy and support (moments of strong affiliation) to the client's

[5] There are, of course, other activities that have social-affiliative payoffs in forging relationships. Displaying immediate recognition of a caller during telephone call openings, based simply on a greeting such as "hi," is another way to display closeness (Enfield, 2006; Schegloff, 2007).

distress without having to assume a close relationship – see Chapters 4 and 5. From my analyses of psychotherapy sessions, inquiries about tracked events tend to occur at the very beginning of the session, before the "actual" therapeutic business gets underway. Making oblique references to shared experiences – for example, therapists offering a second story that conveys a similar experience – seem to appear only rarely (but see Leudar et al., 2006), as do occurrences of therapist laughter following clients' humorous depictions of situations or individuals. Therapists do, however, commonly make references to clients' prior tellings and in this way create "links" between clients' narrated personal experiences (Peräkylä, 2004). Initially, these narrations of personal experience may be seen to be primarily owned by the client. But through the process of dialogue and of therapists' making links between different facets of clients' experiences, the tellings become, in a sense, shared and known-in-common and thus work at creating more intimacy between the participants. But in general, therapeutic sequences are built up such that it is therapists who are responsive to clients' personal experience and conduct, rather than the other way around, and so the opportunities to form emotional connections, bilaterally, are limited.[6]

*Affiliation: A Conversational Building Block of Social Relationships* The sequential patterns outlined by Pomerantz and Mandelbaum (2005) constitute some of the typical resources for how persons may enact "close relationships" in everyday contexts. They also point out that the type of response in each of these sequences plays a key role in showing the quality of relationship that is being enacted. Thus, whereas responses that comply with the requirements of the prior action in each of these sequences potentially result in doing closeness in the relationship (i.e., providing details of personal events, displaying empathy as a recipient to a prior telling, displaying knowledge of a shared event, responding with additional improprieties or laughter), non-complying responses will instead place intimacy at risk and may create a momentary distance in the relationship. Further, having a close or intimate relationship will place expectations on the production of initiating actions for some of these sequences; for instance, not inquiring about tracked events and not telling about one's own problems may involve a breach of intimacy, thus holding those who have made the breach accountable. Another potentially challenging issue may arise in cases where speakers assume "too much" intimacy (or distance). For example, providing *too many* personal details or displaying *too*

[6] To be clear, I am not arguing that therapists and clients are not able to form strong emotional connections. They certainly can. The claim is rather that, *during therapy*, there exists an asymmetry as to how emotional connections are accomplished. There are no real opportunities for therapists to tell their troubles and for clients to be emotionally supportive toward their therapists.

*much* knowledge may also create relational strains, as might be the case when, for example, a psychotherapist is being excessively empathic.

The social actions that we commonly produce in social life (e.g., troubles tellings, inquiring about tracked events) and the way in which we respond to these initiating actions thus have deep interpersonal relevance. This is because, as mentioned in the preceding paragraphs, speakers go publicaly on record to display the extent to which they agree, disagree, comply and resist. The current relationship may be upheld or locally modified through these actions, especially when speakers assume too much intimacy/distance, knowledge or "conversational control," thus exhibiting conduct that is incongruent with the presumed role relationship (e.g., friend–friend or therapist–client). Within CA research, the social implications of these actions/responses have been broadly examined under the following construct: *affiliation*. In general, affiliation has been described as actions that are *pro-social* and often work to show some form of agreement, compliance or support of the other person's social conduct or show consideration of the other's well-being, interests, needs and so on (Heritage, 1984; Jefferson & Lee, 1980; Stivers, 2008). Affiliation has been argued to be a basic conversational principle (Enfield, 2006) and is comparable to other sociological constructs such as *face* and *facework* (Goffman, 1967), in such a way that talk tends to be organized so as to promote social solidarity and avoid conflict and that speakers tend to design their utterances so as to receive affiliative uptake from others and avoid face-threatening situations (Brown & Levinson, 1987; Davidson, 1984; Goffman, 1967; Heritage, 1984; Muntigl & Turnbull, 1998; Pomerantz, 1984).

Affiliation – and its counterpart, disaffiliation – is relevant at any sequential position in an interaction. For this reason, it may be viewed as an essential conversational building block of social relationships. Within each turn at talk, speakers display degrees of acceptance or rejection of others and their conduct, thus influencing their momentary status of intimacy/distance and role relations. Affiliation, as an omnipresent analytic construct for examining conversational sequences in therapy, will be taken up in Chapter 3. More generally, the CA concept of affiliation will be used throughout this book to explore how therapists and clients work pro-socially to create and maintain a "closer" working relationship founded on support and empathy and, in addition, deal with disaffiliation arising from differing viewpoints, unsuccessful displays of empathy or a reluctance (from the client) to engage in therapeutic work.

## 1.6 Outline of Book

The data used to explore psychotherapy conversations were derived from an extensive psychotherapy database, the York 1 Depression Study, that was originally collected by Prof. Les Greenberg in the mid- to late 1990s (Greenberg &

Watson, 1998). Prof. Greenberg and Prof. Angus provided me with restricted access to some of the cases and sessions from that study. I was able to examine twenty cases (with twenty different clients) of video- and audiotaped sessions involving clients suffering from MDD. The clients under investigation were each offered a total of twenty sessions of either EFT (Greenberg, 2002, 2010) or client-centred therapy (CCT; Rogers, 1951, 1957). Three videotaped sessions from each case were made available. These sessions were transcribed according to standard CA conventions (Hepburn & Bolden, 2013) and transcriptions of bodily comportment, multimodality, and non-lexical vocalizations were further informed by Hepburn (2004), Hoey (2014) and Mondada (2018) – a list of CA transcription conventions used in this book is shown in at the front of the volume. Although most of the extracts from this book are taken from emotion-focused interventions, some examples of client-centred conversations have been included to illustrate certain phenomena tightly related to affiliation.

Before delving immediately into affiliation, Chapter 2 sets the stage by providing an extensive overview of the kinds of sequences regularly found in EFT and CCT conversations. Thus, this chapter shows what kinds of initiating actions clients and therapists tend to produce in therapy and which responses typically occur following these actions. Chapter 3 then builds on the overview of sequence types from the prior chapter by outlining the practices in which affiliation or disaffiliation may be achieved in the various sequence types. Associated and relevant concepts important for understanding affiliation, such as alignment and epistemics, are also discussed. Chapter 4 deals with a concept that is related to and closely linked with affiliation: *empathy*. In this part, I draw from past CA research to consider how empathy may be construed in interactional terms that may clearly differentiate it from affiliation and other concepts related to "emotional support." The next two chapters, 5 and 6, take an in-depth look at two kinds of activities that are central to EFT: storytelling and chair work. Storytelling plays an important role in all therapies. By telling stories, clients provide recipients with access to their personal experiences, their life troubles and how these experiences may be causing them considerable upset. In Chapter 5, I show how clients narrate these life experiences using affective stance resources and, equally important, how therapists can affiliate with these stances and provide a unique understanding (empathy) of what has been distressing the client. Chapter 6 on chair work is rather unique to emotion-focused modes of intervention – but also found in gestalt therapy. I show how clients and therapists enter this activity, how therapists formulate their proposals to gain smooth entry and how securing affiliation at each point in the entry process is important for moving forward in this activity. In Chapters 7 and 8, I turn my attention to therapeutic episodes in which clients and therapists are at variance with each other: disaffiliation. Chapter 7 places its focus on how re-affiliation is achieved when clients initially disagree with a therapist formulation. It shows the range of practices, both vocal and non-vocal, that person-centred therapists tend to draw from in getting the conversation back on track. Chapter 8 investigates a topic that is central to psychotherapy research: alliance ruptures. Drawing from an already well-established action terminology of "withdrawal" vs. "opposition," I show the manifold ways in which these rupture-relevant, disaffiliative actions may be accomplished in sequences of talk. Chapter 9 provides a critical reflection of the interactional data presented in this book along two lines: our understanding of how therapist–client relationships are accomplished and of the productive versus detrimental role of dissaffiliation in psychotherapy interaction. Further consideration is also given to the clinical population targeted in this work, persons with major depression, and how CA may reveal some important links between interactional practices and mental disorders.

# 2 Sequences in Psychotherapy Talk

## 2.1 Overview: Action Sequences

When a therapist and client occupy a shared space,[1] have auditory/visual access to each other and are able to jointly construct a common focus, they are said to be in a *focused interaction* (Goffman, 1963; Kendon, 1990). These kinds of interactions have been shown to be highly organized and, thus, enable therapists and clients – and speakers more generally – to do the following: negotiate turns-at-talk, coordinate each other's social actions (e.g., greetings, leave-taking, questioning) and display degrees of engagement or disengagement toward a certain line of activity (Atkinson & Heritage, 1984; Goodwin & Goodwin, 2004; Sacks, 1995; Schegloff, 2007). This becomes possible because each turn at talk occurs within a sequential context that is composed of a series of interlocking turns. Every utterance orients to (i.e., is responsive to) the immediately prior utterance and forms the local context for the next utterance. This phenomenon, in which each utterance is both *context-shaped* and *context renewing* (Heritage, 1984), enables speakers to be in constant intersubjective alignment. This is because each utterance acts as a *display* that documents exactly how the prior speaker's utterance was understood by the current speaker. In this way, if there is a problem in understanding, the speakers may use the immediate next turn to clarify or repair any misunderstandings that have arisen (Schegloff et al., 1977). From this perspective, intersubjectivity is seen as a publicaly displayed, interactional accomplishment that is predicated on what the speakers have visual and auditory access to, rather than simply on speakers' shared mental states (Deppermann, 2008, p. 74). Intersubjectivity, however, is not the only form of alignment between speakers that is ongoingly accomplished via sequence organization. The context-shaping and renewing schema outlined by Heritage (1984) also enables speakers to display affective positions (or stances) toward events/persons and, in turn, allows others to convey support (or opposition) toward these stances. Through these cohesively linked utterances, speakers may constantly build, maintain or alter their affiliative connections toward each other (Enfield, 2006).

[1] Or even therapist*s* and client*s*, depending on the mode of therapy.

Unfolding actions through time adhere to general principles of sequence organization that facilitate the accomplishment of different kinds of interactional work. As Schegloff (2007, p. 2) succinctly phrases it:

> "Sequence organization" … is the organization of courses of action enacted through turns-at-talk – coherent orderly, meaningful successions or "sequences" of actions or "moves." Sequences are the vehicle for getting some activity accomplished.

Thus, through sequences of talk, people co-create activities that are germane to everyday life (e.g., telling stories, gossiping, updating each other on personal events), and also to the myriads of institutional (e.g., service and professional) encounters they engage in on a daily basis. Sequence organization has been able to provide a framework in which to understand and analyze important social interactional phenomena. I mention here but a few: distribution of rights and access to knowledge, mobilizing others to act and creating degrees of closeness or intimacy (or distance) between persons. The first is commonly taken up under the rubric of *epistemics* (Heritage, 2012), the second under *deontics* (Stevanovic & Svennevig, 2015) and the third under *relationships* (Pomerantz & Mandelbaum, 2005).

There has been much research in CA that has worked toward explicating the meaningful connections between actions in sequence. One of the most far-reaching observations is that actions in sequence tend to form basic sequential units that have been commonly termed *adjacency pairs* (Schegloff & Sacks, 1973). Adjacency pairs are composed of two neighbouring, sequential actions that are produced by two different speakers. The two action pairs stand in a unique relation to each other, an initiating first action or first pair part (FPP) followed by a responding action or second pair part (SPP); thus, as a general rule, answers follow questions, acceptances follow requests, a return greeting follows a greeting and so on. Adjacency pairs are also pair-type related. For instance, although questions would project answers as a possible next, greetings would not. This means that certain kinds of responses are appropriately placed subsequent to initiating actions whereas others would not be construed as suitable.

A normative relationship that is termed *conditional relevance* exists between adjacency pair units (Schegloff, 1968). SPPs are relevant and expected following the production of an FPP, and if an SPP is not produced (e.g., the person does not know the answer to the question), it is expected of the second speaker that an explanation or *account* will be given for not being able to produce the SPP. Research has shown that response relevance and expectancy may vary in degree depending on the adjacency pair in question. For example, Stivers and Rossano (2010) found that although requests, offers and information requests tend to strongly mobilize a subsequent response, initiating actions such as assessments, noticings and announcements have a much weaker mobilizing tendency. They were also able to identify a list of response-mobilizing features that largely increased the tendency for receiving a next response. These features included interrogative mood structure, interrogative prosody, speaker gaze and recipient-tilted epistemic asymmetry. Thus by incorporating these features into the turn design of a "weakly" mobilizing action such as an assessment, the speaker of the initiating action was more likely to receive a responsive action.

In this chapter, the focus will mainly be on sequence organization in person-centred therapies (EFT/CCT): how clients and therapists produce sequences of actions that are meaningfully connected in systematic ways. Structural organization and how this relates to specific activities and affiliation will be taken up in later chapters.

## 2.2 Action Sequences in Psychotherapy: An Overview

Psychotherapeutic work is largely accomplished through action sequences. Peräkylä (2019), in fact, views sequences as the main vehicle for spearheading transformations of the client's experience. These transformations, according to Peräkylä, occur at three levels: *referents*, *emotions* and *relations*. Whereas referents are loosely considered to be the "content" of the client's domain of experience (real, imagined or dreamed about), emotion concerns the affectual component of this experience. Relations, on the other hand, pertains to the social relationship between therapist and client and how these relations are, for example, managed via (dis)affiliative displays and claims to knowledge (epistemic status relations).

A collection of studies on psychotherapy talk from a range of different psychotherapy approaches has gone a considerable way in outlining the kinds of actions that do initiating or responding work (Peräkylä et al., 2008). For example, it was found that therapists tend to initiate sequences with questions and respond to clients' initial actions via formulations, extensions or interpretations and that clients produce answers, agreements, elaborations or defensive actions in responding to therapists (Vehviläinen et al., 2008). Even though Vehviläinen et al.'s overview was not meant to supply a complete list of actions in various sequential positions, it does already show the broad variety of interactional work that is done in psychotherapy. In this chapter, I build on this prior work by illustrating the regularly occurring types of initiating and responsive actions that I have found in the many cases and sessions of EFT or CCT examined. These sequence types are differentiated as follows: client initiating actions; therapist initiating actions; and therapist responsive actions. Client responsive actions are not considered here for two reasons: first, they will be given due consideration in the next chapter on affiliation; and second, unlike therapist responsive actions, which perform specific kinds of therapeutic work, client responses are more generic, displaying various degrees of agreement/disagreement or compliance/non-compliance.

Client initiating actions tended to come in two formats – troubles tellings and optimistic tellings, as shown in the following list:

1. Troubles tellings
   a. Complaints
   b. Self-deprecations
   c. Emotional displays
2. Optimistic tellings

The term *troubles telling* is taken from Jefferson (1988) and refers to client reports about their problems or client displays of their current distress. Optimistic tellings, on the other hand, concern instances in which clients report on positive events in their lives, events that often mark a contrast to past problems that have been affecting them. Troubles telling is further grouped into three types: Complaints, self-deprecations and emotional displays.

Therapist initiating actions generally come in two types – questions and directives. Questions are examined with respect to two different grammatical formats: *Wh*-interrogative and Y/N (yes/no) interrogative. Directives were identified as either commands or suggestions.

1. Questions
   a. *Wh*-interrogative
   b. Y/N-interrogative
2. Directives
   a. Command
   b. Suggestion

There was much variation with respect to therapist responsive actions. First, these actions were differentiated with respect to whether they were client-oriented or therapist-oriented. Put simply, client-oriented responses tended to focus on the client's talk (i.e., the client's words or expressions), whereas therapist-oriented responses would emphasize the therapist's point of view, thus going beyond the client's own message:

Client-oriented responses included repetitions (echoing, mirroring) and formulations (summary, upshot), whereas therapist-oriented responses included noticings, extensions, interpretations, challenges and correcting:[2]

**Client-oriented**

1. Repetitions
   a. Echoing
   b. Mirroring

[2] Another type of response, co-completions or *delayed/anticipatory completions* (Lerner, 1991) will be taken up in Chapter 4 on empathy.

2. Formulations
   a. Summary/Gist
   b. Upshot

**Therapist-oriented**
1. Noticings
2. Extensions
3. Interpretations
4. Challenges
5. Correcting

A more detailed overview of each of the initiating and responsive action types, including examples, will be given in the following sections.

## 2.3 Client Initiating Actions

Because clients who enter psychotherapy tend to experience some form of distress (Pennebaker & Segal, 1999), therapeutic conversations typically involve talk about troubles or problems. Many researchers have characterized therapy as involving problem-focused activities such as *problem formation* and *problem resolution* (Walzlawick et al., 1974), *problem-organizing* and *problem-dissolving* (Anderson & Goolishian, 1988), *problem evolution* and *problem dissolution* (Eron & Lund, 1993) and *problem construction* and *problem effacement* (Muntigl, 2004).[3] Research on couples therapy has shown that talk and language use can be different in the initial, problem-focused phase of the therapeutic encounter, compared with later stages when the problem has been dissolved or effaced; for example, problem-focused phases involve client complaints, affective stances of unhappiness/sadness and dissatisfaction and a focus on past and ongoing negative behaviours (realis), whereas "post-problem" phases involve talk that contains positive affect, clients' capability and irrealis (future, possible events)[4] constructions (Muntigl, 2004). Similar kinds of client talk were found in person-centred sessions. Most commonly, clients would engage in troubles telling to report on their problems. These were contrasted with optimistic tellings in which clients would report on alternative behaviours, their positive affect or their ability to act in their relationships in new ways. These kinds of changes, however, may be predicated on whether clients display "recovery" from their depression.

[3] Gaik (1992, p. 276) provides a similar conceptualization of therapy as a speech event. Gaik turns his attention primarily to the communicative structure of therapy and the way in which specific language selections provide "contextualization cues" to the conversationalists that they are in a certain activity rather than another. He argues that therapy consists of two activities or modes, which he labels as therapeutic and counselling. The therapeutic mode is non-directive and is oriented to a discovery procedure of what the problem might be, whereas the counselling mode is directive, focusing more on giving advice or finding a solution to the problem.

[4] See also Gaik (1992).

### 2.3.1 *Troubles Tellings*

One common thread that runs across the different helping professions is the general scenario in which clients seek out professionals for assistance and, in doing so, offer a "report of a problematic experience" (Ruusuvuori, 2005, pp. 204–5). Following Jefferson (1988), these contexts realize what is known as "troubles talk". Client troubles may take on myriad forms. In medicine, for example, troubles often relate to a patient's physical/biological ailments, whereas in couples counselling, relationship troubles tend to get put on the agenda. Jefferson's (1988) work has shown that troubles telling is an activity that is germane to everyday, not just institutional, contexts. Troubles telling has a "tightly ordered" 3-part sequential organization, with the troubles telling as the initiating action, followed by a responsive action from the recipient that often exhibits some degree of affiliation with the troubles conveyed by the teller. Then, in a third action slot, tellers provide their reaction to the recipient's response, often as a form of "return affiliation." Jefferson (1988, p. 428) has found that, for everyday contexts, troubles tellings contain "emotionally heightened talk, 'letting go' and/or turning to or confiding in the troubles/recipient." Further, these contexts often mark a momentary shift in the relationship, as movement from more distant to more intimate and a topical shift in which talk more intensely focuses on the trouble. Three types of troubles tellings were identified in our psychotherapy corpus: complaints, self-deprecations and distress displays.

*Complaints* Clients would complain about non-present others' actions and often treat these actions as involving moral transgressions, thus blaming the other party for having behaved inappropriately (see Drew, 1998). A complaint is shown in Extract 2.1. An overview of the transcription conventions used in this book is provided at the front of the volume.

**Extract 2.1:** 312.02(5)

```
Paula: so I'm just, (4.3) I know tha- (.) t- marriage, (.) °like the
       last years were quite terrible.° e(hh)heh not s- (.) well,
       (0.8)
       there were- (.) were a lot of circumstances, (.) and things
       happening, like which (.) affected our (0.3) °relationship.°
       (2.4)
Paula: and I guess one of the things I was, (0.8) I always have been
       really upset about it is, (0.5) like his family, (0.7) because,
       (.) well since he's- (1.2) ((nationality)), (0.4) like his
       parents really never wanted (0.3) t- to meet ↑me and (.) the,
       [moment] they found out=like that we were actually married
Ther:  [°hm.° ]
       they (.) disowned him as well [hh .hh]
```

```
14 Ther:                                 [↑mm.]
15          (0.5)
16 Paula: but now that we are divorced, like he's welcome back.
17          (0.3)
18 Paula: °yeah so it's,°
19          (0.5)
20 Ther:  so they really didn't accept you.=
21 Paula: =no, no, [not at all.]
```

Paula complains about the unfair treatment she had received from her ex-husband's parents. Her recount is infused with numerous displays of negative affect. Paula begins in lines 01–05 with a few general evaluations of the situation: "`the last years were quite terrible`"; "`affected our (0.3) °relationship.°`". She then elaborates on this stance by providing a few examples: "`parents really never wanted (0.3) t- to meet ↑me`"; "`they (.) disowned him as well`". In line 16, she rounds off her complaint by mentioning that the son has again been welcomed back by the family because they are now divorced. The parents' treatment of Paula has been carefully worked up as a transgression, as being unjust and deserving of blame. The therapist, in line 20, responds to Paula's complaint with endorsement, by pointing out the parents' non-accepting attitude.

*Self-Deprecations* In contrast to a complaint sequence, which in this context is directed at a non-present third party, self-deprecating actions provide a negative appraisal of self. Self-deprecating sequences minimally consist of a pair of interlocking actions (Pomerantz, 1984): An initiating self-critical action by the client, followed by the therapist's response.[5] For "everyday" contexts, Pomerantz (1984) argued that self-critical actions tend to be followed by a form of disagreement (sometimes including praise), rather than agreement. Thus, if a person makes negative claims related to their "imperfections," respondents will tend to contradict the prior speaker and extol his or her personal qualities. This tendency toward disagreeing is argued to have an affiliative function, working to maintain social solidarity and thus strengthen personal bonds (Brown & Levinson, 1987; Enfield, 2006; Pomerantz, 1984). Agreement in this context, however, would work in a disaffiliative fashion, as the respondent is corroborating the claim that the person is flawed. Turning now to psychotherapeutic contexts, one of the challenges therapists face is to support the client's rights to make self-critical claims and to feel pain as a result without actually signalling agreement that the therapist also shares this view. A client self-deprecation is shown in Extract 2.2.

[5] *Self-criticism*, a term commonly used in psychotherapy research, is used synonymously in this book with the term *self-deprecation*.

**Extract 2.2:** 14.3

01 Kris: som- (.) so pr-pr-probably? uhx:.
02 (14.0)
03 Kris: .Hh
04 (0.6)
05 Kris: s::ometimes I have uh (.) m: (0.6) difficulties with uh
06 (0.3) m:. (0.2) °°m- m- y'know.°° (0.4) saying my
07 feelings (huh:.) as(h)uh
t nods, raises eyebrows
08 Ther: su:r[e ]
09 Kris: [.h] a(h)s [we know.hihhuhhuhhuh ]
k smiling->
10 Ther: [^that's what we've been £talking about yeah.£]
t smiling->

Prior to this extract, Kristina had disclosed to the therapist that she had tried to role-play conversations with her mother and that, although she found it difficult, it was easier than if her mother had been physically present. In the current sequence, Kristina provides a self-deprecating utterance by stating that she finds it difficult to express her feelings. The therapist's response of "su:re" in line 08 ostensibly provides confirmation, but as we see later in line 10, this is offered as a way of validating the client's rights to talk about these difficulties, rather than as sharing the view that the client is inadequate.

Because self-deprecations are directed at the self, they may have negative implications concerning agency and blame. Extract 2.3 shows how Ernie has been telling the therapist about how he had been trying to assist his wife (now ex-wife) financially and work-wise, but that his endeavours had been met with no success and substantial financial losses – self-deprecations highlighted in bold.

**Extract 2.3:** Ernie: Case 422.09

01 Ernie: yeah, everything every a- and I I I went to (0.4) y'know I wen-
02 I went to all kinds of efforts.
03 Ther: *[mm hm. ]
04 Ernie: [to assist] under the most difficult >circumstances<*.hh and
t *shallow nods-> shallow nods->*
05 they won't (3.0) I gue- I guess **I have to question myself.**
06 (0.3)
07 Ernie: you know why was + I doing that?
e +looks at T->
08 Ther: *mm hm? mm hm?*
t *shallow nods*
09 (0.7)
10 Ernie: uhm, +
e looks at T+
11 (1.9)
12 Ernie: **it's it's not normal for somebody to keep helping** (0.3)
13 in a +hostile *environment [where that help] isn't a[ppreciated.]

```
14  Ther:                                [mm hm         ]        [mm hm      ]
        e        +looks at T->
        t                  *shallow nods->
15  Ther:   ↑mm hm=that's an interesting ques↑tions.=
16  Ernie:  so (.) why was [↑ I doing] with [that.]
17  Ther:                  [(why)    ]      [mm   ]hm?
18  Ther:   why mm hm so even to yourself it's sort of puzzling
19          why we why would you keep hammering away at something
20  Ernie:  yeah
```

Using extreme case descriptions (Pomerantz, 1986), Ernie conveys the magnitude of his assistance and the degree of hardship surrounding his benevolent actions (`all kinds of efforts.`, line 02; `the most difficult >circumstances<`, line 04). This leads Ernie to question his motives and, in lines 12–13, to negatively judge his behaviour as deviant (`it's it's not normal for somebody to keep helping`). There is also an aspect of self-blame to Ernie's self-deprecation; that is, there is an implication that he should "know better" than to try to provide assistance to someone who is hostile toward him and is not appreciative of his efforts. As a response, line 15 onwards, the therapist provides a more optimistic spin on Ernie's dilemma. She frames it as "an interesting question" and, later, as a puzzle that needs to be worked out and understood.[6] Thus, rather than confirming Ernie's deviancy and self-blame, she subtly shapes the direction of talk toward something that may be therapeutically more relevant.

*Distress Displays* Distress may be conveyed in interaction in either of two forms: through a reporting of a past distressful event or via an *in the moment* expression of distress (Antaki et al., 2015). In the latter sense, distress is something that emerges in the here-and-now and is built up through talk and other non-vocal means to express tearfulness and, in most intense forms, crying (Wootton, 2012). Many vocal distress markers of varying intensity have been identified in Hepburn's (2004) influential work on crying, such as sniffs, pitch changes, aspiration, tremulous voice and sobbing. Other possible distress markers have been noted by Hoey (2014) in reference to sighing.

In Extract 2.4 with the client Lisa, she and the therapist had been discussing a certain pattern in Lisa's life in which she goes through cycles of having happy and sad days. Furthermore, this pattern of cyclical moods is very much contingent on her husband's gambling addiction and whether he is engaging in this behaviour.

**Extract 2.4:** Lisa: Case 306.14

```
01  Lisa:  so that's:(0.3) +I guess something I (0.2) I have to work on,
        l                  +crosses arms-> gaze to T->
02  Ther:  .hh
```

[6] See Vehviläinen's (2008) study of psychoanalytic practices in which therapists focus on client actions as a "puzzle to be explained or accounted for."

```
03            (1.3)
04   Ther:    +*↑well (.) I guess you're saying though
          l   +furrows brow, lowers head gaze downward---+gaze to T
05            that you gist (0.3) kind of (0.7)
06            +stay with+ (0.7) °*whatever co:mes.        *right?°
          l   +nods---   + opens tissue,
          t                         *turns palms side to side*hand together
07            (0.4)
08   Lisa:    +°~↑yeh~°
          l   +scrunches face, wipes eyes, gaze down->
09            (0.6)
10   Lisa:    .snih=
11   Ther:    +=°what's *happening now?°=+
          l   +wipes nose, tissue over mouth---+
          t              *extend finger(s) & head to L-->
12   Lisa:    +=↑uh:m        *(1.9) an I guess ↑accepting?
          l   +hand near/covering mouth->
13            (1.8)
14   Ther:    it's hard to accept this
15            (0.4)
16   Lisa:    +↑yeh
```

Just prior to this extract, Lisa confirms being aware of a pattern in which she has very bad, bleak days and, in line 01, she states that this is something she needs to work on. The therapist's response, however, suggests something slightly different; that is, Lisa tends to remain with or endure these feelings. It is at this point that we see Lisa displaying increased distress such as furrowing her brow and lowering her head (line 04) and opening her tissue (line 06). Then, after a brief pause in line 07, she offers confirmation with a tremulous, quiet voice, while simultaneously scrunching her face and wiping her eyes, followed by another small pause and a sniff (line 10). The therapist, in line 11, orients to this display of distress by asking Lisa "°what's *happening now?°", which then gets Lisa to focus on her distress.

### 2.3.2 *Optimistic Tellings*

Although talk about troubles forms the lion's share of psychotherapeutic work, conversations can, especially in the later stages of therapy, extend beyond problems. These conversations become more focused on positive affect pertaining to alternative life experiences. Consider Extract 2.5 involving the client Joanna, who had been telling the therapist about her recent phone conversation with her mother.

**Extract 2.5:** 412.07(2b)

```
01 Jo:     but=at the same time I can't let them, (1.0) >you know< I kno:w
02         she's been looking at me like ↑oh: wh(h)at's happened to you:.
03         .hhh [and last night on the] phone. >because I wasn't< expecting
04 Ther:        [   mm::.           ]
05 Jo:     it, and I've been having >a really good week,< .hh like I was-
06         (0.6) very h:appy, I [wasn't (0.3) CO:]ld?
07 Ther:                        [mm     ↑h:m.    ]
08         (0.3)
09 Ther:   yea:h. =
10 Jo:     = you know what I mean?
11 Ther:   mm ↑hm.
       t   deep nod
12 Jo:     a:n- .hh ((blows nose)) so:, (0.4) she sa:id that- I said well,
13         (0.8) you know, the therapy is doing ↑good >she goes< I can hear
14         the difference in your ↑voice.
15         (0.3)
16 Ther:   wo:[::w.             ]
       t   slow nod
17 Jo:        [you know, and that ma]kes me really ↑ha:ppy.
18         (0.5)
19 Ther:   and how was that for you:. =
20 Jo:     = yeah↑ =
21 Ther:   = te hear he:[r,]
22 Jo:                  [it] made me feel good?
       j                multiple nods
```

At the beginning of this narrative, lines 01–02, there is already a premonition that good news will be told, as may be implied from Joanna's direct report of the mother's speech, that is, as a quote (↑oh: wh(h)at's happened to you:.). This is followed by a number of positive attributes (having >a really good week,<;very h:appy). Later, after the client had remarked on the benefits of therapy, line 14, she produces another instance of *direct reported speech* (Clift & Holt, 2007), in which the mother notices the benefits (I can hear the difference in your ↑voice.). The therapist then responds with positive appreciation and surprise (wo:::w) and, later, elicits Joanna's reaction to her mother's noticing, to which she responds positively with "it made me feel good?".

## 2.4 Therapist Initiating Actions

Therapists tend to produce two basic types of initiating actions: questions and directives. Each of these will be examined in the following sections.

### 2.4.1 *Questions*

Within linguistics, the category *question* is commonly given a discourse functional interpretation. Quirk et al. (1985) contrast questions with declaratives, directives and exclamations, whereas Halliday (1994) views questions as different in function from statements, commands and offers. Question types may be differentiated in the following way: YES/NO, WH and ALTERNATIVE (Quirk et al., 1985, p. 806). Questions are generally thought to function as seeking information. However, as Stivers' (2010) work has shown, questions may also have other functions such as requesting confirmation and other initiating repair. Further, questions may contain presuppositions and may work to set specific agendas, especially in institutional talk (Ehrlich & Sidnell, 2006; Hayano, 2013; Heritage, 2010).

*Wh-Interrogative* A standard format for doing information requests is the *wh*-interrogative. These questions contain "*wh*-elements" such as *who*, *where*, *why* and *how*, with the respondent being expected to supply the requested "wh" information. Fox and Thompson (2010) claim that *wh*-interrogatives come in two types. The first type consists of *specifying questions*, in which the questioner seeks particular kinds of information. They note that these questions are often used as vehicles for doing other kinds of interactional work such as initiating repair and doing a "pre-request." The other type, *telling questions*, tends to seek more elaborate responses that often appear in the form of stories, tellings, reports and accounts.

Although specifying questions did occur in the person-centred conversations that I examined, they were relatively rare. An example can be seen in Extract 2.6, in which the client Matthew has been reporting on his past experiences with his family.

**Extract 2.6:** Matthew 021.08(4)

```
01 Matt:  >°was about to say°< sumpin °I forget.°
02        (1.0)
03 Matt:  °°geez°°
       m  grabs chin
04        (8.4)
05 Matt:  <li::> (°kinda) lost it.°
       m  flips hand up, slaps hand on arm, shakes head
06        (1.0)
07 Matt:  I=w's jus thinkin bout uh when my mother died.
08        (0.7)
09 Matt:  uhm (2.6) that uh: (1.8) oltha I was f(h)reely >in touch with my<
10        feelings at that point, (0.7) AFTERwards our- it's ↑weird
11        our family kina went apart. instead a together.
```

```
12 Ther:  is [thah=right.]
13 Matt:     [my       fam]ily (stayed) ↑yeah.
14        (0.7)
       t  shallow double nod
15 Matt:  >I=think we jus kina went off on our own little< (1.3) I don't
16        know worlds an. (0.3) jis- an then dealt with it. °whatever way
17        they cou:ld.°
18        (1.0)
19 Matt:  but uh (1.2) >I was< (0.2) ach'ly quite alone at the time, and uh
20        .hh ah member sometimes at work, (0.3) I work (0.5) surprisingly,
21        hh a- a lot of hours of, (0.8) ((lip smack)) lotta part time
22        jobs. .hhh an that's basi'ly how I >kina=avoided dealing with=it
23        for a while< was uh. (.) just working.
24        (0.9)
25 Matt:  like [throw f-]
26 Ther:       [throwing] yourself indo [it,]
27 Matt:                                [↑we]ll ↑yeah an jus running from
28        job ta job an (I liked ta jo) jobs and uh,
29        (0.5)
       m  shrugs
30 Ther:  how old were you when your mom died Ma[tthew?]
31 Matt:                                        [uh::m ] >twenny=one.<
       m                                        looks at T
32        (0.3)
       m  nod
33 Ther:  twenny one, =
       t  double nod
34 Matt:  = yep.
       m  looks away
```

At the beginning of this extract (lines 01–07), Matt launches into a general report about how the death of his mother precipitated a strain in family relations (`our family kina went apart. instead a together.`, line 11). From line 19 onwards, Matt then talks about how his mother's death impacted on his own behaviour, as feeling "`quite alone at the time`", having "`avoided dealing with=it`" and "`jus running from job ta job`". In line 30, the therapist produces a specifying question, asking Matt to provide his age when his mother had died. The question, in this sequential slot, works to shift the trajectory of talk. It does this by not orienting to the emotional implications of the client's prior report (i.e., on the strains in his family relations and how the mother's death impacted on him), but rather to specific features of the event such as the client's age.

*Wh*-interrogatives such as "how are you?" are commonly used at the beginning of sessions to get the conversation going, as shown in Extract 2.7 with the client Ernie.

**Extract 2.7:** Case 422.9.1_Ernie [Beginning of session]

```
01 Ther:  so how are y↓ou,
02 Ernie: +okay.        +
        e +nod, stops smiling+
03 Ther:  yeah=
04 Ernie: =mm
05        (0.9)
06 Ther:  an'ow's your week been?
07        (1.3)
08 Ernie: well (0.5) I (0.2) it's been been-a little better than last week.
09 Ther:  *uh huh.
        t *multiple nods--->
10 Ernie: yeah. a little better.
11        (1.1)
12 Ther:  and what was the:: little better, what made it a little bit
13        better?
14        (2.0)
15 Ernie: well I I finally got (0.4) some (0.3) results on my work for one
16        thing and
17 Ther:  m↑hm.
```

In line 01, the therapist produces the *wh*-interrogative "`so how are y↓ou,`", which is followed by an "`okay.`" response from Ernie. We would note that, in line 02, Ernie stops smiling, which may be signalling some kind of recognition that both he and the therapist are entering into a new phase of talk that is projecting imminent therapeutic business. The therapist then follows up in line 06 with another *wh*-interrogative that narrows the time frame to the events of the past week. After a significant pause and a *well*-preface that signals a non-straightforward answer (Schelgloff & Lerner, 2009), the client admits to experiencing some improvement. The therapist provides a continuer in line 09, which then has Ernie confirming his prior statement. This is then followed by another *wh*-interrogative from the therapist that gets Ernie to expand on his prior turn by having him provide more detail about what was better.

*Wh*-interrogatives are frequently used as follow-up moves to prompt the client to expand on prior talk. In this way, the question both orients backwards (and is responsive) to preceding talk, but it also projects further talk geared toward the provision of more elaborate descriptions, as shown in Extract 2.8.

**Extract 2.8:** 422.3

```
01 Ernie: well I spoke out immediately when- when I arrived the:re. uh I
02        u:m (0.5) I (.) wuz an:: I was immediate- I was very very ↑angry.
03        an I an I jus left in absolute disgust an an .hh jus (0.6)
04        was so angry I r:eally didn't quite know what
05        to do with myself.=
06 Ther:  =mm hm. and what did that feel like when you
07        were so a:ngry, what was it.
08        (1.0)
09 Ernie: f:hxxxx (1.4) frankly it felt good to express those feelings.
10 Ther:  mm h:m?
```

Ernie had been reporting on his disappointing experiences with a former business associate. At the beginning of this extract he speaks of anger and disgust concerning his associate's improprieties. The therapist responds in line 06, first with minimal acknowledgement (`mm hm.`), and then with a *wh*-interrogative that gets Ernie to expand on how it felt like to vent his anger.

*Wh*-interrogatives were also frequently used to focus clients on their present emotional experiencing. These actions, which have previously been identified in the literature as *immediacy questions* and *immediacy instructions* (Kondratyuk & Peräkylä, 2011), are deployed to get clients to recognize and work on their immediate experience. An immediacy question is illustrated in Extract 2.9 with the client Sofia.

**Extract 2.9:** 304.7

```
01 Ther: it seems to me that you really need love and and you need
       s wipes eye, red nose, tilts head
02       somebody's whose there, and someone whos:e (.) understanding,
03       and .hh (0.4) yihkn- [much like you have what you had
04 Sofi:                      [(uh/how?)
05       with this other man. right, .hh and I just imagine that (0.3)
06       not (0.4) not having that right now is very difficult for you
07       (1.3)
08 Sofi: hmm.
09       (0.2)
       s reaches for tissue
10 Ther: (and) what I'm saying is [making you teary right?]
11 Sofi:                          [.h it is it is ver-    ] yeah.
       s                                         wipes eyes
12       (1.0)
13 Sofi: yeah
14       (0.7)
15 Ther: [so what's happen]ing now, when when I (0.3) say this
```

16 Sofi: [uhm ]
17 (0.3)
18 Ther: (° °) .hh
19 Sofi: it is difficult
s wipes eyes
20 (0.4)
21 Sofi: yah it is. .snih
22 (0.9)
23 Sofi: .shih I just the only thing that I am trying to do (1.2)
24 is to cope. (0.3) [at this time]
25 Ther: [right ] right

The therapist and client had been discussing Sofia's current relationship with her husband. The therapist begins by stating that Sofia needs someone who is understanding and is able to display affection. She then, in lines 05–06, asserts that Sofia is not receiving this from her husband and uses the immediacy marker "right now" to highlight its current relevance. Sofia responds with minimal acknowledgement (hmm.) while reaching for a tissue, thus displaying incipient distress. The therapist then responds with a noticing in line 10 (see description of this action in the following text), which draws explicit attention to her present emotional state. Sofia confirms the therapist's turn in overlap as she wipes the tears form her eyes. Then, in line 15, the therapist produces a *wh*-interrogative (so what's happen]ing now, when when I (0.3) say this) that focuses further on the immediacy of the client's distress.

*Y/N-Interrogative* Raymond's (2003) article on y/n-interrogatives has illustrated the range of responses that may follow these initiating actions. First, owing to the grammatical structure, responses may be *conforming* (either a *yes* or *no*) or non-conforming (something other than a *yes* or *no*). Second, the response may offer *confirmation* or *disconfirmation*. In Extract 2.10 with the client Rachel, the therapist's y/n-interrogative not only seeks confirmation from the client, but also clarification on what she had just said.

**Extract 2.10:** 024.02(1)

01 Rachel: >so I< still might wake up. (0.6) with the night light lit.
02 (0.5)
03 Rachel: .hhh but. >when I< wake up. (0.9) like in a panic or whatever I
04 feel, .hhh
05 Ther: >°mm hm.°<
06 Rachel: I look around. there's nothing there automatically I- I just go
07 right back to sleep.
08 (1.1)

09 Ther: .hhh yeah >I don't know. **are you< saying then that the light,**
10 **>having the< light on though does, give you a sense- more of a**
11 **sense of safety.**
12 Rachel: right.
13 (0.5)
14 Ther: because you kno:w that (0.8) it's not so <unknown?> or scary
15 over there.
16 Rachel: ehhh .hhh ↑well i'm not afraid of it ehhh heh .hh per se. >as
17 soon as I< wake up. =
18 Ther: = yeah.
19 Rachel: I'm not afraid of my own roo:m. of course not. =
20 Ther: yeah.

In this session, the client had been telling the therapist about her nightmares or, as she put it, "night terrors" and that a nightlight seems to help her fall quickly back to sleep if she wakes up. The therapist, in line 09, first responds with acknowledgement (yeah) and then launches into a y/n interrogative (are you< saying then) that is prefaced with an epistemic downgrading expression (I don't know). Her question functions as a request for confirmation and clarification about whether the nightlight gives her a sense of security. Although this action appears to be similar to a formulation (see 2.5.2) because it provides an upshot or implication to leaving the nightlight on (i.e., it gives her a sense of safety), its design seeks explicit confirmation due to its y/n interrogative format. Rachel's response in line 12, "right.", is non-type-conforming because it does not provide a simple "yes" or "no". Her response could be interpreted as an upgraded "yes" that not only supplies confirmation, but also takes on a stronger epistemic position that assesses the therapist's view as being "correct." After receiving confirmation from Rachel, the therapist proceeds to subtly challenge Rachel's fears; that is, Rachel's room is not really an "unknown" or "scary" place and so why would she need to make her surroundings more safe? Rachel then contests this reading in line 16 by stating outright that she is not afraid of her own room.

### *2.4.2 Directives*

A large range of *directive*-type actions have been identified in the literature; for example, requests, suggestions, proposals, commands, advice, offers and many more (Couper-Kuhlen, 2014; Halliday, 1994, p. 363; Landmark et al., 2015; Stevanovic and Svennevig, 2015). These directives come with specified *action formations* (Schegloff, 2007) in which speakers draw from a wide range of multi-modal resources to make the action-import of their turns recognizable to other participants. The turn designs of directive actions may display sensitivity to speakers' role relationships involving speakers' entitlements to formulate these actions (Heinemann, 2006), the contingencies associated with granting requests (Curl & Drew, 2008) and agency with regard to who is being mobilized to act, including who will potentially benefit from the future action, if carried out (Clayman & Heritage, 2014; Drew & Couper-Kuhlen, 2014). For example, Curl and Drew (2008) claimed that request prefaces such as "I wonder if" do not presuppose that a certain course of action is possible or even appropriate. Thus, through this type of preface, the requester does not claim any entitlement to make the request. By contrast, they argued that more conventionalized interrogative request formats such as "Can/could you" index upgraded rights to make the request. Further, the "I wonder if" format highlights the contingent nature of the request, as something that is merely possible, whereas the "Can/could you" format seems to treat the request as relatively straightforward.

Directive actions were mainly made in association with chair work. They occurred mainly as two types: suggestions (or proposals) and commands. Extract 2.11 shows an example of a suggestion.

**Extract 2.11:** Case 306.3

```
01   Lisa:   °°it's°°(0.2)°it's° real confusion. .shih
02           (0.3)
03   Ther:   t.hhh (0.8) i- (0.2) me-I think it would be:(0.3)
04           e-good to (0.3) try::(0.2) e-you know
05           last week I sug[gested] uh
06   Lisa:                  [.hh    ]
07   Lisa:   °yeah.°
08           (0.5)
09   Ther:   t.experiment en .hh (.) and e- (0.3)
10           but this time with your da::d,
11           cuz (.) cuz what yer (0.3) describing + is °is°
12           a f:really (0.2) strong (0.4) feeling of anger+
13           [towards] him en .hhhh (0.6) so thet if you were to
14   Lisa:   [.shih   ]
15   Ther:   (0.4) bring him in here that might (0.6)°I mean° (0.3)
16           bring him in here in an imagine way it would
17            [give   ](0.4) you a chance to actually
18   Lisa:   +[°yeah°]+
19         l +nods-   +
20   Ther:   express it towards+ him. .hh
21           +(0.8)          +
           l +shallow nods+
22   Ther:   *w-  wudja be willing to do it?*
           t *turns head towards L---------*
23   Lisa:   +°↑yah°
```

(1.0)

Ther: okay.
1 +begins getting up-->

Following Lisa's assertion pertaining to the confusion about her father's actions toward her mother, the therapist draws from a number of prefacing devices to frame the upcoming suggestion in a cautious manner. These include pauses, downgraders ("I think"), linking the suggestion with potential benefits (it would be: (0.3) e-good to (0.3) try::, lines 03–04), an orientation to past talk (last week I suggested uh, line 05) and, in line 09, a description of the upcoming suggestion as an "experiment." The therapist then proceeds to specify to whom the dialogue will be directed (with your da::d, line 10) and then goes on to justify her suggestion by, first, underscoring that Lisa has "a f:really (0.2) strong (0.4) feeling of anger" (line 12) and, second, highlighting the benefits of doing chair work; that is, it will give her an opportunity to express her anger. Lisa nods throughout this sequence and provides acknowledgement tokens (lines 7, 18), which suggests that she is affiliating with the therapist's project. Finally, in line 22, the therapist designs the suggestion in terms of the client's willingness (w- wudja be willing to do it?) to which Lisa displays upgraded agreement in line 23.

Directives may also be designed in an imperative format, without any modulation markers or expressions. These discursive features are shown in Extract 2.12 with the same client.

**Extract 2.12:** Lisa: Case 306cs3

Lisa: uh::m (1.4) >I feel good< (0.9) °yeah it°Feels good. .hh
(1.3)

Lisa: ah:: relieving hhx
(1.1)

Ther: °uh huh°
(2.0)

Ther: **sta:y with (0.6) the (.) relief** (0.2) if that's what
you feel right?

(0.2)

Lisa: yeah.
Ther: so:: what- (0.6) **tell him. I feel relieved.** [I-I can]
Lisa: [(yeah) ]
(0.5)

Ther: I'm gonna do what I wanna do, it feels better °this way.°
(0.6)

Lisa: I feel relieved and (0.2) I'm gonna do what I wanna do.
(0.5) ↑what's best for me: (.) .shih cuz it feels good.

(1.1)

Ther: uh huh

Lisa and the therapist are currently in chair work and, at the beginning of this extract, Lisa expresses the positive affect at being able to resist her father's demands on her (`°yeah it°Feels good.`). A first directive appears in line 07 in which the therapist instructs Lisa to maintain a certain emotional intensity (`sta:y with (0.6) the (.) relief`). Later, in line 11, the therapist commands Lisa to direct her feelings at the father (`tell him. I feel relieved.`).

## 2.5 Therapist Responding Actions: Client-Oriented

There are a host of ways in which therapists may respond to clients' talk in general and to their troubles tellings in particular. Vehviläinen et al. (2008) list a few common response types such as formulations, interpretations and extensions. Other types have been identified as *repetitions* (Ferrara, 1994), *challenges/corrections* (Antaki, 2008) and *noticings* (Sacks, 1995a, 1995b; Muntigl & Horvath, 2014a; Pawelczyk, 2011). Examples of these response types will be provided in the following sections. I have, in addition, divided response types into client-oriented vs. therapist-oriented and I begin this section with a discussion of the former type. Client-oriented responses are designed to highlight the client's point of view and to primarily work with, or stay close to, the client's talk. They convey B-events (Labov & Fanshel, 1977), in which clients have expert knowledge of their own experiences (i.e., known to client but not to therapist). Clients demonstrate this expertise by being placed in a position to either *confirm* or *disconfirm* the therapist's prior action. Such responses involve repetitions and formulations.

### *2.5.1 Repetitions*

Ferrara (1994) differentiates between two types of repetitions. The first involves the repetition of the prior speaker's utterance (termed *echoing*) and the second involves partial repetition (termed *mirroring*).

*Repeat Utterance (Echo)* According to Ferrara (1994, p. 113), "echoing ... involves the contiguous repetition of another's utterance or statement using the same downward intonation in an adjacency pair." She also claims that this kind of repetition tends to be client-generated, but this data has also revealed instances that are therapist-generated. Further, echoing functions as displaying acceptance or agreement with the prior statement. Extract 2.13 with the client Kristina illustrates how the therapist had been trying to recruit Kristina to engage in chair work, but has not been successful.

**Extract 2.13:** 14.3

```
01  Ther:  ↑what don't you like about [it do you have any sense?]
02  Kris:                             [.HH ↑I don't know,       ]
03  Kris:  .h I=for me it's I I've prefer to imagine some
        k  stops smiling, turns gaze forward, raises hand in air
04         kind(huh)of or i- (0.3) I (0.2) I don't even imagine
05         I feel thet ye'know some kind of a shad(hoh)w (hih)
        k  waves hand in air, smiling-->
        t  nods-->
06         in=a in a co:rner(huh) hx: it's w-uh .hh (0.2)
        k                     smiling->+
        t                                        nods->*
07  Ther:  so this makes it kind've too re:al?
        t  gaze & hand to chair--> gaze to K
08         (0.3)
09  Kris:  .hh
10         (0.4)
11  Kris:  e:[:     ]
12  Ther:    [or too]::=
13  Kris:  =too unreal.
14         (0.4)
15  Ther:  too unreal.
16         (2.6)
        t  tightens mouth, nods
```

In lines 02–06, Kristina tells the therapist how she would prefer to imagine a non-present other in the room; that is, not as someone in a chair but rather a shadow in a corner. The therapist then responds in line 07 that by imagining someone in a chair "`this makes it kind've too re:al?`". What then follows are a number of delay features (pauses, inbreath) that seem to be signalling that agreement is not imminent. The therapist then begins to offer an alternative description (`or too::`), which is then supplied by Kristina in the next turn (`too unreal.`). In line 15, the therapist echoes and thus signals acceptance with Kristina's utterance using the same stress and downward intonation.

Full repetitions of utterances have also been observed during chair work. In Extract 2.14, the client Jennifer is in a dialogue with a version of her younger self as a little girl.

**Extract 2.14:** Jennifer: Case 428_11

```
01  Ther:  °do whatever I can do anything I can if you just love me.°
02         (2.2)
03  Jen:   .HIH (2.9) .hih (1.3) .hih (3.7) .hih.ih
```

04 ( 0.7 )+
j face in her hands-->+

05 Jen: +~**nobody warn me**~
J +raises face slightly-->

06 (0.6)

07 Jen: [.hih] °ihih°
08 Ther: [m:m ]
09 ( 3.4 ) +
j raises face-->+lowers face back into hands-->

10 Jen: .HI:Hh
j crying into hands-->

11 (4.8)

12 Ther: **°nobody warned° me.**
13 Jen: hhh
14 Ther: nobody (0.7) °protected me?°+
j crying into hands-->+

15 (4.4)
j wipes eyes, looks forward, away from T-->

16 Jen: no nobody warned me about the realities of life .hh.shih
j crosses hands, gaze lowered, eyes closed, flushed face-->

17 (1.6)

18 Jen: hhHx

In line 05, Jennifer role-plays the little girl (a version of her former self) by verbalizing that "~nobody warn me~". Her intense distress is displayed both vocally through her tremulous voice and sobbing and non-vocally by having placed her face in her hands. Later, in line 12, the therapist validates Jennifer's talk and emotional state by echoing her previous utterance.

*Partial Repetition (Mirroring)* Mirroring, according to Ferrara (1994), involves a partial repetition of some key component of the client's prior talk. The main function of a mirroring utterance is to request elaboration, as can be seen in Extract 2.15.

**Extract 2.15:** 014.01(4)

01 Kris: so he is- he is very angry and I think (0.9) uh (1.0) I am the
02 (1.2) object(h) .hh ver he. releases his anger.

03 Ther: hm.
04 (1.2)

05 Ther: so you're the brunt,
06 (0.6)

07 Kris: nyeah.

```
08   Ther:  the brunt of his anger, lotta the time,
09   Kris:  ((lip smack)) I- that's how I feel.
10   Ther:  mm [hm, ]
11   Kris:     [yes.]
          t shallow nod
12   Ther:  mm hm,
          t shallow nod
13          (1.2)
14   Kris:  uhm
15          (        3.8                 )
          t                  shallow nod
16   Kris:  so. (5.2) I (0.4) uh(h) (0.8) two years ago (1.3) my daughter and
17          I went to ((name of country))? for a year.
          k               looks at T
          t                                            nod
18          (2.0)
          k looks away
19   Kris:  uhm.
20          (1.2)
21   Ther:  >hm. for a year.<
          t nod, raises eyebrows
22   Kris:  for a year.
          k nod
23   Ther:  h[m. ]
24   Kris:   [for] for year yeah. so she wents to school there.
          t nod
```

This conversation begins with Kristina recounting how she is the object of her husband's anger. In line 05, the therapist replaces the lexical term "object" with "brunt." This substitution is relevant because it changes the meaning from merely being a target to being the target of which his anger achieves the worst impact. A bit later on, in line 16, Kristina shifts the topic to an event two years back in which she and her daughter went abroad for a year, to Kristina's country of birth. The placement of this utterance could be interpreted as bearing relevance to what was discussed earlier; that is, Kristina left with her daughter to escape the husband's anger. Thus, in line 21, the therapist partially repeats Kristina's prior talk (`for a year.`), possibly in order to receive further elaboration on how leaving for a year may have special relevance. After echoing the therapist's talk in line 22, and thus displaying acceptance of the therapist's move, Kristina then proceeds to begin elaborating on her reasons (or implications) for being away for that long: her daughter went to school there.

### 2.5.2 *Formulations*

Formulations have been receiving increasing attention in CA research on psychotherapy (Antaki, 2008; Antaki et al., 2005; Hutchby, 2005). They generally fall under one of two types: *gist* formulations that provide a summary of a prior speaker's talk and *upshot* formulations that point out the implications of prior talk (see Heritage and Watson, 1979).[7] A formulation bears similarity to what Stiles (1992) has termed *reflection*; that is, a therapist's formulation adopts the client's frame of reference and, consequently, maintains the client's ownership of experience. However, while in Stiles' sense formulations are reflective, they are also transformative and often move talk in a more therapeutically relevant direction. Vehviläinen et al. (2008, p. 190) suggest a number of functions that formulations serve in psychotherapy talk such as building a case for interpretation, establishing facts, guiding descriptions toward the psychological and managing the progress of the therapy session. Formulations make confirmation or disconfirmation relevant as a next, responsive action. The important role of formulations in doing empathic work will be taken up in Chapter 4.

*Summary/Gist* Summary formulations provide the gist of the client's prior talk and offer up what the client had just said back to them for confirmation and further reflection. These formulations do not merely repeat client's talk, but also slightly rework that talk often in therapeutically relevant ways. The transformative capability of formulating is shown in Extract 2.16, involving the client Kristina.

**Extract 2.16:** 014.13

```
01   Kris:   I- I don't have the strength really to uh- to uh:
02           leave the marriage. I was thinking about it,
03           why is it- why it didn't come to
04           (1.1)
05   Kris:   a conclusion.
06           (3.5)
07   Ther:   .hhh >so you don't have the< strength to leave- to break
             out.
08   Kris:   mm [hm.   ]
09   Ther:      [yeah.] mm hm,
10           (6.7)
11   Kris:   hm.
12           (0.4)
13   Ther:   .hhh break out've the prison. mm(h)heh
```

7 Weiste and Peräkylä's (2013) research on psychoanalytic and cognitive therapies identified four different formulation types: *highlighting*, *rephrasing*, *relocating* and *exaggerating*. Whereas the first two bear resemblance to gist and upshot formulations, respectively, the other two – *relocating* and *exaggerating* – seem to be restricted to psychoanalysis and cognitive psychotherapy.

In this example, Kristina talks about her lack of strength to leave the marriage. The therapist first summarizes or reflects back what Kristina had said (`so you don't have the strength to leave`), but then elaborates on and self-repairs her turn by transforming the meaning "to leave" to the potentially more therapeutically relevant meaning "`to break out`" and, later in line 13, to "`break out've the prison`". The therapist's *re*formulation of Kristina's talk is interesting because it adds another layer of meaning to what Kristina had said: *Breaking out* lends more intentionality and agency to Kristina's prior formulation of *leaving* – this extract will also be further examined from the perspective of empathy in Chapter 4.

Another example of a summary formulation is shown in Extract 2.17. Here the client Paula has been complaining about her ex-boyfriend.

**Extract 2.17:** 312.09(08)

Paula: w- what ↑I'm wondering about like wis this- (0.8) particular man.
like why: (.) <am I so: hung up> (0.3) on him. like why do I
<have to try:,> (1.2) ↑so hard, (0.5) and at the same time like
it's almost like he doesn't ca:re. (1.5) and why do, (0.4) °why
do I° keep, (3.9) ↑running.
(1.6)
Paula: uh(hh) (.) and why does he say certain things, (0.3) which kind
of make me ↑thi:nk (.)that he cares, but then (0.8) in his
behaviour he doesn't really- (.) live up to it. uh(hh)
Ther: **°t(.hh) so you feel very confused by his behaviour**
(1.0)
Paula: oh ↑yeah. t(h)he he he.
p *rolls eyes to side, laughing*
t *shallow nod*

Throughout Paula's turn, she not only repeatedly questions her commitment to the relationship (`why: (.) <am I so: hung up> (0.3) on him.`, but also makes a number of negative evaluations of what the ex-boyfriend says and actually does (`he doesn't really- (.) live up to it.`). As a response, although the therapist does not actually recycle any of the client's prior words or expressions, she does provide the gist of Paula's complaint: `so you feel very confused by his behaviour.`

*Upshot* A formulation working as an *upshot* is argued to provide "further significance" or implications to the gist of prior talk (Heritage & Watson, 1979), or "presuppose some unexplicated version of gist" (Hak & de Boer, 1996). To count as an upshot, it is important that the action works to maintain the client's expressed perspective, rather than the therapist's. An example of an upshot is given in Extract 2.18 with the client Sofia.

**Extract 2.18:** Sofia: Case 304.07

```
01  Sofi:  yah. When he died dats, dats, (1.0) makes me very s- (0.2)
02         brings (.) very sad memories because we he died, (0.4)
03         .tch (0.3) for a time (1.0) I: (0.8) I did not, I deny? (0.5)
04         that he died?
05  Ther:  mm hm,
06         (0.2)
07  Ther:  you just pretended he was still there=
08  Sofi:  =.h he̲ was a still there. (0.2) [yah.
09  Ther:                                  [°mm hm
10         (0.2)
11  Sofi:  [(      )
12  Ther:  [so it still makes you sad even °when you (0.3)
13  Sofi:  yeah.=
14  Ther:  =talk about it now=
15  Sofi:  =yeah
```

Sofia is recalling past events in which her father died. She identifies these events as bringing "`very sad memories`" and she admits to having denied that he was deceased. In line 07, the therapist offers a gist formulation that focuses on the latter part of Sofia's turn, by re-phrasing her denial as "`pretended he was still there`". She then, in line 12, produces an upshot in which she first recaps the sadness, but then goes on to draw the implication that this emotion is still salient in the here-and-now "`even °when you (0.3)` ... `talk about it now`".

Another example of an upshot formulation can be seen in Extract 2.19 with the client Owen.

**Extract 2.19:** Owen_Case 315_2

```
01  Owen:  >I've be told (.) by women (.) years ago th-that I'v::e (0.5)
02         >sometimes I was a bit pushy.<
03         (0.2)
04  Ther:  *m:↑m:.
        t   *deep nods-->
05  Owen:  I never +(.) realized it at the time. It was jus ( 0.3  )
        o             +tilts head
06  Ther:  mm hm.*
        t  nods->*
07  Owen:  +trying      +to express myself.
        o  +raises hands+
08  Ther:  mm-hm, .hhh so somehow it's like (0.4) I have these feelings,
09         (.)
        o  shallow nods-->
10         I'd li̲ke to express them,+ .hh (0.5) but (.) they might be taken
        o                shallow nods-->+
```

```
11           the wrong wa:y or (.) they might not be appreciated, +.hhh
          o                                              +shallows nods
12           so I better no:t.
13   Owen:   °yeah°.+
          o  nods-->+
```

Owen is recounting his experiences with women. He uses indirect reported speech in claiming that women have generally perceived him as being "`a bit pushy`". In line 05, he then accounts for this behaviour by stating that he was unaware of it and that it was just his way of expressing himself. In line 08, the therapist produces an upshot formulation. She begins by first providing the gist of Owen's prior talk "`I have these feelings, (.) I'd like to express them`" and then, beginning with the contrastive marker "but," goes on to point out some implications: his way of expressing his feelings may be taken the wrong way or not appreciated and, thus, should be avoided (`so I better no:t.`).

## 2.6 Therapist Responding Actions: Therapist-Oriented

Therapists may respond to clients' troubles tellings in ways that highlight their own perspective rather than those of clients. These actions will be referred to as *therapist*-oriented because they index A-events (Labov & Fanshel, 1977), in which therapists position themselves as having expert knowledge or unique access to clients' knowledge domains. Because of this, clients are thus placed in the "weaker" epistemic position of having to "agree with" the therapist (see Heritage, 2002, and section 3.7 for discussions of confirmation vs. agreement as next responses in a sequence). These response types include the following response types: *noticings*, *extensions*, *interpretations*, *challenges* and *corrections*.

### *2.6.1 Noticings*

In everyday contexts, noticings have been argued to halt or alter the progressivity of an interaction (Sacks, 1995). They are actions that create *retro-sequences* (Schegloff, 2007): by noticing something occurring before, they work as a responsive action, but they also initiate a new sequence by projecting further action such as confirmation. In everyday contexts, noticings have been shown to perform a variety of actions (e.g., telling/informing, complaining and blaming) and thus can implicate a range of response types such as offering remedies, accounts, agreements and apologies (Schegloff, 1988). Research in psychotherapy has shown that noticings may also perform a range of functions such as prompting more emotion talk, topicalizing the client's affective stance and moving talk in a new direction (Muntigl & Horvath, 2014a).

A therapist noticing, taken from Muntigl and Horvath (2014a), is shown in Extract 2.20. It is taken from Les Greenberg's (1989) demonstration session video of emotion-focused therapy (EFT) and involves a female client (Dawn), who had reported feeling conflicted about making contact with two other parents from her child's day care centre. Dawn had mentioned feeling "sad and mad" at being ignored by these parents, which led the therapist to initiate an *empty-chair dialogue* (see Chapter 6) between Dawn and the other parents. The main goal of this intervention is to have the client engage in a form of role-play, enabling Dawn to focus on her emotions in a context of being ignored by these parents.

**Extract 2.20:** [Muntigl & Horvath, 2014a, p. 90]

```
01  Greenberg:   tell them about- (1.5) °tell em about-° (.) whichever
02               one is most- (0.3) strong for you.
03               (        3.6          )
            d    gazes towards empty chair
04  Greenberg:   let's go- (.) I can see some sadness [in your] ey:es.
05               right.
06  Dawn:                                             [mm hm.]
07  Dawn:        mm hm. yeah. I'm feeling sa:d.
08  Greenberg:   yeah.
```

This extract begins with the therapist directing Dawn to tell the parents which emotion (anger or sadness) is most prevalent for her. What follows is a silence in which Dawn gazes toward the vacant chair (personified by the two parents). The therapist's noticing in line 04, in which he draws specific attention to Dawn's displayed – but not verbalized – emotion as something occurring in the present moment of the therapeutic encounter (cf. Vehviläinen, 2008 and Kondratyuk & Peräkylä, 2011), does three things. First, it provides an answer to what might be the dominant, presently experienced emotion for Dawn. Second, it *informs* Dawn of what her strongest emotion is, thus opening up a new sequence in which she is invited to supply agreement (or disagreement). This action is *therapist*-oriented because the expression "*I* can see." indexes the therapist's entitlement to know what Dawn is experiencing, which is based on his visual perception. Lastly and pending agreement from Dawn, it works to get a certain trajectory of talk involving the topic of Dawn's sadness underway, one in which Dawn can confront the parents about her sadness in an empty chair activity.

Therapist noticings seem to be the weakest form of A-event action from the preceding list. This is because noticings were often found to be designed with numerous epistemic-downgrading markers, thus tipping the epistemic scales more toward the client as having greater epistemic status and making client confirmation (rather than agreement) a relevant next response. For example, other noticing action formats identified in therapy such as "you look a *little* sad" and "you look (.) like you're (.) getting kinda discouraged (2.0) *is is that right?*" seem to cede much more epistemic authority to clients than in Extract 2.20 – see also section 4.5.3. This is because "softeners" such as "a *little* sad" leave the noticed emotion more open to negotiation. Further, appending a tag such as "*is is that right?*" works especially to invite clients to confirm that what the therapist has noticed also resonates with them, the clients. It may thus be argued that epistemic downgrading may nudge therapist-oriented actions (not just noticings) more toward a B-event and therefore may slightly transform response relevance from agreement toward confirmation.

### *2.6.2 Extensions*

Sacks (1995b) observed long ago that there exist a range of practices for which speakers may collaboratively and jointly produce each other's utterances. Of particular interest is Sacks' observation that utterances, which may seem syntactically complete, can in general be turned into "larger" units through various additions. This phenomenon has been found to commonly occur in therapy (Ferrara, 1994) and the term *extension* has been coined for the practice in which a next speaker adds a further component onto an interactional unit that may be considered syntactically complete (Vehviläinen, 2003). Extensions may also serve as a vehicle for accomplishing intersubjectivity, for showing prior speakers how they are being understood. In general, however, these syntactic additions index the therapist's angle on the client's reported experience. An extension is given in Extract 2.21 with the client Kristina.

**Extract 2.21:** 14.3

```
01  Ther:  so you've bee:n? (1.2).h you've been up and ↑do:wn.
02  Kris:  up and down. yes I I tried to watch .h uh:: °en tuh be:°
       t   slow nods
03         yah. sometimes I felt *(0.7) better and sometimes I y'know
       t                            *slow nods->
04         felt quite worse.
05         (0.9)
06  Kris:  I mean, ye'know +(0.3) really      + (0.5)(°iffy°) *(1.9)*
       t                          slow nods->*          *nod--*
       k             +tilts head
07  Kris:  °uh° (1.3) it does cha:nge.
08         (1.8)
       t   nods
```

09 Ther: **a lo:t?**
10 (0.3)
11 Ther: you find? [very changeable?] °or just°
12 Kris: [.hhh ]
13 Kris: uhx (8.6) tch prob-probably ye'know these are- (0.3) m (0.7)
14 pri- pri̲vate changes within myself. so .hh uh: (0.2)
t *slow, shallow nods-->*
15 but I'd I-ye'know I'd yeah I I I do.

The topic of this conversation involves the client's changing emotional state, which is being described here as "up and down." Following a summary formulation in line 01, Kristina produces confirmation and then goes on to state that her mood is at times better, but also at times "quite worse". In line 07, Kristina emphasizes that "it do̲es cha:nge.", possibly implying that she is not always feeling bad or "iffy". Following a silence, the therapist produces the adverb "a lo:t?", which extends and modifies Kristina's prior turn by adding an element of degree; that is, Kristina's ups and downs may be occurring frequently or that change happens at a large scale (e.g., from "good" to "much worse"). The extension is therapist-oriented because it is not specifically drawn from the client's talk, but is instead independently produced by the therapist. Note that, after a brief pause in line 10, the therapist orients specifically to the client's perspective (you find?), which may be working to "repair" the lack of client-orientation conveyed by the prior extension.

### *2.6.3 Interpretations*

Interpretations make allusions to the *therapist*'s point of view (cf. Stiles, 1992). Work in CA has shown that interpretations are commonly produced with certain design features that index own perspective or a perspective other than the client's such as "I think," "I mean," "from this point of view" or "it seems that" (Bercelli et al., 2008; Peräkylä, 2005). These design features orient to the therapist's own, possibly unique, access to the event in question, thus upgrading the therapist's right to make a claim about the client's experience. Consider Extract 2.22 involving a different client, Sofia.

**Extract 2.22:** 304.07

01 Sofia: before the nervous breakdown. (0.4) I could feel (0.3) sad.
02 but n̲e̲ver sad (0.3) to the point, of wanting to ↑cry.
03 Ther: mm hm. [so this is more recent.]
04 Sofia: [never that sad.]
05 Ther: .hhh >and **I imagine it has something to do with< not**
06 **feeling connected.**

Sofia recounts a recent change in her behaviour in which emotional experiencing of sadness has now become intensified, "`to the point, of wanting to ↑cry.`". As a response, the therapist begins with a formulation by reflecting back the temporal relevance of Sofia's disclosure (`so this is more recent`). However, the therapist continues her turn by emphasizing her own perspective (`I imagine`) and, subsequently, by providing an explanation for why Sofia now feels this way. In this example, the grammatical expression "I imagine" flags the therapist's subjective view; that is, what is about to be said is derived from the therapist, it is a subjective inferential leap, and not necessarily bound to what the client may have specifically said, or to an inference that may be directly generated from that talk.

### 2.6.4 *Challenging*

Another option that therapists have when responding is to challenge rather than summarize, draw implications from, interpret, extend and so on, the client's prior talk. Challenges have been shown as operating to disagree with client descriptions in supportive or non-supportive ways (Weiste, 2015) or to "repair" client talk by substituting a client's lexical term with another contrasting term (Rae 2008). Extract 2.23, involving the client Ernie, illustrates a therapist challenge performed in a supportive manner.

**Extract 2.23:** 422.3 Ernie

```
01  Ther:   =do you think about that that your mother (0.8) sort of
02          was: (0.6) was what. not able to gi:ve to you::?
03          (0.5)
04  Ther:   to: show that she ca:red about you:? >or that you
05          would feel< (1.2) loved by her:? or:, (3.1)
06          what's that sadness. (1.3) °feel like.° °what's that,°
07          (0.5)
08  Ernie:  ye'know I can't even (0.4) get in touch with much of
09          those feelings.
10  Ther:   mm [hm       ]
11  Ernie:     [really.] (.) [truly] I can't.
12  Ther:                    [mhm. ]
13  Ther:   mm hm:.
14  Ernie:  and they're so blocked off.
15  Ther:   ri:ght. but there's a little glimmer of
        e   tilts chair back against wall, gaze forward, hand on neck
16          (0.5)
17  Ther:   [some-]
18  Ernie:  [I get] a glimmer.
        e   gaze to T, gaze down, hand behind neck/head-->
```

```
                (0.5)
     Ernie:     just. I- ye'know uhm=
     Ther:      =>but it< (0.2)
            t   sits back, gaze to chair
     Ernie:     >when I'm< really face to face uh:m (1.1) with a
                situation again uhm. (1.4) I would sort've have a
                glimmer of that but
     Ther:      mm hm,
     Ernie:     not mu[ch    ]of one.
     Ther:            [well-]
```

The conversation begins with the client–mother relationship. Ernie's mother was not able to demonstrate caring or love toward Ernie. In line 06, the therapist introduces "sadness" as the emotion that Ernie must have experienced in this environment of deprivation and attempts to get Ernie to expand on his sad feelings. As a response, however, Ernie denies having access to these feelings and, in line 14, provides an account that "they're so blocked off.". In line 15, the therapist produces an acknowledging "ri:ght.", but then launches into opposition via the conjunction "but" and then states that "there's a little glimmer". There is thus an implication that Ernie may have some access to these sad feelings. The design of the disagreement, through the prefaced acknowledgement (and the downgraded term "little"), is performed in a mitigating manner, showing some support for the client's original point of view. In response, Ernie concedes in line 18 that he does "get a glimmer" but continues to maintain, later on, that it is minor.

The challenge in the prior example had an economy of design; it delicately opposed Ernie's position of non-access to his feelings by suggesting there is "a little" access. Challenges, however, because they are potentially threatening, often require more interactional work to get accomplished. Another example of a challenge is shown in Extract 2.24 with the client Sofia, in which the topic of Sofia leaving her husband is broached.

**Extract 2.24:** 304

```
     Ther:      =meaning [that if you do wanna to get] out you could?
     Sofi:               [(that I meaning           ])
                (0.3)
     Ther:      is that what you're saying?
                (1.0)
     Sofi:      m:?
                (0.6)
     Sofi:      not if I wanted to get out I could n::no. .snih
     Ther:      (0.4)
     Sofi:      is just that the option is not here now? (0.4)
                but the option will be there. soon.
```

```
            (0.5)
Ther:       right.
            (0.4)
Sofi:       is like, (2.1) uh:m (1.3) putting myself in suspense
            (0.9)
Ther:       yeah
            (0.3)
Ther:       .h and yet it seems very difficult for you to put
            yourself in suspense
            (0.3)
Ther:       y yihknow it's not as as if you just put yourself on
            hold .hh an:: (.) you've resolved okay in this ex time
            I'm [gunna leave en until then I'm just gunna
Sofi:           [m:?
Ther:       >hold it together .h< beca- and I imagine thet (0.5)
            thet the difficulty of holding yourself in suspense
            is that (.) you're not getting what you need, .hh
Sofi:       oh °no.°
```

Sofia explains that although leaving her husband is not an option for her at the moment, it may be an option in the near future. In line 15, she then implies that this possibility creates a bit of tension "`is like, (2.1) uh:m (1.3) putting myself in suspense`". As in line 15, the therapist first responds with brief acknowledgement (`yeah`, line 17) before prefacing her turn with the contrastive marker "`and yet`", which signals some form of forthcoming opposition. The challenge, from the therapist's view, is that it is difficult for Sofia to be in suspense. The therapist then continues by elaborating on what she means, which, from its design features, conveys an interpretation; that is, delaying a decision of leaving someone is not a simple matter, because you are denying yourself certain needs. Note the expressions the therapist uses to convey interpretation such as "`it's not as as if`" and "`I imagine thet`". Sofia responds with "`oh °no.°`" in line 29, which signals her agreement with the therapist's claim that she would not be getting what she needed.

### 2.6.5 *Correcting*

Certain responses function to uphold intersubjectivity or to repair possible points of misalignment concerning the therapist's and client's point of view. Extract 2.25 shows the client Bonnie reporting on her fondness of a certain ring that belonged to her husband's aunt, who had moved into residential care. All the aunt's belongings were being appraised and Bonnie, because of her attachment to this ring, asked her husband if she could buy it from the aunt's estate.

The husband originally supported the idea, but then later informed Bonnie that her aunt's wish was that everything was to be sold, the implication being that she might not be able to purchase the ring. This led Bonnie to feel disappointed in what she perceived as her husband's lack of support, but also uncertainty as to whether the husband is really lacking empathy or whether she is interpreting his motives incorrectly.

**Extract 2.25:** 305.02(4)

Bonn: = mm hm. (.) e- ye know no I don't know whether that's me, or
whether it's him. this i- ye know this is what I can't sort
out. .hhh an [I think,]
Ther: [well he ] e:-
Ther: when it y:e say ye don't know if it's: him or you,
Bonn: mm hm.
Ther: I'm not sure what you mean like.
Bonn: .hhh well I don't know whether it's because I'm reading Keith
[wrong] or the[se are my own personal] feelin[gs about thing]
Ther: [.hhh] **[oh: I see, ] [ya mean did he]**
Ther: **really have feelings against [you tak]ing the rin[g. maybe]**
Bonn: [eyea:h.] [a- mu-]
Ther: **he didn't=even mean that.**
Bonn: no you see this is what I find ev- you know like he'll say
then=well I didn't mean that. [an I'll=say well that's] the
Ther: [ uh: huh. ]
Bonn: way it came across to me so. (0.2) you know. .hhh you've
taken the pleasure ou'of it, [I don't want it=anymore.]
Ther: **[ I: see. but ]**
Ther: **your interpretation at the time was. .hhh he's sort of**
**sending me a message? [that I sh]ouldn't be buying this ring?**
Bonn: [mm hm. ]
Bonn: yeah.
(0.4)
Ther: and fer- e: an so even though it was something you loved and
was so ↑beautiful [you gave] up on it.
Bonn: [uh huh. ]
Bonn: yeah.

At the beginning of this extract, Bonnie voices her uncertainty ("I don't know whether that's me, or whether it's him."). The therapist responds by seeking more clarification from Bonnie about her uncertainty (lines 05–07). This can be viewed as a form of other-initiated repair that works to re-establish mutual understanding between the speakers (Schegloff et al., 1977). In line 08, Bonnie produces the repair by providing more detail: She is reading her husband wrong vs. her own personal feelings are clouding her judgement. The therapist then responds by first displaying the acknowledgement of new information with "`oh: I see,`" (Heritage, 1984) and then launches into a correcting action that is prefaced with "`ya mean`" and continues by pointing out that Bonnie's uncertainty may have involved the question as to whether Keith had really been opposed to her taking the ring. But in line 14, Bonnie voices disagreement by stating that the issue for her relates more to the effect that Keith's actions had; that is, he denied her the pleasure of imagining ownership of the ring and, thus, she no longer wanted it. In response, line 19, the therapist produces another correction (`I: see. but`) that reframes the importance of Keith's actions: Keith's message that it would be wrong or inappropriate to buy the ring caused her to give up on something she loved and desired. Bonnie then displays some acknowledgement or agreement with the therapist's second correction in lines 23 and 28.

## 2.7 Third Position Expansions

Initiating and responding actions form a basic unit of the sequence. The first speaker – the one who initiated the sequence via questioning or directing for instance – may, however, expand on the sequence via a so-called third position.[8] There are two general ways in which this can be accomplished. One is by producing a sequence closing third (SCT) (Schegloff, 2007). As this name suggests, these actions work to close off the sequence and often contain "minimal," discourse markers. Another way is to continue to expand on the sequence by somehow re-working or modifying some aspect of the prior response occurring in second position. According to Peräkylä (2011, 2019), these are crucial sequential positions in which therapists are able to continue a certain therapeutic project by modifying clients' descriptions of personal experience in therapeutically relevant ways. These third position actions will be briefly addressed in this section, but they will be given repeated attention throughout the remaining chapters in this book.

### *2.7.1 Sequencing Closing*

Schegloff (2007) identifies many sequence closing markers such as "oh," "okay," "right," "thanks" and assessments ("good," "great"). As shown in Extract 2.26, an abridged version of Extract 2.11, these markers signal that the brief interactional business negotiated in the first two paired actions has been successfully accomplished.

[8] Sequences may also be expanded in other positions, for example, via *pre*-expansion or *insertion* expansion (see Schegloff, 2007). The former is generally accomplished via pre-sequences such as pre-requests, pre-invitations or pre-announcements, whereas the latter is often achieved via repair sequences.

**Extract 2.26:** Case 306.3

```
01   FPP   Ther:    *w- wudja be willing to do it?*
                t   *turns head towards L---------*
02   SPP   Lisa:    °↑yah°
03                  (1.0)
04   SCT   Ther:    okay.
                l   begins getting up-->
```

As can be recalled from Extract 2.11, the therapist was attempting to direct the client Lisa into doing chair work. The initiating action, the proposal, appears in line 01, which is followed by the client's acceptance in line 02. The therapist's SCT in line 04, "okay.", signals the successful negotiating of the proposal sequence and, during this time, Lisa gets up to prepare herself for the upcoming task.

Although SCTs often occur to signal sequence completion, they also function as prefaces to subsequent, cohesively linked therapeutic action. In Extract 2.27, Ernie had been discussing his difficult relationship with his now ex-wife, stating that communication between them was strained and often impossible.

**Extract 2.27:** 422.03

```
01   Ther:    so you're not aware of s: (0.6) >what are you aware of<
02            (0.2) right no:w,
03            (1.2)
04   Ther:    >an you look a little< (.) sa:d to me,
05            (2.0)
06   Ernie:   tc.hh ↑well=I'm w- ye:ah:, I'm feelin sad. uh:m. (0.4)
07            .hh (0.3) because I I've blocked a lot of that off.
08   Ther:    I see.
09            (0.5)
10   Ther:    the sadness [in relation to] your wife.=
11   Ernie:               [yeah,         ]
12   Ernie:   =yeah, cuz I (.) have uh had to close that off.
13   Ther:    ri:ght, I see
14            (0.4)
15   Ernie:   uh:m
16            (1.0)
17   Ther:    so that's feeling closed off inside and as we speak
18            it's sort've
19            (0.4)
20   Ernie:   that's right.=
21   Ther:    =it jars it open a bit. en you get in touch with (0.5)
22            some of those feelings of sadness en
23            (1.3)
24   Ernie:   yeah.
25   Ther:    °mm hm.°
```

While talking about his ex-wife, Ernie had displayed some forms of distress (not shown here) such as sniffs, sighs and tremulous voice. In lines 01–04, the therapist draws attention to Ernie's present emotional state via an immediacy question (>what are you aware of< (0.2) right no:w,) and a noticing (an you look a little< (.) sa:d to me,). Ernie provides some confirmation to feeling sad but also accounts for this feeling (because I I've blocked a lot of that off.). The therapist produces an SCT in line 08, displaying token understanding of Ernie's personal experience, and then in line 10 makes the connection between Ernie's sadness and his wife. Ernie again provides some acknowledgement of the therapist's action (line 12) and again asserts that he has "had to close that off." The therapist again displays token acceptance and understanding of Ernie's talk (ri:ght, I see) and then, from line 17 onwards, makes the link between Ernie's "feeling closed off inside" and his in-the-moment feelings of sadness as he and the therapist focus on his past experiences with his ex-wife.

### 2.7.2 *Expanding*

Rather than using third position in sequence to initiate topic closure, this position may also work to expand the sequence via other-initiated repair, disagreement, topicalization or FPP "reworkings" (Schegloff, 2007). Peräkylä (2011, 2019) has shown for psychotherapy interaction that the third position in sequence may be used as a slot to modify clients' descriptions of their affectively tinged experiences. Thus, rather than working to close off the sequence, or signal a form of sequence closure, therapists can, in the third position, respond to clients by continuing to rework their talk. This is shown in Extract 2.28.

**Extract 2.28:** 014.18(6)

```
01 Ther:  = >is that what you're saying,< that it f-whe- you say it falls on
02        deaf ears he doesn't understand, or h[e doesn't    ]
03 Kris:                                         [doesn't want] to-
04 Kris:  doesn't want to listen.=
05 Ther:  =mm.
        t deep nod
06        (1.5)
07 Kris:  mm. it looks like he is up to his limit of comprehension of (1.2)
        t     deep nod
08        o:f uh: the vorld uh,
        k looks away
09        (1.8)
```

```
10  Kris:  or the family,
        k  looks at T

11         (            10.0                 )

        t  nod→ gazes at K.

        k                 looking down.

12  Ther:  ((lip smack)) so you'd like,
13         (3.8)

14  Ther:  to have your um (1.4) when you wanna do things
15         ta ta not have it ↓undermined an [belittled] an.

16  Kris:                                      [mm hm.    ]
        k                                   looks at T

17         (         0.6        )

        k  fast multiple nods

18  Ther:  uh huh.
        t  nod

19         (          2.0          )

        k   nod→ smiles.

        t  slow multiple nods->

20  Kris:  m-yes. [I would like. e(h)ehheh]
21  Ther:          [↑yeah. ↑yeah.          ] yeah.
        t  slow multiple nods, smiles slightly

        k        looks at T, smiling
```

Prior to this extract, Kristina had been complaining about how her husband does not appreciate her and "spoils her pleasure" by subtly preventing her from doing the things that she really enjoys. In lines 01–02, the therapist seeks confirmation of the client's dilemma by stating that her wishes fall "`on deaf ears`" and that he fails to understand her. Kristina responds affirmatively in lines 03–04 by further elaborating on the husband's behaviour (`doesn't want to listen.`) and, following therapist acknowledgement in line 05, she continues to criticize her husband's limitations in understanding the world around him and his family. A long silence ensues, line 11, leading the therapist to take up the third sequential position. Here, the therapist continues to modify the client's complaints by focusing more specifically on her needs and by presenting a more productive relationship scenario in which she can attend to her needs without having them undermined by her husband. What this brief excerpt shows is how the various sequential positions in therapy can be utilized to accomplish important therapeutic work by constantly re-working a client's descriptions of experience – this kind of sequential work will be illustrated in most of the examples throughout the book. Note also how the therapist's third position action leads to mutual endorsement in a number of ways: reciprocating agreement, nodding and smiling. These displays of affiliation will be taken up in greater detail in Chapter 3.

## 2.8 Conclusions

Following Schegloff's claim that the sequence is a prime vehicle for accomplishing social interaction, I have provided an overview of the kinds of sequences typically found in my dataset of emotion-focused (EFT and client-centred therapy (CCT). Clients tend to initiate actions through various forms of troubles tellings and therapists respond to client tellings through a range of different action types. Further, each of these responsive action types will, following Peräkylä (2011, 2019), work at developing the current therapeutic project in a unique way. Generally, therapist responses will either be client-oriented (indexing B-events), staying close to the client's descriptions of own experience, or will be therapist-oriented (indexing A-events), focusing more on the therapist's view of what the client's talk had meant. Lastly, third position is a potential sequential resource for continuing therapeutic work. Therapists may use this position to close off the sequence and accept the client's viewpoint, before moving on to related or different therapeutic business. Another option is for therapists to continue the therapeutic business at hand by expanding on the developing narrative within the client's response. This can be achieved through subtle or explicit modifications of the client's descriptions of personal experience (i.e., complaint, trouble) or even through more oppositional moves that challenge these descriptions. Thus, sequences may be expanded in this way over many turns, which can facilitate a deeper exploration of the client's problems. The aim of this chapter was to mainly illustrate the various sequence types found in the person-centred therapies under investigation. The remaining chapters will show how sequences may shed light on how various important aspects of social interaction are achieved and how this achievement is relevant for understanding therapeutic interaction. Especially important is the accomplishment of affiliation and empathy and these topics will be taken up in the next two chapters.

# 3 Affiliation: A Conversational Building Block of Social Relationships

## 3.1 Overview

There is general agreement that the organization of talk is biased so as to promote social solidarity and avoid conflict (Brown & Levinson, 1987; Goffman, 1967; Heritage, 1984; Levinson, 1983; Sacks, 1987). This bias, according to Enfield (2006, pp. 399–400), is partly founded upon an *affiliational principle* that "compels interlocutors to maintain a common degree of interpersonal affiliation (trust, commitment, intimacy), proper to the status of the relationship, and again mutually calibrated at each step of an interaction's progression." Some evidence of an affiliational principle may be found in linguistic and CA research: For example, speakers tend to agree with assessments, comply with requests, accept offers and invitations, and so on (Levinson, 1983; Pomerantz, 1984; Schegloff, 2007). In fact, it has been proposed that speakers orient to a "preference principle" in which disagreement, disconfirmation, rejection is avoided and, if produced, these actions should be delayed, mitigated or accompanied by accounts (Pomerantz & Heritage 2013; Sacks, 1987). Further, speakers of initiating actions tend to design their utterances so as to receive affiliative uptake from others, and if a disagreeing response seems imminent, the speaker will re-do the initiating action "in the direction of possible agreement" in order to pre-empt the occurrence of the disagreement (Sacks, 1987, p. 65). It has been suggested that these practices in which agreement is pursued function to avoid face-threatening situations (Brown & Levinson, 1987; Levinson, 1983).

Although much of social life may transpire in a socially cohesive and affiliative manner, there are contexts in which disaffiliation and discord may become especially salient and may even extend over long stretches of time: These may range from everyday conflicts involving children, families or couples (Goodwin, 1990; Muntigl & Horvath, 2005; Muntigl & Turnbull, 1998) to more institutional forms involving court or labour-management disputes (Conley & O'Barr, 1990; O'Donnell, 1990). Affiliation is not always a "coveted" interactional goal and persons may, in the long or short term, have other aims that take priority, such as maintaining differences (i.e., through competition and conflict) or even inducing harm to others (Enfield, 2009; Goffman, 1971). Some researchers have even noted that in conflict situations, the organization of talk may shift its bias to increasing forms of opposition in which there becomes an expectation or "preference" for disagreement over agreement (Bilmes, 1991; Kotthoff, 1993). This suggests that speakers may, in certain contexts, organize their talk to flag the conflict episode, not simply by producing disaffiliative actions such as disagreement but by inviting disaffiliation from the other speaker.[1] By and large, however, interactional research suggests that speakers often display some orientation to an affiliational principle even when dissenting actions are produced. For example, disagreements and refusals not only tend to be "softened" or mitigated through various linguistic-interactional features (Atkinson & Drew 1979; Heritage, 1984; Pomerantz, 1984), but even in contexts in which discord becomes more topically relevant such as in everyday conflict episodes, disagreements are usually designed in less aggravating ways (Muntigl & Turnbull, 1998). It could be, however, that these forms of pro-social sequence organization mainly apply to cases in which relationships matter. As Schiffrin (1984) has shown, arguments may, when performed in "non-serious" ways, promote sociability and thus have a longer-term pro-social effect.

Turning now to psychotherapy, it is commonly argued that a positive relationship, and a productive working alliance, is important for doing productive therapeutic work (Norcross, 2011; Norcross & Lambert, 2018), and that maintaining a good relationship is principally achieved by working affiliatively and empathically with clients (Elliott et al., 2011; Greenberg, 2014; Rogers, 1957). It has also been claimed, however, that affiliation is not necessarily beneficial for all contexts. Rennie (1998), for example, argues that clients can be highly deferential toward the therapist and thus may be reluctant to voice criticism against the therapist or challenge the therapist's viewpoint when it conflicts with their own experiences. Client deference or appeasement may also place strains on the alliance because the client may be seen as withdrawing from the work of therapy and making it more difficult for the therapist to engage with the client's troubles (Eubanks et al., 2015). Thus, rather than generally "go along" with the therapist's project, clients need to, at times, disaffiliate in order to convey their own viewpoint, challenge interpretations that do not fit their experience or question their progress in therapy. Certain contexts are also said

[1] For sequences involving complaints or accusations, however, Dersley and Wootton (2000) have shown that recipients rarely deny accusations. Instead, they admit to having committed the action but deny any implication of guilt or wrongdoing. We may speculate on how this may pertain to affiliation maintenance and social relationships as follows. Outright denials, while preferred next actions, may work to deepen disaffiliation because both parties remain in opposition. By admitting to the action, but by denying the moral implications (i.e., no wrongdoing had occurred or was intended), the recipient may be working to repair damage to face and to minimize the potential harm that may impact on the relationship.

to benefit more from therapist disaffiliation. In psychoanalytic psychotherapy, for example, it is argued that certain client "role offers" invite the therapist to respond in ways that may reinforce the client's neurotic relationship patterns (Bänninger-Huber & Widmer, 1999). Thus, rather than strengthen the neurotic pattern through affiliative acts, therapists are advised to oppose, and thus disaffiliate with, these client offers. This process of opposition, however, should ideally be achieved in a secure and supportive environment to maintain and not unduly strain the alliance. This dilemma of offering support while maintaining a certain degree of conflictive tension has been characterized in terms of a *balance hypothesis* and is described as follows:

> Basically, the therapist has to fulfill a double function. On the one hand, he or she has to provide a reliable working alliance to give the client a basic sense of security. This enables the client to explore his or her experiences and behaviors, and to accept and understand the therapist's interventions. On the other hand, the therapist has to maintain a certain level of conflictive tension by not taking over the client's role offers repeatedly. (Bänninger-Huber & Widmer, 1999, p. 80)

Various multi-modal practices have been identified that can function to maintain this balance, such as therapists smiling at the client while withholding a response, which is termed a friendly refusal (Bänninger-Huber & Widmer, 1999). Here, the smile orients to relationship concerns by offering a token amount of affiliation, whereas the no-response keeps the interactants (especially the client) actively engaged in discussing the conflict (see also Muntigl et al. (2020b) for examples of this kind of practice). There is also some evidence supporting the claim that disaffiliation, as long as it becomes resolved at some point, can be a productive process. This pattern of "rupture & resolution" or "tear & repair" may even be a way of strengthening the alliance in the longer term (Safran et al., 2011b).

In this chapter, I provide a detailed overview of the conversational structures in which affiliation and disaffiliation are accomplished and managed. Drawing from CA methodology, I explain how concepts such as preference and affective stance are fundamental to understanding how (dis)affiliative actions get produced.

## 3.2 Preference Structure

As mentioned earlier, Enfield's (2006) principle of affiliation is highlighted in linguistic and conversation analytic (CA) research: speakers tend to structure their interactions so as to maintain social solidarity (Brown & Levinson, 1987; Levinson, 1983; Pomerantz, 1984; Sacks, 1987). More specifically, the linguistic format of a second pair part (SPP) plays an important role in establishing social relations between speakers. In CA, a strong link has been proposed between the preference type of a SPP and the degree to which the SPP affiliates with the first pair part (FPP). Thus, preferred SPPs are mostly affiliative because they work to strengthen social solidarity and cohesion between speakers, whereas dispreferred SPPs work in a disaffiliative manner by placing social cohesion at risk. Heritage (1984, p. 269) describes the relation between preference and affiliation as follows:

> Preferred format actions are normally affiliative in character while dispreferred format actions are disaffiliative. Similarly, while preferred format actions are generally supportive of social solidarity, dispreferred actions are destructive of it. As we shall see, the uniform recruitment of specific features of turn design to preferred and dispreferred action types is probably related to their affiliative and disaffiliative characters.

After the first speaker (speaker A) initiates a FPP, speaker B has an alternative set of options for responding; for example, offers or invitations may be accepted or rejected, yes/no interrogatives may be confirmed or disconfirmed, assessments may be agreed or disagreed with. These alternatives for speaker B are not equal. One response alternative is referred to as *preferred*, whereas the other is termed *dispreferred* (Levinson, 1983; Pomerantz, 1984; Sacks, 1995b). The linguistic structure of preferred responses is generally "simple," containing few components, and responses tend to be contiguous to the prior action. In contrast, dispreferred responses tend to be delayed and have a more complex structure consisting of pauses, hedges, discourse markers, accounts and/or "pro forma" agreements (Schegloff, 2007, pp. 67ff). These differences between preferred and dispreferred responses may be seen in Extracts 3.1–3.4.

**Extract 3.1:** Sofia Case 304.07(1)

```
01  Sofia:  uh::m. (0.7) whe=was it, (1.2) .hhh oh. (1.4) ((lip smack))
02          I am sunghow, (0.9) lairning to: .hhh (1.9) .hhh control myself
03          better when I s(h)ink that I am having dos:e
04          (0.5)
05  Ther:   the:. (0.4) anxiety? or the=
06  Sofia:  = the anxiety?
07  Ther:   s:k- yeah.
            ...
09  Ther:   [so this-] this ehm (0.2) .hhh the feeling's still there
            (0.6) b-but you know how to cope with it better.
10          is that what's happening,
11  Sofia:  yeap. mm hm?
12        s nod
13        t    fast multiple nods
14  Ther:   yeah.
15        t fast multiple nods
```

**Extract 3.2:** 305.02(5)

```
01   Bonn:   .hhh we=she couldn't see why they couldn't stay for dinner.
02           well=I mean (.) why make it difficult fer people eh?
03   Ther:   [mm      hm:.      ]
04   Bonn:   [e=mean, don't chu] think that's kina mean, hhh huhhuh
05           hehheh
        t                        fast multiple nods. smiles at C
06   Bonn:   [hahhhh             .hhh       ]
07   Ther:   [yeah: I mean it seemed to sorta] bother you that she=was
08           making your daughter feel so [badly.]
09   Bonn:                                [↑ye:ah] I thought ye know ↑that's
        b                                  nod
        t                                         multiple nods--->
10           aw:ful to m- and even her own son.
11   Ther:   y[eah.         yeah.  ]
```

**Extract 3.3:** Kristina Case 014.18(4)(a)

```
01   Kris:   .hh .shih hm, I (.) really don't (0.3) I don feel
02           strong enough to(0.4) quarrel with him to ye know, to
03           yell back or to yell at him ven I,((sniffs)) see because
04           it's-I am m-really uh h(h)m petrifIEd when he starts(0.8)
05           yelling. an I'm- I'm afraid to,
             ...
14   Ther:   ((lip smack)) so maybe the best thing would be to give up
15           on that battle an, put your efforts into, (1.4) >mean
16           this is what you're< saying to yourself maybe the best
17           °thing would be [ta give] up on that, an° put my
18   Kris:                   [mm hm. ]
19   Ther:   efforts inta building my own life.
20           (1.1)
21   Kris:   °.snih n-yeah.°
22           (1.9)
23   Kris:   but I- y'know I think I do do build my own life.
24           (1.1)
```

**Extract 3.4:** 304.03 (3)

```
01   Ther:   feels like you don't even know this man.
02           (1.1)
03   Sofia:  ↑no I feel I ↑know him.
04   Ther:   mm hm.
05   Sofia:  an bec(h)ause I(h)(h) know him. .hhh I-I-I cannot
06           underestan=how can I be with him for twenty years?
```

In Extracts 3.1 and 3.2, client responses following therapist formulations are designed in a preferred format of confirmation. Extract 3.1 shows how confirmation may be done "minimally," which is illustrated by Sofia's immediately adjacent confirmatory response of "`yeap. mm hm?`", following the therapist's formulation. A somewhat more forceful confirmation is given in Extract 3.2. Note the contiguous placement of Bonnie's confirmation in which she overlaps with the therapist's formulation and proceeds to display upgraded epistemic rights (Heritage, 2012) by expanding on her negative assessment of her daughter's mother-in-law. Dispreferred response structures are shown in Extracts 3.3 and 3.4. Extract 3.3 has the "typical" characteristics of delayed disconfirmation such as prefatory pauses, discourse markers (`but`), hedges (`y'know`) and pro forma agreement (`n-yeah but` ...). These interactional features illustrate what Sacks (1987) referred to as, in the first instance, an orientation to the production of an agreement, with a subsequent modification toward disagreement. Extract 3.4 illustrates an account (lines 05–06) for how "knowing her husband," which works to contradict the therapist's previous formulation that Sofia does not know her husband, is a central locus of distress.

The concept of preference provides an explanation as to why dispreferred actions tend to have a more complex structure. The delays, accounts, hedges and so on work to mitigate the potential stress placed on social relations. They are, in Goffman's (1967) sense, *face saving*. Preferred actions, on the other hand, are consensus-oriented. This, however, does not imply that "agreement" always works in a preferred and affiliative manner. As Pomerantz (1984) has shown, the preferred (and affiliative) SPP to self-deprecations such as "I'm so stupid," "I'm so ugly" or "I'm so clumsy" is disagreement rather than agreement.

More recently, affiliation has been given a broader interpretation that extends beyond preference organization (see Lindström & Sorjonen, 2013 for an extensive overview). In one view, affiliative actions match and support the *affective stance* conveyed in the prior action or activity (Stivers, 2008). Broadly speaking, an affective stance refers to the affective components of an utterance, including the range of emotion or evaluative expressions – vocal and non-vocal – that speakers are conveying. In her work on everyday storytelling, Stivers (2008) showed that story recipients would affiliate with storytellers by matching the affective stance communicated in the story; that is, recipients would endorse the affective meanings (e.g., humour, complaint, trouble) that the teller would use to construct his or her stance. From this standpoint, affiliation is not just seen as a response, but as *responsive to* something that the prior had expressed; that is, in conveying an affective stance, speakers provide unique access to their point of view and how they evaluate events. Doing this provides recipients with opportunities to endorse and build rapport with their interlocutors by using matching affiliative expressions. In another complementary view, affiliation is seen as operating more generally at the affective level of cooperative interaction. According to Stivers et al. (2011), "affiliative responses cooperate at the level of action and affective stance. Thus, affiliative responses are maximally pro-social when they match the prior speaker's evaluative stance, display empathy and/or cooperate with the preference of the prior action." With this definition, affiliation becomes further extended from its association with preference and affective stance to also include responses that convey empathy. Yet as I will argue in Chapter 4, although empathic responses tend to be affiliative, the reverse does not necessarily hold; that is, an affiliative response is not necessarily empathic.

Affiliation plays an especially important role in certain activities in which affective stances tend to be prevalent such as storytelling, troubles telling and complaints (Couper-Kuhlen, 2012; Günthner, 1997, Jefferson & Lee, 1980; Lindström & Sorjonen, 2013; Stivers, 2008). Finally, affiliation – and an affective stance – is not only verbally displayed, but rather is built up from a constellation of semiotic modes. Thus, prosodic resources, gestures such as nodding (Stivers, 2008), laughter (Glenn, 2003) and facial expressions work in a complementary fashion to communicate affiliation with others.

## 3.3 Affiliative Responses

Adjacency pairs – but also any sequence type composed of an initiating and response action – are *type-connected*, which means that the set of alternative responses will be coherently bound to the initiating action. Putting it simply, "answers" are coherently produced after questions but not after assessments. The relevance here to affiliation is that what will count as an affiliative next response will depend on the initiating action, the sequence type. Drawing from Levinson's (1983, p. 336) table on preferred responses to some "typical" adjacency pairs in *everyday* conversations, we would note that: acceptance is the affiliative response to requests, offers and invitations; agreements (or second assessments) display affiliation to first assessments (see also Pomerantz, 1984); emotionally reciprocal responses tend to follow troubles tellings (Jefferson & Lee, 1980); expected answers are affiliative in response to (*Wh-*) questions; and denial is the preferred response to blame and accusation. It should also be mentioned that (Y/N interrogative) questions (see Raymond, 2003) will either invite confirmation or disconfirmation, depending on the grammatical design of the interrogative. But, in general, confirmation or agreement are affiliative next responses to many other initiating actions including formulations, interpretations and noticings – see Chapter 2.

Positioning in sequence forms one of the hallmark features of preference. In regard to SPP, responses tend to be *contiguous* with respect to a prior action (FPP) (Sacks, 1987). According to Schegloff (2007, p. 67), contiguous responses are "delivered in a turn which begins after the single beat of silence that composes what is treated by participants as a 'normal' transition space" and they tend to be unmitigated and unelaborated. As Pomerantz (1984) has pointed out, however, SPPs may be adjusted in terms of their strength, via upgrading or downgrading practices, which often results in the recipient having to do additional interactional work.

One of the ways to express affiliation is to cooperate with the preference that a prior action has set in motion (Stivers et al., 2011). The preference is often linked to a generalized form of "agreement" or "compliance," which may be conveyed in various ways. Different terms in CA have been used to indicate agreement, such as acknowledgement, affirmation, confirmation and agreement. In his overview of research on response tokens (e.g., mm, mm hm, yeah), Gardner (2001, p. 2) refers to acknowledgement as actions that "claim agreement or understanding of the prior turn."

Heritage (2002) argues that first positions in assertion sequences generally come with certain rights related to knowledge. For example, being first to make a claim gives the speaker certain rights over the claim in question. Thus, the next speaker in second position is relegated to being a respondent, someone who is confined to providing agreement/disagreement or confirmation/disconfirmation (see section 3.7 on epistemics where this will be discussed in more detail). Next speakers can, of course, do more than agree/disagree – for example, show that they have specialized rights to the claim – but this will take additional discursive work. Certain constraints may also be seen with regard to affiliation. An assertion (description, assessment) or telling will place recipients in the role of "affiliation provider" and, thus, a lack of affiliation (or disaffiliation) will be noticeable and (for everyday contexts at least) accountable. Table 3.1 illustrates different kinds of responsive actions that were found to function affiliatively in psychotherapy. The actions examined are restricted to three kinds of sequential environments: assertions (descriptions, assessments), troubles tellings and directives. Descriptions are understood here in a very broad sense to include many different action types that portray and seek agreement/confirmation of others' conduct, reported experience or viewpoint, for example, formulations, interpretations, challenges and noticings.

The actions in Table 3.1 are shown with regard to relative strength of affiliation, with *acknowledging* actions on the lower end of the spectrum, followed by positive assessment and *upgraded confirmation (agreement)/ compliance* toward the higher end. Upgraded affiliation was found to be accomplished in a variety of ways: *prosodic modification*, oh-*preface*, *expansion*, *repetition* and *collaborative completion*.

Table 3.1 *Action types that work affiliatively in SPP positions of confirmation/agreement or compliance*

| Action Type | Example Realization |
|---|---|
| Acknowledge/Confirm/Comply | "hm," "mm hm," "uh huh," "yeah" |
| Assessment (positive) | "good," "wow" |
| Upgraded ratification | |
| Prosodic modification | "°↑yah." |
| *Oh* preface | "oh ↑yeah." |
| Expansion | (acknowledgment marker) + assertion |
| Repetition | Ther: so a little bit **more at ease**. |
| | Client: **more at ease**. (0.4) yeah. |
| Collaborative completion | Ther: or h[e doesn't] |
| | Client: [**doesn't want**] **to- doesn't want to ...** |

### 3.3.1 *Acknowledging Actions*

An abundance of work in CA has shown how response tokens may function as acknowledging actions (Drummond & Hopper, 1993; Gardner, 2001; Jefferson, 1984, 1993; Schegloff, 1982). Acknowledgement of a prior action, via response tokens, may be expressed in various ways such as with "hm," "mm hm," "uh huh" or even "yeah." Two central issues have percolated out from these studies. The first is that acknowledgement may be displayed with varying strength, ranging from minimal acknowledgment in which "adequate receipt of the prior turn" is displayed (Gardner, 2001, p. 34), to actions in which agreement, affirmation or confirmation of what had been said is conveyed. Whereas assertions tend to make agreement a relevant next action, B-event actions (Labov & Fanshel, 1977), in which it is inferred that the recipient has greater rights or access to knowledge, makes confirmation a relevant next (Stivers, 2005a). Thus, descriptions and assessments will invite agreement, whereas formulations, because they implicate B-events, invite confirmation. Second, the deployment of certain response tokens has implications for impending speakership. It has been found that whereas responses such as "uh huh" and "mm hm" convey that the recipient will not take a bid on the next turn (i.e., will retain his or her role as recipient), "yeah" displays speakership incipiency, in which the recipient will likely take up a speakership role (Jefferson, 1984; Drummond & Hopper, 1993).

Acknowledgements are shown in Extract 3.5. Here, the client Kristina has been complaining about her husband's lack of attention toward her and that she feels betrayed by him.

**Extract 3.5:** 014.18(2)(b)

```
01  Ther:   >so he's [let you<] down.
02  Kris:            [mm hm.   ]
03  Kris:   mm hm.
04  Ther:   °°mm hm,°°
05          (6.8)
06  Ther:   he's not there for you when he, (1.0) he should be.
07          (     0.7          ) (           1.6          )
        k   fast shallow nod.
        t                                  double nod-->
08  Kris:   yeah.
```

In line 01, the therapist produces a formulation that elaborates on Kristina's feelings of betrayal (>so he's let you< down.), thus inviting confirmation from the client. In response, Kristina utters a couple of acknowledgements that occur simultaneously with and immediately following the therapist's turn. Although it would appear that Kristina's *mm hm*s are displaying positive receipt of the therapist's formulation, it also conveys alignment with her role as recipient, with the implication that she will not take up speakership. In what follows, the therapist produces a soft "°°mm hm,°°", which in this sequential location may both be acting as acknowledging Kristina's acknowledgement (a "return" acknowledgement) and as a continuer. Yet, following a lengthy 6.8-second pause, the therapist elaborates on how her husband lets her down, which then receives non-verbal acknowledgment via nodding and, in line 08, somewhat more strongly displayed confirmation ("yeah"). Acknowledgement with "yeah" is shown in Extract 3.6.

**Extract 3.6:** 312.16(1a)

```
01 Ther:  .hhh so almost at- (0.4) I don't know if (.) >this is what
02        you're saying.< but almost at those times you may need some
03        stronger boundaries. .hh you may need to put up those boundaries
04        and say .hhh you can have your opinion, but I [am standing]
05 Paula:                                               [.hhh       ]
06 Ther:  firm.
07 Paula: yeah. (0.2) yeah. =
08 Ther:  = ↑yeah.
09        (1.4)
10 Paula: like(hh) (1.8) yeah acceptin:g like what I want <as well as
11        uh:m,> (3.7) ↑mm::. (2.5) like not be:ing intimidat[ed.]
12 Ther:                                                     [mm ] hm.
```

Here also, the therapist produces a formulation, thus inviting confirmation, and the client Paula is shown to respond with "yeah." in line 07. This response token not only conveys a stronger form of confirmation than in the preceding example – note that it is repeated, but also that the therapist responds with "↑yeah" in line 08, which more strongly endorses Paula's agreement – but also implicates impending speakership, as is evidenced by Paula having taken up the turn in line 10.

Other response tokens such as "sure" and "right" have been argued to display upgraded forms of acknowledgement and to convey certainty (Gerhardt & Beyerle, 1997). This response token type is shown in Extract 3.7 with the client Kristina (also shown as Extract 2.2).

**Extract 3.7:** Case 14.3

```
01  Kris:   som- (.) so pr-pr-probably? uhx:.
02          (14.0)
03  Kris:   .Hh
04          (0.6)
05  Kris:   s::ometimes I have uh (.) m: (0.6) difficulties with uh
06          (0.3) m:. (0.2) °°m- m- y'know.°° (0.4) saying my
07          feelings(huh:.)as(h)uh
        t          nods, raises eyebrows
08  Ther:   su:r[e ]
09  Kris:       [.h] a(h)s [we know.hihhuhhuhhuh                ]
        k              smiling->
10  Ther:                  [^that's what we've been talking about yeah.]
        t              smiling->
```

The therapist's response of "su:re" is placed immediately adjacent to Kristina's self-deprecating statement in which she claims to have difficulty in expressing her feelings. Self-deprecations invite disagreement as the preferred next action (Pomerantz, 1984) and although the therapist's response works to acknowledge what Kristina is saying, it seems that it does not so much affiliate with Kristina's negative self-assessment per se but rather with the importance of Kristina's experience as a topic of talk. Thus, when the therapist continues her turn in line 10, it is "what we've been talking about" that is being endorsed rather than Kristina's self-criticism, her difficulty in expressing herself.

Affiliative response tokens also appear in directive sequences. This is shown in Extract 3.8, which involves a therapist's proposal for the client Lisa to engage in chair work.

**Extract 3.8:** Lisa 306cs.11/EC (CW1)

```
01  Ther:  °somehow it wasn't the right ti-° .hhh
02         ↑d'yu wannu uhm
       t   splays hands in front, turns head, points to chair out of frame
03         (      1.8    )*
```

```
04 Ther:  it might be helpful tuh- (.) t-to- bring(.)
05        your parents, (0.2) °here.°
       t  gaze and splayed fingers towards L.
       t               tilts head to L->
       l  gaze to T.--------------->
06        (0.4)
07 Lisa:  +mkay+
       l  +gaze forward, nods+
```

In line 02, the therapist voices the beginnings of a proposal ("↑d'yu wannu uhm"), while at the same time doing non-vocal work that provides the substance of the proposal such as directing the client's attention to the chair via pointing and gaze. Following a pause in line 03, the therapist then makes the target of future chair work explicit ("your parents") while framing this as a potential benefit ("it might be helpful tuh-"). In line 07, Lisa provides her acceptance that she will participate in the activity.

To summarize, acknowledgement tokens do, in general, offer affiliation with the preceding action. As Heritage (2002) has pointed out, however, if they stand alone, they may imply that the recipient is minimally abiding by the constraints set up by the initiating action: producing the "required" agreement or confirmation. Thus, the endorsement of the prior action may come across as weak and would explain why, for example, therapists often elaborate on their formulations if they only get an "mm hm" or "yeah" from the client.

### 3.3.2 *Assessment*

Pomerantz' (1984) work on assessments has shown that certain actions are specifically designed to do evaluative work. In response position within a sequence, positively assessing actions perform interactional work that is different from mere agreement. As Goodwin (1986, p. 207) says, response tokens such as *wow*, "rather than simply acknowledging receipt of the talk just heard, assesses what was said by treating it as something remarkable." This is shown in Extract 3.9 (also shown as Extract 2.5, Chapter 2).

**Extract 3.9:** 412.07(2b)

```
01 Jo:    = but=at the same time I can't let them, (1.0) >you know< I kno:w
02        she's been looking at me like ↑oh: wh(h)at's happened to you:.
03        .hhh
04 Ther: [    mm::.            ]
05 Jo:    [and last night on the] phone. >because I wasn't< expecting it,
06        and I've been having >a really good week,< .hh like I was- (0.6)
```

```
07          very h:appy, I [wasn't (0.3) CO:]ld?
08 Ther:                   [mm     ↑h:m     ]
09          (0.3)
10 Ther: yea:h. =
11 Jo:   = you know what I mean?
12 Ther: mm ↑h:m
       t nod
13 Jo:   a:n- .hh ((blows nose)) so:, (0.4) she sa:id that- I said well,
14       (0.8) you know, the therapy is doing ↑good >she goes< I can hear
15       the difference in your ↑voice.
16       (0.3)
17 Ther: wo:[::w.                  ]
       t slow nod
18 Jo:      [you know, and that ma]kes me really ↑ha:ppy.
```

Jo is telling the therapist that she has been recently noticing positive changes in her behaviour. She describes a recent telephone conversation with her mother during the previous week in which she was "`very h:appy, I wasn't (0.3) CO:ld`" (line 07). She then proceeds to tell her mother that therapy is having positive benefits, to which her mother responds by stating that she has noticed these benefits in Jo's voice. Then, in line 17, the therapist responds with "`wo:::w`". This assessment not only conveys that what happened to Jo is very good (affiliation), but also highlights the noteworthiness or significance of what Jo has just told.

### *3.3.3 Upgraded Ratification*

There are a number of ways in which acknowledgement with the prior speaker's turn may be upgraded with the effect of strengthening affiliation. This includes *prosodic modification, oh-prefaced confirmation (agreement), confirmation (agreement) + expansion, repetition* and *collaborative completion*. Each of these practices will be addressed in turn.

*Prosodic Modification* The importance of prosody in modifying the function of a response token has been taken up by Gardner (2001). He has shown how intonational contours may alter the kinds of discursive work that the response token *Mm* may be doing. For instance, a falling contour generally conveys acknowledgement, whereas a fall-rising contour transforms the token into a continuer. Finally, a rise-falling contour will convey assessment. The function of a certain intonational contour, however, will depend not only on which response token is being intonationally modified but also on the sequence in which the response token appears. Consider Extract 3.10 (see also Extract 2.11), which involves a directive sequence.

**Extract 3.10:** Case 306.3

```
01  Ther:  t.hhh (0.8) I- (0.2) me-I think it would be:(0.3)
02         e-good to (0.3) try::(0.2) e-you know
03         last week I sug[gested] uh
04  Lisa:                [.hh    ]
05  Lisa:  °yeah.°
06         (0.5)
07  Ther:  t.experiment+ en .hh (.) and e- (0.3)
08  Ther:  but this time with your da::d,
09         cuz (.) cuz what yer (0.3) describing is °is°
10         a f:really (0.2)strong (0.4)feeling of anger
11         [towards] him en .hhhh (0.6) so thet if you were to (0.4)
12  Lisa:  [.shih  ]
13  Ther:  bring him in here that might (0.6)°I mean° (0.3)
14         bring him in here in an imagine way it would
15         [give  ](0.4) you a chance to actually
16  Lisa:  [°yeah.°]
17  Ther:  express it towards him. .hh
18         (0.8)
19  Ther:  w- wudja be willing to do it?
20  Lisa:  °↑yah.°
```

The therapist takes an extended turn at talk to recruit Lisa into chair work entry. First she reminds Lisa of her suggestion to try an experiment in the last session (lines 03 and 07). She then justifies this proposed course of action, first by claiming that Lisa is feeling a lot of anger (lines 09–11) and then by stating that it would allow her to direct this emotion toward the dad (lines 14–17). Finally, in line 19, the therapist produces the proposal (`w- wudja be willing to do it?`). Lisa conveys weak acknowledgement in lines 05 and 16 with falling intonation, but in line 20, her rise-falling intonation following the therapist's proposal strengthens her acceptance to be recruited into chair work. Thus, what might have appeared as an initial reluctance or hesitation to engage with the therapist's proposal, then changes into a stronger display of engagement and willingness to comply.

*Oh-Prefaced Confirmation* Research on *oh*-prefaced actions in second position of the sequence has shown that, although these responses agree with or confirm the prior action and thus convey affiliation, they also index greater epistemic rights and access (Heritage, 2002). As Heritage and Raymond (2005, p. 26) have argued, these response designs offer "a systematic way of claiming that a speaker has independent access to, and already holds a position regarding, the referent." Consider Extract 3.11 (see also Extract 2.17) in which Paula has been explaining to the therapist how her ex-boyfriend's actions often seemed contradictory.

**Extract 3.11:** 312.09.08

```
01   Ther:     °t(.hh) so you feel very confused by his behaviour
02             (1.0)
03   Paula:    oh ↑yeah. t(h)he he he!
```

In line 01, the therapist provides a gist formulation of Paula's prior talk and, because it references a B-event, invites confirmation from the client. Paula then responds with *Oh*-prefaced confirmation that both strongly affiliates with the therapist's formulation, but also signals that she has first-hand experience with and access to the ex-boyfriend's confusing behaviour.

*Confirmation + Expansion* Affiliation may be further strengthened through responses that, in addition to providing an acknowledging or confirming response token, subsequently do elaborative work. In these contexts, recipients are showing that they are doing more than just abiding by the constraint imposed on them of providing confirmation (Heritage, 2002). In Extract 3.12 (see also Extract 3.2), the client Bonnie is recounting an episode in which her daughter's mother-in-law was offended because she and her son could not stay for dinner.

**Extract 3.12:** 305.02(5)

```
01 Bonn:  .hhh we=she couldn't see why they couldn't stay for dinner.
02        well=I mean (.) why make it difficult fer people eh?
03 Ther:  [mm       hm:.      ]
04 Bonn:  [e=mean, don't chu] think that's kina mean, hhh huhhuh hehheh
       t                                fast multiple nods. T: smiles at C
05 Bonn:  [hahhhh            .hhh        ]
06 Ther:  [yeah: I mean it seemed to sorta] bother you that she=was making
07        your daughter feel so [badly.]
08 Bonn:                        [↑ye:ah] I thought ye know ↑that's
       b                                nod
       t                                   multiple nods--------->
09        aw:ful to me-and even her own son.
10 Ther:  y[eah.          yeah.  ]
```

In lines 06–07, the therapist casts Bonnie's actions in a different frame, focusing on her feelings (`it seemed to sorta bother you` ...) rather than on the complaint per se. As a response, Bonnie first offers an acknowledgment token with rise/falling intonation (i.e., prosodically modified) and then continues by explicitly stating how she feels about the mother-in-law's actions. Thus, strong affiliation is displayed via an upgraded confirmation token and by elaborating on the therapist's proposed shift in topic that targets Bonnie's feelings in that situation.

*Repetition* As already discussed in Chapter 2, repetitions found in psychotherapy may be differentiated in two types (Ferrara, 1994): The first, termed *echoing*, that involves the repetition of the prior speaker's utterance and the second, termed *mirroring*, that involves partial repetition.[2] Echoing actions have been argued to work specifically to display acceptance or agreement, and thus affiliate with the prior action. Repetition is shown in Extract 3.13. Here, Sofia has been explaining the contrast between her husband who bosses her around and reproaches her and a male friend who does not.

**Extract 3.13:** 304.07(3)

```
01 Sofia:  jus (0.5) to- in order to:: (0.4) if one is wis(h) a person that
02         is always .hhh uh::m (0.7) bossing around, dere is a lot of
03         energy? that one has to spen all the time?
04 Ther:   mm hm:.
        t  fast multiple nods
05 Sofia:  defend[ing?]
06 Ther:          [mm  ] hm. ↑sure sure.
        t  nod          slow double nod
07 Sofia:  so:: uh::m =
08 Ther:   = so a little bit more at ease.
09 Sofia:  more at ease. (0.4) yeah.
        s  deep nod.       double nod
        t                                  nod
10 Ther:   °°mm hm,°° °°mm hm,°°
```

While Sofia is describing the husband's negative attributes (lines 01–05), the therapist offers token affiliation through an acknowledgement in line 04 (`mm hm:.`) and line 06 (`mm hm.`) and upgraded acknowledgement via "`↑sure sure.`". Sofia then continues with her turn in line 07 with some hesitation, which then leads the therapist to formulate the way Sofia feels with this other man (`so a little bit more at ease.`). In line 09, Sofia immediately provides upgraded affiliation by first echoing the therapist's formulation and then by providing confirmation with "`yeah.`".[3]

*Collaborative Turn Completion* Lerner (2004, p. 225) defines *collaborative turn completion* as "the pre-emptive completion of one speaker's

[2] For everyday contexts, repetitions do a range of discursive work such as initiating repair, sustaining a topical focus, registering receipt of prior talk, targeting a next action, doing confirming or asserting primary epistemic rights from a second sequential position (Kim, 2002; Stivers, 2005a).

[3] Although Sofia has not repeated all of the therapist's prior utterance, I would still refer to her action as echoing as she has re-produced most of the phrasal unit. It could also be argued that, by leaving out the hedge "a little bit," Sofia has modified the therapist's formulation; that is, Sofia is claiming to be more at ease with him and not just slightly.

turn-constructional unit (Sacks et al., 1974) by a subsequent speaker … in a way that transforms its production into a sequence." The prior "turn-to-be-completed" is argued to appear in two general formats: A turn-in-progress that may be hearably syntactically incomplete or a possibly complete syntactic unit that gets extended by next speaker (Oloff, 2018) – see also discussion of extension actions in Chapter 2. Lerner (2004) also lists four features that characterize the *affiliative* accomplishment of collaborative turn completion. These features focus mainly on *next speaker's practices* to complete the prior turn-in progress:

> In summary, affiliating utterances 1. use the format of the [turn constructional unit] TCU-in-progress, 2. maintain the progressivity of the utterance from an opportunity space, 3. bring the turn unit-in-progress to completion and 4. are treated as candidate versions of what was about to have been said. That is, affiliating utterances are built as and treated as a turn-completing action. (Lerner, 2004, p. 229)

Conversationalists' knowledge of grammatical units allows them to anticipate how an utterance may develop and, further, to jointly produce clauses and larger discourse units (Lerner, 1991). The joint production of discourse units is known to be common in psychotherapy (Ferrara, 1994). Further, joint productions appear not only to have an empathic function, but their occurrence also seems to arise from a concerted purpose and to be facilitated by the growing familiarity between client and therapist, as resulting from their regular weekly meetings (Ferrara, 1994). A collaborative turn completion is shown in Extract 3.14.

**Extract 3.14:** 422.3

01 Ernie: I felt tra:pped. I felt anxiety:, I felt trapped. u:m (0.3) uh<br>
02 en I continued to give this person the benefit of<br>
03 the ↑doubt. .hh u::m when in fact I shouldn't. now that was<br>
04 probably oka:y I- if I look back in hind sight, okay th- the<br>
05 first u:m .hh the fact that he didn't u:m: .hh handle- set up<br>
06 the arrangements properly en- en (no) big ↑deal. the fact<br>
07 that he failed to really u:m .hh follow through on something<br>
08 he asked me to ↑do.<br>
09 Ther: °right.° and what=<br>
10 Ernie: **=I- then I should've**<br>
11 (0.6)<br>
12 Ther: **said something.**<br>
13 Ernie: I should have said something.<br>
14 Ther: mm hm::.

Ernie is complaining about his past dealings with a former business associate and how he had been let down and deceived by him. During his complaint, Ernie contrasts behaviour that is in some way pardonable (the fact that he didn't u:m: .hh handle- set up the arrangements properly `en- en (no) big ↑deal.`) to other behaviour (`he failed to really u:m .hh follow through on something`) that is more deserving of sanction. But, in line 10, he stops in mid-clause, without actually specifying what he should have done and remains briefly silent. This leads the therapist, in line 12, to anticipate the missing unit (`said something.`). Following Lerner's (2004) affiliative criteria mentioned earlier, we would note that the therapist's completion aligns with the prior TCU format (i.e., `said something` may sensibly and grammatically follow from the preceding TCU), maintains the progressivity of the unit (i.e., it continues as a telling or description) and also brings Ernie's turn to a possible completion. Furthermore, Ernie then provides strong confirmation by repeating the whole grammatical unit, thus corroborating or affiliating with the therapist's candidate version as being something he would have (or could have) said.

Collaborative turn completions also commonly occur in a different speaker order; that is, with the therapist producing the first turn unit and the client producing the second completing unit. This form of turn completion is shown in Extract 3.15 (see also Extract 2.27).

**Extract 3.15:** 014.18(6)

```
01  Ther:   >is that what you're saying,< that it f-whe- you say it falls
         t  multiple nods
02          on deaf ears he doesn't understand, or h[e    doesn't]
03  Kris:                                            [doesn't want] to-
04          doesn't want to listen.=
05  Ther:   =mm.
         t  deep nod
```

The therapist begins this sequence with a clarification check in which she gets Kristina to explain what "falling on deaf ears" means for her. This is clearly a B-event that invites client confirmation (Labov & Fanshel, 1977). The therapist first provides a candidate reading (`he doesn't understand`) and then proceeds to offer an alternative reading. But before she can continue, Sofia finishes the turn for her. Thus, by providing this alternative reading, the client does affiliative work by collaborating with the therapist's try at finding the appropriate interpretation to the client's prior talk. Even more common completion practices, however, involve therapists actually delaying their turn completion, producing what Koshik (2002) refers to as *designedly incomplete utterances* (DIUs), in which clients become invited to complete the turn. DIUs will be taken up in more detail in Chapter 5 on storytelling. The empathic dimension of collaborative turn completions will be explained in Chapter 4.

## 3.4 Non-Vocal Affiliative Practices

Thus far, the focus has been on how vocalized actions can work to accomplish affiliation. But that is only part of the picture. Social affiliation between speakers is also achieved through resources that are found in what is commonly referred to as the non-verbal or non-vocal dimension of social interaction. In psychotherapy contexts, for example, the sequential organization of laughter and facial expressions has been shown to play an important role in affective regulation and in relationship building (Bänninger-Huber, 1992). Other non-vocal resources such as nodding have been shown to perform valuable interpersonal work in everyday conversations and in storytelling contexts (Kita & Ide, 2007; Stivers, 2008). According to Stivers (2008, p. 37), nods from story recipients during mid-telling are essential for displaying affiliation with the teller's stance or "affective treatment of the events he or she is describing." The placement of nods has also been shown to have implications for the trajectory of talk. For example, in question–answer sequences, whereas timely placed nods may work to close down the sequence, so-called "early answer-nods" may instead lead to further talk, thus expanding the sequence (De Stefani, 2021). In psychotherapy, therapist nods serve the general function of displaying token affiliation with the client and, in contexts of "verbal" affiliation, nods function primarily to reinforce the already established level of affiliation between therapist and client (Muntigl et al., 2012; Vranjes et al., 2019). Further, their manner of production (e.g., simultaneous nods) and duration (e.g., series of nods) indicate the strength of this affiliation.

### *3.4.1 Contiguous Placement of Nods Following Confirmation*

The placement of nods during affiliative sequences tends to have certain structural characteristics (Muntigl et al., 2012). First, clients' verbal confirmations are often produced in conjunction with a nod. This appears to bolster the client's affiliation with the therapist's prior action. Second, therapist nods tend to be immediately latched onto the client's affiliating response or even produced in slight overlap with it. Third, therapist nods seem to be responsive to both the client's verbal and non-verbal display of affiliation and, further, are often multiple in number. One function of the therapist's production of a series of nods may be that it indexes the therapist's and client's co-achievement of an increasingly positive, affective alignment.

Extracts 3.16 (see also Extract 3.1) and 3.17 illustrate how client and therapist nods are placed contiguously (i.e., without delay) with respect to the client's prior affiliating action of confirmation and often lead to simultaneous nodding between client and therapist.

**Extract 3.16:** Sofia Case 304.07(1)

```
01  Sofia:  uh::m. (0.7) whe=was it, (1.2) .hhh oh. (1.4) ((lip smack))
02          I am somehow, (0.9) lairning to: .hhh (1.9) .hhh control myself
         s  looks at T
03          better when I s(h)ink that I am having dos:e
         s  smiling
04          (0.5)
05  Ther:   the:. (0.4) anxiety? Or the=
06  Sofia:  = the anxiety?
         s  nod
07  Ther:   s:k- yeah.
         t  shallow double nod
            ...
14  Ther:   [so this-] this ehm (0.2) .hhh the feeling's still there
15          (0.6) b-know but you know how to cope with it better.
16          Is that what's happening,
17  Sofia:  yeap. Mm hm?
         s  nod.
         t              fast multiple nods
18  Ther:   yeah.
         t  fast multiple nods
```

**Extract 3.17:** Bonnie Case 305.02(2)

```
01  Bonn:  ((lip smack)) an I (h)th(h)ink. .hh ↑what is wrong with me. Why
02         can't I get past this. .hhh [you      know?]
        t  slow nod---------->
03  Ther:                              [so what you'd] like ta be able ta do is
04         (.) do it without resent[ing him?]
05  Bonn:                          [  r:igh ]t. that's [exactly wha]t
06  Ther:                                              [uh      huh.]
        b                      nod, point.     multiple nods-------->
        t                                          slow double nod
07  Bonn:  I'd like ta do=I'd like to feel .hhh
        t                       slow nod
```

For Extracts 3.16 and 3.17, therapists produce formulations that index B-events in which client confirmation becomes relevant. In each case, the clients' nods appear simultaneously with the expression of the acknowledgement token: "`yeap.`" for Sofia (line 16) and "`r:ight.`" for Bonnie (line 05). Also, for each case, the therapist produces a nod immediately thereafter, which helps to co-construct reinforced affiliation between the speakers.

### *3.4.2 Simultaneous Nodding/Smiling between Client and Therapist*

Kita and Ide (2007) observed that in everyday Japanese conversations nod sequences between speakers signalled positive affect and a heightened degree of rapport. In psychotherapy, a similar tendency may be observed. In particular, following the initial client confirmation-therapist response pair, the ensuing interactional sequence often contained additional instances of simultaneous nodding between client and therapist, which seemed to suggest that the speakers were maintaining a strengthened display of affiliation. Simultaneous nodding is shown in Extract 3.18.

**Extract 3.18:** Kristina Case 014.13(1)

```
01  Kris:  hhh yeah av- it's- I uhm (3.5) mm, (3.2) ↑yeah he- he keeps
02         running after me even if he translates, an he c(h)a(h) p(h)retty
03         early qu(h)ick comes to check on me.
           ...
09  Ther:  >so's like he won't< leave you alone ye n[e- y'n- ha-] never
10  Kris:                                           [n:o:.       ]
        k                                             shakes head
11  Ther:  really have any,
12         (1.5)
13  Kris:  no, privacy in [my home. ]
14  Ther:                 [right so-] >so d'ya feel like< you .hhh you
15         crave that? Crave some privac[y, and some space. ]of your own,
16  Kris:                               [↑oh yeah very much.]
        t  nod
17  Ther:  hm.
        t  nod
        k  nod
18         (          3.4            )
        t  multiple nods - -shallow
        k  multiple nods - -shallow
```

In line 16, Kristina provides an overlapping, upgraded confirmation that she desires more privacy and space (↑oh yeah very much.). During Kristina's confirmation (line 16), the therapist nods and thus displays token affiliation with Kristina's strengthened affiliative display. Subsequently, Kristina and the therapist repeatedly display mutual affiliation through a series of simultaneously produced nods.

To illustrate how nodding, in conjunction with other verbal and non-vocal resources, may also work to strengthen positive affect and rapport, consider Extract 3.19 (see also Extract 2.27 and Extract 3.15).

**Extract 3.19:** Kristina Case 014.18(6)

```
01  Kris:  mm. it looks like he is up to his limit of comprehension of (1.2)
        t                                                            deep nod
02         o:f uh: the vorld uh,
        k      looks away
03         (1.8)
04  Kris:  or the family,
        k   looks at T
05         (                          10.0                 )
        t     nod→ gazes at K.
        k                             looking down.
06  Ther:  ((lip smack)) so you'd like, (3.8) to have your um (1.4)
        t  double nod, looks down
07         when you wanna do things ta ta not have it ↓undermined
08         an [belittled] an.
09  Kris:     [mm hm.   ]
        k                    looks at T
10         (       0.6      )
        k  fast multiple nods
11  Ther:  uh huh.
        t   nod
12         (           2.0         )
        k     nod  smile.
        t      slow multiple nods---->
13  Kris:  m-yes. [I would like. e(h)ehheh]
14  Ther:         [↑yeah        ↑yeah    ] yeah.
        t  slow multiple nods, slight smile
        k                   looks at T, smiling
```

In this dialogue, the therapist formulates the upshot of Kristina's prior talk by stating that she would prefer not to be undermined and belittled by her husband (lines 06–08). As a response, Kristina first provides a weak overlapping acknowledgement in line 09 and then produces a series of fast nods. In turn, the therapist responds with a nod that overlaps her weak acknowledgement (`uh huh.`) in line 11. Although therapist and client seem to be affiliated here, the affiliation does not appear to be as strong as in those cases where the client upgrades her verbal confirmation while nodding. It may be for this reason that the therapist somewhat delays her return confirmation and produces only a single nod rather than a multiple one. Subsequently, however, we note that the affiliation displays become augmented in the following ways: First, as line 12 shows, the speakers begin to nod in unison; second, Kristina produces an upgraded confirmation (`m-yes. I would like.`) and the therapist overlaps Kristina's turn, by also responding with upgraded return confirmations. We would also note that positive affect and rapport is being continually built up throughout the interaction through additional features. For instance, in line 12, Kristina smiles at the therapist and, in lines 13–14, both speakers are smiling in unison while Kristina laughs briefly – see Chapter 4 for a discussion on how these sequences may accomplish *empathic moments* (Heritage, 2011).

## 3.5 Disaffiliative Responses

Disaffiliation is the counterpart to affiliation. So, rather than working to foster social cohesion through agreement or compliance, disaffiliative acts may place stress on social relations via disagreement or rejection. As already mentioned in the introduction, however, disaffiliative acts should not necessarily be seen in a negative light, for example, as necessarily damaging the social relationship. In fact, some degree of disaffiliation may be seen as forming a relevant component of the therapeutic process. Recall Bänninger-Huber and Widmer's (1999) claim that one important therapeutic task is to maintain a certain degree of conflictive tension and, for this reason, some level of disaffiliation may at times be necessary. A "good" therapy also does not mean that clients will or should agree with the therapist's understanding of their troubles. Therapists can certainly miss the mark and so clients can certainly call therapists out during such moments. In such cases, client disaffiliation would constitute an appropriate next action, one that maintains the client's ownership of experience (Sacks, 1995b, pp. 242ff; Sharrock, 1974) and possibly repairs the therapist's misunderstanding.

Disaffiliative responses often come in a dispreferred action format. This means that sequences involving dispreferred responding actions are structured differently from affiliative-type sequences. A set of commonly appearing *dispreferred* features, conveying that a disaffiliative response is forthcoming and/or in the making, are identified in Schegloff (2007, pp. 63–73). Disaffiliation may be displayed within sequences in the following ways: a delay in the production of response; elaboration; features of contrast or downgraded action and an orientation of impending disaffiliation from producer of FPP. These features, following Schegloff (2007), are summarized in Table 3.2.

Delays in producing a SPP may be realized in the following ways: through an inter-turn gap or a pause between turns at speaking; through turn-initial delays such as hedges ("uh," "I dunno") and discourse markers ("well"); by prefacing one's response through an other-initiated (OI) repair (Schegloff et al., 1977), eventually leading to a dispreferred response.[4] Elaboration is, in a

[4] Although delays were certainly most common in these disaffiliative environments, there were also instances of *overlapping* disaffiliative responses (see Extract 3.30). These would occur when clients would take a track (i.e., a certain position or topic) that bore no relation to the therapist's track, often working to interrupt or derail the progress of the therapist's course of action.

Table 3.2 *Common features of disaffiliative responses*

**1.** ***Delay in production of response***
- Inter-turn gap
- Turn-initial delay
- Prefacing with an Other-Initiated (OI) repair

**2.** ***Elaboration***
- Anticipatory accounts

**3.** ***Features of contrast or downgraded action***
- "Pro forma" agreement
- Mitigation
- Absence of confirmation or disconfirmation tokens

**4.** ***Orientation of impending disaffiliation from producer of FPP***
- Pre-emptive reformulation with preference reversal (e.g., when therapist does a subsequent version of the formulation to receive a response of opposing (+/-) valence)

general sense, taken to mean doing something more than simply "agreeing" (Schegloff, 2007). Particular instances of elaboration are often expressed through anticipatory accounts that provide some form of explanation or reason for why an affiliative SPP cannot be produced. Disaffiliative responses sometimes contain features that specifically mark its dispreferred character. This may include expressing pro-forma agreement through "yes, but ..." or mitigation through modal expressions such as "perhaps," "maybe" or "probably." At times, the absence of confirmation or disconfirmation tokens may signal a form of disaffiliation; for example, when the respondent is not engaged with (ignoring) the prior speaker and stays on own track (see Extract 3.30). Disaffiliation may also be oriented to by the speaker of the FPP. In these cases, the first speaker may do a *pre-emptive reformulation with preference reversal*; for example, by offering a subsequent version of the initiating action to receive the "opposite," and affiliative, response.

A disaffiliating client move is shown in Extract 3.20.

**Extract 3.20:** Paula Case 312.02(08)

```
Paula:  like I ha- (.) found it difficul:t sometimes (.) to::,
        (2.2) relate to them, and (0.3) their, er- (2.4) their
        problems hh He he he.hh and i- e- (0.8) it worked the
        opposite °way too I guess.°
Ther:   you were just (.) on different wavelengths=
Paula:  = ye- yeah.
        (0.3)
Paula:  but it- (.) like, (0.7) I guess once in a while in
        between we kinda struck it. ehuh he(.h)h.
```

10 (2.3)
11 Ther: but it doesn't sound like (.) e- maybe when you .h (.)
12 rented out the place you thought it might give you some
13 compa:nionship (.) and- (0.3) [it doesn't' sound like]
14 Paula: [**.hhh** ]
15 Ther: (.) that (.) did (0.3) so much °for you?°
16 **(0.5)**
17 Paula: **um, (4.3) yes and no:. like- (.)**
18 I guess my main concern was no I can't cope like [with]
19 Ther: [mm. ]
20 Paula: the mo:ve?=
21 Ther: =mm.

In lines 01–04, Paula talks of the troubles she has had with former roommates and that although she had found it difficult to relate to them, her roommates probably had similar experiences with her. The therapist then provides a summary formulation that captures the differences and incompatibility between them (you were just (.) on different wavelengths). Paula's following disaffiliative move contains a "pro-forma" agreement ("yeah, but"), which is followed by an account for her disagreement. A second instance of client disaffiliation appears a bit further down. The therapist in lines 11–13 subtly challenges Paula's prior talk, stating that her desire for companionship (i.e., getting a roommate) did not come with the benefit that was hoped for.[5] Paula's response is replete with dispreferred elements: delay in the form of an inbreath (.hhh) occurring at a transition relevance place (TRP), pauses and hesitation (um); a qualified agreement (yes and no:.); and an account (like- ...) explaining that she in fact had different concerns at the time.

The preceding dispreferred features play a crucial part in shaping the subsequent disaffiliative action. For sequences in which confirmation or acceptance may be conditionally relevant, I have identified the various disaffiliative action formats occurring in the York 1 data examined, ranging from explicit to more implicit forms of disagreement or refusal (see Table 3.3).

Explicit disconfirmation/disagreement/refusal generally occurs with a disagreement token such as "no" or a contradiction. More covert forms of disagreement/refusal take the following action formats: claiming insufficient access to knowledge; displaying mitigation; other-initiated repair; unexpanded response; and pursuing own agenda or topic.

[5] The therapist's "but," prefacing her turn in line 11, marks an upcoming contrast to what Paula just said.

Table 3.3 *Action formats that do disaffiliative work in SPP positions of confirmation/agreement or compliance*

| Action Type | Example Realization |
|---|---|
| *Overt/Explicit* | |
| Disconfirmation/Disagreement | -*no* [as disconfirming] |
| *or* | -*no* [as declining] |
| Refusal (of proposal) | |
| *Covert/Implicit* | |
| Claim insufficient access to knowledge | -↑*I=dunno.* |
| Displaying mitigation | - *probably.* |
| Other-initiated repair | -°<*if I always needed a lot of love and support?*> |
| Unexpanded response | -*Yeah.* [as confirming] |
| Pursuing own agenda or topic [takes own track] | Features: *overlap; multiple self-repairs; prefacing markers: "I mean," "but," "so"* |

### 3.5.1 Explicit Disagreement and Disconfirmation

Examples of explicit disagreement are shown in Extracts 3.21 and 3.22.

**Extract 3.21:** 014.13(4)(b)

```
01   Ther:   ((lip smack)) >so=i's almost=like you're thinkin I< (.) jus
02           don't know if I could really (0.7) survi:ve in some level.
03           (3.1)
04   Ther:   on my own.
05           (               6.8                   )
         k      gazes at T   looks away
06   Kris:   no=I ↑thin I can ↓ survive on my own,
```

**Extract 3.22:** Sofia Case 304.03(3)

```
01   Sofia:  I don=know whas gonna happen with that too. but the only
02           s(h)ing that I know is=that uh.
         s            shakes head
03           (2.1)
04   Sofia:  .hhh writing to him?
         s                      looks at T
05   Ther:   mm [hm,]
06   Sofia:     [giv]es me (1.9) ((lip smack)) uhm. (1.4) makes me feel
07           better?
         s   double nod, looks at T
08   Ther:   mm hm.
09           (0.7)
```

```
10   Sofia:   because
11            (1.2)
12   Ther:    writing=ta him makes you feel more hopeful?
13   Sofia:   hopeful. noh hop- I .hhh I do=noh have, .hh hopes. (0.9) for
14            that, (2.0) relationship?
            t nod                         shallow multiple nods
```

In Extract 3.21, the therapist provides an upshot formulation that questions whether Kristina could survive without her husband. Following a 3.1-second pause in line 03 that presages upcoming disagreement, the therapist extends her turn with another grammatical unit. This incremental extension, "on my own.", further specifies the conditions or resulting situation that might follow a "break-up." This is then followed by another extended pause (line 05). Here, the client first looks at and then away from the therapist, which might be signalling momentary disengagement and reluctance to respond. A disaffiliative response follows, however, with the disagreement marker "no", which is then followed by a contradiction in which she counters the therapist's suggestive phrasing that she cannot survive on her own.

In Extract 3.22, the client had been discussing modes of communication, such as letter writing, that help her to disclose relevant personal issues with her husband. Sofia asserts that writing to him "makes me feel better?" and then, in line 10, begins to provide an account (because) but then cuts herself off. In line 12, the therapist collaboratively completes the account and slightly modifies Sofia's previous claim that she feels better when writing to her husband, by substituting Sofia's lexical term "better" for "more hopeful". In doing so, the therapist provides a more optimistic interpretation of the client's prior talk (MacMartin, 2008); that is, "feeling more hopeful" has positive implications for the future, whereas merely "feeling better" does not contain this projection. Sofia, however, responds disaffiliatively. She first repeats the term "hopeful", which functions to echo the therapist's prior talk (Ferrara, 1994) and to possibly highlight this term as requiring further elaboration and perhaps even repair. The client then continues with a disagreement that contradicts the therapist and provides the scope of what she does not feel hopeful about (I do=noh have, .hh hopes. (0.9) for that, ... relationship).

### 3.5.2 *Explicit Refusal*

Strong disaffiliation may also occur in *deontic*-oriented, directive action sequences that may involve suggestions, commands, requests or proposals (Couper-Kuhlen, 2014). Disaffiliation is shown in Extract 3.23 in which the therapist makes an attempt at recruiting Kristina into chair work.

**Extract 3.23:** 014.04(6b)

```
01   Ther:    so whaddaya * do:             *as the red °power?°
          t                *nods towards chair*
02            (0.5)
03   Kris:    [>as] the red power not [this] thing +inside?<
04   Ther:    [( )]                   [m    ]
05   Ther:    °yeah.°
06            (0.6)
07   Kris:    °(move)°
08            (1.0)
09   Kris:    uh'I just(huh) .h °I:'m probably° sca::ry
10   Ther:    *okay *scare her.      * scare Kristina.
          t   *nods *points to chair*
11   Kris:    °yeah I've+ fun doing that(hih)°
12            (0.5  *)
          t         *nods->
13   Ther:    >n'ju it out< loud?*
          t                nods-->*
14            (1.4)
15   Kris:    +no.
          k   +turns from chair to T-->
16            (1.0)
17   Kris:    it's ↑quite= ↑it's enough just(.)to I can hih .h
18            just go around. (0.4)
```

During this session, the client had informed the therapist that she had been applying her own form of two-chair work at home to deal with her "self-critic" (see Chapters 1 and 6 for detailed descriptions of chair work). But rather than directing her talk at a vacant chair representing another aspect of self, Kristina imagines a "red power" that surrounds herself and that acts critically toward her. In line 09, Kristina answers the therapist's prior question in line 01, by saying that the red power is scary, which is then immediately followed by a command (`okay scare her. scare Kristina.`). But rather than complying with the demand, Kristina merely assesses the action of scaring herself as something that is fun to do. This then leads the therapist, in line 13, to repeat the command by specifying that she should do this out loud. After a 1.4-second pause, Kristina utters a succinct refusal (`no`), while turning her head away from the chair toward the therapist. She then provides an account, stating that she can "`just go around.`", implying that the red power acts scary not by words, but by its movements around her.

### *3.5.3 Claiming Insufficient Access to Knowledge or an Inability to Act*

Rather than disagreeing overtly through disagreement tokens or contradictions, respondents may instead reference the reasons for not being able to act affiliatively. These accounts often orient to the speaker's insufficient access to knowledge through "I don't know" or to an inability to act. Consider Extracts 3.24 and 3.25.

**Extract 3.24:** 014.04(2b)

```
01   Kris:    .hhh an there's not everything that I mind about him=dere
02            are some(0.6) positive charact(h)er(h)ist(h)icks he has
          t   nod                             slow nod
03            as well,
04            (            9.2               )
          t   shallow double nod
05   Ther:    ((lip smack)) so somehow thes:e .hh these things seem .hh
06            worth (2.3) sacrificing your happiness for?
          t                    shakes head
07            (1.5)
08   Ther:    or worth the pain?
09   Kris:    .hhh well th- th- my question is I don=know what's on de
10            other side. would I- would I be any happier?
          t                                   deep multiple nods ->
11            (    1.6     )
          t   ---------->
12   Kris:    I don=know.
          t   ----------->
13            (    2.0     )
          t   ---------->
```

**Extract 3.25:** 306.03(05)

```
01   Ther:    can you tell him [that?]+
02        k               wipes eyes->+
04   Kris:                     [.shih]
05            (0.7)
06   Kris:    [uh:m    ]
07   Ther:    [tell him] I don't feel accepted °by you.°
08            (1.1)
09   Kris:    Hhx:: ~uh:~ (0.3) +.hih
10            (4.0)
11   Kris:    °uh: I can't s-° (0.2) it seems to be (0.3)
12            blocking outta mind again.
13   Ther:    mm hm.
14   Kris:    .snih
```

In Extract 3.24, the therapist and client are discussing the pros and cons of Kristina staying in her marriage. The therapist interprets Kristina's prior turn as suggesting that, because her husband has some positive characteristics, these may be seen as outweighing all the negatives and as sufficient for her to remain unhappy (`sacrificing your happiness for?`) or in pain. Kristina's response contains typical dispreferred prefacing features (in breath, discourse marker `well`) and is then followed by a claim of insufficient knowledge (`I don=know.`) that accounts for her not be able to provide an affirmative reply. She also further elaborates (or accounts) for her lack of knowledge by stating that the consequences of leaving are uncertain (`would I be any happier?`).

In Extract 3.25, Kristina is currently engaged in chairwork. In line 07, the therapist's action commands Kristina to direct a specific statement to an imaginary person (i.e., her husband) in the vacant chair (`I don't feel accepted °by you.°`). Following this, Kristina displays many features of distress such as sighing, wobbly voice, pauses and crying (Hepburn, 2004). Then, in line 11, she provides an account for why she cannot engage in this task, first by expressing her inability (`I can't s-`) and then by signalling her lack of access to the words she has been directed to utter (`blocking outta mind again`).

### 3.5.4 *Displaying Mitigation*

Disaffiliation can be conveyed through mitigating expressions that either directly soften the dispreferred actions of disagreeing or refusing or considerably weaken the speaker's degree of endorsement. Mitigation is often expressed through modal expressions, through ambivalence markers that imply that the answer can go "either way" or through contrastive expressions that signal other possibilities. I show examples of each of these mitigation practices in Extracts 3.26–3.28.

**Extract 3.26:** 304.07(5): Mitigation

```
01  Sofia:   so my granmother was noh
02           (1.1)
03  Sofia:   did not raise me in a in a very (0.8)
04           like uh:m. oh you kno:w bab[y:,]
         s   swings head and hands side to side, smiling
05  Ther:                                [she] didn °cuddle°
06  Ther:    [mom and cuddle you.]
07  Sofia:   [she didn't         ] yeap.
08  Ther:    b-.hhh but (.) bu=then the same time the message was that
09           those feelings or that part of you .hhh that feels TI:red
10           or feels sa:d (0.5) .hhh i:s (0.8) not allowed to be seen.
11           (2.0)
         t   gazes at S
         s   gazes at T
```

12 Sofia: **probably. (0.4) I-I-I couldn't see .hhh**
s *widens eyes, looks up. looks at T*
13 (0.8)
14 Sofia: **at- that ah=that time. >I couldn=analyze< (.) dat.**
15 (0.8)
16 Sofia: at [that time, ] [because ]

### Extract 3.27: Paula Case 312.02(08): Ambivalence markers

01 Paula: like I ha- (.) found it difficul:t sometimes (.) to::,
02 (2.2) relate to them, and (0.3) their, er- (2.4) their
03 problems hh He he he.hh and i- e- (0.8) it worked the
04 opposite °way too I guess.°
05 Ther: you were just (.) on different wavelengths=
06 Paula: = ye- yeah.
07 (0.3)
08 Paula: but it- (.) like, (0.7) I guess once in a while in
09 between we kinda struck it. ehuh he(.h)h.
10 (2.3)
11 Ther: but it doesn't sound like (.) e- maybe when you .h (.)
12 rented out the place you thought it might give you some
13 compa:nionship (.) and- (0.3) [it doesn't sound like]
14 Paula: [.hhh ]
15 Ther: (.) that (.) did (0.3) so much °for you?°
16 (0.5)
17 Paula: **um, (4.3) yes and no:. like- (.)**
18 I guess my main concern was no I can't cope like [with]
19 Ther: [mm. ]
20 Paula: the mo:ve?=
21 Ther: =mm.

### Extract 3.28: 304.07 (3): Contrastive expressions

01 Ther: uh huh. (0.4) .hhh [so it's just you] just don't fee:l like y-
02 Sofia: [like I woul say]
03 Ther: y-you look at him and what you just .hhh feel numb? or: .hhh
04 Sofia: numb.
05 (0.9)
06 Ther: nothing.
t *shakes head*
s *nod*
07 (0.5)
08 Sofia: numb. (0.3) thas- thas a good word. (0.4) °yeah.° (0.8) °thas a
09 good word.° (0.8) ((sniffs)) (2.0) ((lip smack)) and uh:=
10 Ther: = and that makes you sa:d.
11 (2.3)

```
12   Sofia:   DAs- dat could be one of the s(h)ings. yeah.
           s  shallow double nod
13            (    0.4    )
           t  shallow nod
14   Sofia:   .hhh but (0.6) at dis point (.) I (.) sometimes I think that
15            (0.8) dir are some (0.4) something maybe mo:re?
16            (0.3)
17   Ther:    mm,
```

Mitigation through modal expressions may be seen in Extract 3.26. Here, Sofia prefaces her disaffiliative response with "probably" and then follows this up with an account that outlines her inability to have adopted the therapist's suggested perspective at the time because she was too young. Extract 3.27 (also shown as Extract 3.20) is an example that shows how ambivalence may be displayed by both agreeing and disagreeing (yes and no:.). Qualified agreement may also be expressed via *pro-forma agreement* involving some form of "yeah, but". In Extract 3.28, Sofia begins her response in line 12 with an agreement that has been mitigated using the modal expression "could be" and then, in line 14, proceeds to provide a contrasting and opposing view of what she may be feeling. Each of these types of disagreements has the form of what has been previously described as a *counter-claim* (Muntigl & Turnbull, 1998). These disagreement-act types contain some affiliative elements that attend to the other's territorial preserves and/or face wants (Goffman, 1967, 1971).

### *3.5.5 Repair Initiation*

Responding with a repair initiator, rather than the preferred response, may be construed as *disagreement-implicative* (Schegloff, 2007, p. 151); that is, the repair initiation may be heralding the onset of a disaffiliative action.

**Extract 3.29:** 304.07(5)

```
01   Ther:    [d'ya      ]>I mean d'you think< this goes back to when you
02            were a child? th-it sort've (0.5) .hhh r-it I mean is that s-
03   Ther:    s-[is this] always been true of you? kina=needing a lot of
04   Sofia:     [m-      ]
05            .hhh (0.5) lo:ve, an: (0.5) suppo:rt?
06            (2.3)
07   Sofia:   <if I always needed a lot of love [and support?>]
08   Ther:                                      [mm     hm,    ] mm hm.
           s  squints eyes, inclines head, looks at T
           t                         multiple nods------------->
```

```
09          (1.9)
10  Sofia:  uh::, (2.1) no I don't remember mysel as being,
        s                         shakes head
11          (0.7) uh: I remember mysel (1.1) when I was a little (0.3)
12          girl? [between] ages five? (0.6) an sirteen?
13  Ther:         [mm hm,  ]
```

In Extract 3.29, the therapist seeks confirmation from Sofia that she has always needed a lot of love and support in her life. Sofia's response in line 07, which is preceded by a lengthy 2.3-second pause that already might be signalling some form of interactional trouble, contains an other-initiated repair (<if I always needed a lot of love [and support?>). Although the therapist is quick to provide overlapping confirmation in line 08, another lengthy pause of 1.9 seconds ensues, leading to Sofia's disconfirmation in line 10 (uh::, (2.1) no ...) in which she denies having epistemic access to the event in question that occurred many years past.

### 3.5.6 *Minimal Confirmation without Expansion*

Although disaffiliative responses may often be more discursively complex or elaborate than affiliative responses, such as the occurrence of prefacing material and accounts, responses that remain unelaborated may also signal some form of interactional trouble. Returning to Heritage's (2002) observations on first and second position assertions, by just providing the expected minimal "yes" or confirmation in second position, an inference can be generated that the respondent is merely going along with the sequential constraint of providing agreement but may, actually, feel differently. This kind of orientation to minimal confirmation is illustrated in Extract 3.30.

**Extract 3.30:** 014.18(8)(a)

```
01  Ther:   .hhh I guess as an adult now there are certain things that
02          you do have choices over and do have control (1.0) over,
03          [that you did]n't have when you were a child.
04  Kris:   [mm hm.      ]
05  Kris:   mm hm.
06          (                    45.4                    )
        k   gazes down, hand on chin
        t   gazes at K.               tilts head to side
07  Ther:   ((lip smack)) m'st have been very difficult to have felt so
        t                             looks down.
08          (0.4) powerless so
        t   looks at K, shakes head
```

```
09            (3.1)
         k    gazes at T
         t    gazes at K
10   Ther:    in your young life.
11   Kris:    mm hm.
12            (4.0)
         t    gazes at K
         k    gazes at T
13   Kris:    mm hm?
         k    shrugs
```

At the beginning of this extract, the therapist compares different stages or times of Kristina's life: An older, present-day Kristina who has choices and who has more control over her life versus a younger Kristina who may not have had these options or resources enabling her to act agentively. The therapist's turn certainly makes confirmation relevant as a next response, but the therapist's action may also be inviting more from the client. For instance, the client could address these differences in more detail (e.g., provide examples of how she is able (or unable) to act as an agent now). Kristina could also use this opportunity to speak to her inability to take control and, moreover, to talk about her feelings during these situations. In lines 04–05, Kristina voices acknowledgement but does not take up the floor. The therapist also does not select to continue speaking, thus leading to a long silence of 45 seconds. During this time, Kristina seems to further disengage from the therapist by gazing downwards with her hand on her chin. In line 07, the therapist takes up another turn and orients to the client's feelings of powerlessness in situations where she did not take control. Thereafter, a 3.1-second pause ensues, leading the therapist to produce another TCU that grammatically expands on her prior turn (in your young life.). Kristina responds with an acknowledgement in line 11, followed by a 4-second pause and another acknowledgement with phrase final intonation and an accompanying shrug. Thus, although the client is not conveying disconfirmation per se, her lack of engagement – as manifested by her minimal, unelaborated acknowledgements and non-vocal conduct – seems to be conveying a non-affiliative stance, one that does not endorse the therapist's view.

### *3.5.7 Pursuing Own Agenda or Topic*

Sacks' (1995a) early work on *tying rules* has shown that speaker turns are often tied to each other through some form of grammatical or semantic means, adding a degree of cohesiveness and coherence to the interactional, sequential unit. Thus, next speakers may use referring expressions (i.e., pronouns) or may repeat parts of the prior speaker's talk to show how their current turn forms a meaningful relationship with the previous one. A lack of tying units in the next turn, therefore, may be conveying that the next speaker is ignoring the contingencies and constraints associated with a FPP – resisting the constraints of responsiveness (Stivers & Rossano, 2010) – and is instead pursuing their own agenda or topic and is thus disaffiliating. The client's pursuit of her own agenda is shown in Extract 3.31.

**Extract 3.31:** 304.03(1a)

```
01   Sofia:   that he is becoming (1.7) such a negative ↑person (.)
02            [but I w-] I was- I w- I was looking ba:ck,
03   Ther:    [°mm.°   ]
04   Ther:    °mm hm,°
05   Sofia:   he always been li-that.
          s   shakes head, looks at T
06            (0.3)
07   Ther:    m[m hm,]
08   Sofia:    [he wa]s ↑ALways li-that=I don't know ah hhh=
          t   nod
          s    shakes head
09   Ther:    =so it's kinda hard to figure out righ[t,=bu]t you're
10   Sofia:                                         [so    ]
11   Ther:    starting t- you were starting to think ↑well ((clears
12            throat)) maybe this i[s really ↑bringing him]down too
13   Sofia:                        [I:    like   I me:an     ]
          t                   nod
14   Sofia:   I mean my- I was- I saw my niece. (1.5) and her husband
15            interacting,
16            (0.3)
          s    tilts head forward, gazes at T
17   Ther:    mm hm,
18   Sofia:   and I kno- ok they are newlyweds=and I-one cannot espect
19            .hhh a relationship to go li-that ↑twenty years
          t                                 multiple nods-------->
20            [even  th]ough I don't s(h)ink it's ↑impo:ssible
21   Ther:    [ye a::h.]
22            (0.3)
23   Ther:    mm hm,
```

Before this extract, Sofia had been describing a recent dinner party that she and her husband had attended. Sofia's recently married niece and husband were present and Sofia noticed that they appeared very affectionate and caring of each other. This was then followed by Sofia's negative assessments of her husband "`such a negative ↑person`" that are punctuated with extreme case formulations (Pomerantz, 1986) such as "`he was ↑ALways li-that`" (lines 5 and 8). As a response, the therapist draws an implication by turning the focus of the talk on how the husband's negativity may also be harmful to himself (maybe this is really ↑bringing <u>him</u> down too). During the therapist's turn, however, there are places where Sofia produces overlapping talk that is signalling something other than acknowledgement. For example, her "so" in line 10 orients back to her prior talk and may be signalling an upshot of what she had been saying. In line 13, her "I: like I me:an" could be a bid to take over the floor in order to elaborate on her prior assessment of the husband. In line 14, when Sofia takes up her turn, we see that she does indeed continue on with her turn – note that her prefacing "I mean" orients to her own talk and not the therapist's – by contrasting her relationship with her niece and husband: the implication is that they interact in an intimate, caring way, whereas Sofia and her husband no longer do that. Thus, Sofia's response is disaffiliating because it does not form any grammatical or semantic ties to the therapist's turn. Instead, it essentially ignores or does not acknowledge the therapist's contribution and works to remain on the client's own topic or conversational track.

## 3.6 Affiliation and Alignment

Cooperative actions within sequence are argued to have two main dimensions. An affective/affiliative one in which actions work pro-socially (e.g., agreement, compliance) and a structural/aligning one in which actions facilitate progressivity by aiding the sequence along and by accepting the "terms" of the initiating action (Stivers et al., 2011). In general, affiliative responses will also be aligning; that is, if you agree with or confirm what the other is saying, then you also consent to go along with the activity in question. Returning to Extract 3.8, shown now as Extract 3.32, the client not only produces a pro-social action (i.e., granting the proposal) and thus affiliates, she also accepts the terms of the proposal and moves the sequence forward and thus aligns.

**Extract 3.32:** Lisa 306cs.11/EC (CW1)

```
01  Ther:  °somehow it wasn't the right ti-° .hhh
02         ↑d'yu wannu uhm
        t  splays hands in front, turns head, points to chair out of frame
03         (1.8)
04  Ther:  it might be helpful tuh- (.) t-to- bring(.)
05         your parents, (0.2) °here.°
06         (0.4)
07  Lisa:  +mkay+
        l  +gaze forward, nods+
```

The opposite side of the coin would involve both disaffiliation and disalignment. Consider the abridged version of Extract 3.29, now Extract 3.33, involving client other-initiated repair.

**Extract 3.33:** 304.07(5)

```
01  Ther:   [d'ya       ] >I mean d'you think< this goes back to when you
02          were a child? th-it sort've (0.5) .hhh r-it I mean is that s-
03  Ther:   s-[is this] always been true of you? kina=needing a lot of
04  Sofia:    [m-     ]
05  Ther:   .hhh (0.5) lo:ve, an: (0.5) suppo:rt?
06          (2.3)
07  Sofia:  <if I always needed a lot of love [and support?>]
08  Ther:                                     [mm    hm,   ] mm hm.
09          (1.9)
10  Sofia:  uh::, (2.1) no I don't remember mysel as being,
         s                   shakes head
```

As the therapist is seeking confirmation from Sofia, an affiliative and aligning response would consist of some form of confirmation such as acknowledgement or of upgraded ratification. Sofia's other-initiated repair in line 07 instead works to disaffiliate because it refrains from providing confirmation and is potentially disagreement-implicative. It is also disaligning because it delays the completion of the initial confirmation-seeking sequence by opening up a new repair sequence.

One of the strongest forms of disalignment occurs when the recipient pursues their own agenda and does not in any way acknowledge the prior speaker's turn. This was already seen in Extract 3.31 in which Sofia resisted the therapist's attempt to focus on the husband's affective state – that the relationship is also bringing him, the husband, down – and instead goes on to compare her relationship with her niece's. By disaligning, Sofia does not cooperate with the expectation to continue or complete the sequence. Pursuing own agenda is also strongly disaffiliating because it does not confirm the prior formulation and instead ignores it. Another example of client's pursuance of own agenda is shown in Extract 3.34.

**Extract 3.34:** 304.03(1 c)

```
01  Sofia:  an he walked for about (0.3) ↑tree minutes an den. I'm co:ld.
02          (0.5) [I'm co:l=le]hs go back. [an I said] .hhh how can-it
03  Ther:         [°uh   huh,°]            [.hhh     ]
04  Sofia:  wasn't ↑co::l=it wasn't ↓really ↑co::ld.
         s  shakes head
05  Ther:   so he says (0.2) I'm co:ld and you jus fee::l li::ke
06          (1.3)
```

07 Ther: ↓hm::: what, (0.4) °disappointe::d, or°
08 Sofia: **d-anader b-anader wa-another-ano::ther .hhh wa:::y** (.) that
09 he i::s (0.3) that estops me: (.) fron having fun. (.)
10 [with] him.
11 Ther: [.hhh]
12 (0.2)
13 Ther: oh so a[gain ju:st just da:::shed.]
14 Sofia: [for esample he doesn't he ha::tes]
15 Ther: o:::r:::.=
16 Sofia: = he hates: walking,
s *shakes head*
17 (0.4)
18 Ther: mm hm,
19 Sofia: hates walking, .hhh (0.2) an hates (.) co:ld.

Prior to this extract, Sofia had been complaining about her husband's lack of spontaneity and his tendency to be a spoilsport. She narrates an episode in which she suggests they take a walk, only to have him complain of the cold and put a stop to their joint activity. In line 05, the therapist produces a formulation and adds a DIU (Koshik, 2002), allowing the client to furnish the "missing" material of what she feels in that situation. Following no response from Sofia, the therapist then provides a candidate emotion (°disappointe::d, or°) in line 07. Although Sofia's response in line 08 could be taken as orienting to the therapist's prompt to explain how she feels and it would appear that the therapist in line 13 corroborates this interpretation – that is, his making her feel disappointed is another way that stops her from having fun – there are reasons to reject this reading. As can be seen in lines 14 and 16, Sofia continues by providing another example of his negative behaviour (he hates: walking,) and is thus engaged in an activity that is geared toward listing the husband's complain-able attributes rather than one that explores her emotions resulting from the husband's actions. Further, Sofia's repeated self-repair of the word "another" (d-anader b-anader) seems to be forming a grammatical tie to her previous turn in line 04 and not to the therapist's provision of a candidate emotion, and is also acting as a "pre-telling" (Schegloff, 2007); that is, Sofia had just been recounting a specific behaviour that negatively impacts on her and it would seem, from line 14, that she is proceeding to list an additional behaviour that has this specific effect on her.

Overt forms of disalignment may also be realized when the client does not appear to be actively engaged in working with the therapist's assertion. For example, in Extract 3.30, Kristina only displays minimal acknowledgement of the therapist's formulations. Her non-vocal conduct, gazing down, also suggests a lack of engagement. This kind of client conduct generally results in expanded sequences in which the therapist continues to pursue a response from the client, who keeps refraining from offering unequivocal confirmation of what the therapist is putting forward.

## 3.7 Affiliation and Epistemics

In their article on the "terms of agreement," Heritage and Raymond (2005) argue that, within assessment sequences, agreement with an assessment may be qualified depending on whether or not one of the speakers has privileged access to the experience being assessed. They argue that speakers orient to these differential rights to experience. They cite research that has shown how distinctions between first-hand and derivative access to knowledge, and the corresponding rights to report information, is particularly germane in breaking news stories (Roth, 2002), and how the social categories "victim" vs. "bystander" is especially relevant in 911 emergency calls in terms of how incidents become reported and how they are assessed by call-takers (Whalen & Zimmerman, 1990). In psychotherapy, clients report on their own personal experiences and thus have privileged and unique access to these experiences; for example, what happened, what they felt, who said what. Thus, sequences in psychotherapy – and the person-centred conversations examined here in particular – tend to orient to the client as the primary knower (of own experience). Clients tell their stories and therapists respond in ways that display their downgraded epistemic rights; for example, by mitigating their formulations, refraining from interpreting and assessing clients' conduct in an evaluative manner and by regularly inviting client confirmation.

Sequences of talk may also be organized to favour certain kinds of epistemic roles or status. Many social actions in first position, for example, presuppose a primary epistemic speaker position. As Heritage (2002, p. 200) argues:

> A first assessment can index or embody a first speaker's claim to what might be termed "epistemic authority" about an issue relative to a second or to "know better" about it or to have some priority in rights to evaluate it. ... Moreover, a first assessment establishes a context in which a second can be found to agree or disagree. In such a context, respondents may be vulnerable to the inference that their response is fabricated on the instant to achieve agreement or disagreement and is thus a dependent or even a coerced action within a field of constraint that is established by the first.

For assessment sequences in particular, Heritage and Raymond (2005) have shown that even though initiating assessments may offer speakers with certain advantages of being in first position such as establishing a context in which a range of responses may follow or generating inferences that the first speaker has primary rights to make the assessment, the next speaker has an opportunity to comply with these conditions or make certain adjustments.

Thus, the second speaker may re-work or even challenge these epistemic constraints.

In psychotherapy, clients often tend to take up first positions in a sequence. For example, they often make first position assertions (descriptions, assessments) and narrate about their own experience. This places therapists in second position. Further, therapist responses, even if they appear as assertions that make claims about clients' experiences (e.g., formulations), generally index B-events (Labov & Fanshel, 1977) and thus invite confirmation from clients. In this way, clients are mostly placed in a sequential position in which they can assert epistemic authority from a first position or are invited to assume an upgraded epistemic position by re-working or challenging therapists' views – see also discussion on empathy in Chapter 4. This epistemic organization also has important implications for affiliation. For example, therapists' B-event actions, such as formulations, invite clients to confirm and thus affiliate with the therapist's position. If successful, pronounced forms of mutual affiliation may be achieved, which may work to strengthen the therapist–client relationship.

Extract 3.35, part of which was already shown in Extract 3.17, illustrates how an orientation to epistemic status can work to create strong modes of affiliation. Here, the therapist responds to a prior client telling by making an assertion (i.e., formulation) about the client's personal experience. The formulation, in turn, provides an initiating context that makes confirmation relevant as a next response.

**Extract 3.35:** Bonnie Case 305.02(1b)

```
01  Bonn:  .hhh an then plus the fact. (0.3) that as=e=say he is
02         s:o busy. an so involved in the job right now again. (0.7)
03         that I'm thinking(0.7) tha- e- ye know really. (.) I'm doing
04         his job for'im an although I ↑want to do it to help'im, .hh
05         I ↑resen[t it.]
06  Ther:          [yeah.]
07         (0.3)
08  Bonn:  ((lip smack)) an I (h)th(h)ink. .hh ↑what is wrong with me. why
09         can't I get past this. .hhh [you know?    ]
10  Ther:                              [so what you'd] like ta
        t  slow nod---->
11  Ther:  be able ta do is(.)
12  Ther:  do it without resent[ing him?]
13  Bonn:                      [   r:igh]t. that's [exactly wha]t I'd like
14  Ther:                                          [uh   huh.  ]
        b  nod, point.   multiple nods------->
```

```
      t  slow double nod
15 Bonn: ta do=I'd like to feel .hhh
      t  slow nod
```

Bonnie has been complaining about her husband, explaining that she finds herself taking over responsibilities that he should be attending to first-hand. In line 04–05, Bonnie states that although she wants to help her husband, she finds herself resenting it. She then, in lines 07–08, goes on to negatively assess her behaviour (↑what is wrong with me.). In 10, the therapist provides a formulation that focuses Bonnie's dilemma specifically around her feelings of resentment: She wants to do it without having to resent him. Bonnie responds, in line 13, with an overlapping acknowledgement token (r:ight) that not only strongly aligns with the formulation, but also orients to her greater epistemic rights by confirming the formulation's accuracy (that's [exactly wha] t I'd like). During this time, Bonnie produces a series of nods that convey affiliation with the therapist's formulation and the therapist, in turn, provides a series of responding affiliative nods. Bonnie then, in line 15, continues to assert epistemic authority by stating what she would like to feel in that situation. In sum, two important, complementary aspects of talk are revealed in this sequence organization. The therapist's affiliative, formulating response invites the client to confirm and thus take up an upgraded epistemic position. Also, by confirming, the client offers return affiliation, which creates a sequence of affiliative conduct. Further, the speakers' non-vocal affiliative conduct (i.e., nodding) provides an overlay to the verbal sequence and additionally reinforces the social cohesion being achieved between therapist and client.

## 3.8 Conclusions

Just as the organization of everyday talk appears to be biased in favour of promoting social cohesion (Enfield, 2006; Goffman, 1967, 1971), so psychotherapy conversations adhere to affiliational organizing principles. Clients in the York I person-centred data tend to initiate sequences in the role of troubles teller. By regularly occupying first position in sequence, they take up a role of having primary entitlements to experience, inviting recipients to offer support through agreement or confirmation, or by reworking their descriptions of experience in relation to what the client meant (see also Chapter 5 on storytelling).[6] Even when therapists do re-work and modify client's descriptions of

[6] As will be discussed in Chapter 6 on chair work entry, here therapists do occupy first position in sequence, but they specifically design their proposals by orienting to the client's greater rights in deciding whether to proceed with the task.

personal experience through formulations, *anticipatory completions* or noticings, which may appear to infringe on the client's entitlements and knowledge, clients are still invited to confirm these therapist re-descriptions and thus take up an upgraded position on the aptness or "fit" of the re-description. I have also shown in this chapter how disaffiliation is accomplished and organized in sequences of talk. Disaffiliation – in certain sessions and with certain clients – occurs frequently and this may appear to contradict the affiliational principle proposed earlier. These client disagreements, disconfirmations and rejections do, however, adhere to dispreferred structure as is commonly seen in everyday talk. Thus, disaffiliating speakers (i.e., clients) will generally draw from interactional resources to mitigate the disagreement and thus reduce the threat to the therapist's face. Further, most episodes of disaffiliation seem to, ultimately, orient toward receiving affiliation, or obtaining re-affiliation, in the end. The sequential organizations of disaffiliation, and how re-affiliation is achieved, will be addressed in Chapters 7 and 8.

# 4 Empathic Practices

## 4.1 Overview

Person-centred perspectives on psychotherapeutic practice often orient to Rogers' (1951, 1957) original conception of empathy as the therapist's ability to communicate his or her understanding, to convey support and to refrain from appearing as an expert who has privileged access to another's experience. Over the years, the definition of empathy has undergone various modifications and developments (Duan & Hill, 1996; Elliott et al., 2011; Elliott et al., 2018). These extend from viewing empathy mainly as a personality trait or general ability, to a focus toward empathy being a situation-specific, cognitive-affective state or a multi-phased experiential process (see Duan & Hill, 1996). Some researchers have also been focusing on how empathy may be best put to use as a therapeutic practice, a *talk tool* or *helping skill* to aid therapeutic communication and clients deal with their experiences (Goodman & Esterly, 1988; Hill, 2020). There are also debates on the exact nature of empathy, as being a cognitive, affective or even a cognitive-affective construct (Duan & Hill, 1996). Elliott et al. (2011), moreover, argue that the scope of empathy may also vary considerably: from a single response to the client's present experience (*empathic rapport*) to an ongoing negotiation of that experience on a moment-to-moment basis (*communicative attunement*) and, more broadly, to the therapist's ability to understand the client's experiences that span from past to present (*person empathy*).

In spite of what may be called a lack of consensus on how empathy should be characterized and, moreover, a proliferation of definitions, empathy is considered to be an important relationship element that is responsible for yielding good therapeutic outcomes (Norcross, 2011; Elliott et al., 2011; Elliott et al., 2018). Further, there seems to be a general perception that empathy is almost always something that is "good," provided that it is tailored to a specific client and is offered with humility, ready to be adjusted/corrected when clients become at odds with the therapist's understanding of them (Elliott et al., 2011). Lastly, psychotherapeutic discussions of empathy often highlight the *cognitive* aspect of empathy, as a mental process in which understanding relates to clients' and therapists' perceptions of what the other has intended.

My aim for this chapter is to provide a descriptive, interactional account of empathy that brackets out certain psychological issues concerning the normative (positive vs. negative) and cognitive dimensions assumed in much empathy research. I set out to provide a view of empathy that not only highlights the therapist's action as conveying a certain form of understanding (Rogers, 1951, 1957), but also underscores the accomplishment of empathy as sequentially negotiated between therapist and client (cf., Barrett-Lennard, 1981). In this interactional view, the centre stage is given to how clients and therapists achieve empathy, through a series of interlocking and unfolding actions. The "cognitive-affective" debate surrounding empathy is also re-interpreted in interactional terms with regard to epistemics and affiliation (see also Chapter 3). Further, my examination of empathic action is restricted to a certain sequential context: troubles telling. I argue that empathic actions orient to troubles tellers' epistemic rights and access and to affiliating with the teller's affective stance (Hepburn & Potter, 2007; Heritage, 2011). Drawing from the insights of this afore-mentioned work, I first argue, alongside others (Elliott et al., 2000; Ford et al., 2019; Frankel, 2009), that empathy may be seen as an interactional 3-part sequential unit. Empathic action may thus be examined with respect to a sequential structure that involves three conversational moves: 1) the client's troubles telling; 2) the therapist's "on record" claim of understanding the client's trouble; and 3) client feedback of the therapist's understanding. Next, I deal with each of these sequential components. To begin, I will discuss how a troubles telling may convey a personal experience that might warrant a next speaker to provide empathy as a relevant next action. I then consider how the therapist's responsive action may be used to convey a unique form of understanding of the client's trouble and, at the same time, provide emotional support. Empathic action, it will be argued, tends to consist of certain interactional components or discursive features related to understanding, affiliation and client entitlements (epistemics). Attention will then be given to the last part of the sequence: the client's response. Here I will not only show how the successful accomplishment of empathy may lead to what may be termed an *empathic moment* (Heritage, 2011), but also how an empathic display may result in less productive sequential trajectories or "failed empathy."

## 4.2 The Sequential Organization of Empathy

Rogers' (1951) general observation that practicing empathy involves the ability to communicate one's understanding of another's experience can be re-interpreted from an interactional perspective as consisting of at least two conversational moves: An initiating move by the client who expresses some aspect of personal experience, and a responding move by the therapist who conveys an understanding of the client's experience. Barrett-Lennard (1981), who coined the term *empathy cycle*, slightly expanded on this view by stating that the client, in turn, provides feedback on the therapist's provision of empathy in either of two forms: "One kind is confirming or corrective in respect to the content of A's [the therapist's] just-shared view or sense of B's [the client's] felt experience … . The other possible kind is informative regarding the extent to which B generally is perceiving a relationship of personal understanding with A" (Barrett-Lennard, 1981, p. 94). Thus, in contexts of providing empathy, a third turn or move becomes necessary, one in which client feedback is present.

There is a growing body of CA research on empathy that has examined these first two moves of an empathic sequence (Beach & Dixon, 2001; Hepburn & Potter, 2007, 2012; Heritage, 2011; Hutchby, 2005; Kupetz, 2014; Kuroshima & Iwata, 2016; Muntigl et al., 2014; Pudlinski, 2005; Ruusuvuori, 2005; Weiste & Peräkylä, 2014). The first move is generally considered to involve a troubles telling (Jefferson & Lee, 1980; Jefferson, 1988) and, in psychotherapy contexts, clients will initiate this sequence by expressing a personal event and by imbuing this event with an affective stance aligned with the trouble. The affective components can vary and may include any number of emotions such as upset, sadness, worry, fear or others – this is taken up in more detail in section 4.3. Further, the client's affective stance provides *empathic opportunities* (Suchman et al., 1997) or makes an empathic display a relevant next option for the therapist. The second move consists of the therapist's response to the client's troubles telling, one in which the empathic opportunity is taken up. In terms of Rogers' (1951, 1957) empathic perspective, the therapist's response is meant to communicate understanding of the client's experience in a way that is modulated and somewhat detached, with therapists being careful not to take on and share the client's emotional stance. As Rogers (1951, p. 29) argues,

> experiencing with the client, the living of his attitudes, is not in terms of emotional identification on the counsellor's part, but rather an empathic identification, where the counsellor is perceiving the hates and hopes and fears of the client through immersion in an empathic process, *but without himself, as counsellor, experiencing those hates and hopes and fears*. [italics mine]

Although not originally conceptualized in this way, the concept of empathy may be understood to align with various epistemic components, especially with ownership of knowledge and epistemic rights (Hepburn & Potter, 2012).[1] This means refraining from appearing as an expert who interprets or assesses another's experience and preserving the client's own personal frame of reference or ownership/entitlement of personal experience. Empathy is also considered to be a certain subtype of affiliative action. Other forms of emotional support such as sympathy or comforting, although strongly affiliative, would not be regarded as doing empathic work – see section 4.4.2. Heritage (2011) has argued that troubles telling

[1] In psychotherapy research, ownership of knowledge/ experience is framed instead as "expertise" or as having *expert* knowledge.

Table 4.1 *Empathy in a troubles-telling sequence*

| Sequential Slot | Speaker | General Action | Main Features |
|---|---|---|---|
| 1 | Client | Troubles telling | Conveys personal experience involving upset, sadness, worry, fear, low self-worth, etc. |
| 2 | Therapist | Demonstrating [empathic] understanding of trouble | Stays "close" to client talk<br>Preserves client entitlements as expert/[K+]<br>Supports client's affective stance |
| 3 | Client | Evaluating therapist's understanding | Confirms, disconfirms or assesses<br>Reveals degree of affiliation and/or engagement with prior empathic claim |

situations, especially when persons convey upsetting personal experiences, may create certain interactional challenges. For example, a troubles telling makes next turn affiliation relevant from the next speaker and, in psychotherapeutic contexts, therapists may have difficulty in responding to the client's past or present feelings in an appropriately congruent manner; that is, therapist responses may not necessarily fit with clients' understandings of their trouble, thus infringing on the troubles teller's ownership of personal experience (Sacks, 1995b; Sharrock, 1974). Heritage (2011) has termed this challenge a *problem of experience* – how these challenges arise and are negotiated will be taken up in section 4.6.

The final move or sequential slot is essential for providing troubles tellers with an opportunity to display their understanding or "feedback" of what the "empathy provider" has said (Ford et al., 2019; Frankel, 2009). This feedback may take various forms such as confirmation, disconfirmation or even an assessment of the therapist's understanding claim. Whereas confirmation is affiliative and works to close down the sequence, sometimes producing empathic moments (Heritage, 2011), disconfirmation or negative assessments are disaffiliative and disaligning, requiring the therapist to address the breach and work toward re-affiliation – disaffiliation following therapist formulations is examined exclusively in Chapter 7. These differing interactional trajectories will be shown in section 4.6. Table 4.1 summarizes the components of the 3-move empathic sequence outlined earlier.

## 4.3 Troubles Telling: Affective Stance Displays and Empathic Opportunities

Interactional studies focusing on empathy mostly examine initiating contexts or activities that involve the telling of problems and troubles or forms of distress displays within institutional contexts – such as caller help lines (Hepburn

& Potter, 2007, 2012; Pudlinski, 2005), doctor–patient consultations (Beach & Dixon, 2001; Ruusuvuori, 2005) and psychotherapy (Muntigl et al., 2014; Weiste & Peräkylä, 2014) – and everyday talk (Jefferson, 1988; Kupetz, 2014; Kuroshima & Iwata, 2016). Following Jefferson (1988), these contexts realize what is generally known as "troubles talk" – see Chapter 2, section 2.3.1. A question that arises from this focus on troubles is whether an empathic response necessarily presupposes and orients to a troubles telling event. Although it is beyond the scope of this chapter to properly address this question, it does seem that other kinds of client affective displays, involving some form of happiness, amazement or hope, may invite different kinds of responses from therapists – see discussion in section 4.4.2.

Jefferson's (1988) work has shown that troubles telling is an activity that is germane to everyday, not just institutional, contexts. Further, as already discussed earlier, troubles tellings make a subsequent action of emotional support relevant. Other researchers within the area of doctor–patient consultations, such as Suchman et al. (1997), have viewed these contexts more narrowly in terms of *empathic opportunities*. For example, they have shown that patients' tellings of their troubles created what they term *empathic opportunities* for the physician, especially if the patient expressed emotions when discussing their symptoms. Thus, the expression of attitudes or emotions involving sadness, fear, concern and so on is essential for doing empathic work, because they are affiliate-able; that is, they allow helping professionals to 1) "enter the client's frame of reference" or "walk in the world of the other" (Rogers, 1957; McLeod, 1999) and 2) display their understanding, appreciation and attitude concerning the expressed trouble. In linguistic research, affect and attitudes have been examined within the domain of what is termed *stance*, which has been defined as "the lexical and grammatical expression of attitudes, feelings, judgements, or commitment concerning the propositional content of a message" (Biber & Finegan, 1989, p. 93).[2] Extract 4.1 demonstrates how lexicogrammatical resources work to convey an affective stance. This conversation takes place at the beginning of the second session, where we observe the client, Eve, launching into a complaint about the previous therapy session.

**Extract 4.1:** Evelyn Case 020.02(01)

```
Ther:     °so how's it been.°
          (0.7)
Eve:      mm? (.) °I:? I- (.) I.° I found. I:, (1.1) after the
```

[2] From an interactional perspective, attitudes and feelings are generally not referred to as being *expressed*, as this might presuppose that certain terms or expressions have an inherent meaning or function in interaction. The focus is instead placed on how participants orient to each other's talk in an "emotionally charged way" in support of some interactional task.

```
04              last session I was ↑re:ally like frustrated an:, (0.4)
05              disappointed and I didn't know what to do with it.
06              (0.3)
07   Ther:      ye:s?
08   Eve:       a:nd, I sort of- (1.3) I felt like I'd, (1.4) touch
09              on alotta things an then just walked away from the:m
10              a:nd,
11   Ther:      mm h[m:,]
12   Eve:           [and] it didn't really have any shape and didn't
13              really (.) do anything? an [ didn't-   ]
14   Ther:                                 [so you seem] very
15              dissatisfi:ed?
16   Eve:       ↑yea:h. (0.4) yeah.
```

The client negatively appraises/complains about the previous therapy session, by referencing negative emotions of how she had felt (`frustrated`; `disappointed`) and by upgrading the intensity of these emotions through adverbs (`↑re:ally like`). She also assesses the process of therapy in negative terms (`didn't really have any shape`; `didn't really (.) do anything?`). Thus, the teller's stance is realized through various lexicogrammatical expressions that convey affect, judgement and assessment. A teller's stance, however, may also be displayed through resources that are *not* lexicogrammatical. Stivers (2008, p. 38) has argued that prosody and story prefaces also constitute key stance constructing resources. We can see Eve putting prosody to use in this way by using rising intonation to further intensify her dissatisfaction (`↑re:ally like frustrated`). Tellers may also provide more detail or access to their trouble in a subsequent turn, especially if it appears that the recipient is having trouble affiliating with the telling. Drawing from Schegloff's (2000) work, Stivers (2008, p. 44) argues that tellers often provide more "granularity" to their descriptions by, for example, elaborating with words that specify the action taken or using reported speech. We would note, for example, that the therapist's continuer (line 07) helps Eve to develop and elaborate on her emotions of frustration and disappointment by including a negative assessment of the therapeutic process and how it lacked form and did not seem to benefit her.

Stances that convey upset have been shown to mobilize a large array of resources, vocal and non-vocal (Hepburn, 2004; Hepburn & Potter, 2007), as shown in Extract 4.2.

**Extract 4.2:** 412.18(3)

```
01  Jo:     ~b[ut. ye] know, (1.4) I:'ve seen some behaviour in myself
02  Ther:     [yeah:,]
03  Jo:     the la:st couple weeks that really. (0.3) scares me,~
         j                      wipes eyes          choked up
04  Jo:     >.snih .snih<
05  Ther:   what's been happening.
```

```
06 Jo:     ~we:ll (1.4) I don't <fee:l the measure of control I've had,>~
07 Ther:   yeah::.
        t  slow multiple nods→
        j  shallow double nod→
08         (0.3)
09 Jo:     ~ye know, (.) I ate something, (0.3) I never would have eaten,
        j                    brings hand to chest.  points hand in, shakes head
10         and I made myself throw up?~
11 Ther:   yeah:. =
        t  nod
12 Jo:     = ~an? hhh <i've> done that once in my life maybe.~
13 Ther:   yeah:.
        t  shallow double nod→
14         (0.7)
        t  ------->
15 Jo:     <~once. maybe,~>
        t  shakes head, pulls head back
16 Ther:   ye[ah,]
17 Jo:       [~I ] never belie:ved in anything like tha:t.~
        t  nod
        j          lowers eyebrows, shakes head
18 Ther:   [ yeah.   ]
19 Jo:     [~an I was] so=upset, (0.4) that I a:te i:t, [an I made m]yself
20 Ther:                                                [yeah.      ]
        j  chops hand down. points hand out. flicks hand in, choked up
21 Jo:     throw u:p. (.) >and then I was like,< (0.5) (h)I'm b(h)a:d.~
        j      looks away, crunches face.           widens eyes, sobbing
22         (0.5)
        j  closes eyes, 'silent' sobbing
23 Ther:   you felt really. (.) ashamed of [it, yeah:.  ]
24 Jo:                                     [.snih ↑yeah.]
        t  shallow nod
        j                           dabs eye, multiple nods
```

In this extract, Jo recounts a very upsetting event that happened recently: She ate something that she normally does not eat and then made herself vomit. Her state of distress is consistently conveyed through her tremulous voice (symbolized by "~"), which percolates all throughout her narrative. Her upset is periodically punctuated by sniffs (lines 04, 24) and affect terms such as "`scares me`", "`so=upset`" and "`I'm b(h)a:d`". Most notable, however, is the non-vocal manner in which distress is conveyed: wiping eyes, looking away, crunching face, shaking head, widening/closing eyes and silent sobs. Throughout Jo's turn, the therapist repeatedly provides acknowledgement through "`yeah`" and nodding, allowing the client to continue developing her stance and to provide more granularity to her affective descriptions. In line 23, the therapist then responds by summarizing Joanna's feelings (`you felt really. (.) ashamed of it`).

## 4.4 Connecting with Others' Experience

There has been some debate on what aspect of the client's experience empathy actually targets. Whereas some view this as primarily *emotional* understanding, others see it as mainly cognitive or indeed as both cognitive-affective (see Duan & Hill, 1996 for an extensive discussion). Bachelor (1988), who focused on clients' perceived empathy, further extends the concept of empathy by proposing four general perceived empathy styles: cognitive, affective, sharing and nurturant. Cognitive empathy refers to the ability to accurately recognize the client's own experiences. Affective empathy relates to partaking in the feelings that the client is presently experiencing. Sharing involves contexts in which therapists connect with clients' troubles by disclosing and thus sharing their own related experiences with clients. Lastly, nurturant empathy occurs when clients perceive therapists as being very supportive and attentive. Bachelor's framework seems to go well beyond Rogers' conceptualizations of empathy, which aligns mostly with *understanding* rather than *sharing in* the client's experience (see Pudlinski, 2005 and Ruusuvuori, 2005 for discussions on this topic), and seems to capture instead a vast array of emotional support response types.

There is reason to believe that the preceding different empathic types may actually constitute an artificial separation of phenomena that generally co-occur in conversation. Interactional researchers, for example, have argued that talk about our personal experiences is permeated with affective and epistemic components that reveal what we know and how we know it and also how we feel (Enfield, 2006; Heritage, 2012; Stivers, 2008). Thus, when responding to others' talk about experiences, recipients can take up different options that align in different ways with respect to knowledge and affect. For example, recipients may claim to have more (or less) rights and access to certain information (Raymond & Heritage, 2005) or may assert that they feel similarly, differently, more/less intensively and so on (Jefferson, 1988). Thus, on the one hand, recipients who convey empathy will orient to the client's greater or expert knowledge of own experience. In Goffman's (1971) terms, access to this form of biographical or personal knowledge, which he calls *information preserves*, is under the teller's control.[3] Under a person-centred framework, therapists will work to maintain the client's primary rights to knowledge/ [K+] (Heritage, 2012) or entitlement/ownership to personal experience (Sacks, 1995b; Sharrock, 1974) in showing that they understand the client from his or her own point of reference. On the other hand,

[3] Other researchers have examined this issue in terms of A- or B-events (Labov & Fanshel, 1977) or Type 1/Type 2 knowables (Pomerantz, 1980). Briefly, A-events are within the speaker's knowledge domain, whereas B-events coincide with the recipient's. Type 1 knowables refer to biographical knowledge and Type 2 knowables are what someone knows by some inferential means.

recipients will also display emotional support of the client's trouble by affiliating with the client's affective stance. These two dimensions – knowledge/epistemics and affiliation – may be seen as the interactional counterparts to "cognitive" and "affective" and it would appear that, in conveying empathic understanding, both dimensions will be oriented to. The aim for this section is to show how therapists display understanding and convey emotional support in a way that is consistent with the provision of (person-centred) empathy.

### 4.4.1 *Orienting to Client Ownership/Expertise: "On the Record" Claims of Understanding*

Most studies in conversation analysis (CA) have roughly aligned with Rogers by defining empathy as displaying understanding of another's experience or situation (Beach & Dixon, 2001; Hepburn & Potter, 2007, 2012; Heritage, 2011; Hutchby, 2005; Kupetz, 2014; Kuroshima & Iwata, 2016; Muntigl et al., 2014; Pudlinski, 2005; Ruusuvuori, 2005; Weiste & Peräkylä, 2014). Understanding is meant to target a certain kind of experience, usually related to a problem, concern or trouble – that is, troubles telling (Jefferson, 1988).[4] Further, most studies suggest that a certain kind of understanding is necessary for a response to count as empathic. What seems important is that recipients display a so-called *resonant understanding* (Barrett-Lennard, 1981; Elliott et al., 2018; McLeod, 1999) in which they demonstrate how they have grasped the teller's experience, but without sharing, intruding on or appropriating that experience. One of the most succinct working definitions of an interactional view of empathic understanding comes from Hepburn and Potter's (2007, 2012) research on calls from child protection helplines. In their view, empathic displays are propositional, involving "on the record" claims of understanding. From their examination of what they have termed "crying receipts" (Hepburn & Potter, 2007), they suggest that empathic responses contain two key elements:

1. A formulation of the crying party's business or emotional state.
2. Some kind of epistemic marking of contingency or source of that formulation – crying recipient can claim access to this type of experience while deferring to the rights of the upset party to define the nature of their troubles. (Hepburn & Potter, 2012, p. 210)

[4] Certain definitions highlight the other's "emotional experience" (Kupetz, 2014), or simply "emotion" (Weiste & Peräkylä, 2014), leaving it somewhat open as to whether it is meant to imply a trouble or concern. Heritage (2011), on the other hand, clearly refers to the broad spectrum of emotions, positive and negative, when he speaks of persons reporting on "first-hand experiences of any great intensity (involving, for example, pleasure, pain, joy or sorrow)" (p. 160).

The first point underscores the type of action or response necessary for displaying empathy. Thus, formulations – actions that summarize or draw implications from prior speaker's talk (Heritage & Watson, 1979) – rather than, say, assessments or interpretations. The importance of displayed (negative) affect (e.g., sadness, fear) and recipient next turns that create connections with these emotions is reinforced by Hepburn & Potter (2007, p. 111), who state that "We are cautious about the attribution of empathy to turns of talk that do not construct mental states." The salient role of formulations for doing empathy, as indexing a resonant understanding of the client's experience, will be elaborated on later. The second point aligns with Rogers' insistence that therapists do not come across as authoritative. Epistemic markers of contingency, therefore, maintain the client's ownership of experience and/or their epistemic authority. Further, Hepburn and Potter's work is grounded in CA premises, in which empathy is taken as an interactional accomplishment, managed in sequences of unfolding talk. As Ruusuvuori (2005, p. 206) argues, empathy is examined in terms of "situated actions, achieved in (and defined) in and through concerted actions between the participants in a specific situation."

I have found that person-centred therapists' use of epistemic markings to convey and build up an epistemic stance via formulations may vary considerably. Explicit epistemic markings to express therapist's lesser rights and access do, however, commonly occur. Some formulations make use of evidential expressions such as "sounds" (see Extract 4.6), whereas others may instead (or in addition) use various kinds of modal expressions such as "may," "can," "probably" and so on. A formulation that is replete with epistemic markers is shown in Extract 4.3 (see also Extract 3.6) with the client Paula.

**Extract 4.3:** 312.16(1a)

```
Paula:  yeah like, hh I guess it has bee:n kind of like difficult like
        for a long ti:me like to really say well, .hh (0.5)
        this is what I want, and really stick to it.
        (0.5)
Paula:  and this is who I a:m.
        (0.5)
Paula:  and <that's just> (0.8) it. li(hh) [heh. .hhh          ]
Ther:                                      [uh huh. uh huh.]
        (0.3)
Paula:  a:nd also the:n, (0.4) like wh- (0.3) when people kind of u:m::,
        (2.0) step on my toes. (0.3) °so to speak.° .hh (0.8) that I
        sti:ll. (1.0) that I, (0.4) kind of: (.) still kind of maintain,
        (.) like my, (1.5) sense of self. and also like (.) push ↓back.
Ther:   mm hm. =
Paula:  = not just let them, .hh (.) take over.
        (0.5)
```

```
Ther:   .hhh so almost at- (0.4) I don't know if (.) >this is what
        you're saying.< but almost at those times you may need some
        stronger boundaries. .hh you may need to put up those boundaries
        and say .hhh you can have your opinion, but I [am standing]
Paula:                                                [ .hhh      ]
Ther:   firm.
Paula:  yeah. (0.2) yeah. =
Ther:   = ↑yeah.
        (1.4)
Paula:  like(hh) (1.8) yeah acceptin:g like what I want <as well as
        uh:m,> (3.7) ↑mm::. (2.5) like not be:ing intimidat[ed.]
Ther:                                                      [mm ] hm.
```

At the beginning of this extract, Paula tells of the difficulties she has had in maintaining a strong sense of self (this is who I a:m.) and also to resist other's attempts (push ↓back) at impinging on her selfhood by defining who she is (them, .hh (.) take over.). The therapist begins her formulation in line 17 and immediately starts orienting to downgraded epistemic rights and access with the term "almost". She then self-repairs with "I don't know if … ", before returning to her original "almost at … ". This preface works to display her lesser epistemic access to what Paula has said and meant and it also works as an understanding check: "correct me if I'm wrong but this is what I think you're saying". When she does launch into the formulation segment of the turn, she continues to use epistemic downgraders such as "almost" and "may". This variety of epistemic resources shows the manifold ways in which the therapist defers ownership of experience to the client.

Overt epistemic markers of contingency, although often present in empathic responses, do not seem to be necessary for doing empathic work. Weiste et al.'s (2016) study involving cognitive therapy and psychoanalysis, for instance, has shown that therapists' use of contingency markers may depend on the specific way in which therapists are making connections with clients' experiences. They found that therapist claims remaining "close" to clients' original descriptions (i.e., talk that narrowly summarizes the client's here-and-how descriptions of own experience), tended not to appear in a downgraded manner (e.g., through expressions such as *maybe*, *perhaps*, *it sounds like*, *do you feel*), whereas more interpretive claims that departed significantly from clients' talk (i.e., introduced new and alternative connections or explanations) were produced with more caution and contingency. In Extract 4.4 (see also Extract 2.18), the client Sofia had been discussing the sad memories of her father's death at the time when she was still a child. The example shows a therapist's empathic response produced without overt epistemic markers.

**Extract 4.4:** Sofia: Case 304.07 ~43:30–50:30

Sofi: Yah. When he died dats, dats, (1.0) makes me very s- (0.2)
brings (.) very sad memories because we he died, (0.4)
.tch (0.3) for a time (1.0) I: (0.8) I did not, I deny? (0.5)
that he died?
Ther: mm hm,
(0.2)
Ther: You just pretended he was still there=
Sofi: =.h he was a still there. (0.2) [yah.
Ther: [°mm hm
(0.2)
Sofi: [( )
Ther: [**So it still makes you sad even °when you** (0.3)
Sofi: Yeah.=
Ther: =**talk about it now**=
Sofi: =yeah

Sofia is telling the therapist about her sadness in relation to her father's death and that, for a time, she was even in denial that he was dead. In lines 12 and 14, the therapist formulates Sofia's prior turn by touching upon the sadness and by pointing out that her talking about these past events evokes these emotions in the present moment. Thus, the therapist's understanding of the client's emotional state is being put on record through the formulation and more or less encapsulates (and does not deviate from) Sofia's prior affective descriptions. But even though there is no epistemic marking, the client's greater entitlement to her own experience is still oriented to. This is because the formulation makes next turn confirmation/disconfirmation relevant from the client, thus putting the client in a position of determining the appropriateness of the therapist's viewpoint. Thus, by inviting client confirmation through the formulation, the therapist is indexing her own lower epistemic status vis-à-vis the client (Heritage, 2012).

Can recipients come across as empathic without actually displaying their understanding in propositional form? Hepburn and Potter's (2007) suggestion is that they cannot, thus excluding the large array of response tokens such as "mm," "mm hm," "yeah," "right" or "I see" (Gardner, 2001; Gerhardt & Beyerle, 1997) from being able to have this function. Some researchers, however, have argued that prosody can be used in the service of empathy; for example, by matching or upgrading the prosodic features of the prior speaker's display of anger or indignation (Couper-Kuhlen, 2012) or by continuing the intonation contour of turns that have expressed sadness (Weiste & Peräkylä, 2014). Fitzgerald & Leudar (2010), in turn, argue that continuers may be put to empathic use when they are produced with low volume or spoken quietly (cf. Weiste & Peräkylä, 2014). They claim that this prosodic overlay serves to echo or resonate with clients' strong expressions of affect, thus helping therapists to be with a client's feeling. An example of prosodically modified, therapist response tokens is shown in Extract 4.5.

**Extract 4.5:** 305.02(1a)

```
01  Bonn:  so I had this and, .hhh (0.2) I must admit(h) (0.2) as=e=say I
02         had ↑v'ry mixed emotions I guess, mainly because. .hhh (0.2)
03         she gave=me=a hard time. an I was trying ta understand it
       t                                nod-------->
       b                                                                  nod
04  Bonn:  because my mother had given me a hard time. ye know whad=
05         =[I=mean as far   ]
06  Ther:   [h:m.°°I see.°° ]
       t          shallow nod
07  Bonn:  as um..hhh I was stealing her things. and, you=know an=I did
       t                                            slow multiple nods--->
08         this, and all the things tha'I did wrong.
       t   ----------------------------------->
09  Ther:  [↓right,]
10  Bonn:  [.hhh a ]nd of course ((lip smack)) I was getting this from
11         Aunt Fern. ((lip smack)) and .hhh (0.4) I think in a way I
       t                slow double nod
12         rese:nted=it mainly becau->well first of all I wasn't=doing it
13         (h)< hehhehhehhehheh hehheh
```

Bonnie's affective stance pertains to her feeling "wronged" because her Aunt Fern was suspecting Bonnie of stealing some of her things. Affective expressions such as "`↑v'ry mixed emotions`", "`she gave=me=a hard time`", "`things tha'I did wrong`" and "`I rese:nted=it`" index her troubles, thus providing the therapist with an empathic opportunity in which to display a resonant understanding. In lines 05 and 08, the therapist provides response tokens at very low volume or low pitch, which would seem to be offering some form of affiliation or emotional support. The therapist, however, does not go "on record" by explicitly claiming to understand Bonnie's feelings, as the following invented formulation would have: "So you resent Aunt Fern's wrongful accusations." The therapist's display of understanding via quietly spoken response tokens thus seems limited and non-specific and does not clearly show how the client's trouble is being understood (see Sacks, 1995b, p. 253 on claiming vs. demonstrating understanding). Thus, by displaying emotional support but not explicitly demonstrating understanding, the conditions for conveying empathy have only partially been fulfilled. Thus, rather than showing empathy, the therapist's response tokens may be working instead to convey commiseration and, thus, token sympathy – see subsection "Sympathetic Support" in section 4.4.2.

### 4.4.2 *Affiliating: Displaying Emotional Support*

Various researchers have called attention to what has been termed the emotional or affective component of empathy. For example, Bachelor (1988, p. 230) refers to *affective* empathy as when therapists participate "in the client's ongoing feeling state. The client perceives the therapist as partaking of the same feeling the client is personally experiencing at that moment." In their discussion of *empathic rapport*, Elliott et al. (2018, p. 400) emphasize the attitude that therapists take toward clients as one of compassion and benevolence. Similarly, Suchman et al. (1997) discuss the moral/emotive aspect of empathy, which is referred to as an intrinsic ability to properly attend to another's emotional experience. Hepburn and Potter's (2007) examination of crying receipts also places the focus of empathy on understanding the emotional component of a troubles telling. Heritage (2011) views empathy in affective terms as well, drawing mainly from Eisenberg and Fabes' (1990) paper, which conceptualizes empathy in terms of the recipient's ability to apprehend or comprehend someone's emotional state (of distress), but also the recipient's ability to identify with that person's feeling.

Emotional support may be offered in a variety of ways and, I will argue, some forms of support may be considered empathic and others as doing some different kind of interactional work (see also Pawelczyk, 2011). One broad distinction that is often made is that between sympathy and empathy. According to Ruusuvuori (2005), whereas empathy relates to the recipient's ability to *understand* and *know* the teller's experience (i.e., resonant feelings), sympathy has more to do with *sharing* and *relating* to others' experience (i.e., congruent feelings). Any indication that the recipient is in some way affected by the teller's experience (i.e., sad, concerned, bothered) moves the action toward sympathy rather than empathy (Maynard, 2003, p. 251; Pudlinski, 2005, p. 268). Other actions that display emotional support but do not offer empathy are those that *comfort* or *soothe another*. Thus, there are at least three general kinds of emotional support commonly occurring in social interaction, with only one that may appropriately align with "doing empathy":

1. Empathic support: "I understand your trouble."
2. Sympathetic support: "I feel for you/you matter to me."
3. Comforting support: "I'm here for you."

All three types of support may be seen as performing affiliative work. Empathy and affiliation, from this view, are clearly distinct concepts, whereby empathy may be regarded as one specific practice among others in which therapists may affiliate with clients' troubles.[5]

[5] It should be noted that emotional support types do not always appear in isolation. I have, for example, found instances where empathy co-occurs with sympathetic displays.

*Empathic Support* As explicated earlier, empathic responses go "on record" in claiming understanding of the client's troubles and, in doing so, they affiliate with (some aspect of) the client's affective stance. This kind of action expresses emotional support because it is confirmatory and helps the client to feel "understood" by the therapist. Actions conveying empathic support have already been seen in Extracts 4.1–4.4:

- so you seem very dissatisfi:ed? (Extract 4.1)
- you felt really. (.) ashamed of it, yeah:. (Extract 4.2)
- so almost at- … almost at those times you may need some stronger boundaries. … (Extract 4.3)
- So it still makes you sad even °when you (0.3) … talk about it now (Extract 4.4)

All these empathic responses form tight, semantic connections with clients' own portrayal of personal experience via summarizing or drawing implications from clients' talk and conduct. The responses are designed as a B-event (i.e., known primarily to the client) and thus have the following implications: Therapists in each case cede expert knowledge to clients and invite clients to confirm (or *dis*confirm) thus allowing clients to take up a position of epistemic authority.

*Sympathetic Support* Sympathy refers to actions in which recipients display how they are (emotionally) affected by the teller's trouble or upset (Maynard, 2003; Pudlinski, 2005). Thus, emotional support may be conveyed by being bothered, angered, saddened or by feeling sorry for the teller's hardships. According to Hepburn and Potter (2012), sympathetic responses are often non-propositional and are often conveyed through the use of specific lexical items such as "oh" or "aw" and some form of specialized prosody, as can be seen in Extract 4.6.

**Extract 4.6:** 412.07(7)

```
01 Jo:    = oh yeah. i'm th[inking.] why would people. (.) go: and d(h)o this.
02 Ther:                   [alien.]
       j raises eyebrows.      crunches face holds palms up. laughing
       t                       fast multiple nods, smiles
03        I(h) me:an, .hh (0.3) I ended up in the [hospital.]
04 Ther:                                          [hmhmhm   ]
05        (0.3)
06 Jo:    on our honeymoon.
07        (0.8)
       j blows nose
       t lowers eyebrows, loses smile, shallow double nod
08 Jo:    I bled so much. (0.3) my hymen was almost totally covered. .SHHIH
09        (0.4)
10 Jo:    and [so:, ] (1.3) him not knowing ~what in the heck he was doing,~
11 Ther:      [°mm.°]
       j      looks away. swallows.                      grabs new tissue
       t        shallow double nod
12 Jo:    (0.5) ~penetrated too hard and ripped me to shreds.~
```

```
13          (1.0)
14 Ther:  °oh:[: dea::r.°]
15 Jo:          [and    I bl]e:d like a stuck pig. I bled and I bled and I bled.
16          (0.3)
17 Ther:  °oh: dear.° =
18 Jo:    =((lip smack)) yeah it was ~very painful, .hh so all of th[a:t,~]
19 Ther:                                                              [hhh  ]
        j                 shallow double nod. circles clawed hands in
        t                 slow deep double nod------->noisy outbreath
20          (0.3)
21 Jo:    [~ye kno:w.~]
22 Ther:  [ yea:h.    ]
        t multiple nods
```

The client Joanna is narrating a distressing experience involving her honeymoon night with her husband. A number of distress markers appear such as a sniff (line 08), tremulous voice (lines 10 and 12) and also non-vocal actions such as blowing nose and grabbing tissues (Hepburn, 2004; Hepburn & Potter, 2007). In lines 14 and 17, the therapist's "°oh:: dea::r.°", produced quietly with extended syllable lengthening, displays congruent feelings of commiseration, which works to sympathize with Joanna's painful experience during her honeymoon night. Empathy is not conveyed here, however, because the therapist has not gone "on record" in demonstrating her understanding of Joanna's experience – see also Extract 4.5.

*Comforting Support* Emotional support may also be provided with actions that comfort or soothe a person that is experiencing distress. According to Cekaite and Kvist Holm (2017, p. 112), "*Soothing* is defined here as responses characterized by the caregiver's emotion regulation through the use of positive emotions (talk and haptic means)." Whereas haptic forms are embodied, such as embracing a person in distress, vocal or verbal forms involve talk that works to placate or calm another (e.g., whispering "*shhhh*" or stating that "everything will turn out okay"). An example of haptic soothing occurring in psychotherapy in shown in Extract 4.7, taken from Wynn and Wynn (2006).

**Extract 4.7:** Wynn and Wynn (2006, p. 1391) – Comforting/ Soothing

```
01  P:  it feels like I don't have any friends an nothing … all alone in
02      this world
03  T:  being all alone … it isn't surprising if it feels a little sad and
04      heavy when you are completely alone … it isn't surprising … and
05      then (anonymised) is dead and sort of left you … the only one who
06      cared for you
07  P:  ((the patient starts to cry and the therapist holds her))
08  T:  is it OK that I do this?
09  P:  I can't handle it any more ((cries))
10  T:  cry:
11  P:  I feel so ALONE
```

At the beginning, the patient reports her feelings of being alone in the world without any friends. In response, lines 03–04, the therapist first partially repeats or mirrors the client's talk (`being all alone`) and then draws attention to various emotions (`sad and heavy`) that may arise from being "`completely alone`". In line 07, the patient begins to cry and the therapist responds with haptic soothing by holding her and, afterwards, asks permission to do so.[6]

To summarize, although Extracts 4.1–4.7 all show examples of therapist responses that orient to the client's emotional experience, only Extracts 4.1–4.4 may be considered to be displaying empathy. Whereas Extracts 4.5–4.7 refer to various forms of emotional sharing and thus generate various implications such as "I feel your pain" or "it's going to be alright," the formulations from Extracts 4.1–4.4 seem instead to be getting across the main message of "I understand you."

## 4.5 Reworking Experience from the Client's Perspective

Empathic actions take on, endorse, apprehend, and are resonant with the other's perspective. This, generally speaking, is what Rogers had in mind when he spoke of "entering the client's frame of reference" or "walking in the world of the other." Hepburn and Potter (2007, 2012) have suggested that formulations are the major "action vehicle" through which empathy may be conveyed – see Chapter 2 for a general discussion of formulating actions. A formulation bears similarity to what in psychotherapy research has termed *reflection* or *empathic reflections* (see Elliott et al., forthcoming; Hill, 2020; and Stiles, 1992 for various definitions of reflecting response), as, for example, adopting the client's frame of reference and, consequently, positioning clients as "expert" by maintaining their ownership of experience. Although reflection, in the sense of connecting with the client's talk, is a central feature of this action, the transformative aspect and the ability to often move talk in a more therapeutically relevant direction is also of central importance (see Antaki, 2008). Thus, even when the therapist is seen to mainly "summarize" the client's perspective or trouble, the consequence will most always involve a notable reworking or change in the client's prior stance descriptions. There are many ways in which formulations may work to transform the client's descriptions of experience. Weiste and Peräkylä (2013), for example, identified four general formulating practices common to psychoanalysis and cognitive

[6] It should be noted that no examples of touching or embracing were found in the York I videos analyzed, suggesting that this form of soothing is not generally practiced by CCT or EFT therapists and that it may constitute an "out-of-mode" practice that does not keep sufficient emotional distance between the therapist and client (Greenberg et al., 1993).

therapy – highlighting, rephrasing, relocating and exaggerating – not all of which may be considered as doing empathic work.

In this section, I discuss the different action formats that therapists draw from in order to rework the client's troubles telling in EFT and CCT, while still maintaining a client-centred, empathic perspective. These include 1) summarizing the client's trouble; 2) drawing implications from the troubles telling; 3) noticing; 4) making inferential adjustments; and 5) co-completing the troubles telling.[7]

### *4.5.1 Summarizing the Client's Trouble*

Therapist empathy rests in the ability to convey an understanding of the client's displayed stance that mainly coheres with and not sharply deviates from the teller's original wordings and meanings. In this way, therapists are able to capture or grasp the main thrust of what the client is saying, by apprehending the teller's experience and thus maintaining a fairly close connection to the client's perspective. Summarizing the client's descriptions of experience, via formulating, constitutes one form of practice that gets empathic work underway. Recall Extract 4.1, in which Eve produces a troubles telling that conveys negative emotions and complains about the prior session. The therapist's subsequent formulation, "`so you seem very dissatisfi:ed?`", apprehends the client's experience by articulating her feelings. "Dissatisfied" is a fairly close, readily inferable and accessible approximation or summary of Eve's prior terms: "`frustrated`", "`disappointed`".

Summarizing the client's prior troubles can be achieved in myriads of ways and it is well beyond the scope of this chapter to illustrate these various lexico-grammatical and semantic transformative practices. Instead, I will show two kinds of summarizing practices: one that involves a minimal editing of the client's talk and the other that provides the basic gist of this talk using different lexico-grammatical resources. An example of "minimal editing," involving the client Kristina, is shown in Extract 4.8 (also see Extract 2.16).

**Extract 4.8:** 014.13(1)

```
01  Kris:  I- I don't have the strength really to uh- to uh: leave the
02         marriage. I was thinking about it, why is it- why it didn't
03         come to
04         (1.1)
05  Kris:  a conclusion.
06         (3.5)
```

[7] It should be noted that while most of the action formats that re-work client experience involve formulating, other actions that are also part of this list, such as noticing and co-completions, may also be put to empathic work.

```
06  Ther:  .hhh >so you don't have the< strength to leave- to break out.
07  Kris:  mm [hm.   ]
08  Ther:     [yeah.] mm hm,
09         (6.7)
10  Kris:  hm.
11         (0.4)
12  Ther:  .hhh break out've the prison. mm(h)heh
```

In this example, Kristina talks about her lack of strength to leave the marriage. The therapist first summarizes or reflects back what Kristina had said by virtually repeating Kristina's prior wordings (`so you don't have the strength to leave`), but then elaborates on her turn by transforming the meaning "to leave" to the potentially more therapeutically relevant meaning "`to break out`" and, later in line 13, to "`break out've the prison`". The therapist's *re*formulation of Kristina's talk is interesting because it adds another layer of meaning to what Kristina had said: *Breaking out* implies a greater exertion of force than does Kristina's prior expression of *leaving*; that is, whereas "`not having the strength to leave`" may simply imply that Kristina lacks agency, the expression "`break out`" implies excessive restraints (being placed on her) which may be difficult to free oneself from even with strong agency. Another related transformation involves Kristina's current relationship position of being married. Thus, "`the marriage`" becomes reformulated to the more restraining and more negative version "`the prison.`". Summarizing formulations, as they are being described here, are empathic because they 1) maintain a close semantic (and often a grammatical) tie with the client's prior utterance and, in doing so, 2) imply a client's rather than a therapist's perspective. In the preceding example, the therapist's formulation begins by closely matching the original wording of the client's utterance and then, at the end, offers a slight, but relevant, modification in meaning to the terms "`to leave`" and "`the marriage`". These formulation designs – when the therapist minimally edits the client's prior talk – also do not contain any contingency marking and are thus consistent with Weiste et al.'s (2016) findings for cognitive therapy/psychoanalysis. It may be that, because the therapist virtually reflects back client talk, the client's ownership of experience is not placed at risk and so there is no need to mitigate the formulation through various epistemic expressions.

Summary formulations do not always have this tight grammatical matching. Other summary formats provide the gist of client's troubles by stating what was said *in other words*. This is shown in Extract 4.9 with the client Elke.

**Extract 4.9:** EFT/312.02(3)

```
01  Elke:  and (0.4) u- uh(h) <I guess I:- I have been thinking about(h) uh,
02         (0.3) other:, (1.0) <occurrences like this,> and .hh (3.2) like
03         t- w:hy has it actually happened that people wanted, (2.0) like
```

```
04           to take- m:e to take on ↑responsibility for them? =
          t                            fast multiple nods
05  Ther:    =mm hm, (.)
06  Elke:    <like> (0.6) once, (0.7) I guess: (0.2) that was with my ex-
07           husband? (.) u::m:, like when he:, (0.5) was, °in a ps:ychotic
          t              fast double nod.                 shallow double nod
08           state,° or >whatever you want to call it,< (0.8) uh, (0.4) that
09           he::, (1.7) said >like I am his< mouth-piece? [eh(hhh)]
10  Ther:                                                  [mm:.    ]
          t                                                 double nod→
11           (0.2)
          t  ---->
12  Elke:    and another time with my sista:, (0.2) and she was: (0.6)
          t                                         shallow double nod
13           apparently relating to u:h- an incident a long time ago.
14           (1.1)
15  Elke:    a:nd (0.5) I just, (6.0) I don't ↑know find it (.)
16           somewhat scary, (.) I mean yes, I do like to help people
17           out? and I sometimes feel like I can't really dra:w (0.4)
18           the li:ne,
19           (0.4)
20  Elke:    like once I say yes like I almost go out of my wa:y like
21           to- (.) to [help them] ou:t?
22  Ther:               [mm hm.   ]
23           (0.6)
24  Ther:    you get almost- it feels like you get over involv:ed? =
25  Elke:    = yeah. (0.3) [yeah,  ] eheh .hhh
26  Ther:                  [uh huh,]
          e  shallow nod
```

At the beginning of this extract, Elke's troubles telling constructs a self-critical position in which she cannot seem to control her tendency to help others and acts on this tendency in an extreme way (`I can't really dra:w (0.4) the li:ne`; `I almost go out of my wa:y like to- (.) to help them ou:t?`). In line 16, Elke also frames her self-criticism as "`somewhat scary`", thus providing a more elaborate emotional stance in which she claims to be impacted by her behaviour (i.e., it makes her feel scared), and thus a larger range of empathic opportunities to which the therapist may respond; that is, the therapist has the choice of responding to the client's emotion of being scared or to her self-critical display of not being in control.[8] In line 24, the therapist aligns with the latter by producing a summary formulation that not only conveys a congruent reading of the client's self-critical experience, but also creates a shift in how the client's difficulty may be understood, from not being able to draw the line to being "`over involv:ed`". The therapist's term suggests a more optimistic rendering of the client's experience, as "being involved" can be understood as something positive, although

[8] The therapist could also orient to both affective elements and thus weave together Elke's emotion of being scared with her feelings of lacking control.

the client has taken this beyond its limit. The therapist's epistemic markings such as "almost-" and "it feels like" downgrade the therapist's own rights and access to know about the client's experience and thus work to defer entitlement to the client. Thus, the therapist's formulation summarizes the client's self-critical position *in other words*, which maintains a strong semantic tie to the client's prior talk even if different lexico-grammatical elements have been used.

### *4.5.2 Drawing Implications from the Troubles Telling*

Much of the therapeutic work of formulating lies in its ability to provide new perspectives, by subtly reworking the client's talk in order to introduce new, not previously acknowledged (and possibly avoided) material (Antaki, 2008; Vehviläinen et al., 2008). Some client's troubles tellings, for example, do not contain explicit evaluative terms and thus the trouble is conveyed in an indirect or implicit manner. Thus, certain empathic responses, rather than summarizing, function to draw a direct implication from what the client had said, often by introducing an affective term that was not actually stated but may nevertheless be implied. Extract 4.10 illustrates a formulation that orients to this implicitness by delivering the upshot, or the implications, of the client's trouble.

**Extract 4.10:** 014.01(2)

| | |
|---|---|
| Kris: | uh because when I went(h) uh. not because mm. w- when |
| | uh (1.4) I graduated from high school? an I wanted |
| | to go to university, (0.9) uh. (0.7) no I l- I ↑left |
| | home, (1.2) before that. no. after I- y'after I |
| | (0.4) ye know. when, (0.4) graduated from high school |
| | I, (0.8) I went to live with my boyfriend, |
| | (0.7) |
| Kris: | for a year, which was (0.6) very unusual. for |
| | ((name of country)), then. |
| | (1.9) |
| Kris: | myeah. |
| | (1.2) |
| Kris: | so I think also was in a- a part to. |
| | (1.0) |
| Kris: | to: (.) get awa[y from ] from her, |
| Ther: | [to get away,] |
| Kris: | .hhh and uhm. (0.6) my father was very very nice. he |
| | said I un- I- I understand you cannot stay in thi(h)s |
| | situation. so he actually moved me. |
| Ther: | hm. |
| Kris: | uh he help you know. to take my uh belongings. |
| | (1.2) |
| Ther: | **so the situation then was pretty intolerable.** |
| | (1.1) |
| Kris: | ah- yes. |

Kristina recounts a situation from her youth: a teenager who recently finished high school and who no longer wanted to live at home. Contained within her narrative is an implicit stance in which her home life, and especially her relationship with her mother, is negatively evaluated. Kristina, in line 15, uses various resources that attest to the underlying tension between her and her mother such as the expression "`to: (.) get away from from her,`", which is then partially repeated by the therapist in line 16. This form of repetition, or *echoing* (Ferrara, 1994), seems to highlight this aspect of Kristina's talk as important and noteworthy. The client then continues her story by using quoted speech to exemplify how her father empathizes with her (`I understand you cannot stay in thi(h)s situation.`). Although her stance is implicitly formulated and thus only creates a potential empathic opportunity for her recipient, the therapist does convey her understanding by underscoring the implication behind her "having to move out" and her having garnered empathy from her own father: "`so the situation then was pretty intolerable.`". Further, the evaluative term "intolerable" is slightly downgraded by the adverb "pretty," which may index a slight caution on the therapist's part at having reworked the client's talk in this explicit manner. Interestingly, the therapist's formulation only targets the situation at home with her mother and the therapist's repetition in line 16 already seems to indicate that Kristina's having to get away from her mother is noteworthy. The therapist did not, however, orient to the father's empathy and help that she received from him. Thus, the therapist's choice in affiliating with the home situation facilitates further talk about an "intolerable" past event, whereas an affiliation with the father's help and empathy might have moved the focus elsewhere, possibly toward the father's positive role in providing assistance in times of trouble.

### *4.5.3 Noticing*

Although noticings have been argued to be *therapist*-oriented (see Chapter 2), they are usually epistemically downgraded and invite confirmation, thus maintaining the client's ownership of experience. For examples of noticings that work empathically, see Extract 4.8 and also Extracts 2.19 and 2.26 from Chapter 2. Empathic support is also shown in Extract 4.11, during which the client Sofia reminisces about her father and about the positive experiences they had together.

**Extract 4.11:** 304.07

```
Sofi:   Oh beautiful >because my father was< (.) very eg-uhm
        he: was very (0.5) a very tender man,:
        (0.9)
Sofi:   an:d[ah
Ther:       [(m:)
```

(0.2)
Ther: He was tender with you?
Sofi: Yah.
(1.0)
Sofi: °okay he was very=very=ver- very tender en I have pictures
an it shows
(0.6)
Ther: m:m.
Sofi: what type of man that he was?
Ther: mhm.=
Sofi: =.snih and'uh::m,
(0.5)
Ther: **>it sounds'like it makes you< sa:d when you think**
**about tha:t,**
(0.9)
Sofi: Yah. In a way yes.
(0.5)
Sofi: be-especially because (1.0) when he died,
Ther: °mm hm,
(1.3)
Sofi: I was ten, (0.3)
Ther: °mm,
Sofi: ~an I remember that (.) very well~
(0.4)
Ther: °m:.

Sofia describes her father as being very tender and, following a clarification question from the therapist in line 07, she confirms that this tenderness was directed toward her. She then emphasizes his tenderness and in line 16 produces a sniff, which may be conveying a form of upset or grief – it should be mentioned that her father had died when Sofia was a child. Following a brief pause in line 17, the therapist produces a response that both draws attention to or *notices* (Sacks 1995b, p. 87) Sofia's upset and draws an implication in which her talking about his tenderness brings about this emotion. The noticing also contains a marker of contingency (i.e., an evidential expression) – "`it sounds'like`" – that indicates how the therapist came to draw this inference and thus fulfils Hepburn and Potter's (2007) criteria for conveying empathy. By drawing explicit attention to and affirmatively connecting with the client's display of sadness, the therapist offers the client emotional support by showing that she understands her experience.

### 4.5.4 *Making Inferential Adjustments*

Certain therapist responses empathically connect with client talk by proposing certain adjustments to how clients have described their troubles. These responses, because they suggest an alternative perspective and thus operate to "repair" client descriptions, work to subtly challenge these descriptions. These proposed adjustments to client talk are not oppositional in the sense of disagreeing. Rather, they suggest an alternative view that is done with some contingency and without opposition markers, thus inviting clients to confirm or disconfirm in the next turn. This practice of suggesting an alternative take on what the client has said is shown in Extract 4.12 with the client Owen.

### **Extract 4.12:** Owen 315_15 (a): 2C

```
01  Owen:   sort of try to say okay (0.2)((clears throat)) it's not quite
02          vacation time yet but (1.5) I just need a little bit of a break.
03  Ther:   sounds like that old conflict.
04          (0.7)
05  Ther:   part of you says (0.7) this is appalling,
06          you can't do this.
07  Owen:   °yeah°
08  Ther:   another part of you says (0.3) .hh but I nee:d it.
09          +(   1.1    )+
        o   +shallow nods+
10  Owen:   an'I've been going with +the side that says I need it.+
        o                           +shallow nods->+
11  Ther:   °mm-hm.°
12          (1.2)
13  Owen:   regardless of (1.0) what the consequences might be. .hh
14          just looking for some ways just to get some relief, (1.1)
15          uh::m (0.6) tch visited'uh couple of friends (.)
16          this weekend, down in ((city)).
17          (0.8)
18  Owen:   uh some old friends of mine who'v-
19          +(      1.1           )+ stayin down there
        o   +waves finger towards self+grabs ankle->
20          and decided +what the heck I'll go, *+(1.2) and (0.2)
        o               +shakes head, crinkles nose+
        t                                       *shallow nods
21  Owen:   I + >had a good time,+<
        o     +bobs head---+
22  Ther:   mm-[hm.
23  Owen:      [I didn't regret +(1.9) >any bit + of it< going,
        o                       +shakes head-+nods->
24           (1.0) uh::m +(1.3) +>an me work see-< (.) work
        o                +smiles+
25          seems to be going well,=it's one'uh the things
26          I actually look forward to doing.
27          (0.3)
28  Ther:   *↑mm hm.       *
        t    *shallow nods*
29          (1.7)
30  Ther:   tch.hh sounds like there's a but in there.
31          (1.0)
32  Owen:   there's+ about to be+ a but. it's gist (1.0) I guess
        o          +nods-------+
33          the stability of (1.5) wanting to get something over with (1.2)
34          a::n (1.1) try to find I guess the same sort of stability
35          that I've had last summer.
```

In lines 01–02, Owen informs the therapist that he needs a break despite it not yet being vacation time. The therapist responds with a formulation that reaches back toward an old conflict that had been discussed earlier: "`part of you says (0.7) this is appalling, you can't do this. … another part of you says (0.3) .hh but I nee:d it.`". In the beginning of her turn, line 03, the therapist uses the evidential expression "sounds" to downgrade her epistemic access (`sounds like that old conflict.`). Although Owen seems to confirm the therapist's understanding with a "°`yeah`°" in line 07, he then subtly resists the therapist's implication that the conflict has an active presence in his life here-and-now, by asserting that he is only aligning with one of the sides: "`an'I've been going with the side that says I need it.`" From lines 13 to 26, Owen then recounts how he visited some friends over the weekend in order to get some relief and during the course of this recount he emphasized that he had a good time and that he did not regret going. In line 25, however, Owen downgrades his positive assessment of his work situation with "seems" (`work seems to be going well`), thus possibly casting some doubt on the implication that visiting his friends was not merely an escape from an unhappy situation at work. When responding, the therapist does not seem to fully buy into the client's easygoing attitude. First, in line 28, the therapist responds with "`↑mm hm.`" with the rising intonation turn-initially seemingly conveying heightened involvement in terms of interest, surprise or even slight skepticism (Gardner, 2001). Then, in line 30, following a long pause the therapist responds with "`tch.hh sounds like there's a but in there.`", which works to challenge the client's assessment of his work situation; that is, although the client professes to feel comfortable when visiting his friends and attending to his needs, there is a "but" that suggests some form of conflict or alternative (and unstated) reasons for why he suddenly left for the city to see his friends. The epistemic marker works to downgrade the therapist's position and invites the client to (dis)confirm her understanding. Even though the therapist's response is challenging in nature, it still conveys empathy because it remains tied to the client's and not the therapist's perspective: by calling attention to the "but," the therapist draws an implication that may be heard as emanating from Owen's own narrative and at the same time challenging Owen's claims. Owen then weakly affiliates with the therapist's formulation in line 32 "`there's about to be a but.`" and thus only partially confirms the implication that there might be a conflict at work that is guiding his actions.

### *4.5.5 Co-Completing the Troubles Telling*

Collaborative turn completions have already been discussed in Chapter 3 and have been dealt with extensively in prior studies (Ferrara, 1994; Lerner, 1989, 1991, 2004; Oloff, 2018). In his *Lectures on conversation*, Sacks (1995a, pp. 145–147) discussed how in collaboratively building each other's utterances, speakers accomplish a certain kind of social organization. For instance, it can demonstrate that speakers form a group because they display that they agree on the topic and, furthermore, "know what's on each other's minds" (Sacks, 1995a, p. 147). These kinds of co-completions, therefore, may constitute a major vehicle for doing empathic work because they show that the therapist is immediately able to grasp the trajectory of client's talk and thus display an understanding of the client's experience. A collaboratively completed utterance is shown in Extract 4.13.

**Extract 4.13:** Kristina Case 014.01(1):

Kris: ↑not ↑that I dri- i'll gi- i'll give you a- a- an
(0.8) illostra[tion.]
Ther: [ oka]y?
Kris: it- ye know from u: (0.6) hm. .hhh e: (0.6) she
(0.6)bud this'll de- it could be generalized but this
one is a concrete thing. .hhh she- she would go in uh
in winter in her uh. (0.7) nightgown. (0.6) on the
balcony to hang the clothes?
(0.3)
Kris: t- you know to dry?
(0.3)
Kris: an then uh (.) uhm. she would come back and say
well. well we- (.) my brother and I would be very
concerned you know you should at least have a coat or
something ↑that's when we were children.
(0.4)
Kris: an she would say uhm. (0.8) or if she would be ha-
(0.2) angry or something she would say ser- serves
you well that I am cold.
(1.4)
Kris: **so I think the guilt feeling is uh, (2.3) °yeah.°**
Ther: **something that she (0.8) instilled.**
Kris: .hhh pra- [probably but]
Ther: [in you at lea]st in p[art.]
Kris: [bu- ] v- very
successfully.

In this excerpt, Kristina provides another illustration of her negative relationship with her mother by recounting an event in which her mother blamed Kristina and her brother for making her risk her health by going outdoors in inappropriate clothing. Kristina builds up a specific stance in which the mother's unjust attempts to make her children feel guilty is contrasted with the children's concern for their mother's well-being. This interplay of negatively judging the mother's behaviour, while at the same time positively evaluating own and brother's behaviour is done in the following ways. First, through the use of affect terms, she explicitly contrasts her and her brother's feelings of "concern" with their mother's "angry" feelings; this contrast is further amplified by adding the context, "↑that's when we were children" with a sudden prosodic lift in pitch to emphasize their innocence in relation to the responsibility laid on them by their mother. Second, quoted speech (serves you well that I am cold) is used to vividly illustrate how the mother cruelly admonishes her children for causing her discomfort. Finally, an explicit empathic opportunity is offered to the therapist when Kristina embeds the term "guilt" within an uncompleted clause (so I think the guilt feeling is uh, (2.3) °yeah.°). Here, the long pause followed by the "°yeah.°" shows that the client is hearably at the end of the telling and, in this way, may be inviting the therapist to take up a next turn at talk.

The therapist then conveys her understanding of the mother's practices of blame by completing Kristina's clause and by beginning to explain what consequences, for the client, her mother's actions might have had. The therapist's completion suggests what the client may have had in mind (Sacks, 1995a) and, in doing this, invites Kristina to confirm this understanding. Note also that the therapist first paused before uttering "instilled." (line 22), thus producing what appears as a designedly complete utterance (DIU) (Koshik, 2002), thus giving the client an opportunity to then complete the therapist's turn-in-progress. Although Kristina first responds by downgrading her confirmation (probably but), the therapist, in turn, proceeds quickly to downgrade the certainty of this "in progress" claim through the expression "at least in part.". In this way, the therapist is able to preserve the client's greater rights in knowing how she has been affected by her mother. Kristina then displays her primary rights and access to know by upgrading her confirmation with "very successfully". According to Hepburn and Potter (2007, p. 112), such a turn-completing move may come with certain risks, because the recipient's completion may be misaligned with the teller's prior unit. In psychotherapy, the therapist's attempt to complete the client's utterance may be viewed as too presumptive, inaccurate or as inappropriately overtaking the client's right of turn. This example shows, however, that by implementing epistemic resources at a sequentially appropriate place, therapists can work at smoothly gaining client affiliation.

## 4.6 Client Feedback

Following a therapist's empathic response, clients will normally provide feedback regarding the adequacy, suitability, intelligibility and so on of the response. In Extracts 4.8 and 4.9, for instance, clients readily confirm the therapist's display of understanding, but in Extract 4.12, the client does not initially do so. In this section, I show two kinds of feedback. The first involving strong, upgraded and mutual consensus on the therapists' understanding of the trouble, which may be labelled – following Heritage (2011) – *empathic moments*. The second involves the client's rejection of the therapist's understanding, which may be interpreted as *failed empathy*. Client feedback, following therapist empathic responses, will be examined in further detail for specific sequences such as storytelling (Chapter 5) and formulations involving disagreement (Chapter 7).

### 4.6.1 *Empathic Moments*

Whereas a therapist's response (i.e., formulation, noticing, collaborative completion) may be so designed as to demonstrate knowledge or an understanding of what is "on the other's mind" (Sacks, 1995a) or what the other has felt and experienced, it will take a next turn from the client to ratify the therapist's understanding. Clients may fervently claim to endorse the therapist's view and this kind of enthusiastic display may lead into what may be called an *empathic moment* (Heritage, 2011). During such moments, shared understanding and affect is displayed through speakers' synchronized vocal confirmations and non-vocal affiliation. An empathic moment is shown in Extract 4.14.

**Extract 4.14:** 312.16(03)

```
01 Paula: I: think >at one point in time I was< saying, like
02        (0.7)
03 Paula: u:m,
04        (1.3)
05 Paula: i- it's kind of like starting to- (.) to change and like
06        first it was kind of like a little bit on the aggressive
07        si:de of things? .hh=
08 Ther:  =↑mm:.
09        (0.7)
10 Paula: and that I ↑really wanted like (.) you know like to get into
11        this:,
12        (1.0)
13 Paula: well I guess what you would call <assertiv:e (.) behaviou(h)r,
14        (.) [mode.>]
15 Ther:      [mm hm,] mm hm,
16        (0.4)
17 Paula: a:n-
18        (0.9)
19 Paula: yea:h,
20        (0.9)
21 Paula: u- and for some time I was ↑kind of a little bit worri(h)(h)ed
22        .hh that I wouldn't be able like to:, (.)to find that balance but,
23        (0.4)
24 Paula: <it's comin:g
25        (0.4)
26 Paula: alo:ng
27        (0.7)
28 Paula: alright> (h)e he he.=
29 Ther:  =so you're finding a way (.) to do it but also not to do it too
```

```
30          aggressive[ly,]=
31 Paula:              [.hh]
32 Ther:    =to do it in a way that's, (0.4) works socially, works for you,
          p multiple nods ----------------------------------->
33          works for them.
          p ------------->
34 Paula:   ((lip smack))) ↑yeah.
          p fast deep multiple nods
          t multiple shallow nods
35          (       0.3       )
          p fast multiple nods
36 Ther:    °and isn't,°
37          (0.3)
38 Ther:    you know turning off everyone you [meet,] kind of=
39 Paula:                                     [thet's-]
          p fast multiple nods-------------------->
          t                    smiling
40 Paula:   =that's right. [that's] right,=
41 Ther:                   [yeah, ]
          t double nod
          p multiple nods
42 Ther:    =it's important to think about that too↑ °sure↑°=
          p                           fast multiple nods--------->
43 Paula:   =oh that, it's very important te me(h). [he he.]
44 Ther:                                            [↑yeah.]
          t             multiple nods ------>        smiles
          p smiles------------------------------------------->
45 Paula:   very important. [.hh   ]
46 Ther:                    [yeah,]
          t                 double nod, smiles
```

Before this extract, Paula had reported that she is beginning to be able to move beyond, and overcome, feelings of depression and helplessness by taking a more affirmative stance in certain life events. She reported that, at first, her "assertive behaviour" was "`a little bit on the aggressive si:de`" (lines 05–14), but then in lines 17–28, she noted that she was making some progress. Although aspects of Paula's telling appear optimistic, there are other aspects that convey doubt and uncertainty about her alleged progress. First, in lines 21–22, she admits to having been worried about being able to find the right balance when being assertive. Second, lines 23–28, the speech delivery of her claim that "`<it's comin:g (0.4) alo:ng (0.7) alright>`" is slow and considerably drawn out, suggesting uncertainty and doubt that this is indeed the case. Finally, her turn final laughter (line 28) also may be conveying some problems with what she is claiming. According to Shaw et al. (2013, p. 7), post-position laughter can work to soften or modulate a potentially disaligning or disaffiliative action (see also p. 10). Thus, the laughter may be orienting to Paula's limited success in being assertive in a balanced way. The therapist's response, however, provides an optimistic understanding of Paula's difficulties (lines 29–33). Rather than orienting to Paula's implicit uncertainty, the therapist summarizes Paula's telling as a clear accomplishment without unwanted side-effects (`not to do it too aggressively`) and with pro-social benefits (`works socially, works for you works for them`). Throughout the therapist's formulation, Paula displays affiliation by nodding and then provides upgraded confirmation (**↑yeah.**). At this juncture, both the client and the therapist show that they are on the same page by nodding in synchrony, thus producing an empathic moment. The empathic moment is then further deepened through reciprocating confirmation displays (lines 40/41, 43/44, 45/46) and non-vocal actions such as nod/nod or nod/smile (lines 39, 41, 44, 46).

### *4.6.2 Failed Empathy*

Clients do not, of course, always provide enthusiastic, assenting feedback to what therapists have said and help to accomplish empathic moments such as in Extract 4.14. In fact, client assent is often more subdued – see especially Extracts 4.8–4.9. On some occasions, clients disaffiliate with how therapists have responded by delaying or mitigating their assent or through explicit disagreement or rejection. Sacks (1995b) pointed out that patients often pay close attention to "how carefully the doctor is listening" to their troubles and that patients may topicalize the institutional quality of the interaction if doctors' listening practices do not provide a sufficient endorsement of their troubles. Extract 4.15, taken from Sacks (1995b), shows a telephone conversation at an emergency psychiatric clinic.

**Extract 4.15:** Sacks, 1995b, pp. 387–388

```
pt:    I've got a date coming in a half hour and I (sob)
dr:    I see
pt:    I cant go through with it I cant go through with the evening I
       cant (sniffle)
dr:    uh huh
pt:    you talk I dont want to talk
dr:    uh huh
pt:    (laugh sob) It sounds like a real professional uh huh uh huh uh
       huh sniffle
```

In her analysis of this fragment of talk, Pain (2009) argues that the doctors' responses of "uh huh" are not successful at offering empathy or sympathy and thus do not succeed in building adequate rapport with the client. Part of the reason for this is that the doctor does not acknowledge the patient's emotional displays. In the last line, the patient orients to the "professional" role taken up by the doctor, thus expressing strong criticism of the doctor's inadequate form of listening that does not at all provide her with emotional support. Hepburn and Potter (2007) have argued that responses need to be propositional in form in order to convey empathy and this would partly explain why the doctor's responses in Extract 4.15 were rejected by the patient. Rogers (1957) had also pointed out that empathic displays are intricately tied to what is called *genuineness*, or the therapist's attitude of relating to the client's experience in a transparent manner, without putting on a professional attitude or façade that is incongruent to the client's needs (see also Lietaer, 1993). In the preceding extract, therefore, the patient seems to call into question the doctor's genuineness by implying that he remains rigidly in his professional role and is unable to adopt an attitude that resonates with the client's upset.

Responses that have propositional content such as formulations may also not always come across as being "sufficiently empathic" or as displaying the right kind of understanding of the client's experience. In Extract 4.16, taken from a session of client-centred therapy (CCT) with the client Eve, it is shown how the therapist's attempt at conveying empathy is rebuked. During this session and prior to this extract, Eve had reported her feelings of upset and sadness in relation to her brother's death, occurring some years earlier.

**Extract 4.16**

```
01  Eve:   ~like I never really looked at the fact <that> (1.3) in-
02         in some ways he was the only one who sustained me through
03         my ↑childhood.~
04         (0.7)
05  Ther:  he'd given you so much:. as a <°ch[i:ld,°> an] supported you.
06  Eve:                                     [and he's ]
07         (0.5)
08  Eve:   ~an he=was the only one that uhm, (2.5) really. knew that I
09         existed.
10         (0.3)
11  Eve:   >he=was the only one that< ↑uhm~
12         (1.5)
13  Eve:   ((lip smack)) .hhh HX::.
        e  closes eyes, choked up
14  Eve:   paid atte:ntion::, h- =
        e  wipes eye
15  Ther:  =uh hu::h?
16  Eve:   ~an- and (0.4) uh:m. (0.4) >that=I could< talk to, <and,> (0.5)
17         .hhh °.snih° (1.6) ((lip smack)) an so much of my past and so
18         much of who I ↑am is tied up with ↑him an-~
19         (1.8)
        e  rubs hand across eyes
20  Ther:  so he was your ↓mainstay through your childhoo:d?
        e                                        fast multiple nods→
21         (1.5)
        e  ----->
22  Ther:  he [was- was (someone) who] (.) acknowledged you.
23  Eve:      [   .hhh       hx       ]
```

```
       (0.4)
Ther:  validated you.=
Eve:   HX:::.
       (0.6)
Eve:   °.snih° (.) >I don't know< everytime I- (h)yo(h)u (.)
       use those words >it just< stops me co:ld.
       (0.4)
Eve:   .hhh °it's just-° (.) anyways,
Ther:  they don't fi:t. (.) they-
Eve:   no:. they're jus: su:ch (.)
Ther:  that=he was [your ] companion. (.) that's °t[oo° cli]ché.
Eve:               [k(hh)]                        [↑uh    ]
       (0.9)
Eve:   y(h)eah(h). .hh uhm hx: °.snih°
       (2.2)
Eve:   ~yeh- an he was the o- he was the one
```

At the beginning, Eve launches into an activity in which she praises the virtues of the brother in relation to her own childhood and while she was growing up. Her talk is suffused with a tremulous voice quality and prolonged sighs and, from line 11 onwards, she begins to cry. When responding in line 16, the therapist reflects back or provides a gist formulation of the beginning of the client's turn – compare: "he was the only one who sustained me through my ↑childhood." vs. "so he was your ↓mainstay through your childhoo:d?" – rather than draw more attention to her affective stance display of sadness. Eve then non-verbally endorses the formulation via a series of head nods (line 20). After a 1.5-second pause, the therapist elaborates on the prior formulation by specifying how the brother may have realized his supportive role; that is, by acknowledging and validating Eve. The therapist's empathic understanding can be seen to make cohesive ties to Eve's prior talk about the brother's unique insight about Eve: "really. knew that I existed." (lines 8–9); "paid atte:ntion::" (line 14). Although the therapist's elaboration is subtle, it may generate a variety of inferences that the client may find problematic. First, the therapist's summary formulation that Eve was acknowledged and validated significantly distils the elaborate stance previously built up by Eve, and second, these summary terms (i.e., acknowledged, validated) may appear too specialized or even as bordering on jargon and as not accurately representing the client's frame of reference. As a response, beginning in line 26, the client does not offer confirmation but instead strongly disaffiliates by 1) emitting an exasperated sigh (Hoey, 2014); 2) hesitating and displaying continued distress via a pause and a sniff; and 3) criticizing the therapist's use of terms (>I don't know< everytime I- (h)yo(h)u (.) use those words >it just< stops me co:ld). Here, as in Extract 4.15, the client seems to be drawing attention to the therapist's lack of authenticity or genuineness, in which she uses words, not to develop a strong resonant connection with the client, but to "sound like a professional". In line 29, Eve continues by initiating what appears as an account (.hhh °it's just-°), but then breaks off her turn with "anyways,". Subsequently the therapist orients to the disaffiliation by ratifying the client's objection that the therapist's talk is incongruent ("they don't fi:t.") and by asserting that her wording was too cliché. From here on, the client weakly endorses the therapist's attempt at re-affiliation, before proceeding to continue with her discussion of the brother's positive attributes (yeh- an he was the o- he was the one).

Extract 4.16 also illustrates the "problem of experience" noted by Heritage (2011). Eve's troubles telling created an empathic opportunity and invited the therapist to affiliate with the client's stance of upset. The therapist then takes the initiative by producing a summary formulation that displays her understanding of, and thus makes an epistemic connection to, the client's trouble. Heritage noted that, in regard to epistemic entitlements, an empathic response may encroach on the client's informational preserves (Goffman, 1981) and thus subtly undermine the client's ownership of knowledge/experience. We see Eve in this extract challenging the therapist, as not only failing to have provided a suitable understanding display of the client's trouble, but as not doing so in an authentic manner.

## 4.7 Conclusions

In this chapter, empathy was viewed as a type of emotional support response. Drawing from Hepburn and Potter's (2007; 2012) work, doing empathy was argued to comprise two dimensions: 1) epistemics – orienting to the client's ownership of experience (Sacks, 1995b; Sharrock, 1974) and informational preserves (Goffman, 1981); and 2) affiliation – displaying support of the client's trouble as conveyed through the client's affective stance. For the first point, therapists often express their "on record" claims of understanding the client's experience by using contingency markers, especially when their *re*formulations significantly deviate from clients' original talk. These markers, by for example downgrading their epistemic rights and access, align with Rogers' (1951) conceptualization as privileging the client's experience or "frame of reference." Further, because formulations make confirmation (or disconfirmation) a relevant next response, clients are placed in a sequential slot in which they can demonstrate their greater experiential entitlements or [K+]. The second point reinforces the notion that therapists respond pro-socially to what clients say. This is a unique form of emotional support that does not go as far as sharing in or being affected by the client's trouble (sympathy) and nor does it mean comforting the client as a way of showing that everything will turn out alright. Instead, support is displayed by expressing to clients that they are understood. Empathy, in this view, would only comprise one subtype of the range of affiliative possibilities that therapists (and speakers in general) may draw from when offering emotional support. Thus, this use of interactional terms or concepts such as epistemics and affiliation may offer an alternative way of viewing the cognitive-affective debate within psychotherapy (Duan & Hill, 1996) and instead show how these dimensions are present in interaction, are oriented to and are performing important kinds of discursive-therapeutic work.

The connection between empathy and troubles tellings seems clear enough. Descriptions of personal experience that do not involve troubles but are mainly expressing a "happy moment" probably do not make empathy a relevant next response. This is because someone's happiness does not invite understanding from a recipient but sharing in one's emotion. In psychotherapy, however, client tellings that contain laughter and optimism are often accomplished against a backdrop of former troubles or distress and so empathy may often be appropriate in these contexts. I have tried to use CA to provide more precision in understanding what empathy is, as a social action, what it is responsive to and what kinds of next responses (from clients) it may invite. Because empathy is such an important concept in psychotherapy research and is considered to be a key element of the psychotherapeutic relationship (Norcross & Lambert, 2018), providing a closer look at how empathy is accomplished may contribute to explaining its effectiveness when used in an appropriately responsive manner (Stiles & Horvath, 2017).

# 5 Storytelling: Extended Accounts of Troubles

## 5.1 Introduction

Over the years, the concept of narrative as a fundamental cultural practice has been gaining importance in psychotherapeutic circles. This trend has been linked to postmodernism and the accompanying view that the self is relational and fragmented and that knowledge is socially constructed (Cushman, 1995; Gergen, 1985; McLeod, 1997). Narrative studies seem to be increasingly informing psychotherapy theory and practice. Thus, it is not only therapies with a social constructionist leaning that have incorporated the "narrative turn," but rather a whole range of psychodynamic, experiential and person-centred approaches as well (see Angus & McLeod, 2004). It was Bruner (1986) who pointed out that narrative offers a unique perspective on human thinking and conduct. Contrasting this with what he calls the *paradigmatic mode*, which is concerned with truth, verifiability and cause–effect relations, Bruner argues that the *narrative mode* operates under different principles and assumptions. In Bruner's terms, stories reveal a landscape of consciousness that pertains to human intentions, the moral consequences of our actions, and to what we think, feel and know. Stories, therefore, provide insight into personal experiences and human relationships, topics that are central to psychotherapeutic concerns. Telling stories about one's own distress and suffering has been recognized for some time to have health benefits, especially when done in a psychotherapeutic context (Pennebaker & Seagal, 1999). Research has shown, for example, that a client's narratives can change over time, moving from stories that construe experience as "problem saturated" to ones that are indicative of healing and "preferred" outcomes (Angus & McLeod, 2004; Muntigl, 2004; White & Epston, 1990).

In person-centred approaches such as EFT, clients' provision of their personal experiences in narrative form allows therapists to adopt a relational style, for example, by empathically following the client's experience or by entering the client's internal frame of reference (Greenberg, 2010; Rogers, 1951). What will be explored in this chapter is how clients with depression tell stories about their troubles and display various kinds of stances that display how they feel (i.e., an affective stance) and how they construe themselves as agents – or more specifically as lacking agency – in certain social contexts involving persons with whom they have a close relationship. I show the various practices in which psychotherapists are able to connect or affiliate with the client's troubles and how certain therapist responses to the client's story may be more effective at facilitating mutual affiliation and also displaying understanding or empathy.

## 5.2 Features of Storytelling

One of the first comprehensive linguistic accounts of narrative can be found in the work of Labov and Waletzky (1967). A narrative, they argued, comprises more than one clausal event and has a regular structure that contains various functions of which *complication* (answering the question "then what happened?") and *resolution* (answering the question "what finally happened?") are obligatory. They suggested ways in which narratives got off the ground or were "opened," such as with a story *abstract* that indicates what the upcoming story will be about (Labov, 1972) or with an *orientation* that gives information pertaining to the characters, time, place and setting of the story. Stories are also said to often come to close via a *coda*, which works to move talk out of "story time" and back into present time (e.g., via deictic markers: "and that was that"). Labov and Waltetzky's pioneering work provided many insights into how speakers recount personal experiences and the importance of evaluation in lending one's narrative a unique significance. But, as pointed out by various scholars, their view on narrative was too focused on structure and not enough on how tellings are embedded into the conversational flow, by responding to what the speakers were just doing before and creating a new context for further action. One concern voiced by Edwards (1997) is that the structure proposed by Labov and Waletzky compels analysts to identify pre-determined categories or functions, rather than looking first to what is being said and the variety of interactional business that is achieved via the telling. Schegloff (1997a) goes even further with his critique by arguing that their analysis is basically decontextualized and teller-centred, and does not consider the audience whatsoever in the analysis. I will just mention a few points made by Schegloff that have some bearing on this chapter. First, stories do not simply "tell" but do something, such as complain, boast, inform and explain. Second, storytelling is not a pre-fabricated text that simply materializes from a stored memory. Rather, stories are a co-accomplishment and are *locally occasioned* (Jefferson, 1978), meaning that recipients (i.e., the audience) will play a part in shaping how the story unfolds. According to Schegloff, the audience is not inert but makes vocal and non-vocal contributions that can mould the various next increments in the telling. Finally, what the teller says is *recipient-designed* (Sacks 1995b,

p. 230), dependent on what the recipients know, the number of recipients present and their relationship to the teller. In the next few sections, I review CA work on storytelling pertaining to how stories get opened and closed and how they are formatted with respect to various interactional contingencies.

## 5.3 Opening and Closing a Narrative

Within CA, storytelling is seen as an extended turn that is locally occasioned, sequentially implicative and co-produced by speakers and recipients (Mandelbaum, 1989, 2013; Sidnell, 2010). Because stories take more than one basic turn unit (i.e., turn constructional unit (TCU)) to complete, tellers must have a way of signalling to the audience that they will need audience cooperation, in the form of withholding from constantly making bids at speaking, to tell the story (Sacks et al., 1974; Sidnell, 2010). This form of signalling is done via a *story preface* (Sacks, 1974). In general, these prefaces work to illustrate the relationship between the impending story and what is just being talked about and also to provide an account for why the story will be told at this moment (Jefferson, 1978). Thus, contrary to the Labov and Waletzkian narratives that were always elicited by an interviewer (i.e., "tell me a story about"), CA draws attention to the social contexts in which stories emerge and are launched – not by some external cue – but through impromptu contingencies arising from talk in-the-moment.

A story opening is shown in Extract 5.1. The client Matt begins this excerpt by discussing his tendency to be very self-critical (lines 1–12).

**Extract 5.1:** 021.15(2)

```
01 Matt:  °°and uh°° (0.7) sort've s:elf sabotaging any achievement. (0.3)
02        that I can (1.9) °uhm° (0.4) ↑complete.
04        (0.5)
05 Ther:  mm hm.
06 Matt:  °and uh° an (0.5) den da- (0.7) giving to=myself more (0.6) more
07        material to be negative about.
08        (0.4)
09 Matt:  °°an°° (1.1) °an be self critical about.°
10        (1.2)
11 Matt:  °uhm,°
12        (4.5)
13 Matt:  n:ot (0.8) not allowe- it's funny. (.) a guy at tennis club said
       m                       flips hand out
14        this to me, he said you know=when you play tennis. (0.7) you
15        could play so well but you won't allow yourself.
16        (0.6)
17 Matt:  ta play, (.) up to your potential.
       t  slow double nod-------------->
```

As examples of his self-critical tendencies, Matt first recounts that he self-sabotages any achievements that he could complete and, second, that he gives himself a lot of opportunities to incite his negativity. In line 10 he pauses, before producing an "°uhm,°" which may mark an attempt at producing a third item in what may appear as a 3-part list (Jefferson, 1990). Then following another pause in line 12, we see that Matt does indeed begin with the third self-critical list item "n:ot (0.8) not allowe-", but then cuts himself off by performing a self-repair (Schegloff et al., 1977). What then occurs is a story preface. Jefferson (1978) identified two kinds of conversational strategies for accomplishing a preface. First, tellers may produce talk that signals a topic shift through so-called disjunct markers such as "oh" and "incidentally" and, second, they may use an *embedded repetition* device that "locates, but does not explicitly cite, the element of prior talk which triggered the story" (Jefferson, 1978, p. 221). Matt's continuation of the turn with "it's funny" seems to operate as a shift in trajectory, moving from "listing self-critical attributes" to something else, thus signalling a disjunction. The expression also works to position the recipient by characterizing and evaluating what is to come, that is, as something funny. Matt also simultaneously flips his hands out in an open palm gesture, which may be construed as an offering (Kendon, 1990) or as a request to move toward the story opening. He then immediately does so by recounting a dialogue he recently had with a fellow at his tennis club. In doing this, he provides the setting or the situational grounding in which the recipient can make sense of the story: the characters, where it takes place and what is discussed. In line 15, Matt then makes use of an embedded repetition by locating what he had said just before the story "n:ot (0.8) not allowe-" to the dialogue-in-progress and to his self-critical attitude; that is, he prevents himself from playing to his potential. The following points may be made concerning this story opening. It is, in Jefferson's (1978) sense, locally occasioned because it emerges from what Matt was doing during his turn-in-progress; that is, whereas he began by accounting for his self-critical attitude by producing a list of attributes, this was changed to a storytelling in which he gave a vivid, concrete example of his self-critical behaviour. The story is an illustration of strong argumentation because it provides another's point of view through *reported speech* (Clift & Holt, 2007), the fellow from his tennis club. Thus, it is not only Matt that sees himself in this way, but others do also.

Extract 5.2 is another illustration of how a story may become launched from prior talk using different kinds of conversational resources.

**Extract 5.2:** 423.12(5)

Jan: I=had gone, to this GP doctor ((name)). >now that i've< said his
name, =
Ther: = mm hm.

```
04 Jan:   (h)ah went to=im <yea:rs> before.
05        (1.2)
06 Jan:   an e- hew- he's so friendly. he's so uhm. ((lip smack)) (0.4)
07        °he's° very ebullient=an:, >ye know=he doesn't< hesitate >
08        ta give=ya a big< hu:g. an he's glad da see ya=an=he, treats you
09        nicely, .hhh an (1.0) u- so I had all these nice memories. o:f
10        that, an I completely forgo:t the reason,
11        (0.9)
12 Jan:   [I  had  ] stopped going to=im.
13 Ther:  [you left?]
14 Ther:  (and.)
15        (0.8)
16 Jan:   which is thet he:. (.) d-he never belie::ved(h). (.) me.
          .
          .
          .
17 Jan:   like one day I:- >he=was- ta give=ya an example I was< having
18        all these sweats. well I ↑know now that I was menopausal but w-
19        I >didn't know that< at the time.
20 Ther:  mm hm.
       t  deep nod
21 Jan:   an I r'member telling=im I was having these sweats an. for some
22        reason he took offense to it >an=he said well=then jus< sit
23        there. .hhh until you start sweating.
24        an ↓I like a good little ↓girl. ↓sat there.
25        (0.4)
26 Jan:   an waited while he went out of the ↓office.
```

Jan begins this extract by mentioning that she had gone to a general practitioner/GP some years back. She begins with many upgraded positive evaluative characterizations of her GP (`so friendly`, `very ebullient`, `give=ya a big< hu:g`, `treats you nicely`) but then, from line 10 onwards, begins to deviate from this. She does this by "doing remembering" of what will surface as a contrastive event. Thus, her prefacing expression "`an I completely forgo:t the reason`" is suggestive of something divergent to what came before and then, in line 12, she produces what is not consistent with having a doctor with so many positive qualities ("`I had stopped going to=im.`") and, on line 16, she provides the reason. In some ways, Jan has already furnished her recipient with the necessary materials to launch into a narrative: we know the characters, the situation and the location. In line 17, Jan explicitly opens the narrative with the expressions "`like one day`" and "`ta give=ya an example`" in which it now becomes clear that she will be recounting a specific event that happened in order to corroborate her claim that he never believed her.

Some story openings are carefully orchestrated between the client and the therapist as shown in Extract 5.3.

**Extract 5.3:** 312.09(6)

```
01 Paula:  .hh and I mean uh- (0.2) but e- (.) that affected me:, (2.6)
02         a lo:t. and this- (.) this is again like this thi:ng, (0.4)
03         >like with my ↑present relationship,< I mean things are just
04         going so ter- (.) well, (0.6) °I shouldn't say so terrible.°
05         but they are not going very well because of ↑tha:t. .hh
06         (3.9)
        t  shallow nod
07 Paula:  and I don't, (0.2) I mean (.) I never talked, (1.2)
08         to that m(h)an abo:ut (.) all this, but (1.6)
09         it's almost like he kno:ws,
10         (2.2)
11 Paula:  this whole (.) situation like i- b(h) i- hh (0.3)
12         it just seems like what,
13         (1.5)
14 Paula:  the way my father thinks and feels that, (0.6) that's what,
15         (1.8)
16 Paula:  he ↑does. but then,
17         (1.6)
18 Paula:  °oh I don't know.° .hh hhh
19         (                    9.5                    )
        p  gazes up. flicks fingers up and down, smiles
        t  gazes at P
20 Paula:  he(hhh)
        p  holds fingers at chin, looks at T
21 Ther:   °what happened.°
        t  smiles, straightens head
22         (0.9)
23 Paula:  ↑we:ll, I guess like one of the things is that. (4.3) uh:(hh)
24         (0.6) this guy, (0.3) doesn't talk to me.
25         (5.7)
        t  shallow nod
26 Paula:  u:h he doesn't, (0.7) want to talk about feelings? (0.8) u:m:,
27         (1.1) or (.) uh- (0.2) about ↑too many things. (1.3) and what
        p                                 shallow nod
28         has happened in the pa- o::h. (.) °it's just (.) such a s::-
        p                              throws head back, looks up
29         uh (.) ridiculous story,°
30         (1.3)
        p  gazes forward
        t  shallow double nod
```

In this session, Paula has been discussing the difficult relationship with her father and her boyfriend, but also drawing certain parallels between the two. In lines 01–05 she acknowledges that her relationship with her boyfriend is not going well. From lines 07 to 18, she seems to evince some difficulty in continuing to discuss her relationship troubles. She mentions not having talked with her boyfriend about this situation, but that the boyfriend is presumably aware of their troubles (`it's almost like he kno:ws,`) and she draws a parallel between what her boyfriend and her father think and feel (lines 12–16). She then, in line 18, seems to become a bit exasperated when she produces a denial of knowledge (°`oh I don't know.`°) followed by a sigh. What follows, line 19, is a long pause in which Paula gazes and smiles at the therapist while fiddling with her fingers. This could be taken as a turn offer to the therapist. But, as the therapist does not take up a turn, Paula then produces a brief laugh token while looking at the therapist and holding her fingers at her chin. This laugh token, occurring in a (post) turn-final environment may be performing the following functions: first, it may be signalling the delicacy of which she is not portraying herself and her relationship in a favourable light (Haakana, 2001) and, second, it may be modulating an upcoming disaffiliating action in which the client may voice criticism or complaints against the boyfriend and father (Shaw et al., 2013). This vocal and non-vocal conduct may also be seen as a more explicit request for the therapist to respond and, in line 21, we see that the therapist says "°`what happened.`°" as she smiles and straightens her head. Thus, the therapist is orienting to Paula's sheepishness as her having something specific to say, but as somehow holding back and perhaps needing a slight push. Paula could of course deny that something did happen, but, after a pause, she launches into a story, which at that moment functions to affirm that there is a tell-able event that is relevantly related to the prior topic. Paula produces a disjunctive expression "`like one of the things is that`", a brief summary of the issue (`this guy, (0.3) doesn't talk to me.`) and an evaluation of how her upcoming narration is to be construed (`°it's just (.) such a s::- uh (.) ridiculous story,°`). In sum, Paula's ability to launch into the story was a joint achievement between her and the therapist. Although Paula did seem to signal that she had something potentially delicate and disaffiliative to disclose, it was through the therapist's prompt that got storytelling underway.

Just as there are various practices for opening stories, so are there practices for closing them down. In Extract 5.4, the client Sofia recounts an event in which she went walking with her mother (a full analysis of this extract will be given in Extract 5.9).

**Extract 5.4:** 304.19(4)

```
01 Sofia: ey(h)eah. (0.7) or you care a lot=about an- an be enj↑oyin.
02        I mean .hh w↑alking. (0.6) u::nd uh:m. (1.1) an enjoyin=all
03        th↑ees. this outdoors this: contat with people these
04        firecracker=look a=that. .hhh I mean, (0.4) ah he,
05        an she tells me well, (0.3) I mean d↑ahlin if you wanna do
06        that divorce your h(h)usband an [start] lookin for somebody
07 Ther:                                 [hhh  ]
        t                        smile      laughing
08 Sofia: ↑else. .hhh eh(h)heh .hhh an I, an- and uh::m.
        t                deep nod
09        (1.1)
10 Sofia: so we-I went h↓ome,
11 Ther:  yeah.
```

In the course of this narrative, Sofia is extolling the merits of going for a walk on a beautiful night with someone that "you care a lot=about" – Sofia's husband had earlier rejected her invitation to go for a walk with them. In line 05, she then contrasts this situation with a comment from her mother that radically diverges from the beautiful, serene setting: It is okay for Sofia to divorce her husband and look for someone else. The mother's remark, at this point, could serve as the "punch line" for the story, gaining a response from the therapist. Sofia's ensuing laughter, her repeated self-repairs (line 08) and also the pause in line 09 could be places that mark potential story closure and thus a reaction from the therapist. But, following no response from the therapist, the client in line 10 produces "so we-I went h↓ome", which closes off the event of having gone for a walk, thus more explicitly marking a story ending. The therapist's response in line 11 "yeah." not only conveys acknowledgement but also that she might make a move to take up speakership (Jefferson, 1984).

Although Sofia's line 10 could be construed as a Labov and Waletzkian *Coda*, which potentially ends the narrative about a past event and thus makes it potentially relevant to return to the "present" dialogue between her and the therapist, it should be emphasized that this Coda was produced not because of a structural requirement for producing these kinds of expressions or stages, but because of how the talk between Sofia and the therapist unfolded. For instance, the talk produced in line 08 or the silence in line 09 may have served as resources to signal completion and thus enable the therapist to respond to the narrative. Because the therapist did not do this, Sofia was then pressured to continue and she did so by more explicitly signalling a story ending.

## 5.4 Story Formats: Structure and Function vs. Locally Occasioned

In addition to having an opening and closing, stories also have a middle component in which the teller generally conveys "what happened." Labov and Waletzky's (1967) approach was to examine stories in terms of structure. For the stories they analyzed, two functions were noted: A *complicating action* in which the main events of the story get expressed and a resolution that marks the result of the narrative or how the complication was resolved. Although these two functions seem to work well for the "danger of death" stories analyzed by Labov and Waletzky – the narrator recounts a set of events leading to a "dangerous situation" (i.e., a complication) that then leads to a good outcome (i.e., a resolution) – not all stories centre around problem events that need to be solved. For example, complaint stories generally do not implicate a "resolution." They also claimed that narratives often have an evaluative component, which plays an important role of giving significance to the story.

Emotion-focused psychotherapy researchers adopting a narrative-informed view have been examining stories with respect to two main structural/functional criteria: the presence of *problem markers* or *emergent meaning markers* (Angus and Greenberg, 2011). For example, in studies exploring the interrelationship between emotion processes and narrative organization in depressed clients undergoing emotion-focused (EFT) or client-centred therapy (CCT) (Angus and Greenberg, 2011), it was found that depressed clients tend to narrate personal life events as three different "problem saturated" story types: *same old story*, *empty story* and *broken life story*. The most prevalent story type, "same old story," references maladaptive emotional-agentive themes that correspond with the following markers: a sense of stuckness and helplessness, a flat external voice, ramped-up (or down) adverbial expressions such as "always" or "never" and expressions of low agency (Angus and Greenberg, 2011, p. 60). Empty stories coincide with bare emotional content and focus instead on external details with minimal engagement from the narrator. Broken life stories, by contrast, contain conflicting emotional plotlines and are marked by confusion, uncertainty and frustration, thus creating a narrative that lacks internal coherence. These stories seem to share the common features of low personal agency, helplessness and a "minimal" or depressed emotional content. Stories containing problem markers seem to closely align with what Jefferson and Lee (1980) have called troubles talk or troubles tellings. Narratives, however, do not always focus on troubles but may instead constitute something new, emergent or positive that the client has experienced. These emergent meaning stories fall into three types: *untold stories*, *unique outcome stories* and *healing stories* (Angus & Greenberg, 2011, p. 82). Stories of this type are said to reflect a positive change process happening for the client.

Contrary to the preceding focus on structure and function, CA's approach adopts a view of storytelling as locally occasioned and interactionally produced. Sacks (1974), thus, characterizes stories in sequential terms as comprising the preface, the telling and the response sequence. CA does, however, consider general kinds of functions that tellings perform. For example, stories may be used as vehicles to tell jokes (Sacks, 1974), complain (Drew, 1998; Günthner, 1997) or do a general form of troubles telling (Jefferson, 1988). From the York 1 sessions examined, it was found that clients would tend to narrate their troubles in three different ways: as complaints about non-present others (complaint stories), negative assessments of self (self-deprecation stories) or as a general apprehension or fear concerning personal life events (anxiety stories). Each of these story types will be briefly described.

Complaint stories involve some grievance that the teller has about a non-present third party (Drew, 1998; Günthner, 1997). A complaint is shown in Extract 5.5 with the client Sofia.

### *5.4.1 Complaint Story*

**Extract 5.5:** Sofia 304.03(3)

Sofia: .hhh he is fighting me for any: little thing.
(0.3)
Ther: mm hm.
Sofia: but I know that uh- what's on the back of his- dose uh: estrange
↓misbehaviours. is the lack of .hhh see .hhh by me:, (0.4)
but him having me:, (0.8) to go to work to financially ↓help him.
(0.4) .hhh mea:ns .hhh da:t he ↓no longer is the bread-
the ↑only breadwinner on the home, .hhh he is no longer .hhh
the one (0.4) exerting ↑control.
Ther: mm hm.
Sofia: so bec(h)au(h)e he c(h)anno=↓d(h)o that.
Ther: mm hm,
Sofia: he starts having all of this uh of this all of this uhm .hhh
behaviours.=**for (h)esample I phone hin at work today an I said**
**look. .hhh I am not I cannot (.) make it at home today at uhm**
**(1.0) ((swallows)) early because I have to go .hhh to the place**
**where ↑you know, .hhh a::nd uh:m. (0.7) an I say ↑ok? (0.3) an he**
**says okay. (1.2) an I phone home an he's not ↑home .hhh when ↑I**
**come back home,**
(0.8)
Sofia: **.hhh I bet=jyou where he went. (0.5) he went to a rethstaurant**
**and ate outsi(h)e. even though he knows that we are having**
**financial ↓difficulties. .hhh an we should take care of the**
**money. .hhh but ↓he did that. (0.3) because there=is nos(h)ing in**
**the ↓world .hhh that he would put a pot on top of the kitchen and**
**do some meal. a meal for him.**
(1.8)
Ther: °°mm,°° hhh so you were just feeling pre:::tty:: frustra:te:d
a::nd .hhh resigned. like he's just not gonna
Sofia: ((sniffs)) ↑oh. =
Ther: =change or he's=
Sofia: =↑no.

This excerpt revolves around Sofia's husband who is characterized as "fighting me for any: little thing." (line 1) and for exhibiting "↓misbehaviours." (line 05). After describing the husband as no longer being able to be "the ↑only breadwinner on the home" and as not "exerting ↑control", thus, exhibiting "misbehaviours," Sofia proceeds to a story opening in line 14 (for (h)esample). Following this is the storied complaint in which she recounts an episode where she is not able to make it home early. Even though the couple is having financial difficulties, Sofia complains that the husband goes to a restaurant instead of making himself a meal in order to save money. The husband, according to Sofia, has made a moral transgression because he is placing them in deeper financial difficulties and, further, is acting selfishly – treats himself to a restaurant meal and does not pull his own weight in the household. The therapist, in line 28, responds to the complaint with a formulation that targets Sofia's feelings, thus working to close off the narrative.

### 5.4.2 *Self-Deprecation Story*

In other troubles telling narratives, clients place the trouble squarely on the self, rather than a non-present third part. In these narratives, clients express self-criticisms or self-deprecatory remarks, as seen in Extract 5.6 with the client Eve.

**Extract 5.6:** 020.02(2)

```
Eve:   yeh(h) so trudging >with everything< just that- (0.8) out of my
       control, it's like being la:te again today, >I was actually<
       trying really hard te not be la:te.
Ther:  mm hm[::?  ]
Eve:        [a:nd,] (.) ye know part of it is that. (0.6) >I was trying
       to get something printed o:ut, an: n- n- I was trying to print it
       out< overni:ght an:, (.) I came in, (.) this morning. but later
       than I had intended to:, [an the printer had] cra:shed. an the
Ther:                           [      mm hm,      ]
       program had cra:shed. and we couldn't print, we couldn't print,
       an then I got a phone call, but .hhh
       (.) it's like there's oth- there's other things >that i'm<
       ↑a:lways late because. (1.2) I always >sort of< had this ga:p.
       (0.5)
Eve:   it's like I kno:w I have to leave ho:me <AT.> (.) ten thirty.
       (0.5)
Eve:   s' but ten thirty's when I leave my ↑computer.
       (0.3)
Ther:  m:m hm.
       (0.4)
Eve:   an the:n, (.) of course suddenly I >have to have a conversation
       with Ned.< suddenly I've got to fax something o:ff. (.) su- I
       gotta get off the phone. I gotta find my stuff. an then
       suddenly:, (0.5) you kno:w, like I'm twenty minutes la:te.
       (0.7)
Eve:   °an uhm:,°
       (1.7)
Eve:   a:nd you'd think after ((number of)) ye:ars of this I'd stop
       being ↑surprised.
       (0.8)
Eve:   but-
Ther:  mm [hm ]:?
Eve:      [uh-]
Eve:   by always >doing tha:t, but< (in fact) I always do it.
       (0.6)
Eve:   it's like there's- there's a gap in my brain o:f, (0.7) when I'm
       supposed te le:ave, and what it takes. (0.3) to be ready to
       le:ave?
```

```
39          (0.3)
40  Ther:   <mm: hm:?>
41          (0.4)
42  Eve:    a:nd,
43          (1.3)
44  Ther:   Evelyn, it seems no matter how you, (.) hard you try er'll
45          how much you want to:, (0.5) uhm::, (2.2) °somehow you can't
46          get it together?°
```

In line 01, Eve states that she is "so trudging >with everything<" and that things are "out of my control". These statements are, using CA terminology, self-deprecating (Pomerantz, 1984) and involve some form of negative appraisal of self, such as "I am X = [negative attribute]". Eve then, in line 02 provides a story preface of "it's like being la:te again today" in which she recounts scenarios in which she is unable to be on time. These events work in support of her negative claim that she is "so trudging" and not able to properly control her personal life circumstances. Toward the end of her narrative, lines 34–38, she then produces extreme case formulations (Pomerantz, 1986), "by **always** >doing tha:t, but< (in fact) I always do it." and accounts for her conduct as resulting from a "cognitive dysfunction" (there's a gap in my brain o:f,). Pomerantz (1984) argued that self-deprecations tend to implicate disagreement or praise as the preferred response and agreement as the dispreferred alternative. The therapist's response in line 44, however, seems to opt for neither of these alternatives. Instead, she produces a summary formulation that underscores her experience of having diminished agency: "She is not capable of being on time, no matter how hard she tries."

### *5.4.3 Anxiety Story*

Some narratives involve troubles that neither blamed others for some misconduct nor criticized self. These stories, rather, expressed a general malaise about specific life events in terms of worry, anxiety or fear. This kind of "anxiety narrative" is shown in Extract 5.7 with the client Marlene.

**Extract 5.7:** 407.02(4)

```
01  Mar:   = and if I get this job an go in, (1.5) I mean I- I don't know
02         how I'm=gonna survi:ve, with (1.2) I know exactly what this (.)
03         this particular job entails. I've been dere. before, =
04  Ther:  = <right.>
05         (0.7)
06  Mar:   and I had five years of it.
07         (0.5)
08  Mar:   °and.° just one day jus sat at the computer an got up,
09         an walked out,
```

```
10          (1.0)
11 Mar:     andt uhm, (0.8) went on long tern disability?
12          (1.5)
13 Mar:     and my boss tried da get me back,
14          (0.8)
15 Mar:     an I couldn't, an (0.6) it took (0.9) u- ↑months and months
16          before I=could walk into an ↑office.
17          (0.5)
18 Mar:     I mean not even=working just walk in ta hand somebody something
19          I would start ta shake.
20          (0.5)
21 Ther:    mm:.
22          (0.6)
23 Ther:    °mm hm.°
24          (1.0)
25 Mar:     °°so°° I(h)'m scared.
26          (0.5)
27 Ther:    <sca:red.> so th- (0.3) scared.
28          (1.3)
29 Ther     mean you say that an there's such a (1.4) kin've a:
         t  looks at m, shrugs, holds clawed hands in front of stomach.
         m                       turns and bobs head back. grimaces, claws hands in
30          ↑shakine[ss in there]
31 Mar:             [↑ooh:.     ]
31 Ther:    or.
         t  shakes hands
```

Marlene has been expressing her concerns about beginning a new job (lines 01–06). She seems to look upon this potential future event with some apprehension because she is uncertain how she will survive it because she knows "`exactly what this (.) this particular job entails`", she has "`been dere. before`" and "`had five years of it.`". Then, in line 08, she opens her story about her previous job experience "`°and.° just one day`", explaining how she suddenly felt the need to leave her job and go on long-term disability and how it took months before she was able to return to work. In line 19, she conveys an affective stance of anxiety by recounting her conduct (`start ta shake.`) and, in line 25, speaks of her emotions (`°°so°° I(h)'m scared.`). This story is different form the former two because, first, Marlene is not pointing out someone's transgression (e.g., someone's conduct that led to her becoming shaky or scared) and, second, she is not really criticizing herself by saying, for example, that she is incompetent, a failure, or an emotional wreck. Instead, she seems to be mainly recounting her dread and fear when she is in this specific work environment. There is, of course, implied diminished agency because she construes herself as not being able to control or master this job situation. In response, the therapist first repeats or *mirrors* the emotional component of Marlene's talk in line 25, thus potentially serving as a request for elaboration (Ferrara, 1994). Yet when no response is forthcoming, the therapist, in line 30, produces a formulation that focuses on the shakiness and fear that Marlene had expressed. The therapist also simultaneously makes a clawed hand gesture in front of her stomach, thus providing visual access to how the fear or shakiness might feel in an embodied sense.

Telling about troubles in a story format has implications that pertain to affective stance and agency. Troubles imply some kind of negative affect and so various emotional expressions will tend to be conveyed during the telling. Clients' troubles tellings also generally do not come with a kind of "resolution" and thus there is often the implication that clients are not able to effectively deal with the trouble. These two resources that are of key importance in storytelling will receive further attention in the following section.

## 5.5 The Teller's Affective Stance[1]

The action a story performs (e.g., to complain, criticize self or express anxiety) and the specific way in which the story becomes discursively designed provides a recipient with access to the teller's unique portrayal of personal experience and, in particular, to the ways in which the teller has positioned her- or himself (and others) in terms of authority, knowledge, affect or identity. A teller's positioning with respect to these various dimensions generally falls under the rubric of *stance* or *stancetaking* (see Jaffe, 2009 for an extensive overview). Interactional approaches tend to view stancetaking as locally occasioned and "emergent." In this way, speakers may take up positions that index differential rights and responsibilities – regarding knowledge, affect, identity and so on – and these positions may be negotiated or even contested in and through talk (Goodwin, 2007; Heritage and Raymond, 2005).

Stories tend to contain explicit evaluative components in which tellers convey their assessments of certain situations, their own personal feelings and their appraisal of others' actions. These evaluative components are generally seen as indexing the teller's *affective* or *emotional stance* (Günthner, 1997; Stivers, 2008) – see also Chapter 4. A wide range of interactional resources for doing affective stance work in stories has already been identified in the literature. These include: story prefaces (Jefferson, 1978; Sacks, 1995b), prosody (Günthner, 1997; Stivers, 2008), "extremely formulated" and metaphorical expressions (Günthner, 1997), reported speech (cf. Drew, 1998; Holt, 2000; Günthner, 1997; Clift & Holt, 2007; Labov, 1972), reenactments (Sidnell,

[1] Although I have already written about affective stance in Chapter 4, this treatment of stance is more specific, dealing with the interactional environment of storytelling.

2006) and facial expressions (Ruusuvuori and Peräkylä, 2009). Stories that involve complaints about a non-present third party (i.e., "complaint stories") have been found to be heavily saturated with evaluative meaning (Drew, 1998; Günthner, 1997). According to Günthner (1997), everyday complaint stories facilitate intense co-alignments between teller and recipient that are characterized by "emotional reciprocity" and "dialogues of indignation."

Successful storytelling requires the cooperative participation of others present. Story recipients need to 1) recognize that a story is about to be launched and that the teller will need to take an extended turn at talk to successfully bring the story to completion and 2) produce a relevant response to the telling, one that displays suitable understanding and affiliation with the story (Bavelas et al., 2000; Coates, 1996; Jefferson, 1978; Lerner, 1992; Mandelbaum, 2013; Sacks, 1974). Stivers (2008) has described two main interactional issues that story recipients need to address when storytelling gets underway. The first involves *aligning* with the in-progress activity of storytelling and the second concerns displaying *affiliation* with the teller's affective stance – see also Chapter 3. Further, these two interactional issues – alignment and affiliation – are managed by different response tokens. Whereas alignment tends to be displayed through vocal continuers such as "mm hm" and "uh huh" (Schegloff, 1982), affiliative responses that claim token access and understanding of the teller's stance are accomplished through nods. Stivers (2008) has also argued that by offering provisional support for the teller's displayed affective stance, nods in mid-telling project "preferred uptake" and a matching of the teller's stance from recipients at story completion. Some attention has already been given to recipient responses following complaint stories in everyday contexts and whether the responses affiliated or disaffiliated with the teller's stance (Couper-Kuhlen, 2012; Günthner, 1997). Affiliative responses included claims of understanding, congruent negative assessments and accounts that justified the teller's stance, whereas disaffiliation was conveyed through factual follow-up questions, minimal responses and withholdings.

The question of how therapists respond to and affiliate with the affective stances conveyed through client stories is an important one. In narrative-informed EFT, stories are viewed as crucial sites in which strong personal bonds between clients and therapists may be created and maintained (Angus and Greenberg, 2011). During psychotherapy, clients disclose distressing personal events and therapists are called upon to empathize with and validate the client's "emotionally permeated" experience. In doing so, emotion-focused therapists work at building and strengthening a collaborative alliance in which the therapist may not only be present as "witness" to the client's troubles, but may also work at shaping and co-editing the client's lived experience (Angus & McLeod., 2004). Thus, an examination of the practices through which therapists draw attention to the affective stances that are implicitly or explicitly conveyed via storytelling will shed important light on how empathic relations may be achieved and how "core emotional themes" emerging from the telling of stories may be developed and transformed.

## 5.6 Agency in Storytelling

Enfield (2017) has argued that agency is centrally tied up with social semiotic elements pertaining to *control* and *accountability*. Some of the key features of control involve the ability to direct and compose one's conduct and accountability pertains to potential evaluations from others and to entitlements and obligations to do a certain behaviour. Agency may be examined at different levels of discourse such as 1) during present, in-the moment conduct; and 2) in reported conduct. In the former, agency can be related to how speakers are directing, composing and accounting for own conduct in the present moment. In storytelling, for example, client agency may be reflected in terms of how clients determine when to tell their story and which story, what aspects to reveal and which to keep hidden. Thus, by telling a version of their story, tellers already exhibit some form of agency. The narrative, however, is also a report of what happened. In this way, tellers' selections or choices may position themselves and others as being more or less agentive within a certain social situation. The Labov and Waletzkian narratives are good examples of how agency may be realized. Tellers recount how they get into a difficult (danger of death) situation and then get out of it or resolve it. Agency, therefore, is expressed in terms of their ability to overcome the odds and come out on top. When clients talk about their troubles in psychotherapy, however, there tends not to be a *resolution* to the trouble. In Extract 5.1, for example, Matt reported that someone from his tennis club perceived him as not playing to his potential and, thus, as having limited agency. In Extract 5.6, Eve claims to always be late and not to have any control over this conduct. Also, in Extract 5.7, Marlene reports not being able to overcome her anxiety and fear of resuming work. Extract 5.8 shows another example of reported diminished agency.

**Extract 5.8:** Trudging along; CCT 020.02

```
01 Eve:  .hh like I should be able to do it differently. I should be
02       able to::.hh °you know° (0.5) get a grip on things an .hh be-
03       strong and creative and have fun and be happy an .hh ha:ve
04       good frie:nds an .hh live a good life and then, you know,
05       and instead I just sort've like- (0.8) trudge along.
      e  moves right hand outwards while tapping index finger up/down
06       (0.7)
07 Ther: °mm hm::.°
```

Eve produces what is termed a self-deprecating action. In general, these are actions that provide a negative appraisal of self, such as "I feel helpless/useless," "I'm always late" and "I'm extremely ugly" (Pomerantz, 1984) – see also Extract 5.6. Her self-deprecating action is expressed in terms of what she *should* be able to do. By framing this as her obligation or her entitlement, she makes herself accountable for not acting differently (e.g., living a good life). The implication here also is one of diminished agency. Because narrative utterances such as self-deprecations are often multi-functional (i.e., make appraisals of self and other and draw implications about agency), it becomes important to examine these actions with respect to how issues of control and accountability become implicated and relevant. This would involve detecting how certain affective stance constructions tend to implicate certain agentic themes (e.g., control, evaluation, entitlement or obligation), how therapists would target these themes in their response and how these themes became points of contention and negotiation in the ensuing discourse.

## 5.7 Therapist Responses to Client Complaint Stories

In the psychotherapy sessions analyzed from the York 1 corpus, most client stories revolved around a particular client "trouble" (see Jefferson, 1988 on "troubles talk") and, more specifically, tended to function as a complaint about a non-present third party (Drew, 1998; Günthner, 1997). The main interactional unit of analysis that will be focused on in this section consists primarily of two sequential slots in which clients would recount a past personal event followed by therapist responses to "hearably complete" tellings; that is, after the teller had produced a *narrative climax* (see Günthner, 1997). Within this sequence, attention will be placed on clients' affective stance displays and on therapist responses that targeted what the client felt during the event – therapist orientations to client agency will be taken up in section 5.8. But because the interest here is on the collaborative construction of stories and emotions, the analytic focus will be extended to include therapist responses in mid-telling and also how clients would respond to therapists in next turn. Thus, within this sequential context of storytelling, particular attention is paid to how the client's displayed affective stance is built up and negotiated and how affiliation around the client's stance is accomplished moment by moment.

In the stories analyzed, although clients would convey an explicit affective stance in which they would complain about others' actions – and often treat them as moral transgressions (see Drew, 1998), the way in which these actions affected the client in emotional terms was left inexplicit. In these contexts, it was found that emotion-focused therapists would respond to the client's telling by drawing attention to what the client felt. Three types of therapist responses were identified that targeted the client's tacit feelings and emotions. These involved *eliciting*, *naming* or *illustrating* the emotional impact of story events on the client. "Illustrating" responses would not only display the strongest form of affiliation with the client's affective stance, but would also garner subsequent affiliation in the client's next turn. By themselves, eliciting responses indexed the weakest form of affiliation and, further, seemed to challenge the "completeness" of the narrative; that is, they created an implication that there is more to the client's story than was said.

### *5.7.1 Eliciting the Emotional Impact from the Client*

Elicitations tended to come in two different formats. In the first, therapists would design their turns as questions that directly prompted the client to identify the emotional impact: "what did you feel?"; "how did it end up leaving you feeling?'. In the second, the therapist would first summarize or provide the gist of the client's stance through a *formulation* (Heritage & Watson, 1979), before eliciting the emotional impact. I argue that the latter format does more affiliative work than the former. Each of these elicitation formats is discussed in the following text.

*Question-elicitation: "What did you feel?".* An example of a therapist response that directly prompts the client to name the emotional impact is shown in Extract 5.9 – part of this dialogue was already shown in Extract 5.1. Here, the client Sofia is recounting a conversation with her mother during a recent visit they made to an outdoor festival. The context for this conversation is that Sofia's husband has rejected her invitation to join them.

**Extract 5.9:** 304.19(4)

```
01 Sofia:  an we were walking the night was beautiful, thah was
02         Monday night.
03 Ther:   yeah.
04         (1.2)
05 Sofia:  AN WHEN I was coming, (1.8) okay? the: uh:m. (0.4) walking, to
06         the car. I tol my mum. mum le digo- m-I- ((lip smack)) mum (0.5)
       s                                             shakes head, smiles
07         sometimes I mix °spanish° .hhh uh mum, ((sniffs)) uh:m,
       t                                         smiles
08         (0.4) >look at the night.< I mean i=was a beau:tiful night
09         ih was [cle:]ar, de stars you cou=see the star, .hh mean dis is
10 Ther:          [euh ]
11 Sofia:  a night to be wis somebody,
12         (1.0)
       s   gazes at T
       t   gazes at S
13 Ther:   °you love.°
       t   inclines head, smiles at S
```

```
14          (0.5)
15 Sofia:   ey(h)eah. (0.7) or you care a lot=about an- an be enj↑oyin.
        s   nod
        t                                     nod
16          I mean .hh ↑walking. (0.6) u::nd uh:m. (1.1) an enjoyin=all
17          ↑thees. this outdoors this: contat with people these
        t                shallow multiple nods----------->
18          firecracker=look a=that. .hhh I mean, (0.4) ah he,
19          an she tells me well, (0.3) I mean ↑dahlin if you wanna do
20          that divorce your h(h)usband an [start] lookin for somebody
21 Ther:                                    [hhh   ]
        t                          smile    laughing
22 Sofia:   ↑else. .hhh eh(h)heh .hhh an I, an- and uh::m.
        t                deep nod
23          (1.1)
24 Sofia:   so we-I went h↓ome,
25 Ther:    yeah.
26 Sofia:   and [uhm.       ]
27 Ther:        [wha=did you] wha- what happened when she said that to you.
28          (1.2)
        t   gazes at S, smiling
        s   gazes at T, smiling
29 Ther:    wha=did you feel.
30          (               3.1               )
        s   gazes at T. S: looks away, loses smile
        t   gazes at S. T: loses smile
31 Sofia:   well the firs=(s)hings that- the firs=(s)hing I- I tol her
32          yes mum. you know, e-everys(h)ing is so easy for you.
        s       fast double nod
```

Sofia begins by conveying some general features of the story's setting: She and her mother were out together walking at night and, further, the night is assessed as "beautiful." From line 06 onwards, she then reports on the dialogue she had with her mother using *direct reported speech*. By quoting what was said, the act of narrating is rendered more vivid or dramatic, thus providing recipients with unique access to the story details and fostering recipient involvement in the story's production (Holt, 2000; Labov, 1972; Schiffrin, 1981; Tannen, 1986, 2007). This is because the direct reported speech does more than merely inform; rather it *shows* the recipient how something was said by portraying the reported speaker in a particular way (such as through the use of prosody or voice quality; cf. Besnier, 1993; Günthner, 1999). At the same time, the marked prosody of the reported utterance makes it possible for tellers to convey their own implicit attitude toward the utterance (Clift & Holt, 2007; Labov, 1972; Schiffrin, 1981), thus creating what Günthner (1999) refers to as a "layering of voices."

Sofia's direct reported speech (`mum ... >look at the night.<`) first constructs a past dialogue in which she calls the mother's attention to her surroundings. Second, it conveys her use of prosodic resources to construct a positive assessment of the night. Her subsequent elaboration further upgrades her assessment by mobilizing a number of descriptive features (`beau:tiful`, `cle:ar`, `you` cou=see the star) and by highlighting the significance of this event as something to be appreciated and shared (dis is a night to be wis somebody). Third, in this reported dialogue, Sofia initiates an assessment sequence or activity in which the mother is invited to affiliate with Sofia's assessment by offering a next – preferably upgraded – assessment (Goodwin and Goodwin, 1987; Pomerantz, 1984). Fourth, Sofia's positive appraisal of the night also invites an assessment relevant action from the therapist. But rather than offering a return assessment, as might be common in contexts of everyday interaction, the therapist in line 13 grammatically extends Sofia's clause in turn-final position with "°you love.°". By doing this, the therapist seems to take an opportunity to re-direct the focus on the husband's absence and on his refusal to have joined them; that is, it is a night that may best be appreciated and shared with "someone you love" and yet her husband had declined to take part. The therapist also smiles while delivering her turn, thus providing Sofia with an opportunity to return her smile and establish affiliation between the two speakers.

Sofia's response to the therapist's extension in line 15 is ambivalent. On the one hand, she offers upgraded agreement by producing an acknowledging "ey(h)eah" and by nodding. But on the other, she seems to resist taking up an alignment with the therapist's attempt at focusing on her husband's absence. Instead, she casts the referent of who may be involved to share the experience in more general terms, "or you care a lot=about", thus allowing a range of people, her mother included, to be potential candidates for sharing. She then goes on to list the various *assessables* (Goodwin & Goodwin, 1987) of which could be enjoyed during that night such as walking, the outdoors, contact with people and the fireworks. Sofia then delivers the mother's response to her initial assessment in the form of direct reported speech (lines 19–22). In this narrative account, the mother's utterance is the so-called climax of the story that represents the potentially complainable aspect of "what happened?" (Drew, 1998; Holt, 2000). The mother's reported response is portrayed as completely ignoring the import of Sofia's prior action and, hence, as not affiliating with her local aim of gaining positive appreciation of the events that they just shared or of their immediate surroundings. Instead, the mother is cast as abruptly shifting topic to Sofia's relationship with her husband and to the possibility of an impending divorce. The prosody used to report the mother's utterance also plays an important role in depicting the inappropriateness of her response. The "well, ... ↑dahlin" seems to portray a deprecating or perhaps a mock innocent tone of voice (see Drew, 1998, p. 321). Sofia's production of laugh tokens (lines 20, 22) during her utterance (h(h)usband, .hhh eh(h)heh .hhh) also renders the mother's response as highly insensitive or even outrageous, and thus, gives the recipient of her story (i.e., the therapist) opportunities to affiliate with the client's assessment of the mother's misconduct. Note that affiliation is successfully displayed at both opportunities: In the first, the therapist responds with a smile and a laugh token (line 21) and in the second, line 22, the therapist nods to display token affiliation with Sofia's affective stance (Stivers, 2008).

After having produced the "punchline" of her story and having secured affiliation with the therapist, Sofia closes off the reported dialogue between her and her mother (`so we-I went h↓ome,`), thus making a bid at ending the story (line 24). CA research has shown that story closings create opportunities for recipients to respond by demonstrating their understanding of the story (Jefferson, 1978; see also Sacks, 1995b on "second stories"), thus displaying greater affiliation with the affective stance built up through the telling (Stivers, 2008). Yet what the therapist does instead is elicit Sofia's reaction to what the mother had said (`wha=did you wha- what happened when she said that to you`). Following a "no response" from Sofia, the therapist reformulates her elicitation to focus more specifically on her feelings (`wha=did you feel.`). This move from the therapist has a number of implications: First, it treats Sofia's story as not-yet-complete; second, it introduces another very important affective dimension to Sofia's story – how she felt when her mother made that insensitive remark; and third, it subtly transforms the affective import of the story from simply "an amusing, outrageous story to tell" to a story in which Sofia may have become emotionally affected and perhaps hurt. The therapist's shift toward what the client might have felt shows an orientation to what Angus and Greenberg (2011) call the *internal narrative mode*: "The *internal* narrative process mode entails the description and elaboration of subjective feelings, reactions, and emotions connected with an event and addresses the question of "what do I feel?" during the event (Angus & Greenberg, 2011, p. 49). The aim is to share feelings with the therapist that are associated with the event in question, which may lead to the articulation of new emotions and understandings during the therapy hour.

There may, however, be certain risks involved in introducing this affective dimension to Sofia's story in this way; that is, the therapist's elicitation works to change the relevance of her story as being about how the mother's comment has affected her emotionally and yet the therapist has done little preparatory work to secure affiliation with Sofia in this regard. We would note that Sofia's response is significantly delayed (line 30) and that when she does respond, she proceeds to complain about her mother rather than discuss the emotional impact. In the next section, we show an example in which the therapist does more affiliative work before launching into her elicitation and demonstrate that this technique seemed to be more successful at getting the client to discuss the emotional impact of the event.

*Formulation preface as a step-wise entry into elicitation.* As shown in Extract 5.9, clients may articulate their affective stance through direct reported speech in which some third party's morally deviant conduct is made evident to the therapist. Another resource that clients may draw from in displaying an affective stance is what Sidnell (2006) has termed *reenactments.*

This involves a teller's re-presentations or depictions of an event and is often realized through non-verbal means involving gestures and facial expressions. Reenactments are also initiated through a "frame shift" in which tellers withdraw their gaze from the other participants in order to make their conduct more visible, *as it happened.* According to Sidnell (2006, p. 383), "gaze, talk and gesture are combined to reenact the event being described." Extract 5.10 (also see Extract 5.3) illustrates how a therapist affiliates with a client's affective stance – realized through the client's reenactment – before launching into an elicitation that targets the emotional impact on the client. In this way, therapists are able to secure affiliation around the client's expressed affective stance before probing the more implicit kinds of emotions that the story event may have set in motion. This extract involves the client named Paula and the story opening of this extract was already shown in Extract 5.3. Prior to her telling, she had noted that her relationship with the man she is currently dating reminded her of how she was mistreated by her father. As an example of this strained relationship, she had previously detailed how she felt unable to approach the man when she found him sitting with a group of people at a cafe. Paula returns to the same situation in this excerpt to discuss his unwillingness to talk to her, despite appearing to be conversing easily with others at the cafe.

**Extract 5.10:** 312.09(6)

```
01 Paula:  ↑we:ll, I guess like one of the things is that. (4.3) uh:(hh)
02         (0.6) this guy, (0.3) doesn't talk to me.
03         (5.7)
        t  shallow nod
04 Paula:  u:h he doesn't, (0.7) want to talk about feelings? (0.8) u:m:,
05         (1.1) or (.) uh- (0.2) about ↑too many things. (1.3) and what
        p                                   shallow nod
06         has happened in the pa- o::h. (.) °it's just (.) such a s::-
        p                             throws head back, looks up
07         uh (.) ridiculous story,°
08         (1.3)
        p  gazes forward
        t  shallow double nod
09 Paula:  and it's, (3.2) like I w- I didn't, (0.9) I don't f:eel like I
10         want to <take o:n like this:> (0.5) nurturing role, this mother
11         role of like- (1.4) tr:ying so hard like to:, to make him: (0.3)
        t  nod
12         talk or make him relax. (0.3) .hh and what- (.) actually
        p                  shallow nod
13         happened this afternoon is, (2.6) that I w(h)alked around this
        p                                         flicks hand out, smiles
14         ↑corner and here he is sitting like in a group of people
        t                                      shallow nod→ multiple nods→
        p                         throws arms out to sides, palms up
15         having obviously no problem talking to ↑them.
        t  continues nodding---------------------------->
16         (0.3)
```

17 Ther: °h:m.°
t *slow double nod→*
18 (2.8)
p *blinks, mouth agape, holds palms up*
t *----->*
19 Paula: and it's just like, (0.8)(h)h:old on a moment (.) here.
p *shallow double nod*
20 (.) like- (0.3) it (0.3) uh(hh).
p *smiles, circles hands in*
t *slow shallow nod----------------->*
21 (0.9)
22 Ther: **somehow that really got to you:,**
p *shakes head*
23 (0.4)
24 Paula: ↑yeah.
p *shallow nod*
25 (0.4)
26 Ther: **°that he has no problem talking to th↓em,°**
27 (1.0)
28 Ther: **.hh >so maybe before you thought well maybe this is just the way**
t *points hand to side. waves hand around*
29 **he i:s< an- .hhh (.) somehow now you see him there totally**
p *fast shallow double nod*
30 **comfortable.**
31 (1.3)
p *fast shallow multiple nods*
32 Ther: **°and wha:t.°**
33 (0.8)
34 Ther: **what did that feel like? (.) somehow,**
35 (1.0)
36 Paula: uh. well it's almost like with my father like. (.) he never,
p *looks away, multiple nods, flips palms up*
37 (0.4) I hh (.) he never talked to me, he never, (.)we never had
p *shakes head*
38 like- (2.2) an honest decent convers↓a:tion, (1.3) with each
p *looks at T*
t *slow shallow ...*
39 other, >where I really could say< well this is what I think
t *... double nod*
40 and this is like how how I feel about it,
41 (1.0)
42 Paula: and this is like the same way I feel:,
43 (1.8)
44 Paula: with this gu:y?

Paula begins with a complaint sequence in which she criticizes her boyfriend's actions – referred to as "this guy"[2] – in terms of what he perpetually fails to do: "doesn't talk to me", "he doesn't, (0.7) want to talk

[2] Sacks (1995b, p. 502) claims that expressions such as "this guy," when used to complain, may function as hostile characterizations of persons; that is, references to "guy" often occur when the person being referred to is not well known, but when the person is, for example, the teller's husband or boyfriend, expressions such as "this guy" may have unfavourable connotations and provides recipients with access concerning the speaker's relationship to this other person.

about feelings". She then, beginning in line 05, launches into a story opening in which she assesses that which she is about to tell as "ridiculous". The story's projected absurdity is further reinforced through her prefaced "o::h" and accompanying body movements of throwing her head back and looking upwards, which together seem to depict a reaction of astonishment. The main event of the story is then told in lines 12–15, when Paula had inadvertently observed her boyfriend casually and easily talking to a group of people at a cafe. By constructing the events of the story in this way, the boyfriend's actions may be seen as an offence or transgression, especially since the boyfriend apparently does not speak to her. While Paula conveys the boyfriend's actions, the therapist offers token displays of affiliation through a series of nods. She also, in line 17, produces a continuer (Schegloff, 1982) that seeks to elicit more talk from the client (see Muntigl & Hadic Zabala, 2008), but may also, due to its realization in "soft voice," be working to resonate with and affiliate with the client's expressed affective stance (Fitzgerald & Leudar, 2010). After the therapist's continuer, the client then produces a reenactment that conveys astonishment or shock through the following non-verbal features: *blinks*, *mouth agape*, *holds palms up*. Immediately thereafter, Paula makes an attempt at expressing her astonishment (it's just like, (0.8) (h)h:old on a moment (.) here), but seems unable to explicitly verbalize how she felt.

At this point, the therapist responds to Paula's talk with a formulation that attends to and offers the gist of Paula's general reaction to the boyfriend's actions (somehow that really got to you:). After having garnered an upgraded confirmation from Paula (line 22), the therapist then elaborates on her formulation by specifying what Paula finds objectionable (°that he has no problem talking to th↓em,°) and then moves on to more explicitly point out Paula's potential worry; that is, his lack of desire to talk may have more to do with her than with his general character. Toward the end of the therapist's turn (lines 29–30), Paula nods enthusiastically, thus displaying token affiliation with the import of what the therapist had said. Thereafter, the therapist selects another turn that works to elicit how this worry may have impacted upon her emotionally (°and wha:t.° (0.8) what did that feel like? (.) somehow,). In this way, the therapist seems to be attempting to get Paula to consider something beyond her initially articulated emotional reaction of astonishment, such as for example feeling sadness or anger that he speaks easily with others but not with her. We see by Paula's response that she does engage with the therapist's prior formulation by pointing to similarities in terms of how her father made her feel; that is, the father also did not talk to Paula. Yet we would also note that by making comparisons with her father, Paula seems to be skirting the issue of the direct emotional impact that these kinds of actions have on her. Thus, it would appear that the therapist's goal of getting Paula to identify how the boyfriend's behaviour makes her feel has not been fully realized.

### 5.7.2 *Naming Client Emotions*

When responding to client storytellings, therapists were also found to put into words how the client may have been affected emotionally from a certain story event. One such practice involves *naming the client emotion* (cf. Pudlinski, 2005), in which therapists would express the emotional impact through clausal constructions such as "you felt X." Examples include: "`so you were just feeling pre:::tty:: frustra:te:d a::nd resigned`"; "`you felt really. (.) ashamed of it`"; "`you musta=been terrified`". These kinds of actions, however, seem to constitute a certain subtype of formulation, but one that is focused specifically on the client's emotional stance display.

In the discussion leading to Extract 5.11, the client Kristina and the therapist have established that Kristina receives no appreciation or support from her husband. Kristina then launches into a story in which she recounts a specific instance of her husband failing to introduce her to one of his students at the opera despite clearly acknowledging the daughter's presence. She designs her story as a complaint sequence that implicitly conveys the moral offence of the husband's actions, but she does not express how his misconduct had affected her.

**Extract 5.11:** 014.01(5)

```
01  Kris:  yeah. .hh an even as I said when we go to the op↑era so it-
02         sometimes it's. very ((clears throat)) (1.2) .hhh uh
03         frustrating to me because uh (0.9) there he would not (1.2) mm.
04         (0.7) v- i'm giving you ye know impressions over the past
05         let's say six years uh, .hhh not just uh most recently. (1.8)
        t  fast multiple nods
06         but e- (0.6) we went once? (0.3) an he met somebody there.
        k  opens palm up
07         (1.1)
08  Kris:  one of his students.
        t  fast shallow multiple nods
09         (0.4)
        t  fast shallow multiple nods
10  Kris:  ((sniffs)) you know from (0.6) uh- ((name of university))
        t                                          fast shallow double nod
11         .hhh and uh, (1.5) uh: su: (0.7) so he would you know dey would
12         °you know.° exchange the formalities whatever? .hhh an then
        t                              shallow double nod
13         he would uh m- ye know push our daughter in fron an he would say
        k                              pushes palm up
14         this is my daughter.
15         (1.1)
16  Kris:  an (0.3) an they- he introduced them and he did not introduce me?
        k               circles hand, inclines head.   hand to chest
17  Ther:  hm:.
        t  shakes head
18  Kris:  which was uh
19         (0.3)
```

```
20  Ther:  you musta felt so sl↑ighted. so(h)[o(h)o? ]
21  Kris:                                    [it's ve]ry bad.
22  Ther:  [yeah::.   ]
23  Kris:  [yeah. very] bad because …
```

At the beginning of the extract, Kristina assesses her general experiences with her husband as frustrating, which then seems to provide the impetus for her to begin her story at line 06. The crux of the story centres around the husband having encountered someone whom he knew at the opera. Kristina gradually provides the therapist with access to who this person was and subtly involves the therapist in co-constructing the person's identity; for instance, in line 06 she mentions that "he met somebody there" and then pauses. The word "somebody" works here as a *prospective indexical* (Goodwin, 1996), signalling that more detail is forthcoming from the speaker. After the pause, Kristina then continues her turn by elaborating with "one of his students" (line 08). It is here that the therapist then begins nodding, thus displaying her understanding of who is being referenced. What follows is another short pause in which the therapist continues to nod. This then leads Kristina to provide yet more information about the student (you know from (0.6) uh- ((name of university))). Thus, it appears that by initially withholding from responding until Kristina had provided more detail and then by responding through nods when added information was presented, the therapist and Kristina worked together to build up an appropriate description of one of the story characters, thus providing more *granularity* to her telling (Schegloff, 2000).

After having described the relevant features of the story setting, Kristina then begins to recount the events leading up to the husband's misconduct: The husband and the student first "exchanged formalities" and then he introduced his daughter to the student. The way in which the husband introduced the daughter deserves some mention. Kristina describes the husband's action as having "pushed" the daughter in front and uses an accompanying gesture to reinforce this physical movement. By pushing, therefore, the husband may be viewed as having applied undue force and, by implication, as being somewhat brutish. The spatial reference to "in front" is also noteworthy, as it implies that she, Kristina, is left "behind" and thus has a lower social standing in the eyes of all conversationalists. Following Kristina's account of what happened is a pause (line 15) in which the therapist could make an assessment-relevant response but does not. This then leads the client to make the husband's transgression explicit: "an (0.3) an they- he introduced them and he did not introduce me?", following which the therapist conveys affiliation through a non-verbal head shake with an accompanying reflective "hm:.". Kristina then, in line 18, begins to produce an action that has the appearance of an emerging assessment (`which was uh`), but stops mid-turn. At this point, the therapist formulates what the client may have felt but also uses prosody and adverbial intensifiers to upgrade the strength of the emotional impact. For example, Kristina did not just feel slighted but "`so slighted`". The adverbial intensifier "so" shows that the therapist herself is partaking in the assessment activity launched by the client (Goodwin & Goodwin, 1987). The use of rise-falling intonation and emphasis also works to draw more attention to what Kristina must have felt at the time (`sl↑ighted.`). Thus, this heightened participation from the side of the therapist in co-constructing the client's affective stance strongly helps to create an account of the husband's action as a moral transgression.

The therapist's response also was successful at securing affiliation from the client in the following turn, as seen from line 21 when the client produced an overlapping assessment that was upgraded in strength (`it's very bad.`). One resource that may have facilitated that is the therapist's use of evidential "`musta`" (i.e., must have), which gave the client a next opportunity to display epistemic authority of her personal experience by, for example, providing upgraded confirmation (Heritage & Raymond, 2005). Another resource is the therapist's prosodically drawn out "so" occurring in turn-final position. Goodwin and Goodwin (1987) have shown that adverbial intensifiers designed in this way give next speakers an opportunity to provide an overlapping assessment. Thus, the way in which the therapist designed Kristina's emotional impact led to increased involvement between therapist and client and also allowed Kristina to take up greater epistemic rights regarding her personal domain of experience.

### *5.7.3 Illustrating Client Emotions*

Another technique for expressing the emotional impact on clients is for therapists to use elaborate or vivid language in illustrating what clients had felt. Rather than naming the emotion, here therapists use graphic terms, metaphorical expressions or non-verbal resources to more vividly convey the feeling that the client may have had. These multi-modal practices work empathically by revealing the therapist's depth of understanding of what the client felt. In doing so, they tend to invite an affiliative response from the client, one that confirms and engages with the therapist's prior turn.

Consider Extract 5.12, which follows a bit later in the session from Extract 5.10. While still on the topic of her boyfriend, Paula tells the therapist about a comment he had made discouraging Paula to become too intimately involved with him. Although Paula's talk clearly conveys the boyfriend's action as indexing a moral transgression, here again she seems unable to clearly articulate her own emotional reaction to the boyfriend's misconduct.

**Extract 5.12:** 312.09(8)

```
01 Paula:  and there- there is uh- (.) u(hh). (0.5) he is- (0.6) there are
02         a:ll these set ups. and it's almost, (0.3) like the same way °as
03         with my father.° .hhh (1.6) uh:m.
04         (2.2)
05 Paula:  °when was this one thing.°
        p  lowers forehead into fingers
06         (6.7)
07 Paula:  o:h. it's just outrageous. (.) i:t's j(h)ust outrageous like-
        p                                     laughing
08         (0.6)
09 Paula:  y(hhh)
10         (10.0)
        p  brings hand to mouth, gazes down
11 Paula:  u:(h)m, (4.2) I guess one of the things was like- (0.4)
12         when we were talking: once about (.) relationships,
13         friendships, .hh (0.8) um. (5.3) he just- (2.3) no.
14         >(h)↑how this was actually very interesting.< .hhh (0.3)
15         he goes (.) <well don't,> (0.4) don't fa:ll:.
16         (0.7)
17 Paula:  I don't want you to fall in love with me:.
        p  multiple nods---------------->
18         (0.3)
19 Paula:  °um,° (0.3) we are just frie:nds.
        p             fast shallow multiple nods
20         (1.5)
21 Ther:   this was this ma:n?
22 Paula:  yeah.=
23 Ther:   = uh °huh.°
        t  multiple nods
24 Paula:  that- that's:: some time ago. =
        p  waves hand out to side
        t  continues nodding
25 Ther:   = mm [hm.]
26 Paula:       [a- ] a fe:w (0.8) °two months ago whatever.° (0.3)
27         .hh and I'm just (0.3) hh (2.1) the:re and I'm thinki:ng,
28         <o(.)ka:y,>
29         (1.6)
30 Paula:  and I couldn't really, I didn't really want to comment
31         on it bec(h)ause >I was just like< (0.5) u(hh) heh .hh (.)
        p                           shakes head.     opens mouth, shakes head
32         what's [going on here.      ]
33 Ther:          [you're just stu:nned]
        p                           looks at T
34 Ther:   sorta like a slap in the face?
35         (0.3)
36 Paula:  yea:h. °e- euh s-° (.) literally.
        p  multiple nods
        t           shallow nod
```

At the beginning of this extract, Paula complains that the boyfriend generally tries to set her up (`there are a:ll these set ups.`) and that this behaviour finds a parallel in her father's behaviour toward her. In line 05,

Paula then does a "memory search" in which she makes a display of trying to recall a past episode of her personal life (°when was this one thing.°), while simultaneously lowering her forehead into her fingers as if "portraying a cognitive process" (Heritage, 2005). Subsequently, Paula then continues with her story opening by making an intensified assessment (just outrageous) of some event that is relevantly tell-able. This assessment, made with accompanying laughter, already provides the therapist with a degree of access regarding Paula's affective stance, thus supplying the therapist with a scaffold in which she may construe and appreciate the upcoming telling.

The moral offence is recounted in lines 17–19 through direct reported speech "I don't want you to fall in love with me:. (0.3) °um,° (0.3) we are just frie:nds.". Note that here, Paula has quoted what the boyfriend had said to her without actually stating what was reprehensible about the boyfriend's actions. According to Drew (1998, p. 321), by deploying quotes in this way, "the complainant leaves the complained-about's words to 'speak for themselves,' as it were. ... Hence the complained-about behaviour is animated in such as way that the recipient can appreciate how rude, unjust and thoughtless the other was, without the complainant needing to categorize the particular offence that was thereby committed." Paula's action, therefore, creates a potential opportunity to negotiate a narrative closing in which the therapist may offer an assessment-relevant response. Instead, the therapist initiates repair by seeking confirmation about the identity of the person who committed the misconduct. The therapist also slightly reformulates the original referent used by Paula in Extract 5.10 (this ma:n vs. this guy) when referring to her boyfriend.

The therapist's withholding from displaying affiliation with the boyfriend's misconduct then seems to set in motion an extended turn in which Paula slightly expands on her narrative. First she specifies the time frame of the story (i.e., about two months ago) and then she provides some insight into how she had responded to her boyfriend. She begins by stating what she thought in non-specific terms (I'm thinki:ng, <o(.)ka:y,>) but then, in line 31, she produces a reenactment that provides the therapist with more access in terms of how she felt. The design of her reenactment is similar in structure to what Sidnell (2006) has observed; that is, the left-side boundary contains a direct reporting verb (I was just like) and the right-side boundary contains the demonstration of the action: opens mouth, shakes head while producing gasping-type sounds. Following the reenactment, Paula then returns her gaze to the therapist while making a meta-commentary that assesses the boyfriend's action (what's going on here.). At this point, the therapist then overlaps Paula's speech by putting Paula's reenactment into words, thus verbalizing how Paula had felt (you're just stu:nned). In the next line, the therapist's language becomes more figurative by drawing an analogy between the boyfriend's words and receiving a "slap in the face." Through her formulation, the therapist displays a strong understanding of the emotional impact that the boyfriend's words had. Paula, in line 33, offers upgraded confirmation, thus displaying affiliation to the therapist's understanding of how the boyfriend's conduct may be viewed as a moral offence.

When engaging with the lived experience conveyed through the client's story, therapists may also draw from non-verbal resources such as gesture to more graphically display the emotional impact on the client. Consider Extract 5.13 with the client Kristina in which she recounts an incident involving her husband that she considered offensive.

**Extract 5.13:** 014.13(1)

```
01  Kris:  let me think about(h) huh .hh my quarrels. .hhh (0.6) uh: for de
02         last week,
03         (11.1)
04  Kris:  don't remember any big quarrel, ah don't reca:ll.
        t                                           double nod
05         (      1.0         )
        t  shallow double nod
06  Kris:  uh:. (0.5) except uh:. a rema:rk of my husband which I found also
07         very. uh offensive.
08         (1.1)
09  Kris:  uhm.
10         (4.4)
11  Kris:  an I don=know what I said.
12         (3.0)
13  Kris:  but it was m- more a joke than anything else.
14         (1.1)
15  Kris:  uh.
16         (4.8)
17  Kris:  uh- not a- not a joke or something uohm, (1.2) let's say
18         I=would ask him to move in de sof- move on de sofa
19         little bit. (0.2) more to the s- something.
        t      multiple nods
        k                    shallow multiple nods→
20         you kno[w uh:m,] totally (1.2) uh (1.1) °like° everyday talk?
21  Ther:         [mm hm, ]
        k  -------------->
        t  double nod
22         (1.1)
        k  looks away
        t  fast shallow multiple nods
23  Kris:  an he- he would uh. get- he- he got upset, (1.2) an he said
24         oh uh:. (3.1) if I am::. (1.1) sending him: back to work?
25         (0.6) like let's say in the evening. instead of watching
        k  tilts head, tilts hand side to side
        t  slow nod---------------------------->
```

```
26          television or something dat I would uh be sending.
       t                                          shallow double nod
27          (0.4)
28  Kris:   >uh he=said.< .hhh uh should I go: uh::m. (1.3) back (0.4) to
29          translate or. to de computer whatever, .hhh an:. an then
       t     slow nod
30          he said OR I will. (0.8) take an axe and will: chop(h)
       k    holds hand up. K: flips hand back, chops fist across
31          everything into pieces.
       k                       looks away
32          (0.5)
33  Ther:   °°hm.°°
       t    nod
34  Kris:   so. so=I don't really know what to say (anaymore.)
35          (1.1)
36  Kris:   mm. occasions °like=that.°
37          (0.8)
38  Ther:   so sounds like that kina s:topped you cold it kina
       t                                         throws fist down
39          (0.7)
       k    bobs head back, shakes head
40  Kris:   [absolutely. yeah.     ]
41  Ther:   [almost like kina .hhh]
       t                         sharp inbreath, bobs head back
42  Ther:   hold your (0.6) breath [an not know wh]at ta hm
43  Kris:                          [mm       m.   ]
       t                                                slow nod
       k                                   shallow nod
44          (1.0)
45  Kris:   ((lip smack)) zis h↑orrible. it's really horrifying.
       k    bobs head back, lowers eyebrows, shakes head, looks down
```

At the beginning of this excerpt, Kristina produces a potential story opening in which she recalls an offensive remark made by her husband (lines 06–07). Immediately thereafter, she downplays her own role in this incident by *defensively detailing* her own conduct (Drew, 1998); for example, first she claims not to have remembered what she said (line 11), then she refers to it as a joke (line 13) and, finally, casts her initial comment to her husband as "°like° everyday talk?" (line 20). Thus, Kristina's request for the husband to "move over on the sofa a little bit" is formulated to be construed as innocuous and certainly not as warranting an upset reaction from the husband. But then in lines 23–27, Kristina provides the husband's perspective by revealing his rationale for being upset; that is, the husband felt that she was sending him back to work in the evening, rather than letting him watch television. Afterwards, in line 28 onwards, Kristina shifts into direct reported speech to proceed with her story. First she elaborates on his response that accuses her of trying to send him back to work (>uh he=said.< .hhh uh should I go: uh::m. (1.3) back (0.4) to translate or. to de computer whatever,) and then produces the climax of her story by reporting his potentially serious and violent remark (`I will. (0.8) take an axe and will: chop(h) everything into pieces.`). Toward the end of her turn in line 31, Kristina looks away from the therapist thus possibly indicating that her story has come to a close. Here, as with most of the previous examples, the client reports on the speech of someone else but does not herself explicitly assess others' talk. Instead, others' talk is treated as a straightforward moral offence that does not seem to need further comment.

Although the therapist could, at this point, start engaging with the client's affective stance by exploring the emotional impact of the husband's remark, she adopts a different approach. Instead, the therapist first withholds from responding and then produces a quiet-voiced continuer (`°°hm.°°`) that is accompanied by a single moderate nod. Through this practice, the therapist seeks to elicit more granularity from the client in order for her to more fully develop her affective stance – compare Extract 5.10 involving the client Paula in which a different therapist uses the same practices to elicit Paula's reaction to her boyfriend's misconduct. As a result, Kristina offered more granularity to her description by describing her husband's effect on her (`I don't really know what to say (anaymore.) … mm. occasions °like=that.°`). This extra detail from the client in which she provides more specific access to her affective stance leads the therapist into producing an explicit assessment relevant response in which she affiliates with the client's inability to respond to her husband. What is noteworthy is the range of interactional resources that the therapist draws from to make Kristina's stance more explicit and to show how she understands Kristina's reaction to the husband's remark. Her use of metaphors such as "`s:topped you cold`" and "`hold your (0.6) breath`", her deep inbreath and her "clenched fist" gesture depicting the fall of the axe provide the client with explicit access to how the therapist understands the effect of the husband's offence on Kristina. By upgrading the detail of the event in this manner, the therapist may be taking a risk in that it may be demonstrating greater or "expert" access to Kristina's feelings. But, several points may speak against that. First, the therapist repeatedly downgrades her formulations with "kina" and "almost" and, second, she receives affiliative displays from Kristina during her turn-in-progress; for example, during the brief silence in line 37, Kristina seems to be showing strong affiliation with the therapist's response when she bobs her head back and shakes her head; and, following that, she displays additional affiliation by offering upgraded confirmation (line 38) and by nodding (line 40). Thus, by continuously monitoring Kristina's affiliation, the therapist may be encouraged to continue with her detailed expressions of empathy. As a third point, we note that the therapist's responses seem to fully align with Kristina's viewpoint; that is, the expressions "stopped you cold" and "hold your breath" develop the client's emotive reactions of being unable to speak during these encounters with her husband and, in this way, preserve her ownership of that experience. At the end of this extract, Kristina then produces an upgraded assessment (`it's really horrifying`) that is further strengthened through her non-verbal displays (*bobs head back, lowers eyebrows, shakes head, looks down*). Thus, it appears that the therapist has been successful in not only accurately identifying what the client had felt, but also in getting the client to strongly endorse and engage with the therapist's formulation of the emotional impact.

## 5.8 Therapist Responses that Orient to Agency

In the complaint stories examined so far, the clients generally did not explicitly convey their emotional stance, or more specifically, their emotional reaction to another's misconduct. Sofia did not mention how her mother's insensitive remark affected her and both Paula and Kristina did not convey in words how their partner's transgressions were hurtful. There is also an implicit aspect of agency that surfaces from these narratives; that is, clients narrate situations in which someone wrongs them and they, in turn, do not seem able to act on the misconduct by, say, confronting the transgressor. Although therapists would generally orient to the client's unarticulated emotional response to misconducts in complaint narratives, there were cases in which therapists would instead focus on clients' inability to challenge the wrongdoer. In Extract 5.14, the client Marlene has been complaining that she is the victim of others' transgressions and that she is constantly "`getting slapped in the ↑face.`" (not shown in transcript). Then, at the beginning of the extract, she produces a number of complaint/victim narratives in series, but rather than respond to the client's emotions or how she feels, the therapist focuses on the other's transgressor role and on Marlene's diminished agency in these situations.

**Extract 5.14:** 407.09(2)

```
01  Mar:   e- well and- and I hate ta do that. (.) >I hate ta say that.<
02         because all=ah can hurr in the back, hh is my husman going
03         ↑y'always feel like a victim. ↑y'always feel like a victim.
        m  nasal voice, shakes head around, sneers ------>
04         ye know ↑poor ↑little ↑Marlene. ↑you're always a victim. .hhh
        m  ------------------------------------------------->
05         an that's (.) what I hear all the time.
06         (0.7)
        t  shallow double nod
07  Mar:   ((lip smack)) but (1.4) that's way I ↑see it. ah-
08         I jus can't see it any other way.
        m  shallow multiple nods---->
09         (0.5)
        t  ---->
10  Ther:  mm hm,
        t  ---->
11  Mar:   so that ye know uh, if I talk ta my husband about ih- (.)
```

12 like something serious that's bothering me he (0.3)
*m fast multiple nods->*
*m shakes hand*
13 the middle=of my conversation he just turns aroun an wa:lks away.
*m shakes hand*
14 ( 0.9 )
*m widens eyes, opens mouth, shakes head*
15 Mar: (h)an i'm just (0.6) oka:y?
16 (0.6)
17 Mar: an my kids, ye know I say=aw ye know I sa=oh well I went ta see my
18 mother an she didn't know me.
*m looks at T, nods*
19 (0.6)
20 Mar: and (0.5) I mean I- I almost had a- an anxiety attack g- driving
*m shaky voice, shakes head*
21 an I didn=even realize what was happening
22 they=go .hhh ↑well ↑fer ↑heaven's sakes=shu know
23 it's coming fer- you know, so .hh why be so upset about it.
*m shrugs repeatedly, shakes head.*
24 an they walk ↓away?
*m looks at T, flips hand out*
25 Ther: mm=hm.
26 (0.4)
27 Mar: an
28 ( 1.0 )
*m shakes head, holds palm up*
29 Ther: **so somehow fer you it- ah mea[n:.]**
30 Mar: [hhh]
*t points hands inward*
31 (0.7)
32 Ther: **n- nobody's really listening to the fact that you are upset**
**[an. ]**
33 Mar: [that's]
*t circles hand leans forward multiple nods*
34 Mar: right like ↑somebody listen.
*m looks down, flips palm up*
.
.
.
35 Mar: an (0.6) that's like (0.7) n- ye know. an then
*m smiles, throws hands out, shakes head*
36 I get=a- a- a- phonecall .hhh I- on- on my answering machine
*m shakes head shrugs holds palms up*
37 because I- I .hh called an agency?
38 (0.3)
39 Mar: cause they had a perfect job in the paper=an
40 i've already applied to them,.hhh an she gets on,
*m shakes head, flips palms up*
41 ye- I mean she=was on the answering machine=say'ng=well,
42 ((lip smack)) your skills aren't really qualified
*m claps hands, shakes head, looks up*
43 an you're not this an you're not that an you're not this an.
*m bobs head to sides,*
44 ((lip smack)) uhm uh if we have anything else ye know we'll

```
45           call you an- an bang.
        m          flicks hand towards T
46           (       2.0         )
        m    opens palms to sides
47  Mar:     an I go oh my god. (.) every which way I ↑turn.
        m    covers cheeks with hands, shakes head, holds hands up.
48           (0.5)
49  Mar:     it's like the doors are like ↑closing.
        m              clasps hands           shakes head
50           (       1.2         )
        m    shallow multiple nods
51  Mar:     [and   ]
52  Ther:    [so rea]lly feeling trapped a[n:    there's no] way out.
53  Mar:                                  [o(h)h it's just,]
        t                                shallow double nod
        m                                  closes eyes, opens mouth wide
54           (            0.2             )
        m    lowers eyebrows, shakes head
55           that's ↑right.
        m    shakes head
```

Marlene begins this excerpt by berating her husband for his belittling tendency: "ye know ↑poor ↑little ↑Marlene. ↑you're always a victim.". Then, in lines 05–08, she complains that she is always being told this and that she is unable to perceive her situation differently. This then sets the stage for a couple of narratives in which she exemplifies others' maltreatment of her. She begins with a short narrative involving the husband, lines 11–15, in which he just walks away from her during a serious conversation. Following this is a pause in which she produces a series of non-vocal actions that convey her emotional reaction to the misconduct (line 14): *widens eyes*, *opens mouth*, *shakes head*. This conduct is very similar to Paula's non-vocal reactions to her boyfriend's transgressions in Extracts 5.10 and 5.12, as is her subsequent verbal reaction "(h)an i'm just (0.6) oka:y?". But following no response from the therapist in line 16, Marlene continues with another complaint narrative involving her children. Here, the client recounts a distressing episode in which she goes to visit her mother who no longer recognizes her. When she tells her children, however, she describes their callous response via direct reported speech as ".hhh ↑well ↑fer ↑heaven's sakes=shu know it's coming fer- you know, so .hh why be so upset about it." After basically challenging the severity of the situation and, further, the mother's right to be upset about it, Marlene then recounts how they simply leave her to deal with this distressing event by herself (line 24). The word initial falling pitch and word final rising pitch on "↓away?" seem to convey complete incomprehensibility on Marlene's part, that her children would be so utterly unsupportive. There is again, at this point in the sequence, an opportunity for the therapist to respond to Marlene's complaint. What happens, however, is that the therapist first offers an acknowledgement that conveys passive recipiency (mm=hm.). This is then followed by a pause, Marlene's brief attempt to continue her turn (an) and another pause in which Marlene shakes her head and makes a open palm gesture that may be conveying a request for the therapist to display some form of emotional support, by taking up an empathic opportunity or something else. In line 29, the therapist begins her turn by first drawing attention to how the client may be experiencing this (so somehow fer you it-), but then self-repairs (ah mean:.) and focuses the attention on the other's behaviour instead (n- nobody's really listening to the fact that you are upset). In contrast to the other extracts, the therapist does not attempt to elicit the client's feelings, formulate the emotion or illustrate it. Rather, the therapist formulates the misconduct (nobody's really listening) and, in a way, underscores the client's experiences of helplessness, diminished agency and tendency not to get help in these situations of upset.

A bit later, Marlene resumes with another narrative that conveys helplessness in her everyday life. She recounts an incident when a woman from a job agency called her back and left a message on her answering machine. The response was negative, with the person stating that she was not at all qualified (line 42) and that she was lacking in many skills (an you're not this an you're not that an you're not this an.). The end of the call is described as terminating abruptly, "an- an bang.', which seems to reinforce the harshness in which this news was being delivered. Following this, in line 46, is a 2-second pause in which Marlene makes open palm gestures with both hands as if to say "what can I do?', possibly conveying her powerlessness in this situation. At this place in sequence, the therapist could respond to Marlene's narrative but withholds from doing so. Thus, Marlene resumes her turn with a response cry "an I go oh my god." (Goffman, 1981), while simultaneously covering her cheeks with both hands, which seems to convey shock and astonishment at what had happened. She then continues by emphasizing not only her helplessness to act but also the hopelessness of having these events change in the future "every which way I ↑turn. it's like the doors are like ↑closing." At this point in the conversation, line 50, the therapist has choices in which to respond, for example, clarifying the client's affective stance in terms of how she feels when people do not listen or do not value her qualities or basic human needs. But perhaps because Marlene has oriented so strongly to her powerlessness in these contexts, the therapist in line 50, following a significant pause, orients to her diminished agency with regard to her ability in changing her circumstances: "so really feeling trapped an: there's no way out'.[3]

Thus, this extract has shown how, by closely following the client's construction of her narrative, therapists may be given materials to connect with clients that do not necessarily involve how clients felt in a certain situation. In this case, it was the client's diminished agency brought on by others who do not listen to her. This does not mean that the client's emotions are not relevant here, but it may mean that it was at this time more productive to affiliate with the client's experience of diminished agency first, before exploring how she generally feels when these events occur.

## 5.9 Conclusions

From an EFT standpoint, a change process gets underway when clients – with the help of therapists – are able to work with their emotions. The client's exploration of intense feelings of vulnerability and emotional pain may also have an added benefit of providing a context of safety and a sense of trust in the client's conversational partner, the therapist. Investigations that have addressed the interrelationship between storytelling and emotion processes in EFT treatments for depression have established that the transition toward a more emotionally differentiated view of personal experience seems most successful when it was first preceded by the client's active exploration of their own experiential responses to a personal story disclosure (Angus, 2012; Angus et al., 2012). Further, these transitions toward a more in-depth understanding of how one's emotions are coupled to own experience are argued to stimulate the emergence of new and more elaborate perspectives on self and others in the world (Angus & McLeod, 2004).

Clients draw from a wide range of interactional resources to build up their affective stance and, subsequently, therapists can work with the client's prior affective displays in different ways. It has been observed that in everyday complaints, storytellers often report their overt reaction to another's misconduct by expressing their outrage (Günthner, 1997; Drew, 1998). Depressed clients from the York 1 sample, however, would repeatedly refrain from considering how they felt in response to someone else's wrongdoing. In other words, although clients were able to construct a well-defined stance by fully elaborating on another's moral transgression, what seemed to be missing is a clearly articulated statement of how these transgressions affected them, the clients. Confronted with these specific affective stance displays, emotion-focused therapists would respond by targeting the emotional impact brought

[3] Although the therapist responses also convey emotional impact (you are upset; really feeling trapped), I would argue that they are embedded within the main action of formulating the client's powerlessness in these situations.

on by the misconduct. Within EFT, therefore, indicating "how I felt" is treated as an essential component of a telling and when this is not mentioned, it will be oriented to by therapists as relevantly absent. Further, by construing themselves as a victim of another's moral transgression, clients reveal the lack of control that they have in important personal situations and this finding is consistent with the general claim made in psychotherapy research that depressed clients portray themselves as helpless and as having low agency (Angus & Greenberg, 2011).

Therapists are able to draw from different response types when focusing on the client's emotions – eliciting, naming and illustrating. These responses display varying degrees of affiliation with the client's prior affective stance displays, with *eliciting* conveying the lowest and *illustrating* the highest amount of affiliation. In fact, eliciting practices on their own could even be regarded as *disaffiliative* because they do not directly engage with the client's affective stance. Instead, they reposition the affective focus toward how the client felt, often in contexts where the client had laid prime emphasis on another's moral offence. Therapist elicitations in these contexts may be revealing an orientation to the *balance hypothesis* (Bänninger-Huber & Widmer, 1999), in which therapists find themselves in a dilemma of having to challenge clients somewhat while still providing some degree of affiliation. The challenge here would be to momentarily turn the prime focus away from the other (e.g., their misconduct) and focus instead more on the client and the emotional impact of others' behaviour. A more productive way of dealing with this interactional dilemma and to achieve "balance" occurs when therapists preface their elicitation with a formulation that displays empathy with the client's grievance. With this practice, therapists could secure affiliation around the complaint before launching into an elicitation that targeted the client's feelings. On the other end of the affiliation continuum, illustrating responses often used vivid/descriptive language, metaphors or gestures to reveal the therapist's intricate grasp and appreciation of the story's emotional impact on the client. By establishing an empathic context in which therapists demonstrate their understanding of the client's emotions, illustrating responses – but also naming responses – seem to create a next opportunity for clients to offer affiliation with the therapist's turn through upgraded forms of confirmation. Elicitations, by contrast, prompt clients to perform additional affective work, rather than primarily confirm or affiliate with the therapist's prior action. Naming the client's emotion also does not always lead to an affiliative uptake by the client; that is, clients at times would disagree with the therapist's reading of how the client felt, thus compelling the therapist to repair the disaffiliative moment at the next opportunity – see some examples in Chapter 7 where therapist emotional naming responses were met with disagreement. It seems, therefore, that illustrating responses operate effectively at establishing and reinforcing a shared context of affiliation between the therapist and client. With this response type, therapists are in a strong position to not only develop the emotional facets of the client's emerging story, but to also secure the client's endorsement of the therapist's displayed understanding of the client's lived experience.

# 6 Chair Work

## 6.1 Overview

Person-centred therapies tend to operate within a client's epistemic domain by being attuned to the client's ownership of personal knowledge and experience. Such therapies are inclined to be *non-directive* as they place a premium on what clients are saying and offer validation and support to clients' emotional distress. Certain therapies within the person-centred paradigm such as emotion-focused therapy (EFT), however, make systematic use of different interactional styles (Greenberg, 2010). In the non-directive style, EFT therapists *follow* the client's internal experiences by remaining within the bounds of what clients have said and felt and by heightening awareness of and validating their emotions. What is meant here is that when clients portray their personal experience of troubles or upset, as for example through storytelling, therapists would *follow clients* through practices of affiliation such as by displaying understanding/empathy through formulations rather than offering up their own interpretations or challenging the client's viewpoint. Emotion-focused therapists also make use of a more directive style, hence *leading* the client, by selecting and facilitating a particular process-guiding intervention targeted to resolving an identified emotional processing difficulty in adaptive ways (Elliott and Greenberg, 2007; Goldman et al., 2006; Greenberg, 2014).

The practices of both following and guiding the client during therapy make it incumbent on EFT therapists to appropriately navigate two central domains of interaction. The first refers to *epistemic rights* and *responsibilities* (Heritage & Raymond, 2005) and the second to *deontic entitlements* (Stevanovic and Svennevig, 2015). Whereas the former involves the degree of authority participants have with respect to rights and access to knowledge and personal experience, the latter concerns a speaker's authority to guide or direct others to do things. Thus, by following their clients, therapists are often attuned to clients' epistemic entitlements and their primary rights and access to *own* their experiences. In contrast, guiding clients orients more to deontic concerns of getting clients to engage in EFT tasks. One such task that plays a central part in doing EFT is called *chair work* (Greenberg, 1979, 2002) and more recently *chair task intervention* (Angus and Greenberg, 2011). Chair work involves a mediated dialogue between the client and a "personified vacant chair" that is occupied in an imagined sense by a non-present "significant other" or a conflicting aspect of self. During chair work, the client strives to re-engage with an unresolved, problem-laden interpersonal situation in a kind of role-play, giving voice, in turn, to different aspects of a two-sided internalized conflict ("split"): The "empty-chair" variant most often involves a relationship with a significant other person, while the two-chair version most often focuses on two (or more) alienated aspects of self within the client, commonly referred to as "splits,"[1] In all instances, the goal is to bring the deep-seated unresolved/split dynamics into the present, here-and-now, of the therapy session, and to help the client move toward resolution or accommodation of the "split" elements (Greenberg & Higgins, 1980). Because chair work is an expressive, here-and-now enactment that uses imagery and active expression, it is often accompanied by the activation and intensification of painful emotions. For this reason, hesitation, performance anxiety, shame, and/or awkwardness may be associated with this task. As a consequence, some clients may not feel "ready" – or *are reluctant to engage in the task* – to participate in what can be an unfamiliar and emotionally intensifying experience. It is for this reason that securing clients' active endorsement and collaboration to participate in activities, such as engagement in chair work, is a core mission in EFT. Thus, a dual-tracked objective in this therapy is the negotiation between therapist and client to move beyond such reluctance to potentially effective therapy activities and, at the same time, maintain positive relational affiliation between therapist and client.

In this chapter, I explore how emotion-focused therapists secure affiliation with clients to engage in chair work. It will be shown that chair work entry is regularly accomplished through four distinct interlocking interactional phases and, thus, that affiliation is required at each phase of the process. Each of the phases were found to align with certain interactional challenges involving either epistemic or deontic entitlements (see also Smoliak et al., 2021). Epistemically, the therapeutic interaction focuses first on gaining client confirmation about what is experientially and emotionally relevant for the client. On the deontic side, therapists and clients then negotiate rights regarding who has authority in deciding whether chair work should be done. Successful initiation of chair work is predicated on the client's approval or consent toward a therapist's proposal for action. It is argued that chair work involves the delicate interplay between both deontic and epistemic orientations in which

[1] For a fuller description of techniques involving the chair, see Perls (1973), Elliott and Greenberg (2007) and Greenberg et al. (1993).

therapists and clients must first work out epistemic concerns before moving forward toward deontic ones. Thus, failure to gain client confirmation or agreement will impede or delay chair work entry. Thus, to successfully accomplish each of these phases, and for moving forward, it becomes necessary for therapists to secure affiliation from clients for each step of the process. I also demonstrate how chair work is an embodied activity that relies strongly on co-ordinated bodily actions for its achievement. When clients are mobilized to speak with a personified vacant chair, therapists and clients draw on a range of non-verbal, bodily resources such as gaze, hand gestures and facial expressions to enter into new participation frameworks and to facilitate intersubjective understandings pertaining to what *is* being done now or what *will* sequentially follow.

## 6.2 EFT and Chair Work

The foundation of EFT's therapeutic effectiveness is emotional support inside therapy following three person-centred emotion processing principles: increasing awareness of, enhancing regulation of, and transforming emotion (Greenberg, 2004). Greenberg (2010) outlines the three stages of treatment within EFT. Stage one is developing a therapeutic bond, understanding the client's story, and building emotional awareness; stage two is evoking and discovering core maladaptive emotion schemes; and the final transformative stage is constructing alternative emotional experiences and new narrative meaning making. In-session activation of maladaptive emotion schemes are evidenced by indicators of emotional processing difficulties that prompt process-guiding therapist responses, as well as signal the client's possible *in-the-moment* readiness to work on a specific problem and implementation of chair task interventions (Greenberg, 2010, 2014). These interventions, which are usually implemented in stages two and three, draw from techniques and principles rooted in gestalt therapy and psychodrama (Perls et al., 1951; Yablonsky, 1976). Chair task interventions have been adapted and developed within EFT to provide a framework within which clients can "activate and experience the affective base of their self-organizations in conflict" (Pos and Greenberg, 2012, p. 89); reduce indecision, self and marital conflicts, and interpersonal difficulty (Wagner-Moore, 2004); and uncover and tap into negative or unresolved emotions with regard to self or significant other (Goldman et al., 2006). Importantly, chair task interventions help clients to access healthy primary adaptive emotions, needs and action tendencies (= emotional transformation). Two forms of chair task interventions are *two-chair* work and *empty-chair* work.

### 6.2.1 *Type 1: Two-Chair Task Intervention for Self-Criticism or Self-Interruption*

Two-chair work targets aspects of the client's relationship with self. Described as two parts of self in an internal struggle (Clarke and Greenberg, 1986; Greenberg, 2010; Wagner-Moore, 2004), these conflicts stand in the way of "the full expression of a more adaptive and fundamental aspect of self" (Elliott et al., 2004, p. 220). In-session, two types of emotional conflicts may prompt two-chair work: 1) events involving self-criticism that reveal an inner critic who denigrates or bullies another part of the self, referred to as the "experiencing self" (Pos and Greenberg, 2007); and 2) events involving self-interruption that reveal one part of self as interrupting, restricting emotional expression, or disowning parts of self (Mackay, 2011; Pos and Greenberg, 2007).[2] Once such emotional conflicts are identified, the client is guided to alternatively assume and keep separate the two parts of self engaged in this inner turmoil. One self is assigned to the experiencing chair from which he/she expresses needs, wants, and deep-seated instinctual emotions, along with expressing how it feels to be criticized. The other self is assigned to the inner critic chair from which he/she speaks from a critical perspective, often using "should" language and negative self, parental or societal evaluations (Greenberg, 2010; Wagner-Moore, 2004).

### 6.2.2 *Type 2: Empty-Chair Work for Unfinished Business*

Empty-chair work for unfinished business is implemented when the client attunes to long-standing or unresolved feelings or unmet needs toward a "significant other" (e.g., spouse, parent, business partner), and is generally used for two categories of emotions: one relating to neglect or abandonment; and a second relating to abuse or trauma (Paivio and Pascuale-Leone, 2010). As with two-chair work, the therapist empathically follows the client's experience and guides by facilitating a dialogue between self and significant other, who is brought into the session in an imaginary sense, channelled through an empty chair. To maintain a necessary division between self and other, the client switches chairs, alternating between presenting their own perspective and that of the significant other. Guided by the therapist, the client dialogically processes experiences and emotions and comes to be better able to assert themself, to understand, to forgive, and/or to hold the significant other to account (Goldman et al., 2006; Wagner-Moore, 2004).

[2] In EFT terminology, these would be referred to as specific *problem markers* (Angus & Greenberg, 2011; Greenberg et al., 1993), which work to guide process-directive interventions, such as chair work.

## 6.3 Participation Frameworks in Chair Work

In getting clients to enter into chair work, therapists and clients must shift into a new activity and, further, they must accommodate new and modified speaker roles. A conversation analytic (CA) study of two-chair work to perform a self-soothing task has shown how Goffman's (1981) work on *framing* and *footing* may be particularly helpful in conceptualizing the chair work activity (Sutherland et al., 2014). To begin, chair work involves movement into a different *participation frame* and, hence, speaker actions will be understood with respect to this new frame. For instance, Sutherland et al. (2014) refer to therapist–client dialogue as occurring within the *ordinary frame*, whereas self-soothing talk related to chair work as the *soothing frame*. Further, therapists and clients construct different stances or footings with respect to each other and their utterances. For example, chair work involves bringing in an additional non-present participant, giving clients two different potential addressees to which they may direct their talk. In addition, therapists tend to adopt a different conversational role during chair work, as they do not directly participate in the client–chair dialogue, but rather observe and guide the client to speak.

## 6.4 Deontics: Stance and Status

Getting others to do things is a pervasive activity in social interaction. These action types, commonly referred to as *directives*, involve some future event or task to be accomplished, orient to speakers' rights and responsibilities, and make relevant some form of acceptance or compliance by the recipient or commitment to carry out the task (Couper-Kuhlen, 2014). Various additional pragmatic dimensions are important to consider when examining directive environments, especially involving imperative formats, such as participant role distributions (e.g., who is the agent? who benefits from doing the action?), the relation to the ongoing activity and the degree of immediacy or urgency (Sorjonen et al., 2017). Directives may include a variety of action types such as requests, commands, proposals, or suggestions (Couper-Kuhlen, 2014; Landmark et al., 2015; Stevanovic and Svennevig, 2015). The ways in which directives are formulated (e.g., the expressions, words used to design the directive) tend to orient to certain kinds of general principles that involve *entitlement* and *contingency* (Drew & Couper-Kuhlen, 2014) – for a related discussion, see Chapter 2. For example, the degree of entitlement to direct another's actions (e.g., assigning homework, giving advice concerning a problem) is often realized in the linguistic design of the directive, such as whether imperative or declarative formats or whether certain modality markers (e.g., will, would, could, should) are used (Craven & Potter, 2010; Heinemann, 2006). These displayed sensitivities to the speakers' role relationships have also been shown to take account of the participants' agency with regard to who is being mobilized to act, including who will potentially benefit from the future action, if carried out (Clayman and Heritage, 2014; Drew and Couper-Kuhlen, 2014). There may also be various reasons for which a recipient may refrain from complying with the directive. Thus, a speaker can orient to these contingencies by delivering the directive in a format less likely to be refused. For example, prefacing a directive with "I wonder" displays that the recipient may have other (perhaps better) options (Curl & Drew, 2008), and this sensitivity to the other's concerns can make it easier for the recipient to accept the terms of the directive. How speakers design their directives will also be predicated on what Rossi (2012) has termed "low cost" vs. "high cost" actions. Thus, therapists will presumably not need to do much discursive work in getting their clients to "take a seat," but for "higher cost" actions, such as getting clients to engage in chair work, presumably more work will need to be done.

More recently in CA work, this broad spectrum of actions that involves directives (but also *commissives*, such as offers and invitations) has been examined under the general rubric of *deontics*, and more specifically *deontic stance* and *deontic status* (Stevanovic & Peräkylä, 2014). According to Stevanovic and Svennevig (2015, p. 2), "Deontic stance refers to the participants' public ways of displaying how authoritative or powerful they are in certain domains of action relative to their co-participants, and deontic status denotes the relative position of authority and power that a participant is considered to have or not to have, irrespective of what he or she publicly claims." Further, entitlement and contingency hold a central place within this framework for understanding how these kinds of (authoritative) role relationships are negotiated turn by turn.

Directive sequences are commonly found in therapeutic approaches. For example, in chair work, a technique that is regularly used in EFT and gestalt therapies, therapists need to recruit clients into this activity, *in situ* (Muntigl et al., 2017; Smoliak et al., 2021; Sutherland et al., 2014). In cognitive behavioral therapy (CBT), therapists often make proposals to clients for homework or future behavioral change (Ekberg & LeCouteur, 2015).

## 6.5 The Four Phases of Chair Work Entry

A consistently occurring overall interactional trajectory has been found for successful first-time entry into chair work. This refers to either first time for the therapy or first-time entry within a given session.[3] This trajectory comprises

[3] A different trajectory for initiating chair work has been proposed for the smooth step-wise entry into a directive (Smoliak et al., 2021): 1) T's *Wh*-question; 2) C's answer; 3) T's directive; 4) C's compliance. The extracts presented in that study, however, appear to involve chair work dialogues already in progress and not first time entries.

four distinct phases: 1) *formulating the trouble*; 2) *recruiting participation in chair work*; 3) *readjusting the participation frame*; and 4) *making contact*. Each phase is marked by specific EFT practices of following or guiding the client, thus orienting to either epistemic or deontic concerns. Overall, therapists and clients work toward gaining entry into an activity that is primarily contingent on the client's approval of the therapist's initial suggestion and commitment to the proposed future action. In some sessions, movement from one phase to the next proceeds in a smooth, step-wise fashion. In other sessions, owing to problems in understanding or resistance, entry into chair work extends over the course of the session, with phases being recycled. At times, participation within chair work for an identified conflict is withheld or abandoned when a new emotional conflict is revealed and then pursued – see also Chapter 8.

Extract 6.1 is a prototypical example of entry into two-chair work, with all phases being carried out sequentially in fewer than 100 lines. It appears approximately 14 minutes into the session. The ensuing analysis of the four phases merely illustrates "typical" interactional features of each phase. More detailed analyses and descriptions are given in subsequent sections.

**Extract 6.1:** Owen: Case 315.9 (Two-Chair)

**Phase 1: Formulating the trouble**

```
1        Owen:  and (.) there's still * all sorts of things (0.4) that
           t            shallow nods->*
2               I would like to do.
3               (*    3.0      *)
           t    *shallows nods*
4        Ther:  [°mm hm,               ]
5        Owen:  [>but I guess I keep<] in the back of my head
6               cuz=↑um (0.9) and I guess that brings th-(0.6)
7               again that brings up a question of (0.5)
8    →          relationships, (1.6) >n'maybe this< is where I (0.6)
9    →          +kinda get a little fearful on the relationship * side is*
           t                                                     *nod--*
10   →          (2.6) >am I ready?< do-I often equate relationships
11   →          with settling down.
12              (1.4)
13       Ther:  *mm hm,*
           t    *nod-*
14   →   Owen:  rather than sort've going out and having a good time.
15       Ther:  mm hm, somehow .h getting involved in a relationship (.)
16              means that .h (0.4) it's the inevitable (.) question
17              of + (.) is this the person I'll settle down [with.]
           o       +shallow nods->
18       Owen:                                              [yeah.]+
           o                                                nods->+
19              (1.5)
20       Ther:  m:m.=
21       Owen:  =I know that's pretty unr- (0.2) that might be
```

```
22  →         unrealistic. considering my (1.1)sort'of avoiding
23  →         dating issue entirely.
24            (*    2.7      *)
       t       *shallow nods*
25     Owen:  an'I guess in in the midst of all this (0.5) activity
26            that's going on around me, that's=that's: still one
27            element that I kind of (0.8) wish I could (.)
28            incorporate.
29            (0.5)
30     Ther:  *mm hm,*
       t      *nods-*
31            (0.3)
32  →  Owen:  >but again + it's a question'of< (1.0) well- (0.4)
       t                 +gaze forward->
33  →         number one=+do I?     +
       o                 +gaze to T+
34            *(0.9)
       t      *nods->
35  →  Owen:  in the midst* of all (0.2) all this activity, (1.5)
       t           nods->*
36  →         uh:m (1.3)+or:,
       o                +shrugs
37  →         (0.5) >is it really< ye'know? (0.2) >is it really<
38  →         necessary or (1.2) + could I be able to incorporate it.
       o                         +turns head to T->
39            *(0.7)
       t      *slow nods->
40  →  Owen:  rather than +sort'of dismiss it +entirely.*
       o                  +waves hand sideways+
       t                                     slow nods->*
41  →  Ther:  so it's .hh a lot of conflict there in terms of .h (0.4)
42            do I want it, am I ready::,
43            (1.8)
44     Ther:  en-th- en we kno:w,(0.4) also from (.) previous times
45  →         *it's a s'rta lo:nging,*
       t      *raises shoulders--    *
              (0.2)
46  →  Owen:  +°yeah.°+
       o      +nods-  +
47            (0.5)
48     Ther:  *mm hm.
       t      *slow nods->
```

**Phase 2: Recruiting participation in chair work**

```
49            (    3.5      )*
       t      slow nods->*
50  →  Ther:  °m?° * ↑wanna work with that today?
       t           *tilts head, raises eyebrows->
51            (0.3)
52  →  Owen:  +I think so yeah.
       o      +nods->
53     Ther:  *mm hm.*
       t      *nods- *
54            (0.3  )+
       o      nods-> +
```

**Phase 3: Readjusting the participation frame**

```
55  →  Ther:  *.hh ↑where (0.2)* where do feel like *you are right now? *
          t   *gets out of chair*                    *extends cupped hands*
56            *(0.5)
          t   *exits frame->
57     Ther:  °what's° * (0.6)
          o             *gaze forward/downward->
58     Owen:  ↑uh::m Hx::m
59     Ther:  *what's the feeling about it today.(.)°thet?°
          t   *brings new chair into frame, returns to seat->
60            (6.4)
61     Owen:  I guess toda:y it's (2.3) it's more on the side of
62            (6.1) probably I could just sort'of (2.3) not deal with it.
63     Ther:  *mm hm,
          t   *slow nod->
64            (0.8)
65     Ther:  .hh * th'part that sez:: (0.3) is this what
          t   nods->*
66            I really want right now?
67     Owen:  +yeah. (0.3) the part that says well,+ (2.2) +↑yeah exactly.
          o   +nods, smile/ sneer -----------------+    +nods->
68            is this *what I want right now.+*
          o                                   nods->+
          t           *slow nods--------------*
69            (0.8)
70     Ther:  so what is it that you question?
71            (1.7)
72     Owen:  hx:
73            (0.3)
74     Ther:  is'it you're wondering (.) °about°
75            (3.8)
76     Owen:  I guess I'm wondering (3.7) >how I would< present myself
              (.)
77            in a situation where (3.0) °I might want that.° (0.6)
78            >I mi-I might< (0.6) want that longing.
79            (1.8)
80     Owen:  and somehow trying to (2.3) maybe* (1.8) accept a
81            part of myself that says + okay,(0.6) >this=seems t'me<
          o                            +shallow nods->
82            something I would like.+
          o           shallow nods->+
83            (*     2.5     *)
          t   *shallows nods*
```

**Phase 4: Making contact**

```
84  →  Ther:  ↑tell this*(0.5)+tell this part of yourself (1.2) what it *
          t             *reaches out and pulls in empty chair closer--*
          o                   +gaze to empty chair->
85            *is you <think you wa:nt,>
          t   *gaze to C--->
86            (3.6)
87  →  Owen:  >I'dunno?<=I think I would wa:nt, (3.1) j'st'a be able
88            to: >either pick up the< telephone or (2.1) find some
```

time to (1.2) go visit that (0.4) special someone:, (1.8)
>jus talk about what I'm feeling.<
(1.4)

Owen is a 26-year-old student, working part time at his school newspaper, and finding his way in the world. In the beginning of this extract, Owen delivers a *troubles telling* (Jefferson, 1988) and gradually develops a detailed affective stance that portrays himself as struggling with self-doubt and uncertainty, resulting in procrastination, avoiding romantic relationships and an unfulfilled longing. For example, he mentions: "I (0.6) kinda get a little fearful on the relationship side" (lines 08–09); "my (1.1) sort'of avoiding dating issue entirely." (lines 22–23). Later, in lines 32–40, Owen frames possible courses of actions that he may take as competing alternatives: "number one=do I? ... or:, ... ". Phase 1 consists of the therapist orienting to Owen's dilemma by reformulating Owen's description of his desire for and uncertainty about wanting a relationship as a source of conflict (lines 41–42) and connecting it to previous discussions (not shown in transcript) as a kind of longing (line 45). Here, the therapist follows the client and endorses his epistemic entitlement of having ownership of his emotional experiences. Owen affiliates with this formulation (line 46) through verbal acknowledgement and nodding, thus completing Phase 1 of chair work entry.

The therapist then launches into Phase 2 – recruiting the client's involvement to do therapeutic work on the identified issue. In line 50, the therapist transforms this conflict into something that deserves immediate therapeutic attention: "°m?° ↑wanna work with that today?". By drawing from a deontic modality targeting the client's "willingness" (i.e., ↑wanna), the therapist orients to the client's greater entitlement to decide over the suggested future course of action. Her granting Owen the prerogative to proceed or not is also conveyed through hesitation, heightened pitch, rising intonation and head tilting. What is implied through this turn format is that Owen will not only be the agent of the future action, but will also be the main beneficiary; that is, what is being suggested will have therapeutic gains for the client (not the therapist). Owen's verbal response of "I think so yeah.", while nodding, endorses the suggested project (line 52), thus completing Phase 2 and readying the stage for Phase 3.

Within Phase 3, the therapist draws upon multiple, and often repeated, interactional practices to orient the client to a new participation framework, by preparing the client to move from a therapist–client interaction to an interaction between the client and an imaginary self or significant other. In this segment (lines 55–83), the therapist re-arranges the setting by bringing a third chair into the room (lines 55–59), and most of the talk involves an extended negotiation of what Owen could say to an aspect of his "self":"not deal with it."; "is this what I want right now."; ">this=seems t'me< something I would like.". The therapist then works to remodel some of Owen's talk by using subject position "I" and simulating the client's voice: "th'part that sez:: (0.3) is this what I really want right now?" (lines 66–67). Owen affiliates with the therapist's suggestions in lines 66–67. He first offers agreement (yeah.), then begins to report what he would say but cuts himself off (the part that says well,). He then does a repair by producing more upgraded agreement (↑yeah exactly.) and then repeats the therapist's prior wording in what could be taken as a self-critical utterance that tries to block his present needs (is this what I want right now).

After having established what Owen could say, the participants then move into Phase 4 (lines 84–91). This involves the therapist's use of directives to guide future dialogue (line 84) "↑tell this (0.5) tell this part of yourself (1.2) what it is you <think you wa:nt,>". These *imperative-designed* directives appear to index a reconfigured deontic status between the therapist and Owen as compared with those in Phase 2, suggesting that the therapist now has greater rights to shape client talk. It also marks the shift from the ordinary client–therapist participation frame to a new client-self/other frame. The therapist's alternate participant role is now someone who orchestrates talk from "outside" of the immediate client dialogue with *own* self. Finally, by complying with the directive, Owen verbally establishes contact with his *other* self (line 87).

### *6.5.1 Phase 1: Formulating the Trouble*[4]

The emergence, identification and endorsement of a specific emotionally laden trouble connected with self or significant other, considered Phase 1, appears to be consistent precursors to the subsequent phases of entry into chair work. *Troubles talk* (Jefferson, 1988) realized mainly in terms of a personal conflict or emotional distress is often expressed via the client's affective stance displays. Whereas stances are often directly expressed as a negative feeling, they may also be conveyed non-verbally through crying or, more subtlety, through such means as a wavering voice, scrunched face or downward gaze. In this

[4] The term used for this phase – *formulating the trouble* – is meant to capture the more general interactional, sequential quality of what is going on: client engages in troubles telling, therapist formulates (i.e., identifies) the trouble and client then (usually) confirms the formulation. This phase may also be viewed through a psychotherapeutic lens as *identifying and elaborating key client process markers*. From this EFT standpoint, the chair task intervention does not start, or will not be engaged until there is evidence of client markers and readiness for engagement (Greenberg et al., 1993).

phase, the therapist follows the client's lead by further exploring and drawing attention to the client's affective stance, most often by *formulating* the client's talk and sometimes by responding with a *noticing*. By doing this, the therapist orients to the client's greater entitlements to own their emotional experience – see Chapters 3 and 4 for discussion on action formations and entitlements. Subsequent client affiliation with the therapist's formulation of an identified emotional conflict demonstrates an in-the-moment readiness to work on this specific maladaptive emotion. When the conflict is not clearly identified or is weakly ratified, it may hinder the development of subsequent phases or may derail chair work altogether.

In Extract 6.1, it was shown how troubles talk may be realized in terms of a client's uncertainty about relationships and the emotional repercussions of either avoiding or trying to pursue a relationship. A trouble, however, may also be conveyed in other ways, such as the client's unresolved feelings about persons or events. In such cases, therapists may work at identifying an unresolved feeling as a precursor to subsequent chair work. An example illustrating how a salient emotion becomes identified is given in Extract 6.2. The client, Lisa (Angus et al., 2008), is a mother of young children, in a non-communicative marriage, employed part time to make ends meet. Growing up, she was expected to take care of her younger brothers, sidelining her own needs. By accepting these responsibilities without complaint, she felt confined to being the good little girl, a role she has carried into adulthood. Maintaining this behaviour, she has struggled to express her unhappiness with her husband's gambling addiction and to assert herself within their marriage. Previous to Extract 6.2, she describes herself as feeling stronger and better able to express her own needs as a result of therapy. This extract illustrates how an emotion-to-work-on is revealed and identified.

**Extract 6.2:** Lisa: Case 306.11 (Empty Chair)

```
1    Lisa:   so that's where I guess uh the strength has come in.
2            (0.3)
3    Ther:   uh huh
4            (0.4)
5    Ther:   ye- (.)°yeah° (0.3) you feel more strong,
6            (0.4)
7    Lisa:   yeah.
8            (0.5)
9    Ther:   °mm hm:°
10   Lisa:   °yeah it's uhm° +(3.6) I guess it's +beca- uhm
          l                  +gaze downward      +opens hands,
11           +~being an indivisual(0.2)+ ↑that I uhm (.)↑I never was?~
             +gaze to T----------------+lowers head->
12           (0.2)
13   Ther:   +mm hm, (.) mm hm,
          l  +gaze to T->
```

```
14                +(*0.7)
            l     +nods, gaze to hands->
15    Lisa:       +uhm
16                (1.5)
17    Ther:       tch (0.5)* you +feel °sa:d when you say that,°+*
            t                *gaze to C--------------------------------*
            l                      +gaze to T--------------------------+
18                (1.3)
19    Lisa:       .h +uh:: yeah I feel sad uhm (1.7) towards my parents? uhm
            l        +hand to mouth, wipes nose, tenses face, gaze down--->
20    Ther:       *uh huh
            t     *slow nods--->
21                ( 1.6  )*
            t      nods->*
```

After Lisa asserts and the therapist endorses her newfound strength, Lisa switches to quieter, hesitant speech, characterizing herself as being an individual that she never was with a tremulous voice and a higher pitch (lines 10–11). Following a couple of continuers and significant pausing, the therapist produces a *noticing* (Muntigl & Horvath, 2014a; Sacks, 1995b; Schegloff, 1988) that draws attention to Lisa's new affective stance: "`you feel °sa:d° when you say that.`" (line 17). Then, following a 1.3-second pause and hesitation markers (`.h uh::`), Lisa confirms that she feels sad and then elaborates by tentatively proposing that her sadness is directed at her parents (line 19). In this way, her parents are offered as potential candidates for empty-chair work, and thus implicating her in-the-moment readiness to work on the targeted emotion sadness.

Emotional conflicts may become especially germane in the interaction when an identified emotion is mutually and collaboratively developed and ratified over the course of talk. Extract 6.3 demonstrates how Lisa's anger toward her father in response to her mother's situation becomes topicalized and expanded. Lisa's dysfunctional relationship with her husband echoes that of her parents'. For instance, Lisa's mother does not stand up for herself with regard to her own husband's long-standing gambling addiction and to managing the problems arising from the dangerous behaviours of her schizophrenic son who is still living in the parental home and is no longer taking his medication.

**Extract 6.3:** Lisa: Case 306.3 (Empty Chair)

```
1     Ther:      so there's kinda + [both.] right?+ [like you]
2     Lisa:                         [.snif]         [yah     ]
            l                     +gaze to T, nods+
3     Ther:      can [acknowledge]
4     Lisa:          [a bit con  ]fused.
5                (0.7)
6     Ther:      that (.) and yet
7     Lisa:      .snif
8                (3.0)
```

```
9    Ther:   +^and yet. (.)
        1    +gaze to T--->
10   Ther:   [you do have this,]
11   Lisa:   [.hhhh            ] Hhx: the anger[hhh   ]
12   Ther:                                     [anger] towards him.
13   Lisa:   +°yeah° (0.8) °yeah° +(   1.5     )   + it's like
        1    +gaze down->         +shallow nods+ gaze forward->
14           ye'knowed, (0.8) doesn't he ~ca:re?~ (0.8) if something
15           happens to her? or'um
16           (0.6)
17   Lisa:   tch ~hadn't she been through enough?~ um
18           (0.5)
19   Ther:   [mm hm.]
20   Lisa:   [.snif ]
21           (0.3)
22   Ther:   mm hm.
23   Ther:   tch.hh (0.2) yeah like +how much (0.5) longer+
        1                           + gaze to T, nods----  +
24   Ther:   [can he keep doing this.             ]
25   Lisa:   [°yeah >I dunno how much< + ~mo:re]~ can she take?°
        1                              +rubs eye->
```

When further exploring Lisa's confusion about her father's behaviour to her mother, the therapist projects a slot for producing a candidate emotion (line 10), which is followed by Lisa's *anticipatory completion* (Lerner, 1991) of "anger" (line 11). In line 12, the therapist continues by completing her utterance (`anger towards him`), thus affiliating with Lisa's identification of anger as the prominent emotion and offering further elaboration by naming the target of the anger. What then follows is Lisa's confirmation in lines 13–15 and an emotionally charged complaint about the father (`doesn't he ~ca:re?~ (0.8) if something happens to her?`). Afterwards, in lines 23–25, the therapist and client co-construct another sequence that underscores the extremeness and the negative effect of the father's behaviour toward the mother. Through these linked sequences displaying deepened mutual affiliation around Lisa's emotions of anger and frustration, the participants create a strong warrant for further exploring the client–father relationship through a dialogue in which the client may, for example, confront the father about his behaviour toward her mother.

### 6.5.2 *Phase 2: Recruiting Participation in Chair Work*

Following the identification and differentiation of a client's articulated and currently experienced expressions of self-interruption, self-criticism or unfinished business (Phase 1), the therapist may "test the waters" by suggesting or proposing the implementation of chair task interventions. Chair work may be introduced a single time and be agreed to immediately, with Phases 3 and 4 following in a consecutive, orderly fashion (see Extract 6.1).

Alternatively, guiding participation may necessitate multiple turns, especially when the possibility of chair work needs to be reintroduced. This often occurs when agreement is tacit or ambiguous, when a new emotional conflict is introduced and exploration of the previously identified conflict is abandoned, or when client agreement is not readily forthcoming – see also Chapter 8.

Talk in this phase is organized in such a way as to grant the client greater deontic status in ultimately deciding on the course of events. This may be because, ultimately, the client will be the main agent and sole beneficiary of the future action. Therapists perform a variety of different kinds of deontic stance work to realize this aim. First, proposals were designed in a highly contingent manner (e.g., involving hesitation, heightened pitch, deontic modality of "willingness," rising intonation, head tilting), orienting to the client's greater entitlement to decide over the suggested course of action.

- `w- wudf be willing to do it?`
- `↑d'yu wannu uhm`
- `>so is that< something that you'd like to try tuh (.) do:?`
- `↑wanna work with that today?`
- `.h >so is that< something that you'd like to try tuh (.) do:? then is .hh at least try to (0.8) work toward:`

High contingency was also conveyed by framing the proposal as merely a possibility or as an activity with an "uncertain" outcome (e.g., "an experiment"). Common interactional features for introducing chair work include indirect hesitation (e.g., notable pausing before and within utterances, questioning intonation), modal expression ("could") and softeners such as "a little bit" and "sort've focus" (see also Muntigl & Horvath, 2014a).

- `would you be willing to (1.5) actually try an experiment where you could express some of these feelings toward him.`
- `jus'sorta work< that through in some fashion`
- `en I (.) throw it out as a^ ehm (0.8) ↑I guess it's like an experiment. I mean just to see what might happen.`

Additionally, therapist proposal turns commonly feature either a deictic reference of "that" only or "that conflict" as something to work on, displaying that the therapist and client have come to a clear, shared understanding of the in-the-moment conflict. This feature can also frequently be found in turns proceeding agreement, and after previous more extensive turns have been made in scenarios with dissent or rejection.

- `so we can work with that some more today?`
- `>so is that< something that you'd like to try tuh (.) do:?`

- `↑wanna work with that today?`
- `.hhh is that conflict something that (.) we should (.) spend some time on?`

Further, the successful completion of the key components of Phase 2, which are suggesting/proposing *and* accepting a conflict or emotion as something to work on, appears necessary to ultimately reaching the final Phase 4. Client affiliation to the proposal may be expressed with various degrees of acceptance, ranging from strong agreement/commitment to weak acquiescence. An example of high commitment is shown in Extract 6.4.

**Extract 6.4:** Jennifer 428_12/2C

```
1   Ther:   *so we can work with that some more today?
       t    *raises eyebrows--->
2           (+          + 1.2          *)
       j     +shallow nod+
       t        raises eyebrows--->*
3   Ther:   or
4           *(2.6)
       t    *extends hands - open hand supine - to J
5   Ther:   pick up (0.9) anything else? thet
6   Jen:    oh no +this is very interesting+
       j          +raises eyebrows, looks up/down->
7   Jen:    °[I have nothing] come up.°
8   Ther:    [mm * hm *       ]
       t           *nods*
```

Following the therapist's proposal (line 1), there is a significant 1.2 second pause during which Jennifer gives a shallow nod. The therapist then, in line 3, appends an *or* onto her prior turn, which functions in a couple of ways. First, it treats Jennifer's nod as insufficiently displaying acceptance and, second, it gives Jennifer an opportunity to suggest an alternative course of action – thus obviating the need for her to refuse the therapist's proposal if need be – and downgrades the force of the proposal. Further, the extension of the therapist's hands, as an open hand supine (OHS) gesture, toward the client may be seen as an offer (Kendon, 2004) and works to reinforce the downgraded deontic stance set in motion by the stand-alone *or*. Following no response from the client, the therapist continues her turn by supplying an alternative course of action (line 5) and this then immediately receives acceptance by Jennifer of the therapist's original proposal of line 1. With this response, the client both strongly opposes the suggestion that there could be "`anything else?`" to work on with "`oh no`" and expresses an upgraded form of interest and commitment to engage in chair work (`this is very interesting`).

Instances of strong, but less enthusiastic, commitment are shown in Extracts 6.5 and 6.6.

**Extract 6.5:** Lisa: Case 306.3 (Empty Chair)

```
1    Lisa:    °°it's°°(0.2)°it's° real confusion. .shih
2             (0.3)
3    Ther:    t.hhh (0.8) i- (0.2) me-I think it would be:(0.3)
4             e-good to (0.3) try::(0.2) e-you know
5             last week I sug[gested] uh
6    Lisa:                   [.hh    ]
7    Lisa:    °yeah.°
8             +(0.5)
          l   +shallow nods,gaze to T--->
9    Ther:    +t.experiment+ en .hh (.) and e- (0.3)
          l   +shallow nods+
10            but this time with your da::d,
11            cuz (.) + cuz what yer (0.3) describing + is °is°
12        l             +shallow nods-------------------------------------+
13            a f:really+(0.2)strong (0.4)feeling of anger+
          l               +shallow nods-----------------------------+
14            +[towards] him en .hhhh (0.6) so thet if you were to (0.4)
15   Lisa:    +[.shih]
          l   +gaze down/nods--->
16   Ther:    bring him in here that might (0.6)°I mean° (0.3)
17            bring him in here in an imagine way it would
18             [give   ](0.4) you a chance to actually
19   Lisa:    +[°yeah°]+
          l   + nods---+tightens lips--->
20   Ther:    express it towards+ him. .hh
          l   tightens lips--->+
21            +(0.8) +
          l   +shallow nods+
22   Ther:    *w- wudja be willing to do it?*
          t   *turns head towards L----------*
23   Lisa:    +°↑yah°
          l   +nods, gaze down--->
```

**Extract 6.6:** Paula 312_10/2C

```
1    Ther:    >°cu-°< (0.2) * ↑I wanna try some thing, °if that's okay?°
          t   points finger *nods, raises brow, gets up to get chair->
          p                                     smiles, uncrosses legs
2             (1.3)
          t   gets & brings in chair, walking backwards, back to P->
          p   legs forwards, hands separated on lap
3    Ther:    >is that alright? (cuz I'm gunna=)<
          p   straightens skirt
4    Paula:   =sure.
          p   smiles, tilts head
5             (1.3)
```

In Extract 6.5 (see also Extract 2.11 and Extract 3.10) following Lisa's assertion pertaining to the confusion about her father's actions toward her mother, the therapist draws from a number of prefacing devices to frame the upcoming suggestion in a cautious manner. These include pauses, downgraders (I think), linking the suggestion with potential benefits (it would be: (0.3) e-good to (0.3) try::), an orientation to past talk (last week I suggested uh) and, in line 09, a description of the upcoming suggestion as an "experiment." The therapist then proceeds to specify to whom the dialogue will be directed (with your da::d) and then goes on to justify her suggestion by, first, underscoring that Lisa has "a f:really (0.2) strong (0.4) feeling of anger" and, second, highlighting the benefits of doing chair work; that is, it will give her an opportunity to express her anger. A sensitivity toward the potential distress that such a confrontation might evoke is illustrated in lines 16–17. The therapist first suggests to "bring him in here" but then self-repairs to underscore that the confrontation will not be "real" but "in an imagine way". Finally, in line 22, the therapist designs the suggestion in terms of the client's willingness (w- wudja be willing to do it?) to which Lisa offers strong agreement (°↑yah°) while nodding in line 23.

In Extract 6.6, The therapist produces a proposal followed by a confirmation-seeking question with turn-final rising intonation (°if that's okay?°). A 1.3-second silence follows during which the therapist brings the chair into the scene. Then, the therapist again seeks confirmation with turn-final rising intonation (>is that alright?), which receives immediate confirmation from the client Paula. The client's emphasis on "sure" along with her smile indexes commitment to engage the task.

Weaker forms of commitment are shown in Extracts 6.7 and 6.8.

**Extract 6.7:** Lisa 306cs.14/2C

```
01 Ther:  .h +*>so is that< something that you'd like *to try tuh (.) do:?
       c    +looks at T.->
       t     *looks at nails-----------------picks nail->
02        then is .hh at least try to (0.8) +work *towards:
       c                              looks at T.->+looks down, wipes eyes->
       t                                            *extends palm up hand to C.->
03        (1.2)
04 Ther:  tryin to=
05 Lisa:  =uhm
06 Ther:  get'in (0.2)* touch with [(.)] these two parts? er in
       t                *puts hands on lap->
07 Lisa:                           [shih]
       c  looks at T.,finger on mouth->
08 Ther:  the next
09        (0.6)
10 Lisa:  +yeah,+ that would be good. °I think.°
       c  +nods-+
11 Ther:  yeah.
          (0.4)
   Ther:  +okay.+
       c  +nods-+
```

**Extract 6.8:** Ernie 422.9/2C

```
1  Ther:  right, (.)* and if we (.) * try that here?'en      *
       t             *hands on knees *hands up, forward & back*
2         uh* I'll sit over there. (.)     *
       t    *looks and points to 3rd chair*
3         *like we've done this before? (0.2) + and .h *just (1.0) *
       t  *looks at E.-------------------------*extends hand to 3rd chair*
       e                                     +tightens lips->
4         *that's o↑kay?
       t  *looks at E.->
5            (0.4)+
       e  lips--->+
6  Ther:  to [do that?*     yeah? ]
7  Ern:     +[yeah+ (.)+ I think-]+think so=
       e    +nods-+              +gaze forward
       t        *gets up to bring in second chair--->
8  Ther:  *=ya'think so. (0.2) okay. (0.2)
       t  *looks back towards E.--->
```

At the start of Extract 6.7, the therapist makes a proposal that orients to Lisa's willingness to engage in chair work (`something that you'd like to try tuh (.) do:?`). She then, in line 2, mitigates the proposal through high contingency markers such as (**`at least try`**) and (**`work toward:`**) and by extending her hand in a palm up position toward Lisa. Following no response from Lisa in line 3, which may be indexing impending reluctance to comply, the therapist reformulates the proposal (`tryin to`) by appending more specificity to the task to be done (`get'in (0.2) touch with (.) these two parts?`). During the therapist's proposal, Lisa exhibits upset on numerous occasions, through wiping away tears (line 2), sniffs (line 7) and silence. Eventually, Lisa does offer affiliation in line 10 by agreeing and evaluating the proposal as "`good`", but then weakens her commitment to act by appending "`°I think.°`" to the end of her turn.

In Extract 6.8, the therapist articulates a proposal (`if we (.) try that here?'en`) while gesturing toward a vacant chair. Then, following a silence in which Ernie could show compliance but does not, the therapist seeks confirmation (`that's o↑kay?`). At this point Ernie's lips are tightened and he appears somewhat tense. In line 6, the therapist continues to seek confirmation and, in overlap, Ernie voices compliance at which the therapist then gets up to retrieve the chair. Ernie's response is weakly affiliative and indifferent, uttering his agreement with flat intonation and a downgrading expression (`I think-think so`). The therapist immediately orients to Ernie's low commitment by repeating his weakly designed compliance (`ya'think so.`), which is then followed by an acknowledgement token (`okay.`).

### 6.5.3 *Phase 3: Readjusting the Participation Framework*

Phase 3 begins after the point at which chair work is ratified by the client (completion of Phase 2) and proceeds until the client makes contact with an imagined self (experiencer or critic) or a significant other. Readjusting the participation framework from speaking to a therapist, a co-present, real person, to an imaginary version of self or a non-present significant other often requires a fair bit of interactional work and is, therefore, particularly challenging. Some of the main activities occurring in Phase 3 include 1) *rearranging the setting* to include a third participant (i.e., personifying the chair); 2) *priming clients* for them to get a sense of the third participant in the personified chair; and 3) *clarifying* what the client wants to say to self or other (in the chair). Therapists would draw from one of two types of practices – one orienting more to deontic entitlements and the other to epistemic entitlements – in order to accomplish this phase. In the first, therapists would continue to solicit client participation into chair work through a series of guiding actions. In the second, therapists would work instead to readjust the participation framework by following clients through actions that endorse their ownership of experience (e.g., formulations, information requests). Extract 6.9, which continues on from Extract 6.5, illustrates a more deontic practice in terms of how the therapist manipulates the setting and brings the client to focus on a significant other in order to prepare the client for subsequent empty chair work.

**Extract 6.9:** Lisa: Case 306.3 (Empty Chair)

```
24              (*1.0)
        t        *gets up to bring in chair--->
25    Ther:     +okay,
        l       +begins getting up->
26              (0.5)
27    Lisa:     .shih
28              (0.4)
29    Ther:     en I'll sort'of +(0.2) [show] (.) I'll tell you
        t                        +brings chair in frame->
30    Lisa:                              +[oh  ]
        l       rises from chair---> +sits back down->
31    Ther:     [how to]
32    Lisa:     [okay.  ] >you want me to stay here.<
33    Ther:     ye:ah.
34              (0.4)
35    Ther:     *+°>we'll bring it<° (0.5) the chair here.
        t       *adjust chair location, begins to sit--->
        l       +gaze to tissue, gaze to chair--->
36              *(1.5)
        t       *sits down--->
37    Ther:     e:n (0.3) an >what + I want you to do: + is (0.5)
        l                          +gaze to T--------+gaze to chair->
```

```
38             >first of all< [(.) can] you actually imagine+
        t      +gaze to chair, extends hand to chair---+
39   Lisa:                        [.snih  ]
40   Ther:     him (0.3) being here? in a sense in +your mi:nd.+
        1                                                  +nods---+
41             .h bring him in here?
42             (0.8)
43   Lisa:     °mkay°
44             (0.4)
45   Lisa:     .sHih
46             (0.5)
47   Ther:     >can you get a< sense + of him?
        1                             +tightens lips->
48   Lisa:     +mhm.+
        1      +nods+
49   Lisa:     +hih
        1      +closes eyes->
50             (    0.2    )+
        1      eyes,lips->+
51   Ther:     +tch (1.0) <wh-what do you fe:el whe-
        1      +gaze down, forward->
52   Ther:     [when you see] him °here. °°>
53   Lisa:     [.shih        ]
54   Lisa:     +hhih hih (0.8) ~↑I just feel like cr(hi)ying↑~
        1      +scrunches face, lowers head, wipes eyes->
```

After having received Lisa's agreement to try working with the empty chair, she brings in the chair (lines 24–29). She then begins to prime Lisa for the upcoming encounter by instructing her to first try to envision the father in the chair and, second, to imagine what she feels at that moment. The therapist both gazes and motions toward the chair to guide the client's gaze (line 38). To facilitate priming, the therapist uses expressions that guide Lisa's entry into this "imaginary realm" such as "`can you actually imagine him (0.3) being here?`", "`in your mi:nd. bring him in here`" and "`can you get a< sense of him`". During this time, Lisa begins to display an incipient form of upset, as expressed through a sniff (line 45), tightening lips (line 47) and closing of her eyes and lips (lines 49–59). The therapist, in line 51, proceeds with a *wh*-interrogative that targets Lisa's feelings. As a result, for Lisa, the empty chair transforms into her father, as evidenced by her emotional distress in line 54 that is conveyed through a sniff, crying and tremulous voice (see also Hepburn and Potter, 2007). From here (transcript not included), the therapist nudges the client toward expressing her emotions directly to her imaginary father by such means as issuing directives and modelling language (`tell him I don't feel accepted °by you.°`), and personifying the chair (`you don't wanna face him?`: *while pointing at the chair*).

Extract 6.10 shows a more epistemically oriented method of priming the client, in which the therapist provides affective descriptions involving the person in the chair. This creates a vivid scenario, specifying in detail the difficulties that Ernie is experiencing with his ex-wife, thus providing a scaffold through which Ernie may begin to make contact by expressing these difficulties and emotions.

**Extract 6.10:** Ernie: Case 422.4 (Empty Chair)

```
01   Ern:     this's a person that's: (2.3) quite vulnerable.
02            (0.3)
03   Ther:    oka:y?
04            (0.7)
05   Ther:    *so there's a vulnerable: (0.5) person. sitting there+
        t     *gaze to chair->
        e     +gaze to T---------------------     ------------------+
06            +who's just trying *to shield herself.(0.2)[from life.]
07   Ern:                                               +[yes.      ]
        e       to chair->
        t                         *gaze to C->
        e                                                +nods
08   Ther:    *from (0.6) hurt'en:d (0.2) en (0.3) pa:in'end
        t     *gaze to chair->
09            (0.9)
10   Ther:    things that are gonna *cause her distress. .hh (0.2)
        t                           *gaze to chair->
11            ^and *as you look at (0.2) * her (.) sitting there,
        t          *raises hand towards chair*
12            what (0.5) what goes on inside, for yo:u.
13            what are you feeling.
14            (0.8)
15   Ther:    what (0.2) comes into your awareness as you see
16            her sitting there.
17            +(20.9)
        e     +gaze down, to chair->
18   Ern:     I I just feel so sad that I (.) that I (0.2)
19            I-I cahn't get (1.0) uhm
20            (3.9)
21   Ern:     .h underneath the surface. that I can't (.) really
22            reach (0.6)+ ~uh~
        e                +lowers hands,gaze forward,downturned mouth->
23            (2.5)
24   Ther:    so it's hard for you:, (0.2) to reach her.
25            =you-you want to reach her but somehow
26            it's (0.4) it's hard to reach her
```

Ernie begins by describing his former wife in the chair as someone who is "`quite vulnerable`". Following a prompt in line 03 that makes more talk from the client relevant, the therapist produces a summary formulation in line 05 (Antaki, 2008; Heritage and Watson, 1979) that lists some of the ex-wife's attributes already mentioned by Ernie (`vulnerable`, `shielding herself from hurt`, `pain`, `distress`) and then proceeds to further direct Ernie's attention to his ex-wife in the chair, getting him to focus on his feelings toward her at that moment via a number of *wh*-interrogatives. Following a lengthy

20.9-second silence in line 17, Ernie articulates his emotion (`I I just feel so sad`), but then struggles to provide a detailed account of this sadness. His emerging upset also comes to the fore in line 21, when he begins to speak in a tremulous voice, as he lowers his hands and cuts off his speech while gazing forward. Ernie's difficulty is then topicalized by the therapist in a formulation that emphasizes how hard it is for Ernie to connect with his ex-wife. This dialogue prepares the way for Ernie to begin talking to his ex-wife about his difficulty in "reaching her" and the intense sadness he feels for not being able to do so (see Extract 6.11).

### *6.5.4 Phase 4: Making Contact*

Phase 4 of entry into chair work comprised the first time within the session in which the client makes the imaginary self or significant other the intended recipient of his or her utterance. This is most overtly displayed through the client's gaze, physical orientation to the chair, use of second-person singular pronouns and other indexical vocabulary selections. This phase begins with a therapist-initiated directive, followed by the client's action of compliance. Further, the directive is most often realized in an imperative format (`tell him`) and, much less frequently, in an interrogative format (`can you tell him`). In contrast to Phase 2, the therapist's turn is now produced more directly, thus driving these actions more along the scale toward *non-contingency*; that is, now that the client has agreed to participate in chair work, the therapist no longer needs to further negotiate the deontic status of the encounter. Thus, the imperative formats of the directives seem to index the client's tacit agreement that the therapist will now orchestrate the dialogue between the client and the non-present other.

Extract 6.1 at the beginning of this chapter shows a fairly quick transition into Phase 4 and also how the client, Owen, readily complies with the therapist's directive. It is also common for clients to display hesitation and marked distress before actually conversing with the "other chair." Consider Extract 6.11, which occurs soon after Extract 6.10. Believing his ex-wife has not listened to him, Ernie successfully enters Phase 4 by making contact with Nora, and eventually takes a long extended turn in which he vents his feelings about her blocking his attempts at communication.

**Extract 6.11:** Ernie: Case 422.4 (Empty Chair)

```
40          (1.1)
      t     >>gaze to chair->
      e     >>gaze to chair, downturned mouth->
41  Ther:   *can you tell Nora     * what (1.7) what it is,
      t     *extends hand to chair* rubs chin->
42          you w- (.) would li̲ke,
```

```
43          (*     2.8              *)
      e     *quick glance to video*
44    Ern:  +tc.hhh
      e     +raises hands in front, gaze to chair->
45          (3.2)
46    Ern:  hx uh.(1.0) Nora what I er'really
47          want is is for you to .hhh (0.6) listen to things
48          that I've got to sa:y. +(0.3) I (2.5) tch (0.4)
      e                            +plays with, gaze to hands->
49          *they're really (2.1) they may be hurtful but
      t     *turns head to E, gaze intermittent between E, chair->
50          they're not s: (1.2) + intended to hurt you.=+
      e                          +gaze to chair----+
51          +=they're really (+ 3.9     +) my feelings
      e     +gaze to hands->  +in-breath+ gaze to chair->
52          + which I've not been able to express to you,
      e     + gaze to hands->
53          an and you've never +allowed me to express
      e                         +gaze to chair->
54          them. (0.2) you've +(0.7) .snih tc.hhh + you've always
      e                        +gaze to hands--to chair->
55          blocked me + by (0.4) telling me about all of the
      e                + gaze to hands->
56          + things that I've done, (0.2) that I regret.
      e     + gaze to chair - ->
57          en shouldn't've done. + and (1.3) by (+ 2.4)+
      e                           +gaze to hands-> +visible inbreath+
58          throwing (0.9) all these issues at me the minute
59          I want +to try and reach you uh (0.3)
      e            +gaze to chair->
60          +I'm (1.0) .snif (1.4) tch I'm at my wit's end
      e     +raises hands, gaze to hands, gaze to chair->
61          I + don't know+ how to get through to you
      e       +shrug--+
            ((continues for several more lines))
```

In line 41, the therapist initiates a sequence by recruiting Ernie's involvement in beginning an emotionally challenging dialogue with his ex-wife Nora. Note that *what* Ernie is able to say is left open to his discretion. This is in some ways not surprising because, as can be recalled from Extract 6.10, there were a number of issues involving his ex-wife that Ernie had mentioned (i.e., feeling sadness, unable to reach her, dealing with a shield). Disruption to the contiguity of Ernie's response (a glance to the camera, notable pauses, an audible, extended inbreath and an affect-laden sigh) may not only indicate his hesitation to participate in this new framework, but also the mounting distress that he is feeling as he is about to confront his ex-wife in the chair. However, at line 46, Ernie complies with the therapist's directive, which simultaneously serves as a complaint that launches an imaginary dialogue with his ex-wife.

Confirmation of contact is demonstrated through person-reference, indexical vocabulary (second-person singular pronouns), and fluctuating gaze between the chair and his hands.

Within all phases, similar to the Phase 2 example from Extract 6.5, there may be client resistance or ambiguity which the therapist attempts to work through, in order to gain affiliation and move the therapeutic project forward – see also Chapter 8. Extract 6.12 is taken from a highly emotionally charged session in which Jennifer describes her inability to communicate or to have close relationships, and considers the necessity of loving herself as the ultimate failure. Prior to this extract the therapist asks "`so how d'yah end up being silenced.`" and Jennifer responds with "`fear`". With this client-identified conflict involving emotion, the therapist then makes a proposal "`can we work with the chairs a little bit with that.`", working to jumpstart intervention, by bringing in a new chair. Jennifer's ambiguous response is limited to shallow nods.

**Extract 6.12:** Jennifer: Case 428.18 (Two Chairs)

```
1    Ther:   there's the part of you (0.5) that (.) has (.)
        t    >>returns to frame, sits in new chair, gaze to J->
        j    >>arms crossed on stomach, gaze to chair->
2            so much more to say +(0.6) then she ever says.
        j                        +opens mouth, shallow nods->
3            (1.2)   +
        j    nods-->+
4    Ther:   howda +you? (1.7) scare her. (0.5) °into being silent,°+
        j          +gaze to T---------------------------------------+
5            (+ 8.7                         +)
        j     +gaze to chair and downward+
6    Ther:   she + wants (0.4) to say to people I need to be loved,+
        j        +gaze to T----------------------------------------+
7            +(0.5) I need to be listened to,(0.5) I need to
        j    +gaze downward->
8            be understood,(0.7) +bu'she never gets a chance+
        j                        +looks at T.---------------+
9            +to say °that?°
        j    +gaze downward->
10           +(0.4)+
        j    +nods-+
11   Ther:   °why:.°
12           (1.1)
13   Jen:    .hh (1.9) ↑because nobody's gunna listen.
14           +(1.1)                    +
        j    +tilts head, gaze to ceiling+
15   Ther:   +°right.°
        j    +lowers head, closes eyes
16           (0.2)
17   Ther:   say that to her again.+ (.) don't even bo:ther,
        j                          +shallow nods->
```

```
18   Ther:    (0.5) nobody's gunna listen.+
         j                  shallow nods->+
19            (1.3)
20   Jen:     +>nobody's gunna listen nobody's listening< at all.
         j    +small head shakes, gaze down, eyes closed?->
21   Ther:    [mm.]
22   Jen:     [.hh]
23            (0.9)
24   Jen:     Hh nobody cares. + ~.hh~ (0.2)
         j                     +lowers head, scrunches face->
25   Ther:    [>nobody] cares< about you,
26   Jen:     [.snif  ]
27   Jen:     hh
28   Ther:    nobody's interested in you, (0.7) nobody gives a shit.
```

In lines 01–02, the therapist makes a claim that a part of Jennifer, the one sitting in the other chair, has "so much more to say". After Jennifer provides weak acknowledgement through nodding, the therapist then utters a directive in interrogative format (howda you? (1.7) scare her. (0.5) °into being silent,°), thus giving the client the opportunity to make contact with her other self by "scaring her" into silence. However, a lengthy 8.7-second silence ensues in which the client does not verbally respond and, ultimately, withdraws her gaze from the chair. The therapist then provides more interactional context by stating what the other may want or need to say, but is unable to do so. Then, in line 11, the therapist initiates a direct question to prompt Jennifer to make contact with her fearful self and to get her to focus on how she is being silenced. Following various delay markers (inbreaths, pauses), Jennifer responds with heightened intonation by giving the reason (↑because nobody's gunna listen.). However, as there are no clear references for displaying with whom Jennifer is connecting, her response could be directed to the therapist, to her imagined self, or even both. Following a pause in line 14 and the therapist's minimal confirmation in 15, she then, using an imperative format, directs Jennifer to "say that to her again" and, immediately afterwards, directly models what the client could say (don't even bo:ther; nobody's gunna listen.). By using the word "again", the therapist tweaks the participation framework, presupposing that she was, in fact, already in the contact frame. Subsequently, the client not only begins to make direct contact with her other self, but the lack of compassion toward the other becomes increasingly intensified from ">nobody's gunna listen nobody's listening< at all." to "nobody cares." (lines 20, 24). During this time, Jennifer's emotional distress becomes more audible, as evidenced through her tremulous voice, sniff, facial expression and downward head position. Finally, the therapist responds by first making the target of everyone's indifference explicit (nobody cares< *about you*) and second by intensifying the indifference to "nobody gives a shit".

## 6.6 Conclusions

This chapter has shown that chair work entry regularly comprises four interconnected phases, with each phase orienting to either epistemic or deontic concerns. Whereas Phase 1 (*formulating the trouble*) mainly orients to the clients' greater entitlements to their own experience, Phase 2 (*recruiting participation in chair work*) and Phase 4 (*making contact*) orient to deontic concerns. Phase 3 (*re-adjusting the participation frame*), on the other hand, fluctuates orientation between deontic and epistemic concerns. Further, there appears to be a consistent trajectory in which the interaction first works through epistemic matters before moving on to deontic ones. This regular sequential pattern seems also to point toward a general, person-centred, EFT premise concerning *following* and *guiding*; that is, therapists first follow clients' emotional experience by seeking confirmation from them about what is especially salient. Thereafter, therapists move on to guide clients by recruiting them into chair work with the goal of having them address emotional conflict and unfinished business in the here and now of therapy. By following and/or guiding the client within chair work phases, the participants are able to demonstrate mutual affiliation and achieve task alignment around the client's willingness to work on salient emotional experiences. When initially recruiting client involvement in chair work, in Phase 2, therapists construct a deontic stance that indexes clients' greater authority in deciding the future course of events (i.e., whether to do chair work). But, as the analysis of the four phases has shown, client confirmation in Phase 2 seems also to provide implicit consent for therapists to take up greater deontic status in Phase 4, where they begin to explicitly orchestrate clients' actions. Finally, by confronting an aspect of self or significant other, clients become able to provide a voice to their emotional conflict, thus empowering them to take up greater experiential rights, not only in terms of better understanding the reasons for their depressed state, but also in terms of acting on this understanding within a dialogic context.

This chapter also points out the clinical relevance to therapists who use chair work in their treatments. While chair task interventions are well documented as having successful outcomes, Elliott et al. (2004) have found that introducing these dialogues is challenging for novice therapists. Wagner-Moore (2004) additionally highlights the potential risk of chair work for novice therapists if the client is not ready to explore a particular emotional experience. Pos and Greenberg (2012) also argue against engaging in two-chair work when there is an absence of explicit self-conflict events. It has been shown how the provision of turn-by-turn descriptions of in-session interactional sequences can inform our understanding of how conversations with a personified chair are facilitated and co-constructed within these key EFT interventions. It also offers insight into the interactional practices through which therapists may successfully recruit clients' active participation, the ways in which clients may display hesitation (ambivalence or uncertainty) being recruited and how therapists may then work to repair these task misalignments. More attention to explicit client resistance to chair work and how this resistance is interactionally managed in the unfolding conversation in order to offset further intervention implementation risks will be given in Chapter 8.[5]

[5] Whereas this chapter has focused primarily on first-time chair work entry in a given session, up to the point at which clients first make contact with an aspect of self or significant other, other work has begun exploring directives during in-progress chair work (Smoliak et al., 2021). An understanding of how these dialogues further unfold moment-to-moment and how the therapist helps to orchestrate these recurrently shifting participation frameworks warrants further exploration.

# 7 Repairing Disaffiliation in Therapy

## 7.1 Overview

Emotion-focused therapy (EFT) is based on two major treatment principles (Greenberg, 2002): the provision of a therapeutic relationship and the facilitation of therapeutic work. An important component of the former principle, securing a positive relationship, was already discussed in Chapter 4 on empathy. It was argued that the EFT relational style is person-centred, which involves a way of being with clients characterized by entering the client's internal frame of reference and empathically following the client's experience. The other principle, taken up in Chapter 6 on chair work, focused on facilitating clients into task-based activities by leading them into a form of person-centred engagement with their problems.

Conveying an understanding and acceptance of what clients are telling you is considered to be a fundamental component of a person-centred relational stance in therapy. Recall Rogers' (1951, p. 29) claim – from Chapters 1 and 4 – that therapists are called upon "to perceive the world as the client sees it" and "to lay aside all perceptions from the external frame of reference while doing so." From this perspective, actions that interpret, evaluate or disagree with what clients say or do are avoided and, instead, preference is given to empathic modes of understanding that reflect and validate client experience (Elliott & Greenberg, 2007; Elliott et al., forthcoming; Greenberg et al., 1993; Rennie, 1998; Rogers, 1951). Thus, to achieve a person-centred relational stance in therapy sessions, therapists should refrain from appearing as "experts" who have special rights in knowing what clients *mean* or *feel*.

The vast benefits of formulating what clients have said, by summarizing or pointing out the implications of their talk, have already been addressed in prior chapters. For instance, formulations form key practices through which therapists can affiliate with client's troubles; that is, therapists can show that they support the client by conveying that they understand the client's distress. Formulating is also considered to be a powerful vehicle for doing empathy. Hutchby (2005), for example, has argued that formulations often index a practice known as "active listening," in which empathic understanding is conveyed to the client. Nonetheless, clients may choose to disagree with how therapists have reworded their talk. In these moments of disaffiliation, clients may view therapists as having intruded on their *epistemic rights* (Heritage, 2012) concerning personal events and, by implication, that the therapist is displaying specialized or greater insight into the client's life and experiences. Thus, when clients do not express agreement with how therapists have formulated their talk, therapists adopting a person-centred relational stance are faced with a dilemma: On the one hand, they have suggested a line of activity or exploration that may be therapeutically relevant and thus worth pursuing; yet, on the other hand, they should privilege the clients' viewpoint of their own experience (Rogers, 1951, p. 29) and, therefore, accept the client's version of events over their own. This dilemma, termed the *problem of experience* by Heritage (2011), thus has consequences for the provision and maintenance of affiliation and empathy – see also discussion in Chapter 4. Therapists are called upon to affiliate with clients' troubles tellings and yet certain affiliating practices such as providing empathy may be seen as infringing on their ownership of experience or information preserves (Goffman, 1971; Sharrock, 1974). So, clients may ultimately consider the formulation to be disaffiliative and a violation of these rights or "territorial preserves," leading them to oppose the therapist's understanding of their situation.

In this chapter, formulation sequences containing client disagreements are examined to explore the following question: How do (EFT) therapists realize the person-centred relational practice of privileging the client's unique, yet contrasting, standpoint during moments of disaffiliation/disagreement? Emotion-focused therapists in this sample were found to re-affiliate with clients using a small set of regularly occurring practices. First, therapists would withdraw or retreat from their previously formulated description of the client's prior talk. Withdrawing or retreating is taken to mean that therapists would withhold from responding verbally and wait for clients to develop their diverging perspectives. These therapists would also, during the retreating phase, make explicit non-vocal displays of nodding. These nods worked to *affiliate* (Stivers, 2008) with the client by claiming some access to and endorsing the client's alternative position. Thus, nodding indexed a delicately accomplished maneuver of what may be termed *active retreating*, in which the client's position becomes foregrounded and validated and in which a mutually supportive environment becomes restored. It was also found that, after having made a display of retreating from their own position, therapists would sometimes work to further strengthen affiliative ties with the client by explicitly supporting, displaying understanding of and developing the client's contrasting position through a range of verbal practices.

Although there seems to be a general tendency in which emotion-focused therapists actively retreat from their own prior position and work with the client's divergent position, therapists do, at times, also call attention to (or even advance) their own position. In these contexts, therapists orient to the client's disagreement as a problem of intersubjectivity (i.e., understanding) that is in need of *repair* (Schegloff et al., 1977; see also Pomerantz, 1984 on how speakers may modify their position in contexts of impending disagreement). Two strategies of repair have so far been identified: one that emphasizes a *convergence* of views between client and therapist and the other that maintains a *divergence* of views. For the former practice, therapists attempt to underscore the similarities of their positions. In this way, therapists are able to retain an empathic tie with clients, while at the same time not having to fully rescind on their own previously formulated position. For the latter practice, the interaction tends to become increasingly *off-track*, in the sense that therapist–client disagreement is sustained rather than resolved. Thus, maintaining differences seems to index a *non*-person-centred activity, one in which both therapist and client are more concerned with defending their own standpoints and less so in displaying empathic understanding of the other's standpoint.

## 7.2 Retreating from Therapist's Own Position

In order to maintain a person-centred relational stance, client disagreement following a therapist formulation makes a response from the therapist relevant and expected. The therapist should somehow address any breaches to the client's epistemic primacy that may have arisen and resolve the disaffiliation and disalignment that has ensued. Important epistemic and social implications arise when clients do not confirm or agree with a therapist's formulation. To begin, the disagreement indexes a divergence of views and, possibly, that the therapist's formulation did not, from the client's perspective, adequately cohere with the client's initial telling. The client's opposition may also imply that the therapist is taking the conversation down a certain road that the client cannot endorse or may not feel comfortable with. Disagreements are also disaffiliative and may put social cohesion between the therapist and client at risk, if the disagreement is not resolved (Safran and Muran, 1996; Eubanks et al., 2018). Finally, disagreement runs the risk of getting the therapeutic talk initiated in the sequence "off track" (i.e., disalignment), in the sense that subsequent talk may come to focus on resolving the conflict or misunderstanding, rather than on exploring a therapeutically relevant topic (e.g., the client's feelings). In these contexts of opposition, therefore, therapists who adopt a person-centred relational stance with their clients are confronted with a three-way task. The first task is to maintain an empathic posture by privileging the client's viewpoint. The second task is to mitigate the threat to solidarity by resolving the disagreement. The third task is to get the action re-aligned toward a therapeutically relevant trajectory.

When displaying affiliation with the client's position in contexts of disagreement, there is a strong tendency for therapists to retreat from their own position. This therapist practice can be considered client-centred (Roger, 1951), as it displays a readiness on the therapist's part to accept and focus on the client's frame of reference. Retreating is also better conceptualized as an *active*, rather than a passive achievement; that is, although therapists let go of their own position, they actively engage and affiliate with the client's position both non-verbally and verbally. An important non-verbal resource to achieve affiliation and to *re-establish* a context in which agreement or collaborative aims may be pursued is nodding. Verbal resources are also used by therapists to strengthen their support of the client's divergent position and to re-align both parties toward a common goal. These resources include mirroring repeats, collaborative completions and second formulations.

The practice of retreating tends to undergo a unique temporal development. First, therapists withhold from responding, allowing clients to develop their contrasting position. Second, therapists affiliate with the client's position only when the client expressed some overt "affiliate-able content": an explicit disagreement or fully articulated stance (i.e., appraisal of a person or event). This therapist practice of retreating from one's own position on the one hand, and affiliating with the client's contrasting position on the other, will be explored in the next sections.

## 7.3 Nodding to Affiliate

Conversational conduct that supports or endorses another speaker's perspective or stance is affiliative (Stivers, 2008; see also Drew and Walker, 2009 for a related view). Stivers (2008) showed that, during storytelling, nods from a recipient constitute a key affiliative resource. This is because nods display that the recipient is able to access and show an appreciation of the teller's affective treatment of an event. In contexts of client disagreement, nods from the therapist were also found to display affiliation, but of the client's *divergent* viewpoint. In the subsections that follow, I show how the sequential position of nods indexes a person-centred relational practice in EFT by affiliating with clients in two ways: 1) delaying the nod until the client has fully disagreed and 2) displaying an appreciation of the client's affective treatment of an event.

### *7.3.1 Nodding to Affiliate with the Client's Divergent Position*

In the sample for this study, emotion-focused therapists would often position their nods immediately following a client disagreement. These nods were often "stand alone," produced without any accompanying verbal utterance.

An illustration of this practice appears in Extract 7.1 (see also Extract 3.3), which shows the client disconfirming the therapist's formulation and the therapist, in turn, retreating from her own position and delaying the production of a nod until the client fully completes her disconfirmation (A=Advice; D=Disagreement; F=Formulation).

**Extract 7.1:** 014.18(4)

```
       01 Kris:  .hh ((sniffs)) hm, I (.) really don't (0.3) I don feel strong
       02        enough to(0.4) quarrel with him to ye know, to yell back or
       03        to yell at him when I, .snif see because it's-I am
       04        m-really uh h(h)m petrifIEd when he starts(0.8) yelling.
       05        an I'm- I'm afraid to,
                 -
                 -
                 -
A→     14 Ther:  ((lip smack)) so maybe the best thing would be to: give up on
A→     15        that battle an, put your efforts in:to:, (1.4)
F→     16        >mean this is what you're< saying to yourself maybe the best
F→     17        °thing would be [ta give] up on that, an° put my efforts
       18 Kris:                  [mm  hm.]
F→     19 Ther:  inta building my own ↑life.
       20        (1.1)
D→     21 Kris:  .snif n-yeah.
       22        (1.9)
D→     23 Kris:  but I- y'know I think I do do build my own life.
       24        (      1.1              )
nod→          t             slow nod→
       25 Kris:  mm,
       26        (3.8)
       27 Kris:  because I ye know did go to school I. .hh did get degrees
              k  looks at T
              t                                               nod
       28        and I went uh (2.0) mm. to-to work right away,
```

At the beginning of this extract, Kristina relays her difficulty in quarreling with her husband by accounting for the negative emotions that these quarrels conjure up in her (`petrifIEd`; `afraid to`). The therapist's response draws the implication that Kristina's not feeling "`strong enough to quarrel`" and her being petrified and afraid when the husband yells may be construed as her not wanting to confront the husband and, instead, her wanting to engage in more productive activities. The therapist first designs her utterance as a form of advice (`the best thing would be to:`) but then, after a 1.4-second pause, she does a repair by recasting her utterance as a formulation of what the client had herself said (`>mean this is what you're< saying to yourself`). Through this repair, the therapist underscores that the "best thing" is derived from the client's prior talk, rather than what the therapist has concluded from this talk. The therapist then continues with her upshot formulation that focuses on what Kristina might prefer to do rather than stay in perpetual conflict with her husband. When uttering the formulation, the therapist takes on the client's voice (`put my efforts inta building my own ↑life`), thus speaking *as if* she were paraphrasing or quoting the client's message. Following the formulation are various dispreferred markers (Schegloff, 2007, p. 67) such as pro-forma agreement (`n-yeah. ... but`) and inter-turn delays (lines 20 and 22) that explicitly signal impending disconfirmation – see also Chapter 3 for a full list of disagreement/disconfirmation markers. When Kristina does finally disagree, in line 23, she counters the implication that she has not build her own life. Note that the therapist's nodding is not contiguous to the client's response but is delayed until Kristina has finished her disconfirming move and a silence has begun. The slow rate of the nod and its delay in execution seems to match the client's prior disaffiliation and show that the therapist has slightly disengaged from the interaction with her client. However, by providing a nod, the therapist makes up for this potential rupture by allowing the client some space in which to expand upon her disconfirmation. In this way, the therapist is able to display a willingness to accommodate the client's stated viewpoint. In effect, the therapist's own position recedes in the background, thus allowing the client to further expand on how she has worked at building her own life.

### *7.3.2 Nodding to Affiliate with the Client's Affective Stance*

In the majority of examples, therapists do not nod to affiliate with the client's disagreement as such, but rather further delay their production of nods until the client had displayed a clear *affective stance* or has communicated an affective position – see also Chapter 5 for a full list of stance resources. Stance-taking resources include story prefaces (`I have a friend. (1.4) who .snif (0.7) became depressed. (0.8) a long time ago.`), prosody (`like how he did it, (.) was just, (1.7) really ↑goo:d`) and lexical choices realizing affect (`so funny; really ↑goo:d`). The nodding environments in contexts of disagreement bear a similarity to what Stivers (2008) had noted in storytelling contexts; that is, recipients (i.e., therapists) tend to nod in order to convey an appreciation of the teller's (i.e., client's) affective description of an event. These affiliative displays involved a two-step manoeuver: First, therapists decline to engage with the client's potentially conflicting view by withholding from speaking; second, therapists re-engage with the client by timing their nod in such a way that it endorses the client's affective stance. This process is shown in Extract 7.2 involving the client Paula (see also Extract 2.17).

**Extract 7.2:** 312.09(08)

```
     01   Paula:  I guess for me like, (1.3) to have like h- harmonious
     02           balanced.hh (0.9) relationships with people is
              t               shallow nod          shallow nod
     03           something very important.
     04           (          2.8          )
              t   slow nod--------------->
F→   05   Ther:   °so part of you really wants t- g- (0.5) make this work.°
              t                                    shrugs shoulders
     06           (.)
              p   fast double nod
D→   07   Paula:  .hhh (.) ye:ah? but- (.) eh(hh) (0.5) at the same ↑ti:me,
     08           (3.3)
D→   09   Paula:  if it doesn't work it doesn't ↑wo:rk.
     10           (0.5)
              t   slow double nod->
     11   Paula:  and it's just really hard, (0.8) to say oka::y (1.3) this
              t   -------------------------->
     12           person, (2.0) ((lip smack)) doesn't make me feel good,
              p                                                 takes tissue
     13           (3.4)
              t   slow shallow double nod
     14   Paula:  a:n- (.) like jus- (.) just to ↓leave it like just to
              t                                             shallow nod
     15           sa::y, like f::- (.) ↑f:orget it. like just drop it an-
     16           and move o:n. >like it< doesn't work.
     17           (2.5)
     18   Ther:   and is there (.) a feeling of somehow, (0.9) I fa:iled
              t   leans into hand
     19           if tha- I do tha:t or °I-°
     20           (1.1)
D→   21   Paula:  .hhh::: hhh:::
     22           (8.8)
              t   gazes at P
              p   gazes away
D→   23   Paula:  .hh >I- euh< no:. like- (.) w- what ↑I'm wondering
     24           about is like wis this- (0.8) particular man. like
              t                                        shallow multiple nods
     25           why:: (.) <am I so: hung up> (0.3) on him. like why do
     26           I <have to try:,> (1.2) ↑so hard,
              t    slow double nod------------------------>
     27           (0.5)
              t   shallow nod
     28   Paula:  and at the same time like it's almost like he
              p                                            looks at T
     29           doesn't ca:re.
     30           (1.5)
              t   deep nod.
     31   Paula:  and why do, (0.4) °why do I° keep,
              t                     slow nod.
```

```
32            (3.9)
          t   slow nod
33  Paula:    ↑running.
34            (    1.6     )
          t   multiple nods→
35  Paula:    uh(hh) (.) and why does he say certain things, (0.3)
          t   nods------------------------------------->
36            which kind of make me ↑thi:nk (.) that he cares, but
          p                              double nod
37            then (0.8) in his behaviour he doesn't really- (.)live
38            up to it. uh(hh)
          p                 smiles
          t                 nod
39  Ther:     °t(.hh) so you feel very confused by his behaviour
          p   looks down
40            (1.0)
41  Paula:    oh ↑yeah. t(h)he he he!
          p                 rolls eyes to side
          t                   shallow nod
```

When speaking about her relationships and her current boyfriend (lines 1–2), Paula states that she finds it important to have "`h- harmonious balanced .hh (0.9) relationships with people`". After a long pause in line 4, the therapist produces a formulation that contains an implication about what she desires; that is, because relationships (and more specifically, the relationship with her boyfriend) are so important to her, she "`really wants t- g- (0.5) make this work.`" The therapist adds markers of contingency to her formulation, using the expression "`part of you`" and a shoulder shrug, which cedes epistemic primacy to the client. In response, line 7, Paula's turn begins with dispreference markers such as an inbreath, pauses and proforma agreement, thus signalling impending disagreement. This then occurs deeper within the turn as Paula opposes the implication that she always desires a certain relationship outcome (`if it doesn't work it doesn't ↑wo:rk`). As in Extract 7.1, the therapist waits until the disagreement has been fully expressed before producing nods (line 10).

Paula then continues with an affective stance in which breaking up with a partner because of an inadequacy in the relationship (`doesn't make me feel good; >like it< doesn't work`) is evaluated as "really hard." Paula, thus, creates an opportunity for the therapist to affiliate with this stance in her next turn. Although there are many possible ways of making affiliative connections to what Paula has said (e.g., confirming the difficulty in breaking up; exploring Paula's emotions when she has ended a past relationship), the therapist chooses to target a possible reason for her not wanting to have the relationship end, thus presenting it as an implication that arises from Paula's expression of difficulty. It should also be noted that, similar to a different therapist's formulation in Extract 7.1, this therapist also uses first-person pronouns (a feeling of **somehow**, (0.9) I fa:iled if tha- I do that), thereby designing "the reason" as something that Paula *could have* said or thought. Thus, by using the first-person pronoun "I" in subject position and by drawing an implication that has arisen from her talk, the therapist is able to speak directly from the client's perspective and build on or expand what Paula has said. Paula, however, responds by rejecting this implication. Her disagreement is slowly ushered in through a prolonged sigh (line 21) and is then followed by a long pause in which she remains stoic. Paula then voices explicit disagreement (.hh >I- euh< no:.) and, after that, continues to develop her turn by bitterly complaining about why she remains with "this- particular man" even though he does not live up to her expectations.[1]

In contrast to the therapist's non-vocal conduct following the first disagreement – and also in Extract 7.1 – the therapist's first overt display of token affiliation through nodding does not occur immediately after the client's disagreement, but after her first conveyance of stance (↑I'm wondering about is like wis this- (0.8) particular man.). The client's affective stance would involve either self-avowals (e.g., being so hung up on him, trying so hard, keeping on running) or ascriptions (*he* doesn't care) of blame. Further, nods were found to occur systematically in a certain sequential position: immediately following the client's production of an affective stance within a complete clause. The therapist's systematic positioning of nods to synchronize with the client's completed stance display is shown in Extract 7.3. Here, the client's initial five-stance displays are listed, but this synchronous matching of nods with the client's expression of stance is continued throughout the rest of Paula's turn.

**Extract 7.3:** Nods contiguously placed after stance expressions by Paula

1. Paula: ↑I'm wondering about is like wis this- (0.8) particular man.
2. Paula: like why:: (.) <am I so: hung up> (0.3) on him.
   t *shallow multiple nods* *slow double nod→*
3. Paula: like why do I <have to try:,> (1.2) ↑so hard,
   t *nod---------->* *shallow nod*
4. Paula: (0.5) and at the same time like it's almost like he doesn't
5. Paula: ca:re. (1.5) and why do, (0.4) °why do I° keep, (3.9) ↑running.
   t *deep nod* *slow nod* *slow nod*
   ( 1.6 )
   t *multiple nods→*

To recapitulate, there are two general non-vocal practices of displaying affiliation in response to client disalignment: The first is to delay affiliation until

[1] The potential pejorative implications of terms such as "this man" or "this guy" (see Sacks 1995b), also used by Paula in a different conversation, is discussed in Chapter 5.

the client has had time to develop her disagreement or opposing agenda; the second is to display affiliation only once clients have made clear the affective stance that they are taking, in which case the therapist's nods work to affiliate directly with that stance. But why delay affiliation in this manner? Sacks (1995b, p. 573) remarked that in the context of telling news, recipients tended to wait until the storyteller finished before expressing joy or sorrow. According to Sacks, assessments that come too early may be perceived as interruptions or cutting the speaker off and, therefore, may ultimately discourage the teller from developing the story in such a way that the recipient may properly appreciate it. A parallel may be drawn in these therapy extracts. If the therapist were to affiliate too early by nodding, the client could interpret the therapist's move as interrupting or even as insincere; that is, the client may feel that 1) the therapist is trying to discourage her from disagreeing or pursuing her own agenda, or 2) the therapist is merely feigning affiliation because the client had not yet even had a chance to fully express her contrasting view. For this reason, withholding from affiliating until clients actually produce some kind of affiliate-able content may constitute a particularly effective form of emotional support, showing a degree of caring or concern from the therapist. Nods occurring in the immediate environment of a client disagreement (i.e., contradiction) might only be seen as acknowledging that the client has disaffiliated. Yet, by waiting for the client to expand on her disconfirmation and, further, by waiting for the client to develop her affective stance (as shown here), the therapist may be in a better position to 1) accede primary rights or ownership of experience to the client, 2) display genuine understanding of the client's point of view, and 3) re-align with the client by endorsing her trajectory of talk such as, in Extract 7.2, providing the client more opportunities to elaborate on her criticisms regarding her own and her boyfriend's actions.

## 7.4 Verbal Practices: Supporting and Developing the Client's Divergent Position

The person-centred relational practice of retreating from one's own position and affiliating with the client's counter-position represents a first step in securing epistemic primacy for the client and a context in which the client and therapist become re-affiliated. Although nods were found to accomplish much of the groundwork for establishing this kind of empathic connection, often more discursive work was required to ensure that the interaction could move toward a more therapeutically relevant track. Therapists drew from a range of interactive practices that worked to explicitly support or develop the client's divergent position. Included are *mirroring repeats*, *collaborative turn completions* and *second formulations*. Each of these practices will be discussed in turn.

### 7.4.1 Mirroring Repeats

Repetition has already been explored for its occurrence in affiliating sequences – see Chapters 3 and 4 – and here the focus will instead be placed on the interactional work they do following client disagreement. To recap: "mirroring is strategic word or phrase iteration using the same downward intonation" (Ferrara, 1994, p. 119). Mirroring tends to function as a prompt by getting the prior speaker to elaborate on the word or phrase that has been repeated. In the context of prior disaffiliation, it would seem that therapist use of mirroring also works to affiliate with a specific part of the client's disagreement. It displays a complete letting go of one's own position and operates to align with the client's newly articulated trajectory of talk. Mirroring is shown in Extract 7.4 (M=Mirroring) (see also Extract 3.5).

**Extract 7.4:** 014.18(2)(a)

```
    01  Kris:  and uh. of course my husband he doesn't (.) help(h) me in(h)
                   t                                                 nod
    02              .hhh .snif many of my uh. (1.3) doesn=make me happy at
    03              all(h).
    04              (     5.3     )
                   k   gazes down
                   t   nod
    05  Ther:  .hhh so you're wanting him to be supporti:ve and.
                   he['s not.]
    06  Kris:     [↑mm hm.]
                   k     nods
    07  Kris:  yes or at [least be int'rested, ]
    08  Ther:            [you feel unsupporte:d] an
    09              (0.9)
                   k  nods
                   t  nods
    10  Kris:  yeah.
    11              (0.7)
    12  Kris:  y-I would exp[ect at least]
F→  13  Ther:                    [very  ↑alone] it sounds like in (a hair)=
D→  14  Kris:  = I ↑was thinking about=it-is- I ↑don't know if it is:
                   k  looks down
    15              feeling alone I:,
    16              (1.0)
D→  17  Kris:  .hhh it's more betrayed den alone.
                   k                  looks at T
                   t                 slow multiple nods→
    18              (            5.7            )
                   t  nods------------>
                   k  shifts gaze away
M→  19  Ther:  .hhh betrayed. yeah.
    20              (2.2)
    21  Ther:  >so he's [let you<] down.
    22  Kris:           [mm  hm. ]
                   t    shallow multiple nods→
```

```
23   Kris:   mm hm.
        t    ---->
24   Ther:   °°mm hm,°°
        t    ---------->
```

Kristina has been complaining that her husband neither helps her nor makes her happy. In line 04, the therapist reformulates Kristina's complaint as a plea for having her husband become more supportive toward her. This formulation receives affiliative uptake from the client and leads to sequences in which mutual affiliation and consensus on Kristina's situation is displayed. Somewhat later on (line 12), the therapist seems to push the implications of the husband's actions a bit further through an upshot formulation that focuses on the resulting affective state (`very ↑alone`) caused by her husband's lack of attention toward her. Kristina responds with disagreement, claiming that she feels "`betrayed`" rather than alone. The therapist works to retreat from her initial position by withholding a response and by affiliating with Kristina immediately after her disagreement. Affiliation is achieved through a series of nods that stretch over a period of 5.7 seconds. Following this lengthy silence, the therapist provides another affiliative display: She first mirrors Kristina's prior talk by repeating the word and matching the original prosody "`betrayed`", and then produces an acknowledgement. Through this move, the therapist demonstrates her readiness to work with Kristina's claimed feeling of betrayal, thus relinquishing epistemic primacy to the client. Kristina, however, does not elaborate on her position, which leads the therapist to produce another formulation that elaborates on and empathizes with Kristina's feelings of betrayal (`>so he's let you< down.`) – see section 7.4.3 for more discussion of second formulations. As a consequence, mutual consensus is restored, as evidenced by Kristina's acknowledgements that occur simultaneously with the therapist's nodding and acknowledgement.

### 7.4.2 *Collaborative Turn Completions*

The affiliative and empathic functions of collaborative turn completions have already been discussed in Chapters 3 and 4. The collaborative production of an utterance, in which one speaker begins the utterance and another extends it, is a carefully orchestrated accomplishment requiring considerable attentiveness and skill from the second speaker; that is, the second speaker must be able to project when *turn constructional units* (TCUs: Sacks et al., 1974) are nearing completion and, at the same time, must be able to immediately build upon the utterance by adding an appropriate grammatical unit that semantically coheres with what has come before (Lerner, 1996; Sacks, 1995a, pp. 144–145). Lerner uses the term *anticipatory completion* in referencing how the turn design of the first speaker furnishes the resources through which a second speaker may continue or complete the TCU-in-progress. These co-constructed utterances also have considerable social relevance, because they index a high degree of cooperation, solidarity and involvement between the participants (Ferrara, 1994, p. 147). Joint, collaborative productions have also been shown to imply relevant social categories such as "husband and wife" (Goodwin, 1987; Muntigl and Hadic Zabala, 2008) or group membership (Sacks, 1995a, p. 175).

Certain turn elements may be specifically deployed to invite completion from others, such as in Extract 7.2a. In this example of invited completion, also commonly referred to as designedly incomplete utterances (DIUs) – see also Chapter 3 (Koshik, 2002), where the therapist uses a turn-final *or* + subject as an opportunity for the client to produce her own version of what she feels, a version that may or may not align with what the therapist had proposed.

### Extract 7.2a

```
18   Ther:  and is there (.) a feeling of somehow, (0.9) I fa:iled if tha-
         t  leans into hand
19          I do tha:t or °I-°
```

Another example of a collaborative production is shown in Extract 7.5: Sofia has just described a violent incident with her husband. The context for the incident involved a snowball fight that Sophia initiated by throwing a snowball at her husband. According to Sofia, her husband then reacted violently by rubbing snow in her face and, because Sofia was holding a dish in her hands at the time, the dish ended up hitting her in the face (CP=Collaborative Production).

### Extract 7.5: 304.03(1d)

```
      01  Sofia:  an he was (.) an I mean (0.3) the reaction was (0.6) violent
               s                                                 double nod
      02          (0.3)
      03  Ther:   yeah.
               t  nod
      04          (0.4)
               t  nod
      05  Ther:   [sca:red yo:u.]
      06  Sofia:  [pretty   vi::]-violent, .hhh a:nd uh::m.
      07          (2.3)
F→    08  Ther:   like >a little bit< jarring or sca:ry::. or
D→    09  Sofia:  ↑scary? .hhh no not scary, I don't (.) I don't
CP→   10          [I don't feel sca:re.  ]
CP→   11  Ther:   [you don't feel scared.]
      12  Ther:    (     0.6     )
               t  multiple nods→
D→    13  Sofia:  of him anymore=no. ↓not scary:=sad.
               t  -->
      14          (0.4)
      15  Sofia:  sad because I mean.
               t  shallow nod
```

In response to this telling (line 08), the therapist formulates a couple of emotive reactions (jarring, scary) brought about by the husband's actions. Although these therapist formulations seem to work empathically by naming the other's feelings – thereby conveying a strong sense of how the client feels (Pudlinski, 2005, p. 272) – Sofia resists this identification (line 09). Non-vocal affiliation is achieved through the production of multiple nods after Sofia completed her disconfirmation (line 12). But just prior to that, the therapist makes an even stronger affiliative display by extending Sofia's turn and voicing the contradiction simultaneously with her. By constructing the disagreement concurrently with the client (you don't feel scared.), the therapist not only *echoes* the client's speech (Ferrara, 1994, p. 113), but also demonstrates that she is able to anticipate what the client is going to say. In this way, the therapist displays a keen understanding of the client's contrastive position, and that she is prepared to affiliate with that position, by making transparent the therapists' willingness to adopt Sofia's perspective over her own.

### *7.4.3 Second Formulations*

Mirroring and collaboratively extending the client's talk were shown to index specific practices in which therapists affiliated with the client's contrasting position. These practices revealed how the therapist was able to accommodate the client's view by allowing the client to develop her own track and even to encourage her in doing so. The next practice will show how therapists take an even more active role in helping clients to advance their contrasting viewpoint. These are second formulations. In most cases, these formulations signal a complete abandonment of the therapist's prior line, because the therapist is now explicitly working with the client's elaborated divergent position. Thus, second formulations constitute a re-alignment in which the therapist explores a slightly new path that originated from the client's disagreement with the therapist's original formulation. Examples of second formulations have already been shown, but not discussed, in prior extracts. For example, in Extract 7.2, after a number of stance displays from Paula that were mainly critical of her boyfriend's behavior, the therapist, in line 37, formulated her talk as "°t(.hh) so you feel very conf<u>us</u>ed by his behaviour". That the formulation does take the interaction in a different direction can be seen if it is compared with the therapist's prior intervention (and is there (.) a f<u>eel</u>ing of somehow, (0.9) I <u>fa:i</u>led if tha- I <u>do</u> that or °I-°): Thus, the focus of talk moves from Paula possibly "feeling that she failed with her past relationships" to her "feeling confused by her present boyfriend's behaviour".

A different example of a second formulation is shown in Extract 7.6 (see also Extract 3.4). This example highlights not only how the formulation effects re-alignment but also how it can be used to secure affiliation and epistemic primacy by getting the client to jointly produce the formulation. This episode occurs some minutes after Extract 7.5, and although the topic still involves the husband's behaviors, Sofia now begins to question why she persists in staying within the relationship (F2=Second Formulation).

**Extract 7.6:** 304.03 (3)

```
     01  Sofia:  at this ↑point. (.) I f:eel (3.2) u::m
     02          n:o:thing towards him.
     03  Ther:   ↑yeah.
     04  Sofia:  emotionally.
F→   05  Ther:   (clears throat) it's that- (.) n:umb feeling right?
     06  Sofia:  mm hm.
F→   07  Ther:   you feel- (.) blo:cked off from him.
     08  Sofia:  I mean, uh, some people after twenty years they say well,
     09          you know still it's my husband, .hhh .snif sometimes (0.8)
     10          at some points I don't even feel that.
     11  Ther:   mm hm.
              t  nod
     12          (          1.9          )
              t  shallow multiple nods
F→   13  Ther:   feels like you don't even know this man.
     14          (1.1)
D→   15  Sofia:  ↑no I feel I ↑know him.
              s  slow multiple nods, raises eyebrows
     16  Ther:   mm hm.
              t  shallow double nod
D→   17  Sofia:  an bec(h)ause I(h)(h) know him. .hhh I-I-I cannot
              s     laughing
              t               smiles at S
D→   18          underestan=how can I be with him for twenty ↑years.
F2→  19  Ther:   .hhh uh huh. so you: look at him and feel like-
              t  fast multiple nods      lowers eyebrows
     20          (1.5)
F2→  21  Ther:   how=did=↑I (0.3) give all [this up, or]
     22  Sofia:                            [what'm=I do]ing here.
              t     shrugs shoulders
              s                                 looks away
     23          (0.4)
     24  Sofia:  what=am I doing. wha have I been doing.
              s            looks at T
     25          (0.5)
              t  fast nod
     26  Sofia:  for all this time with this man?
     27  Ther:   yeah,
              t  fast shallow nod
     28          (1.4)
     29  Ther:   yeah.
     30          (0.4)
```

```
31   Ther:    how've I lost all these yea:rs.
32   Sofia:   mm hm:?
           s  raises eyebrows, slow deep nod→
33            (     1.2      )
           s  ------->
```

Sofia is disclosing her increasing difficulty in perceiving her spouse as *her husband.* She claims to feel "n:o:thing toward him." (line 02) and then, in line 04, appends the term "emotionally.". The therapist responds with a summary formulation (it's that- (.) n:umb feeling right?), which receives minimal affiliative uptake from Sofia (mm hm.), and then continues by drawing an implication (you feel- (.) blo:cked off from him.). But rather than offering confirmation, Sofia seems to instead continue on her own track by reiterating her lack of feelings toward her husband (lines 08–10).[2] This disalignment is displayed via Sofia's repair marker (I mean) in which she ties her talk back to what she had said earlier. In response, the therapist offers minimal acknowledgement while nodding and then continues to nod throughout a prolonged silence (line 12). The nods appearing in this sequential environment could be responding to the disalignment that has arisen over the past few turns.

Following the silence, however, the therapist seems to continue on her own track by providing an upshot formulation implying that she is disconnected or blocked off from him (feels like you don't even know this man.). Sofia disagrees through a forceful contradiction and the therapist, in turn, affiliates by nodding, smiling and acknowledging Sofia's opposition (lines 15–17). Sofia ends her turn by accounting for her position (how can I be with him for twenty ↑years.), to which the therapist responds by producing a second formulation that is incomplete, appearing in the form of a DIU, and contains an intra-turn silence (so you: look at him and feel like- (1.5)). Various researchers have argued that for everyday conversations, although the silence belongs to the current speaker in these constructions, the recipient is allowed an opportunity to complete the TCU (Lerner, 1996, p. 260; Sacks et al., 1974). This also appears to be going on in our therapy data; that is, the therapist is giving the client an opportunity to complete the formulation by designing it as an *anticipatory completion* (see also 3.3.3 in Chapter 3 and 4.5.5 in Chapter 4); through the formulation's DIU format and the intervening silence, Sofia could "take over" and determine the content of the therapist's initiated turn, thus demonstrating epistemic primacy over what she feels about her husband. Although the therapist's first attempt did not succeed in securing completion from Sophia, the therapist's next turn

[2] Sofia's prior minimal acknowledgement/affiliation may have already been presaging upcoming and deeper disaffiliation in her next turn.

does. She offers Sofia a possible interpretation (how=did=↑I (0.3) give all this up, or), albeit in mitigated form: The therapist's shoulder shrug (line 21) and the appended "or" in turn-final position considerably weaken any claims to epistemic primacy concerning the therapist's rights to knowledge over the client (Drake, 2015). Sofia then takes up epistemic primacy by providing her own version of what she feels in a turn with an interjacent onset (Jefferson, 1986) before the therapist has completed her turn. Thus, Sofia seems to shift the focus of talk to the consequences of not having any feelings for her husband (what'm=I doing here) rather than taking on the therapist's position of further exploring how she feels. This ultimately led to mutual affiliation around Sofia's affective stance of having been so deeply dissatisfied with the relationship for so long.

## 7.5 Contending with Disagreement: Operations of Repair

When encountering disagreement, there is an overwhelming tendency for person-centred therapists to retreat from their own position and affiliate with the client's divergent position. There are instances, however, in which therapists treat client disagreement as a form of interactional "trouble" that, from the therapist's perspective, is in need of *repair* (Schegloff et al., 1977); that is, the disagreement is viewed as a form of misunderstanding between therapist and client that has arisen from the interaction. There are two general types of repair: The first type implies an underlying congruency of perspectives between therapist and client, whereas the second type does not. For the former, therapists try to maintain a person-centred relational stance by affiliating with the client's counter-move while, at the same time, endorsing their own previous position. For the second type, therapists momentarily exit from their person-centred relational stance by disaffiliating with the client's position. In doing so, therapists create an implication that the client may not have understood the therapist correctly.

### *7.5.1 Re-Aligning: Assuming a Congruency of Perspectives*

This section shows how therapists conduct repair work to ultimately re-align with clients around what they, the therapists, claim to be comparable viewpoints. Although this practice runs the risk of threatening the empathic relationship between therapist and client, the therapists are able to circumvent this difficulty by safeguarding the client's epistemic primacy. Therapists accomplish this task by using a range of affiliating devices such as nods and repair initiators that convey consensus expressions (e.g., that's what I meant; yeah yeah I'm saying that yeah). Extract 7.7 shows how the therapist's repair work is successful, whereby she and the client are able to re-align and affiliate with the therapist's view as one that is actually shared between them (R=Repair).

**Extract 7.7:** 014.13(3)

```
    01  Ther:  .hhh so how could you change your behaviour. e-wonder
    02         .hh you talked about s- not. uh not avoiding
    03         (0.6)
            t  looks at K
    04  Kris:  uh y[es.]
    05  Ther:      [issu]es anym[ore.]
    06  Kris:                   [yeh ] so I- but I wou- you know
            k                   looks away.
            t                                     looks at K
    07         I would like to change my behaviour,
    08         (    0.6     )
            t  shallow nod
    09  Kris:  an feel comf(h)ort(h)ab(h)le (h)or .hhh y'know of e:
            k  looks at T
            t                                    nod
    10         meaning uh being able to handle .hhh uh the situations,
    11         (0.7)
F→  12  Ther:  ((lip smack)) so sounds like you're. (0.3) .hhh afraid
            t                    multiple shallow nods.
F→  13         of the consequences of (0.7) whether=not you could
            t  shallow double nod
F→  14         handle the consequences of.
    15         (0.9)
D→  16  Kris:  ↑not=the consequences no but the situation itself. let's
            k           shakes head
D→  17         say f- my (0.3)yeah I don=know what to do=if my husband
D→  18         uh starts uh, (1.0) uhm yelling uh=
R→  19  Ther:  = >that's what I meant< like if you stopped avoiding
            t              fast double nod
R→  20         what- how his w-how he would react you don't know if
    21         you could handle.
    22         (0.4)
    23  Kris:  that's righ[t. ye]ah.
    24  Ther:             [yeah.]
            t              nod
```

At the beginning of this interaction, the therapist poses a *wh*-interrogative, asking the client how she could change her behaviour, and then begins to connect this question with a remark about what Kristina had said earlier, but does not finish it, and then directs her gaze at the client: "not. uh not avoid-ing". In doing so, the therapist creates an environment for the client to do *anticipatory completion* in a DIU format and thus finish the therapist's turn. Instead, Kristina first offers confirmation (uh yes.) while the therapist completes the turn herself (issues anymore.). In lines 06–10, Kristina lists two areas of potential change (feel comf(h)ort(h)ab(h)le; being able to handle .hhh uh the situations), but seems to frame these as merely hypothetical (would like) and produces them while laughing and with some hesitation. The therapist then orients to these elements of hesitation and uncertainty (so sounds like) by providing an upshot of Kristina's turn and by positing that she is "afraid of the consequences" of change. The therapist again ends her turn in a DIU format with the preposition "of", thus giving Kristina the opportunity to co-construct what these consequences are. In line 16, however, Kristina refrains from further extending the turn and instead responds with a disagreement (↑not=the consequences no). During this time, the therapist withholds displaying affiliation until after Kristina has fully articulated her affective stance concerning the husband's extreme behavior (I don=know what to do=if my husband uh starts uh, (1.0) uhm yelling). At this point, the therapist nods to affiliate with Kristina's stance, but at the same time she initiates repair work by highlighting her own perspective and by claiming that the two perspectives are actually in alignment (>that's what I meant<); that is, whereas for Kristina the fear or concern had to do with the situation rather than the consequences, the therapist was careful to point out that by changing her behaviour (if you stopped avoiding), Sophia might have to deal with these situations involving the husband, implying that there might also be consequences. Further, the repair initiator and the nods are produced simultaneously and at a fast rate, which works to strengthen the therapist's claim to mutual agreement and affiliation. A congruency of perspectives is achieved at the close of this sequence when Sofia claims epistemic primacy through her upgraded confirmation (that's right. yeah.) and when the therapist simultaneously nods while producing an overlapping agreement.

Misalignments may also occur due to a misunderstanding. Extract 7.8 shows an instance in which the therapist uses a term that is misconstrued by the client Sofia, thus requiring the therapist to engage in repair work.

**Extract 7.8:** 304.07(4)

```
01   Sofia:   not even in my dating time.
          s   widens eyes at T
02   Ther:    ye[ah,]
03   Sofia:     [in-] during=de time that I was dating him.
04   Ther:    yeah,
05   Sofia:   uh: I had a good relationship.
06            (1.0)
07   Sofia:   a relationship that made me,
08            (    0.9           )
          t   slow multiple nods
09   Sofia:   uh:m- m- (0.6) the ↑real me.
```

```
10              (         1.1           )
           t    shallow multiple nods→
11   Ther:      yeah. yet you- that you did (0.5) not even in your dating
           t    -->                                 shakes head
12              relationship did you ↑feel .hhh
           t    double nod
13   Sofia:     that I- [what I felt   ]
14   Ther:              [like So-Sofi:]a was really [being]
15   Sofia:                                         [yeah.]
           s            deep nod                     deep nod
16              (0.3)
17   Ther:      [see::n, °or°]
18   Sofia:     [what I      ] fe:lt,
19              (0.2)
20   Sofia:     yeah. mm hm? so::
           s    nod
21   Ther:      °touched, or°
22              (1.0)
23   Sofia:     .hhh >pardon=me?<
24   Ther:      .hhh well that your self wasn't really being °tou:ched.°
25              (3.2)
           s    gazes at T
           t    gazes at S
26   Sofia:     that's not-
           s    turns head, looks away
27   Ther:      .hhh is just a terminology thing.
           t    smiles, shakes head
           s           smiles at T
28   Sofia:     [a(h)heh(h)]
29   Ther:      [I     mean] just that- that your
           t    double nod
30              (1.0)
31   Ther:      your th-your self. like the real Sofia was not being seen
32              or [heard.]
33   Sofia:        [yeah. ] or not was-
34              (0.6)
35   Sofia:     us- o::r was uh sunghow not be'in able to (.) come ↑out.
36              (1.1)
           s    raises eyebrows, looking at T
37   Ther:      ((lip smack)) yeah. yeah. (0.3) °uh huh.°
           t    deep multiple nods-------------->
```

Sofia provides a serious critique of her relationship with her husband by stating that she did not feel like "`the ↑real me.`" even when they first began dating (lines 01–09). The therapist begins her formulation in line 11, which continues on intermittently until line 21. In line 12, the therapist takes a deep inbreath after the word "`↑feel`", which is then taken as an environment for doing *anticipatory completion* by Sofia in line 13 "`that I- what I felt`" and, thus, to expand on her feelings. But rather than allow Sofia to continue her turn, the therapist resumes speaking in line 14, thus creating overlapping talk before briefly pausing in line 16. Then, both the therapist and the client resume speaking simultaneously, which results in the therapist ceding the turn to Sofia. The client, however, does not complete her utterance "what I fe:lt," and, in line 20, voices an acknowledgement token, followed by a continuer (mm hm?) and a turn-final "so::". Thus, the conversation up until this point is characterized by repeated misalignments in which the therapist pushes forward with her formulation, while the client attempts to engage in *anticipatory completions*. The participants seem here to be talking past each other and are not engaging with each other's actions in an affiliative manner. Then, in line 21, rather than inviting Sofia to, perhaps, conclude her turn by mentioning how she feels, the therapist further extends her formulation from line 17 by offering up another attribute: "see::n, °or° ... °touched, or°" that may be subsequently ratified or rejected by Sofia. For the former practice of inviting the client, Sofia would have stated how she felt, which would have strongly oriented to her epistemic primacy. But by producing an action that simply gets the client to confirm or disconfirm the therapist's proposed attribute, Sofia's ownership of experience may be somewhat downgraded.

The therapist's final term, "touched", seems then to launch a misunderstanding; that is, the claim that, in her dating relationship, Sofia did not feel that she "was really being touched" can be construed in different ways, literally and metaphorically. In line 23, Sofia produces an other-initiated other repair (.hhh >pardon=me?<) that presages interactional trouble and potential disagreement. The therapist then produces a repair that re-iterates the potential claim that Sofia's needs were not attended to, again using the term "touched" (.hhh well that your self wasn't really being ° tou:ched.°). This then sets off a long pause and the beginnings of a disagreement in which Sofia turns her head to look away (that's not-). In line 27, the therapist performs another repair by orienting to the term that she had used (.hhh is just a terminology thing.), while smiling and shaking her head. Thus, it seems that the therapist has now realized, at this moment, that the term "touched" may have been taken literally and is therefore causing Sofia some uneasiness. Sofia then deals with this awkwardness (and perhaps embarrassment) by smiling back at the therapist and by briefly laughing (line 27). In turn, the therapist launches another repair (I mean just) that now deals directly with the misunderstanding by explaining what she actually meant by not "really being ° tou:ched.°". The therapist's concurrent nod displays affiliation, and perhaps a consensus in viewpoints, and in line 33 Sofia begins to affiliate with an acknowledgement (yeah.), followed by an alternate yet similar interpretation to the one that the therapist is putting forward. Following this is the therapist's return affiliation, via nodding and the production of repeated acknowledgement tokens (yeah. yeah. (0.3) °uh huh.°).

### 7.5.2 *Disaligning: Maintaining Incongruent Perspectives*

The therapist's attempt at repairing the misaligned points of view, rather than leading to successful re-affiliation, may temporarily deepen the disagreement between therapist and client. These instances of unsuccessful repair work often involve repair initiators that contain contrastive markers that oppose the client's perspective in some way (e.g., `no I mean I thought that's what you were saying`; `yeah of course of course. but`). An example of unsuccessful repair is shown in Extract 7.9 (see also Extract 3.26). In this extract, the disagreement is over the message that the grandmother intended to convey to Sofia when she was a child.

**Extract 7.9:** 304.07(5)

```
    01 Sofia: an I said granma I feel lis- I:. (.) I wanna go to sleep.
    02 Ther:  [mm hm,]
    03 Sofia: [an he ] said wa:ke? u:p.
           t  double nod
    04        (0.3)
           s  smiles at T
    05 Ther:  mm:. uh [huh,]
    06 Sofia:         [a:nd] uh::m.
    07        (0.6)
F→  08 Ther:  so it's=like your natural state °y'know it's° >you
           t                     bobs head back
           s                                                 shallow nod
F→  09        weren't allowed< to have it.
           t  opens palms
D→  10 Sofia: so my granmother was noh
    11        (1.1)
           t  clears throat
D→  12 Sofia: did not raise me in a in a very (0.8) like uh:m. oh you kno:w
           s                                    swings head and hands
                                                side to side, smiling
D→  13 Sofia: bab[y:,]
    14 Ther:     [she] didn °cuddle° [mom and cuddle you.]
    15 Sofia:                        [she didn't         ] yeap.
    16 Ther:  b-.hhh but (.) bu=then the same time the message was that
    17        those feelings or that part of you .hhh that feels TI:red or
    18        feels sa:d (0.5) .hhh i:s (0.8) not allowed to be seen.
    19        (2.0)
           t  gazes at S
           s  gazes at T
D→  20 Sofia: probably. (0.4) I-I-I couldn't see .hhh
           s  widens eyes, looks up.       looks at T
    21        (0.8)
D→  22 Sofia: at- that ah=that time. >I couldn=analyze< (.) dat.
    23        (0.8)
D→  24 Sofia: at [that time,    ]    [because    ]
R→  25 Ther:     [yeah of course] of [course. but] I'm just saying
           t       raises hand, double nod, smiling
R→  26        y'didn't think about it like that when you're a ↑kid
```

```
              s   sniffs
R→ 27             you're a kid you're a [kid  ] but
   28 Sofia:                            [yeah.]
              t   shrugs
   29 Sofia:  mm h[m:?]
R→ 30 Ther:      [jus] somehow that was the >message,<
   31             (3.4)
              s   looking up
D→ 32 Sofia:  hm. (1.0) .hhh ↓maybe, but (1.6) .hhh s(h)inkin it about
D→ 33         logically wha=happens my granmother was (1.3) divorced when
              t                                           smiles
D→ 34         she was (0.7)very young?
              s                               looks at T
   35 Ther:   mm [hm,    ]
   36 Sofia:     [an from] that age she had to .hhh uh:m. ((lip smack))
              t     double nod
   37         fight de world. with tree children?
              t                         multiple nods
   38         (       1.6        )
              t   fast multiple nods
```

At the beginning of this extract, Sofia is just finishing a story illustrating how her grandmother "taught her to be tough." The example she provides is of her grandmother not allowing Sofia to fall asleep while they were waiting for the train and that serious consequences would result if Sofia did fall asleep (i.e., the grandmother would leave her behind at the train station). In response, the therapist provides an upshot formulation in which the grandmother deprived her of certain needs (`>you weren't allowed< to have it.`). Sophia, however, ignores this utterance and instead continues to expound on her strict upbringing. At this moment, the therapist and client are in disaffiliation and disalignment – disaffiliation because Sofia has not confirmed the therapist's formulation and disalignment because they are pursuing different activities: The therapist is attempting to explore Sophia's deprivation at the hands of her grandmother and Sophia is elaborating on her grandmother's "educative" tactics.

In the therapist's next turn at talk, the disaffiliation is addressed and momentarily resolved when 1) the therapist confirms and jointly produces Sofia's utterance (line 14) and 2) Sofia produces a return confirmation (line 15). But as the therapist continues with her turn, she attempts to pursue her original interactional project by providing a subsequent version of her previous formulation. In doing so, the therapist provides more specificity about the grandmother's *message* to Sofia, that she was not allowed to put her emotions on display (`part of you .hhh that feels TI:red or feels sa:d (0.5) .hhh i:s (0.8) not allowed to be seen.`). Subsequently, Sofia disagrees. This is first signalled by her delay in responding, followed by a weak confirmation (probably) and then a disconfirmation that rejects the claim of her having *primary access* to this interpretation as a child.

What follows is a move in which the therapist openly contests, rather than retreats from Sofia's disagreement, by initiating repair (line 25). This repair, however, is not characterized by consensus as in Extracts 7.7 and 7.8, but instead deploys a range of interactional resources to index an incongruence of views and to even challenge the client. Most notably, the therapist interrupts the client. This is accomplished by overlapping speech and an *open hand prone* gesture, which commonly functions to interrupt an ongoing line of activity (Kendon, 2004, p. 248). Further, challenge is realized through the disagreement marker "yeah ... but" and through "of course".[3] Stivers (2011) has shown that, for question sequences, responses containing "of course" contest a presupposition of askability. In this interactional environment, it would appear that "of course" contests the relevance of the prior speaker's counter claim; that is, it implies that, although the client is correct in stating that she could not analyze the grandmother's motives as a child, this does not have any bearing on the therapist's aim to explore the effects of the grandmother's actions on Sofia. Finally, the therapist's continued repair implies not only that Sophia had misconstrued the therapist's actions, but also that her reservations about what the therapist is proposing are unwarranted; that is, the therapist's agreement with Sofia that as a child she could not have deeply analyzed her situation (y'didn't think about it like that when you're a ↑kid. you're a kid you're a kid) does not work to affiliate, but rather shows that what Sofia is claiming is beside the point.

It should also be noted that the therapist produced a double nod and a smile in conjunction with her repair initiation (line 25) and that these most likely did work to maintain a level of affiliation with Sofia's contrasting viewpoint. However, these affiliative displays were minimal and were clearly overshadowed by the numerous ways in which Sofia's disagreement was contested. This lack of affiliation was evidenced by Sofia's continued disagreement (line 32), which was realized in such dispreferred features as inter-turn delay, the reluctance marker "hm.", an inbreath and pro-forma agreement "↓maybe, but". Both therapist and client did, however, become re-affiliated when Sofia proceeded to give a personal account of her grandmother's life (line 33 onwards). Rather than continue with the activity of repair, the therapist instead adopts the role of story recipient and nods with increasing rate and frequency in order to display her affiliation with Sofia's projected activity. In the end, most likely to secure affiliation and alignment, the therapist eventually

[3] Hill (1978) refers to therapist responses that are often prefaced with "but" and points out a discrepancy or contradiction in client talk as *confrontations* – see also Chapter 8.

withdraws from her previously articulated position (or activity of repair) by working with the client's chosen trajectory of action.

In sum, it was shown how repair initiations from the therapist contest, rather than retreat from, the client's diverging perspective. Repair in these contexts orients to client disagreement as a problem in understanding. But, depending on its turn design, repairs do different kinds of interactional work and have different outcomes. When the repair practice aimed toward a consensus of views, clients tend to respond affiliatively. The therapist was thus able to re-establish an affiliative context and alignment on a proposed therapeutic activity, while not placing the client's epistemic primacy at risk. By contrast, the repair practice that emphasized incongruent perspectives and that placed the burden of misunderstanding *on the client* seemed to foster disaffiliation and disalignment rather than resolve it. As a consequence, the client's epistemic primacy was challenged, partly because the client's disagreement was treated as irrelevant and partly because the therapist tenaciously tried to carry out her agenda of exploring her interpretation of the grandmother's message to the client. For these reasons, the first form of repair may be considered as conforming to person-centred relational aims congruent with the EFT practice model (Greenberg, 2010), whereas the latter does not.

## 7.6 Conclusions

The focus of this chapter was placed on what happened during interactional contexts in which clients disaffiliate with emotion-focused therapist formulations of client experience through disagreement. These contexts of disagreement made relevant a response in which therapists should orient to the clients' standpoint rather than their own, if a person-centred relational stance is to be maintained. For the most part, these therapists would use nods to signal that they are retreating from their previous formulations and, by implication, that they are endorsing the clients' diverging viewpoint or disaligning interactional project. These observations thus provide added support to the claim that one of the central functions of nods is to affiliate with another's affective stance (Stivers, 2008). A range of verbal practices such as mirroring repeats, collaborative productions and second formulations are also consistently used by therapists. These practices help to strengthen and upgrade the therapist's display of endorsement. Retreating from one's own position (e.g., nodding, delaying the production of a response), endorsing and aligning with the other's position (e.g., mirroring repeats, collaborative productions) and working with the client's divergent view (e.g., second formulations) thus illustrate how talk is organized in an EFT model that endorses a person-centred relational stance to safeguard the client's epistemic primacy.

The strategic placement of nods and supportive utterances following disaffiliation not only allows emotion-focused therapists to prioritize the client's perspective but also helps to avoid potential disputes over who has epistemic primacy in construing or representing the event under discussion. The affiliative (and perspective aligning) use of these interactional practices, therefore, has important implications for the trajectory of client–therapist talk. Owing to their affiliative function, they can "liberate" clients from having to defend their contrasting position, thus allowing both speakers to work primarily toward re-aligning on the issue of client experience under negotiation. On a more general level, these person-centred relational practices show how, when disagreement arises due to an incongruence of perspectives, potential conflicts may become neutralized. These findings, therefore, have relevance for how disagreement may be managed and avoided in other helping profession contexts (e.g., counselling, medicine, social work), but perhaps also in more politicized face-to-face contexts in which negotiation and mediation form a central component.

Furthermore, it can be argued that a person-centred relational stance does not necessarily imply that therapists renege on their own interactional aims at all costs. If a therapist suspects that the client has not understood or fully considered the import of the formulation, a practice of withdrawing and allowing the client to continue may not be a productive line to take. This chapter has shown instances in which emotion-focused therapists draw the client's attention to the misunderstanding and attempt to repair the misunderstanding by re-formulating or clarifying what she (the therapist) had initially meant. Such a practice does not necessarily run counter to a person-centred ethos. In fact, resolving misunderstandings may even be a necessary precursor to being genuinely empathic and, according to Sacks (1973), may be a way to preempt conflict because it treats the disagreement, in the first instance, as a potential problem of understanding of hearing.[4] Thus, therapists' initial line of action, attending to intersubjectivity and its maintenance may demonstrate to clients that the therapist does not simply feign affiliation, but rather, when there is interactional trouble, actually makes an effort to achieve a congruency in perspectives. The therapist's attempts at repair, however, do not come without certain risks. This is because establishing the verity of the "facts of the matter" (i.e., what the client and therapist *really* meant) may be tangential or in opposition to the emotion-focused therapist's goal of maintaining an empathic link with the client. This pertained especially to contexts in which the therapist would contest the client's disagreement. Thus if the repair is unsuccessful, clients may defer, withdraw or even continue to oppose the therapist.

[4] Taken from Schegloff (lecture XV min 45:10–47:25): www.conversationanalysis.org/schegloff-video-lectures/. For a related discussion, see also Guxholli et al. (2021).

Organizations of talk that secure client epistemic primacy have also been observed in other therapeutic contexts. Peräkylä and Silverman (1991), for example, have shown how a patient's *ownership of experience* (Sacks, 1995b, pp. 242ff; Sharrock, 1974) is oriented to and preserved in question sequences by counsellors adopting a Family-Systems approach. There may, therefore, be a tendency across a range of therapeutic orientations for privileging the client's standpoint on his or her personal experience, but caution should be exercised when making generalizations beyond person-centred treatment modalities. For instance, how would therapists adopting a more expert position, in which client experience is sometimes interpreted or evaluated rather than formulated, tend to respond to disagreement? Or, when client disagreement indexes avoidance or resistance to talk about personal experience, do therapists tend to openly challenge the client's avoidance and run the risk of deepening the conflict and of appearing as more knowledgeable about the client's private domain? CA studies on different therapy approaches focusing on disaffiliative contexts have already shed light on some differences and similarities. Cardoso et al.'s (2020) examination of narrative therapy (White & Epston, 1990), for example, has shown that narrative therapists respond in two general ways following what they term a *collaboration break*: by maintaining or retreating from their prior action or position. Further, two formats were identified in maintaining own action/position. This was achieved by proposing a new client experiential meaning or highlighting the client's agency and by guiding or making exploratory questions to deepen the client's experience. In the former practice, therapeutic collaboration was usually re-established, whereas in the latter it was not. For the second response type, retreating from one's previous action/position, there was a tendency for therapeutic collaboration to become re-established. According to Cardoso et al. (2020), the differences between their narrative data and my EFT data may be explained by the therapists' adherence to the different therapeutic models; that is, although both models adhere to preserving the client's ownership of experience, narrative therapists also deem it necessary to persist in using externalizing language in order to dissociate the client from the problem and, thus, may find it important to maintain this position rather than retreat from it. A different CA study on disaffiliation in psychoanalytic psychotherapy focused on how therapists used collaborative moves in response to client disagreement (Guxholli et al., 2021). They found that these therapists would use what they term "collaborative moves," such as collaborative completions, formulations and extensions, to perform the following kinds of discursive work: temporarily mending the disaffiliation while commonly maintaining their position and also re-affiliating with clients. In this way, therapists were able to maintain a balance between different, and at times opposing, therapeutic requirements, by sustaining a certain level of relational affiliation and, at the same time, pursuing a therapeutic agenda with which clients may be at odds (see also Muntigl et al., 2020b and Bänninger-Huber & Widmer's 1999 discussion of the *balance hypothesis*).

Psychotherapy researchers have argued that maintaining affiliation with the client is one of the most significant common factors in all forms of therapy across a variety of contexts (Horvath et al., 2011). This study involving EFT, but also the other studies mentioned earlier involving narrative therapy and psychoanalytic psychotherapy, seem to offer some support for this at the "in the moment" interactional level, by showing how therapists and clients orient to maintaining some degree of affiliation even in moments of conflict. Thus, whether therapists tend to adopt an expert role or not, retreating from one's own position may constitute a generic practice, especially to ensure that social relations between the participants do not derail. Further research into client disagreement in different, non-person-centred therapies, will be needed to better explore the differences in which affiliation, epistemic status and therapeutic agendas become negotiated.

# 8 Extended Disaffiliation: Withdrawing and Opposing

## 8.1 Overview

It is commonly observed in psychotherapy that the interactions between therapists and clients sometimes get off-track. Clients do not always agree with the therapist's perspective, comply with the proposal to do a certain activity or enthusiastically engage with a given therapist intervention. Further, such disaffiliation may persevere, extending over many sequences and turns at talk. There is much research in psychotherapy that addresses problems and breakdowns in communication between the therapist and client. One such area is termed *resistance*, originating in Freud's (1999b) psychoanalytic work on hysteria. The concept of resistance is used in the psychotherapy literature in a number of different ways: Psychodynamic theorists beginning with Freud (1999a) saw the patient's resistance to a therapist's interpretations as primarily caused by an unconscious reluctance to confront underlying psychodynamic issues. Cognitive behaviourists tend to use resistance in a more lexical sense; as a challenge to treatment progress and signalling the client's reluctance to follow the therapist direction or logic (Beutler et al., 2002, 2011; Newman, 2002). It has been suggested that the concept of resistance in psychotherapy often comes with considerable unwanted baggage. As Arkowitz (2002, p. 221) argues, "the term resistance implies the locus of responsibility in the client, when it actually may be with an ineffective therapist or therapy." Certain therapy approaches that have a person-centred, experiential or humanistic ethos (e.g., client-centred, emotion-focused, gestalt) tend to refrain from using the term *resistance*. One reason is that a resistance model might presuppose that the therapist has superior knowledge over (i.e., knows better than) the client (Engel & Holiman, 2002). In these approaches, rather than positing theories about why something might not be working, focus is instead placed on working with the client's perspective and trying to jointly manage clients' reluctance to engage the task or self-disclose, on clients' difficulties in dealing with potential overwhelming emotions in the moment and on a possible breakdown in the trusting relationship (Watson & Greenberg, 2000).

Another perspective on "off-track" therapist–client communication falls under the general rubric of *alliance ruptures*, in which therapist–client mis-attunements, breakdowns, stresses/tensions, impasses and so on are examined (Eubanks et al., 2018; Safran & Muran, 1996) – see Chapter 1 for a discussion of the *alliance*. Alliance ruptures have been argued to come in two different formats: *withdrawing* versus *confronting* (Eubanks et al., 2015, 2018). Withdrawal involves actions through which clients *move away* from the therapist, such as denial, minimal responses, shifting topic, deference/appeasement and self-criticism. Confrontation, on the other hand, involves actions that *move against* the therapist such as complaints (e.g., about therapist, activities, progress of therapy), rejection of interventions, being self-defensive and controlling/pressuring the therapist (see Eubanks et al., 2015). One of the main aims of this alliance rupture model is to identify the range of practices through which a lack of collaboration between therapist and client may be organized. Although the focus is mainly on *clients'* practices of withdrawing/confronting, the model takes both client and therapist contributions into account and leaves open the possibility that therapists may be mainly responsible for the rupture (Eubanks et al., 2015).

In this chapter, I examine therapist–client interactions involving some form of "resistance," rupture or lack of collaboration through a conversation analytic (CA) lens as primarily consisting of extended episodes of disaffiliation. I principally draw from CA studies of sequence organization and how initiating actions of sequences (from therapists) may set up various possibilities and constraints that next speakers (clients) may conform with or resist (Heritage, 2010; Stivers & Hayashi, 2010). In this way, resistance or opposition is not seen as *client*-based, but rather as a *joint* achievement that gets played out through norms and constraints that are set in place via sequences of talk. Further, in order to flesh out notions of resistance or opposition, I draw from the conceptual distinctions of withdrawal vs. confrontation found in Eubanks et al. (2015, 2018). But rather than use the term *confrontation*, which has been used in psychotherapy research to refer to a *therapist response* that points out contradictions or discrepancies in client talk and conduct (see Hill, 1978), I will draw from M. H. Goodwin's (1990) and Goodwin and Goodwin's (1990) CA-informed characterization of *building opposition*. These are actions that convey some form of (at times aggravated) contrast or disagreement with another speaker. These terms (withdrawal and opposition), however, will not be used simply as categories with which to identify resistance. Instead, they provide a general kind of action framework for describing, in detail, the ways that client disengage with or oppose the sequential, interactional constraints being placed upon them.

## 8.2 Ruptures and Resistance as Discursive, Interactional Achievements

Within CA, therapeutic constructs such as *resistance* or *alliance ruptures* are examined for the discursive work that they perform within the local confines of therapist–client interactions. Peräkylä (2004, p. 290) succinctly summarizes this position by stating that CA "concentrates on 'how' (rather than 'what' or 'why') questions, describing how interaction is so as to produce coordinated actions such as questions and answers, openings and closings of conversation, or turn taking." Thus, explanations as to *why* a client is disagreeing or withdrawing are bracketed off in favour of exploring the variety of discursive practices in which a client draws from to engage in this form of conduct. Another approach that is consonant with the aims and methods of CA has taken a rhetorical or discursive psychological view of resistance. In his innovative re-interpretation of Freudian repression, Billig (1999, p. 3) argues for the conceptualization of resistance as a rhetorically situated activity: "Instead of hypothesizing what goes on in the mind, we should be analyzing the details of conversation, paying careful attention to the micro-features of talk." Thus, Billig proposes that by examining *how* clients actually respond, discursive evidence for resistance can be presented. For example, what makes a client's "no" an act of resisting may not so much lie in the denial itself, but in the interactional details; the denial was perhaps made too vehemently or was accompanied by an over-abundance of protest. Close inspection of client denials can also show that they are sometimes made as a way of defending oneself against unmade accusations (Billig, 1999, p. 204). In these cases, the client may be attempting to block a certain avenue of therapeutic investigation even before it gets underway.

CA studies have so far shown how opposition or withdrawal are realized as client disaffiliative actions that in some manner do not conform to the interactional aims of the therapist or counsellor. Most notable is Hutchby's (2002, 2007) examination of child counselling. Hutchby examined instances in which a child used the expression "I don't know" as a way of avoiding answering. As Hutchby (2007, p. 120) argues:

> The repeated use of "Don't know" as a response to questions is a particularly powerful resistance strategy as it is capable of frustrating any line of questioning the counselor seeks to pursue, while at the same time inoculating the child against being held to account for, or expected to explain or develop, any thoughts or feelings that he might actually have on the matters in question.

Other studies that have drawn attention to specific practices of resistance and opposition vs. withdrawal include withholding agreement or disagreeing after therapist formulations (Antaki, 2008; Muntigl & Horvath, 2014b), mis-aligning with therapists' "optimistic" questions (MacMartin, 2008), making claims of not remembering (Muntigl & Choi, 2010) and identifying and managing client resistance in psychoanalysis (Vehviläinen, 2008).

Research from other institutional contexts has recognized that resistance may be performed with different degrees of "strength" or "explicitness": In her analysis of treatment decisions in acute care encounters involving a physician and the parent of an ill child, Stivers (2005b) suggested the terms *passive* and *active* resistance. In passive resistance, parents would withhold acceptance, whereas in active resistance, parents take a position against the treatment being offered. Similar kinds of strategies for resisting advice have been identified in Heritage and Sefi's (1992) examination of interactions between British health visitors and first-time mothers examined: *unmarked acknowledgement* and *assertions of knowledge or competence*. In the former, mothers would avoid acknowledging the advice as informative and, in the latter, they would claim independent access to the advice being given (i.e., that they are already knowledgeable about the advice being given to them). Drawing from Heritage and Sefi's work, Silverman (1997) also found these practices of resisting advice to be operative in HIV counselling interactions. A slightly different framework for identifying practices of resistance has been undertaken in research on news interviews (Clayman, 2001; Clayman & Heritage, 2002). Two general forms of practices used by interviewees to resist or evade answering the interviewer's question were identified: *Overt* forms that operated by shifting the agenda or refusing to answer the question and *covert* forms that surreptitiously depart from the topical agenda contained in the question.

## 8.3 Conforming to vs. Resisting Sequential Constraints

The general framework used to examine how opposition and withdrawal are accomplished in sequences of talk draws from Boyd and Heritage (2006) and Heritage (2010). They have shown that an initiating action such as a question can project various constraints on an addressee's response by 1) setting topical agendas, 2) embodying presuppositions, 3) conveying an epistemic stance, and 4) incorporating preferences. Thus, when answering, clients may either conform to some (or all) of these constraints or may not conform to them through some manner of opposition or delay/reluctance. Non-conforming responses tend to work in a disaffiliating manner, because they often fail to work prosocially by not endorsing the evaluative stance or preference of the prior action (Stivers, 2008; Stivers et al., 2011, p. 21) – see also Chapters 3 and 7. Thus, by applying this framework, the dimensions of the therapist's initiating action being resisted – and the special kinds of interactional resources used to accomplish this specific form of resistance – can be readily identified. For example, therapist formulations and proposals to engage in chair work also project various constraints related to agenda-setting, preferences, epistemic/deontic stances and presuppositions. Thus, client non-conforming responses to these initiating actions will also orient to one or some of these dimensions.

Consideration is also given to the relative strength of the client's non-conforming response and to its contextual orientation within the sequence; that is, it is important to consider not only the strength of opposition with respect to the design of the therapist's action and the constraints being placed upon the client, but also how it might project certain kinds of interactional trajectories that affect affiliation and progressivity in productive or non-productive ways. The work of Stivers and Hayashi (2010) was used as a guide in determining the ways in which disaffiliative responses to initiating actions such as questions index different degrees of resistance. For example, responses that deny knowledge ("I don't know") or that involve other-initiated repair (Schegloff et al., 1977) were shown to constitute especially strong forms of disalignment, as they disrupt the progressivity of the sequence.

In keeping with the tenets of experiential therapy and especially EFT, I will not make use of the term *resistance* in the remainder of this chapter but instead will draw from the action-based categories of "moving away" (withdrawing) vs. "moving against" (opposing) another speaker (Eubanks et al., 2015; Goodwin, 1990). I do this partly because of the conceptual baggage associated with the term *resistance* as used in psychotherapy (see Arkowitz, 2002), and partly because I feel that the terms *withdrawal* versus *opposing* better capture the general practices through which clients may take up a position of not conforming to the constraints set up by a prior action. I also do not refer to the upcoming extracts as necessarily constituting alliance ruptures because, in this CA-informed view, the focus lies primarily on how (extended) moments of disaffiliation are organized and negotiated rather than on whether various "social contracts of agreement" have broken down or whether emotional bonds have become unduly strained.

## 8.4 Withdrawing and Disengaging

In Eubanks et al.'s (2015) framework, withdrawal occurs when the client moves away from the therapist. This *moving away* can be characterized in interactional terms as when clients refrain or withhold from engaging with the prior action and with the constraints associated with this action. By withdrawing or disengaging from the interaction (or from certain interactional constraints), clients may simply delay their response (or not respond), provide some form of weak confirmation, agreement or compliance, deny having the requisite knowledge to give a response, display a reluctance to respond, provide an account stating the difficulties in meeting the constraints of the prior action, maintain own topic, and so on. All these types of responses are disaffiliative because they do not make a clear display of assenting to or going along with the proposed course of action. Instead, clients may be seen as disengaging from the conversation or as avoiding or evading the prospective option of taking up a firm position. These actions are also disaligning because they resist the *progressivity* of the sequence that was laid down by the therapist's initiating action (Stivers & Robinson, 2006). Five different types of withdrawal or disengagement are examined here: 1) withholding/delaying; 2) acknowledging/weakly conceding; 3) displaying reluctance; 4) denying the relevance of what is proposed; 5) challenging the validity of an intervention; and 6) pursuing own agenda or topic – see also Chapter 3.

### *8.4.1 Withholding from Responding*

One of the most overt forms of disengagement occurs when clients withhold from providing a response to the therapist. In these cases, clients do not display any form of conduct – or only minimally do so – that conveys a stance or attitude toward what the therapist had said. In Extract 8.1, the client Ernie had been expressing his frustrations regarding his ex-wife. The therapist orients to Ernie's feelings by preparing the way toward a potential "empty chair" confrontation between him and the ex-wife.

**Extract 8.1:** Ernie: Case 422.4 (Empty Chair)

```
01  Ther:  +I don't have a sens:e (.) at this point.
        e  +gaze to T, then downward, still->
02         * I don't (.) know about you*
        t  extends hands to e--------->*
03         what really your feelings are:?
04         (1.0)
05  Ther:  uh:m
06         (0.5)
07  Ther:  *all about fully? * I know I sense some resentment
        t  *extends hands to E*
08         towards your wife some anger you've mentioned sadness,
09         *feelings of sadness.* .h
        t  *extends cupped hand-*
10         (0.2)
11  Ther:  uh:m
12         (0.9)
13  Ther:  *in relation to your wife.
        t  *extends hand to side->
14         (0.3)
15  Ther:  in particular.
16  Ther:  *and I guess (0.5) I'm suggesting uh (.) sort've uh * (0.2)
        t  * gaze to chair, hand extended to chair------------*
17         tch (0.4) a very structured way of working (0.3)
18         with that. uh: that=ma- makes it very concrete.
19         *and I think helps          * bring to awareness
        t  *extend hand, gaze to chair *gaze to E-> brings hand in->
```

```
20          your feelings and your needs,
21          (0.3)
22  Ther:   and then (0.3)* a way in which you can express those too,*
       t                  * extends hand to chair -------------*
23          (0.5)
24  Ther:   uh:m here.* (0.2) to an ima:gined (0.3) person. *
       t               * gaze to chair, hands directed to chair*
25          *as opposed to the real thing.
       t    *gaze to E--->
26          (1.5)
27  Ther:   cuz you can't do that in real life. that seems to be
28          the (0.8) the stumbling block.
29          (0.5)
```

In lines 01–03, the therapist portrays her knowledge of Ernie's feelings in a highly downgraded manner. Using epistemic expressions such as "`I don't have a sens:e`" and "`I don't (.) know`" and the turn-final rising intonation (line 03) not only convey her low knowledge status, but also gives Ernie the opportunity to supply the therapist with this knowledge, that is, to "fill her in." The therapist's extended hand/arm gesture to the client also functions to invite Ernie to possibly take up a turn. What follows, however, are a series of pauses and delays, lines 04–06, in which Ernie refrains from doing any conduct whatsoever. This leads the therapist to then extend her prior turn at talk (`all about fully?`) by providing more detail, or granularity (Schegloff, 2000), to the utterance, while making another turn-offering gesture to Ernie. Given that knowledge about Ernie's feelings lies in the client's epistemic domain (a B-event from Labov & Fanshel, 1977), it is only Ernie that can "fully" provide this information. But the therapist then goes on to suggest certain feelings Ernie might have, such as resentment and anger, based on what he had reported previously. But again, in lines 10–15, this is followed by pauses, delays and extensions in which Ernie does not articulate any form of acknowledgement and response and thus completely disengages with the therapist's efforts at getting him to expand on what he feels toward his ex-wife.

In the remainder of this extract, the therapist then begins to provide a rationale for implementing an in-session activity – that is, empty chair work – to help get Ernie to focus more on his feelings in this context. Throughout her talk, however, Ernie remains impassive and does not signal any form of engagement with what the therapist is proposing. Declining the turn – that is, withdrawing from the vector of inquiry that the therapist is suggesting – could also indicate that therapist and client do not share a common "vision" for the goal of the session. It might be that Ernie is not yet convinced that re-engaging with his "ex" is what they *should be* doing in therapy. If this was the case, the misalignment is at the *goal level* and (according to the "rupture repair model") it would need to be topicalized before forward movement can be attempted (i.e., repair). Instead, the therapist seems to ignore the lack of shared purpose and proposes a "solution" to a problem the client may not have bought into.

### 8.4.2 *Acknowledging and Weakly Conceding*

Somewhat more engagement, and a less overt display of withdrawal, is seen when clients provide weak acknowledgement or weakly concede the import of what has been said. In Extract 8.2, the topic of the discussion centred around Kristina's relationship with her husband and how that is filled with tension and unpleasantness. Just before this extract, Kristina muses about various possibilities (or "exercises") that might enable her to deal with her troubles or to "let go."

**Extract 8.2:** 014.04(2)

```
01   Ther:   .hhh well that's a really good question=I mean how do you (.)
02           how do people- how does one .hh let ↑go o:f (2.5)
03           painful things. painful.
04           (3.2)
05   Ther:   experiences.
06   Kris:   .hhh >an is it< letting go of uh (1.3) m- as you say the
07           ex↑periences o:r.
08           (0.8)
         k   turns head to side, looks at T
09   Kris:   or de whole per:son.
10           (2.2)
         t   slow nod
11   Kris:   o:r
12           (5.4)
13   Kris:   or ju=the ↑feelings or just certain feelings,
         t                                               slow nod→
14           (1.6)
         t   -->
15   Kris:   mm.
16           (5.4)
17   Ther:   so=it's hard t'understand what that concept really (0.8)
         t   shakes head
18           really means or what it=might mean in terms of your .hh
19           >relationship with your< ↑husband anyway °would it°=
         k                                                      double nod→
20   Kris:   = mm hm.=
         k   --->
21   Ther:   = uh huh,
         t   multiple shallow nods→
22           (                 10.8               )
         t   ---> multiple shallow nods-->
         k   gazes at T
23   Ther:   how it might co:me to be:: (2.5) not a source of pain anymore.
24           not a source of-
```

```
25          (           2.7         )
        t             shallow nod
26   Ther:  for you.
27   Kris:  mm hm.
28          (                47.2                    )
        t   deep nod multiple shallow nods
        k         gazes down
29   Ther:  .hhh I=guess I wonder would it b- continue to be a source of pain
30          for you were you ta .hh leave him?
        t                             looks at K, shakes head
31          (1.3)
32   Ther:  or=is that whatch=yer sorta thinking y'know does this mean
        t          waves hands inward, shakes head
33          that I should leave him? ↑or.
34          (1.0)
35   Ther:  is tha what-
36          (0.9)
37   Kris:  mm ↑hm.
        k   nod
38   Ther:  letting go:: en↑tails,
39   Kris:  y'i[t  can   e-be   v-one] v-one vay of letting go::.
40   Ther:     [or what it might (mean) ta]
        t                                                 double nod
41   Kris:  .hh either I would not be disturbed ↑by: (1.5) what's going ↑on,
        k                                          looks at T
42          (2.6)
        k   looks away
43   Kris:  what he doe:s.
44          (17.6)
45   Ther:  ih seems that something prevents you from doing that.
46          (2.1)
47   Kris:  mm hm?
48   Ther:  °from leaving him.°
        t   multiple nods→
49          (               23.5               )
        t   -----------> gazes at K
        k   multiple nods------> gazes away
```

The therapist responds to Kristina's prior question by posing another question: "how does one let go of painful experiences" (lines 01–05). The question is non-specific, not necessarily pertaining to Kristina or to any experience in particular. But rather than answer, Kristina subtly questions whether it is "experiences" or rather "de whole per:son" or "the ↑feelings or just certain feelings" from which one could be liberated (lines 06–13). Further, Kristina does not proceed to provide an answer and instead produces an "mm." and then remains silent (lines 15–16). The therapist then responds with a formulation by drawing attention to the complexity of the concept of "letting go" in terms of what it exactly means but also how this specifically relates to the client's relationship with her husband. This receives weak acknowledgement from Kristina in line 20 (mm hm.) and a return acknowledgement from the therapist (uh huh,). After a long pause, the therapist continues on the topic of "letting go" by asking how her relationship with her husband would stop being a source of pain. In line 27, Kristina briefly acknowledges the therapist's turn (mm hm.) but then refrains from continuing, which results in a very long silence. During this time, Kristina also draws her gaze downwards, which could be conveying further disengagement. The therapist then utters a series of questions that do not receive a response. The first is in declarative and embedded Y/N format (I=guess I wonder would it). The second, lines 32–33, is in Y/N format and is designed as an alternative to the first (or=is that). This question also contains a turn-final "or," which indexes a downgraded epistemic stance or commitment to what is being asserted or claimed (Drake, 2015; see also Muntigl et al., 2020a). The therapist's third attempt (is tha what-) eventually receives a form of acknowledgement (mm ↑hm.), in line 37, that expresses deliberation or uncertainty. Perhaps for this reason, in line 38, the therapist then completes the question (letting go:: en↑tails,). When Kristina does respond in lines 39–43, however, she does not agree with or confirm the therapist's assertion of what letting go might entail and instead merely concedes that this is a possibility (y'it can e-be v-one v-one vay of letting go::.) and then goes on to state that she would then not be disturbed by his behaviour anymore. The client, however, begins to look away from the therapist at the end of her turn and does not resume speaking. This again results in a long silence. The therapist then asks what prevents her from leaving, but this *wh*-question does not receive an answer. Thus, throughout this extract, Kristina repeatedly produces weak acknowledgements, concessions and *generalized disengagement practices* (gazing down/away, remaining silent) that enable her to resist having to engage with potentially painful emotions involving her relationship with her husband.

### *8.4.3 Displaying Reluctance*

Clients may also give responses that are non-committal or ambivalent in terms of whether they endorse the therapist's point of view or proposal. These actions imply a reluctance to engage with the task or material introduced by the therapist. Extract 8.3 shows a dialogue with the client Kristina and, as in the previous extract with this client, the topic involves her relationship with her husband and the advantages or disadvantages of becoming divorced.

**Extract 8.3:** 014.13(6)

```
01  Kris:  so I think no matter-
02  Ther:  °°hm.°°
03         (3.6)
        k  brings tissue to nose, wipes nose
        t  shifts posture, sits back in chair
04  Kris:  °.snif° who my husband is o:r how he behaves, or whatever
```

05 I should be able to:
06 (1.2)
07 Kris: u:h
08 (0.9)
k *circles hands out from chest*
09 Kris: liberate <myself.>
10 ( 7.5 )
t *slow shallow multiple nods*
11 Kris: enlighten first? e(hh)heh=and liberate °second.° .hhh
k *laughter*
12 ((blows nose)) heh after watching
k *looks at T*
13 the historical mov(h)ies?=eh[hh heh heh]=I (h)am
14 Ther: [°mm::.° ]
k *laughter---------------->*
t *slow shallow nod---------> smiles, lowers chin*
15 Kris: getti(h)ng the right, .hhh steps. .hhh at least in theory.
16 (0.3)
17 Ther: .hhh so you should be able to: overcome
t *looks down, flips palm out from chest*
18 (2.4)
t *shakes head, looks at k*
k *gazes at T, wipes nose*
19 Ther: whatever obstacl:es:.
20 (1.3)
21 Ther: he pla:ces in your ↑path. >no matter what he's like.<
22 you should be able tuh-
23 (.)
24 Kris: **m-↑yeah-s. don't you think so?**
k *looks down, looks up, clasps hands together*
t *slow shallow nod. double nod*
25 (0.8)
26 Kris: hhheh (0.6) heh hehheh .hhh .SHHIH
t *raises eyebrows at K. smiles*
27 (1.6)
28 Kris: .hhh uh:m.
29 (2.4)
30 Kris: [↑why:]
31 Ther: [so ] sounds like you're angry at your↑se:lf,
32 that you can't ↑do this.
33 Kris: °.snih°
34 (10.7)
35 Kris: **>no I'm st-< hhh hehheh .hhh (0.4) still <reluctant.> .hhh ↓uh.**
k *opens palm*
t *slow shallow nod*
36 (1.0)
37 Kris: **an to admit °that I would be angry with myself,°**
38 (0.9)
39 Ther: wha maybe you're no:t. I mean I'm just- it's just an observation.
40 Kris: .hhh yeah uh y-y:
k *nods, throws palm out then pulses hand and nods at T.*
41 (5.4)
42 Ther: ((lip smack)) maybe it's not anger maybe its just determination
43 you know or I will (1.6) °overcome this at some point or. I du↑nno.°
44 ( 13.1 )

k *gazes ahead, left fingers on chin*
45 Kris: ((lip smack)) **yeah. I- I <haven't (.) deci:ded.>**
46 ( 20.5 )
t *shallow double nod. lowers chin, gazes at K*
k *gazes down, takes long deep breath*

Kristina begins this extract by presenting an "extreme version" of her relationship with her husband. Using the expression "no matter- ... who my husband is o:r how he behaves, or whatever" implies that the husband may behave in whatever manner he wishes toward Kristina (by implication, even if the husband's acts are cruel). In contrast to this, Kristina claims to have only one choice in the matter, that she should in some way rise above these acts (liberate <myself.>). A long silence ensues, after which Kristina jokingly states that she needs to be enlightened first, before becoming liberated. Thus, the joking and laughter may be working in part to reframe her prior talk as being meant ironically; that is, it need not be the case that she always remains impervious to her husband's acts of cruelty. The therapist's response, however, orients to Kristina's claim as "serious" rather than ironic (17–22). By summarizing and slightly elaborating Kristina's talk, "liberating" becomes transformed into the upgraded version of "overcoming obstacles" unconditionally (no matter what he's like.).

Kristina's response is disaffiliative (line 24) and not only expresses covert or mitigated disagreement, but also a reluctance to engage with the therapist's proposition. The initial part of her turn expresses ostensible agreement (m-↑yeah-s), but the rest of her utterance clearly disaffiliates with the therapist. Her subsequent "don't you think so?" followed by ensuing laughter is expressed in a mocking tone and works to maintain her ironic stance. In a way, Kristina not only ridicules her own position toward her husband's behaviour, but also the therapist's attempt at merely reflecting back Kristina's portrayal of the relationship dynamic. Thus, rather than engage with the therapist's formulation, it is treated as "non serious." In this way, Kristina withdraws from having to work with the therapist's prior talk. The ironic manner in which Kristina responds, however, does offer the therapist "access" to how she may be emotionally experiencing everyday situations with her husband. Thus, the utterance "don't you think so" and the ensuing laughter may be disclosing and recreating her sense of frustration at always having to endure unacceptable behaviours.

In lines 31–32, the therapist reacts by drawing attention to the affective component of what Kristina had said; that is, she is angry with herself at always tolerating the husband's actions, rather than acting differently, perhaps more confrontationally (that you can't ↑do this.). The therapist's reaction marks a substantial inferential leap from Kristina's original utterance and, thus, is no longer reflecting back Kristina's own words, but extrapolates to her present (as opposed to hypothetical future) emotional state. The therapist's utterance, therefore, borders on interpretation and thus may be considered as more a reflection of the therapist's than the client's perspective. That the therapist has perhaps taken her interpretation of the client's state too far may be indicated by Kristina's response. Her disagreement that she is angry with herself is inexplicit and couched within a mitigating expression that she may be "reluctant to admit" what the therapist proposed, thus indicating that this may still be open to negotiation. Here, Kristina is being evasive in terms of whether or not she supports the therapist's viewpoint.

The therapist, in line 39, then opts to retreat from her standpoint that the client is angry with herself (wha maybe you're no:t.). Various mitigation strategies are also employed by the therapist such as modality (maybe) and repair in which she frames her turn as stemming from her own personal perspective (I mean I'm just- it's just an observation.). Kristina, however, responds with ambivalence: She does not ratify the therapist's assertion, as evidenced by the disagreement markers (Pomerantz, 1984), such as the inbreath and the aborted attempt at producing more talk, surrounding her minimal agreement. But, her use of non-vocal resources such as nodding and placing her palm outwards toward the therapist imply a minimal endorsement of the therapist's utterance. The therapist then proceeds to retreat from her claim that the client experiences anger and instead suggests that "determination" may explain her behaviour. With this move, the therapist backs away from a potentially conflictual theme and attempts to secure affiliation around a different theme, one that positions the client as an *agent* who resolutely tries to overcome difficulties rather than a passive participant who feels anger due to her lack of agency.

However, the therapist's attempt at securing affiliation is, at best, only partially successful. The wording of the client's utterance in line 45 is relevant here because, on the one hand, the client asserts primary rights to interpret own experience, and, on the other hand, she remains non-committal. By emphasizing "I" in "I- I <haven't (.) deci:ded.", Kristina asserts that any interpretations regarding her personal experience (e.g., what emotions are at play, whether she is an agent of certain events) clearly rest with her and not the therapist. But, because she refuses to decide on this issue, she blocks any further progress to explore her anger or determination. By not committing herself, Kristina withdraws from cooperatively negotiating the reasons behind her inability to confront the husband. On a more productive note, however, the client's disagreement is very weak (line 45) and may be signalling that the prior negotiation over her emotional state has garnered some acceptance from the client and that if the therapist is able to gain and display further understanding of the client's experience, then more exploration and therapeutic work may be accomplished.

### *8.4.4 Denying the Preconditions Needed for Cooperative Engagement*

Another way of withdrawing or disengaging is for clients to deny that the preconditions exist to enable cooperative engagement in the task. Clients may, for instance, claim that they are not yet "ready," that the task is too difficult or, as shown in Extract 8.4, that the aim of the task is not achievable. This conversation is a continuation from Extract 8.1.

**Extract 8.4:** Ernie: Case 422.4 (Empty Chair)

```
30  Ther:  right, you're not going to work anything through with her
31         cuz it doesn't (.) seems like there's a wa:ll there
32         that just can't be penetrated [at all]
33  Ern:                                 +[yeah I] can't +[so    ]
       e                                 +shakes head, gaze to T->
34  Ther:                                                 [yeah.]
35  Ther:  *.hh but we don't need (0.2)            *<your real wife.>
       t   *turns head, extends hands & gaze to chair*gaze to E->
36         (0.8)
37  Ther:  tuh [tuh     ]
38  Ern:       [there's] only one person that can deal with
39         the wall and that's her, not me,
40  Ther:  yes. (.) right. (.) exact[ly. ]
41  Ern:                           +[yeah]
       e   >>downturned mouth->    +shrugs, gaze downward->
42  Ther:  so we can only have yo:u *(0.3)+ however within yourself+
       t                            * gaze to chair->
       e                                  +gaze to T-----+
43         +there still is >it's like< (0.2) insi:de you there
       e   +shakes head, gaze downward->
44         is your wife. if you know what I mean? like in (0.4)
45         those feelings are in relation to another +person.
46         (0.4)
47  Ther:  and *we can sort've +bri:ng (0.2)+
       t       *gaze, extended hand to chair ->
       e                       +gaze down-+
48         *+what's going on inside you out. <here.>
       t   *gaze to E, mimes weighing two sides--->
       e   +gaze to chair, downturned mouth-->
49         (0.4)
50  Ther:  without *having (0.4) your real wife here.
       t           *glance, extended hand to chair, gaze back to E->
51         (0.5)
52  Ther:  >[without] you having *to a talk to her< *re:ally.
53  Ern:    [ye+ah +]
       e       +nod+
       e           +downturned mouth, gaze to chair->+
54         (0.4)
55  Ther:  uh::m
56         (1.0)
57  Ther:  [>jus'sorta work< that *through.]
58  Ern:   [+.hh hhx                       ] * hhh
```

```
       e   +visible in/outbreath-->
       t                            *gaze to E-*gaze upward->
59  Ther:  [in some fashion.* ^en I](.) throw it out as a^
60  Ern:   [hhh                      ] +
       e       visible outbreath-->+
       t                 *sits up, mimes throw, gaze to chair->
61  Ther:  ehm (0.8) ↑I guess it's like *an experiment. I mean
       t   ((clears throat))            *gaze to E->
62         just to see what might happen. .h **↑nothing might happen:(.)*
       t                                     *shrugs, gaze forward--*
63  Ther:  *something might happen we don't really know. but I know,
       t   *gaze to chair->
64         .h (0.3) uh:m it <can be useful,>
65         (0.7)
```

As can be recalled from Extract 8.1, the therapist drew attention to the variety of emotions that Ernie is experiencing with regard to his ex-wife, such as resentment, helplessness, anger and sadness, and stated that there is some uncertainty about which emotion might be most salient. The therapist then suggested engaging in "a very structured way of working" in which Ernie may confront an imaginary person – rather than "the real thing", his wife in actual life – and express the emotions "here." that he feels toward her. The therapist, lines 30–32, emphatically states that Ernie is unable to talk to his ex-wife in real life because "there's a wa:ll there" that is impenetrable, the implication being that he might be able to do so in a chair work setting. As a response, however, Ernie confirms that an existing barrier prevents him from making a connection with his ex-wife (yeah I can't so) while shaking his head, rather than orienting to the potential benefits implied in the therapist's suggestion. Ernie's response may be seen as underscoring the futility of what the therapist has proposed and, thus, as implying that there is no point in proceeding with this proposed course of action. To counter Ernie's opposition, the therapist re-emphasizes that it is not necessary for him to talk to his wife in person (but we don't need (0.2) <your real wife.>, line 35). But here again, Ernie seems to oppose the relevance of confronting his wife by asserting that only she can remove the barrier that separates them (lines 38–39). The therapist, in turn, offers upgraded confirmation of Ernie's opposition (yes. (.) right. (.) exactly., line 40) – displaying that they are aligned in their viewpoints – with the added condition that they can sidestep this difficulty by having Ernie direct his "inner" thoughts and feelings outwards toward his wife without actually having to face her in an actual situation (lines 42–52). This account then garners minimal acknowledgement from Ernie in the form of a "yeah" and, non-verbally, a nod. Faced with the client's repeated hesitation/resistance and building skepticism about the proposed therapeutic activity, the therapist now designs her suggestions with high contingency, especially concerning the benefits accrued through chair work. This gets expressed through softeners (`jus' sorta work< that through`, line 57), metaphorical expressions and gestures marking contingency (`throw it out`, line 59), contingency labelling (`it's like an exper̲iment.`, line 61), epistemic markers of uncertainty (`what might ha̲ppen. .h ↑nothing might happen. ... so̲mething might happen we don't really kno̲w.`, lines 63–64) and allusions to the possibility of benefit (it <ca̲n be useful,>, line 64). During this time, Ernie conveys some distress through repeated sighs (lines 58, 60) and hesitation and by not providing a verbal response to the therapist's suggestions. Thus, in sum, it may be that Ernie finds the possibility of engaging with his ex-wife too painful or threatening and that the therapist's offer to do so "remotely," via chair work, does not appear safe or attractive enough. The therapist's proposal to resolve the problem through engagement is thus met with disaffiliation and with Ernie placing the blame on the ex-wife.

### 8.4.5 *Challenging the Validity of an Intervention*

Certain in-session tasks in therapy, such as chair work, require that clients engage in a form of role-play in which conversations between oneself or with others are imagined and enacted – see especially Chapter 6. Clients may resist these kinds of tasks because they do not appear entirely "genuine" or "real." Extract 8.5 with the client Ernie, occurring a bit later on in the conversation after Extract 8.4, shows his difficulty in accepting and going along with this imaginative aspect of chair work.

**Extract 8.5:** Ernie: Case 422.4 (Empty Chair)

```
               ((lines omitted subsequent to extract 4))
01   Ther:     .hh ^so I've^ *(0.5) throw* that out again as a
         t                  *mimes throw*
02             possibility and'uh: (1.3) °uh::m° (0.4) yihknow,
03             we can see today where (1.3 +)*where you feel you're
         e                                +gaze to T->
         t                                  *gaze to E->
04             at. and if that would (0.8)[yihknow] work at some point,
05   Ern:                                 [°kay°   ]
         e     >>downturned mouth->      +gaze to hands->
06   Ther:     [if yer (0.9) if you (.)] wanna give that a whirl
07   Ern:      [°.hhh°                 ]
08   Ther:     *and see what happens? er
         t     *gaze to chair->
09             (0.6)
10   Ther:     *> I dunno wha̲t< you think about that.
         t     *extends hands out, gaze forward/to E, leans forward->
11             (0.8)
12   Ther:     +that ide:ah,+
         e     +shakes head-+
```

```
13              *(0.6)*
           t    *smiles*
14   Ern:       tch (0.6) I don't know either,=°°I°° °i-it° uh:m
15              (6.2)
16   Ern:       it seems a little contrived I-I-I-[I °uh w°] yihknow,
17   Ther:                                        [*mhm:.  ]
           t                                       *nods->
18              (0.2)
19   Ern:       uh::m
20              (0.7)
21   Ern:       @hihm (0.2) s:huh
           e    @gaze to T, wide smile->
22              +[what e(h)l(h)se] can I sa(h)y[(hh.Hih)]
23   Ther:      [mhm:           ]              *[mhm. *  ]
           e    +extends arms out-
           t                               nods->*smiles*
24   Ther:      [so something not quite]tuh: real about it, er it's
25   Ern:       +[hihuhuh hh            ]              +
           e    +gaze forward, peaked hands to mouth-> +stops smiing->
26   Ther:      [sort've] uh
27   Ern:       [yeah   ]
28   Ern:       [yeah] but [I mean I] I'm I'm open to anything
29   Ther:      [.h  ]     [yeah,   ]
30   Ern:       +that's why I'm here. +[huh. ]
31   Ther:                             [ye:ah] right. (.) right*
           e    +gaze to T->           +quick nod, smiles->
           t                                              nods->*
32              (0.4)
33   Ther:      so:,(0.5) and (0.3) uh::m (0.7) I mean I've done it myself.
34              +so I kno:w what it's like. to: (0.4)+ to (0.3) to do that.
           e    +gaze to T, slight smile------------+
35              en it's ↑quite surprising sometimes what (0.5)
36              what can come up.
37              (0.3)
38   Ther:      °uhm° (0.5) I mean it * it can be very * useful.
           t                          *shrugs, gaze down* gaze to E
39              *>I guess I'm just trying< * to say thet'[it]
40   Ern:                                               +[eh]m.+
           t    *extends hand to E---*
           e                                             +nod-+
41              (0.4)
42   Ther:      °uhm° *it can be   *   very useful and
           t                *extends hands*
43   Ther:      [I think *it's worth a try] anyway.*
44   Ern:       [.hhh                     ]
           t    *sits up, extends hands*
45   Ern:       °okay. well,°=
46   Ther:      *=justa se:e.*
           t    *shakes head-*
47              (0.2)
48   Ther:      what [what cou-           ](0.4)* could come of it. *
49   Ern:            [°let's let's try it°]
           t                          *leans head forward, extends hand*
```

The therapist, in lines 01–04, makes another attempt at suggesting chair work. First, as seen in Extract 8.4, she orients to the high contingency associated with the suggestion through a number of turn design features that cast it as unmotivated and conditional on the client's interest: "`throw that out again as a possibility`" (lines 01–02); "`if that would ... work at some point`" (line 04). The many pauses, the term "`possibility`", the expression "`where you feel you're at`" and conditional *if* all work together in constructing this proposal as highly contingent on the client's acceptance, but also display a moment-by-moment orientation to his lack of affiliative displays. For instance, Ernie does not only refrain from accepting at numerous places where he could have, but he also delivers muted agreement that is accompanied by non-vocal actions that signal displeasure and disengagement (line 05) – and possibly indifference by looking at his hands with a downturned mouth – and a long whispered inbreath possibly displaying distress (line 7). This leads the therapist to redo her suggestion by orienting to Ernie's willingness (`wanna give that a whirl`, line 06). Following no response from Ernie, she then solicits an assessment (and confirmation) from him pertaining to her suggestion to do chair work (`> I dunno what< you think about that.`) and, later in line 12, provides more granularity (Schegloff, 2000) to deictic *that* by elaborating with "`that ide:ah`". At this point, Ernie's lack of enthusiasm to engage becomes more overt. He shakes his head in line 12 and then, following a few pauses and a "`tch`", he grammatically ties his turn to the therapist's (line 14) by offering a parallel claim of uncertainty about engaging in chair work (`I don't know either`). Although, at one level, Ernie's response is disaffiliative because he is clearly revealing his hesitation to comply, it may also be understood as an affiliative move that displays both participants' being "in agreement" regarding each other's uncertainty about whether to engage the task.

In line 16, Ernie makes his discomfort explicit by pointing out the artificiality of the proposed task: "`it seems a little contrived I-I-I-I °uh w° yihknow,`". He afterwards makes a number of bids to continue his turn but then, in line 22, makes the plea that there is nothing more he can say while extending his arms outwards. This seems to work not only to defuse his act of disengaging by making an offer to the therapist, but also seeks re-affiliation with the therapist through smiling and laughter. In lines 17 and 23, the therapist displays affiliation with the client's initial reluctance by a number of acknowledgement tokens (`mm hm`), nodding, smiling and then by producing a formulation that endorses Ernie's unease concerning the artificial quality of the proposed activity (`so something not quite uh: real about it`). These therapist actions, which work to re-affiliate with the client's opposing viewpoint, engender a movement toward realignment with the activity (see also Chapter 7). Ernie voices his willingness to comply (`but I mean I I'm`

I'm open to anything), showing that they are in the process of re-aligning toward doing chair work. The therapist, however, continues to provide a rationale and justification for doing chair work, lines 33–43, which seems to indicate that an "agreement to engage" has not quite yet been reached. It is only in lines 45 and 49 (°okay. well,°; °let's let's try it°) that Ernie's readiness to work becomes more overtly displayed.

Engaging in chair work requires that clients are ready to experience and engage with their emotions in the presence of an imagined other or conflicted self. According the Watson and Greenberg (2000, p. 181), "they [clients] may find the activities required of certain tasks too artificial and contrived, and feel silly performing them, for example, when asked to talk to an empty chair." The successful realignment shown in this extract illustrates the level of attention required to track subtle non-vocal indicators (a shift in gaze, pausing, head movements, gestures), but also how the therapist reacts by downgrading her epistemic position responsively. These numerous contributions from the therapist can work to offset mounting and pending disengagement *in the moment* but, importantly, preserves the alliance suggesting that the momentum in therapy, which was at risk, is not interrupted.

### 8.4.6 *Pursuing Own Agenda or Topic (Taking Own Track)*

When responding to client's troubles tellings, therapists often subtly transform the reported troubles via formulations. The basic response alternatives available to clients are to ratify or oppose the action but there is one other option that clients do regularly make use of: ignoring the therapist's formulation by pursuing own agenda or topic – see also Chapter 3. In such cases, as seen in Extract 8.6 with the client Sofia (part of this extract was shown previously in Extract 3.31), the client takes her own track by sticking with her original topic of comparing her interactions with her husband versus her niece's interaction with her (i.e., the niece's) husband.

**Extract 8.6:** 304.03(1a)

```
01 Sofia:  so .h we went to ~this pa:rty.~
02         (1.3)
03 Sofia:  a:nd uh:m
04         (2.4)
05 Sofia:  and we started joking,
06 Ther:   °mm [hm° ]
07 Sofia:      [with] other people. not with him.
        t  nod                    shallow double nod
08         (0.8)
09 Sofia:  .shih and I look at him ~ah one point in the pa::rty. and he was~
10         .hhh serious,
11         (0.5)
```

12 Ther: mm: hm:,
13 Sofia: com-com-<pletely> .hhh uh::m (0.6) so:: (.) fo:rmal,
14 (0.3)
15 Sofia: he lacked (0.5) a sponta::neity (.) so much.
*t* *shallow nod* *nod*
16 Ther: mm hm,=
17 Sofia: and I started to s(h)ink about ↑maybe (1.1) dis marriage
18 (0.3) is hurting him as much as- as I as it is hurting me::
*t* *nod*
19 .h en he is becoming so: (0.6) so:: (0.9) how could I say.
20 Ther: hm.
21 Sofia: .shih (.) that he is becoming (1.7) such a negative ↑person
22 (.) [but I w-] I was- I w- I was looking ba:ck,
23 Ther: [°mm.° ]
24 Ther: °mm hm,°
25 Sofia: he always been li-that.
*s* *shakes head, looks at T*
26 (0.3)
27 Ther: m[m hm,]
28 Sofia: [he wa]s ↑ALways li-that=I don't know. ah hhh=
*t* *nod*
*s* *shakes head*
29 Ther: **=so it's kinda [hard] to figure out righ[t,=bu]t you're**
30 Sofia: [.shih] [so ]
31 Ther: **starting t-**
32 **you were starting to think ↑well** ((clears throat))
33 **maybe this i[s really ↑bringing him do:wn] too.**
34 Sofia: **[I: like I me:an .shih]**
*t* *nod*
35 Sofia: **I mean my:- I was- I saw my niece.**
36 (1.5)
37 Sofia: **and her husband interacting,**
38 (0.3)
*s* *tilts head forward, gazes at T*
39 Ther: mm hm,
40 Sofia: and I kno- ok they are newlyweds=and I-one cannot espect .hhh
41 a relationship to go li-that ↑twenty years [even th]ough
42 [ye a::h.]
*t* *multiple nods---->*
43 I don't s(h)ink it's ↑impo:ssible
44 (0.3)
45 Ther: mm hm,
46 Sofia: ↑BU:t °.shih°
47 (1.3)
48 Sofia: I looked at my: (.) niece and-and her
49 husband interacting=and >I mean< .hhh (0.6) they were having
*s* *looks at T*
50 such a good time.
51 Ther: mm [hm, ]
52 Sofia: [an I:] loo:k (.) at .hhh u::hm my husband and I,
*t* *nod, shakes head*
53 (0.5)

```
54 Ther:   yeah? and you [just       fee:::l,]
55 Sofia:                [and I     <looked at] the way .hhh I cannot>
56         (0.6)
57 Sofia:  uh:::m
58         (1.3)
59 Sofia:  I cannot en↑JOY myself.
       s                throws hand down, palm up, looking at T
60         (0.3)
       t   fast multiple nods
61 Sofia:  .hhh >because I mean if I wa-< if I was by myself I ma- I might be
62         l↓onely, but I m- I might find ways to .hhh (.) to-to (0.3) to be::
       t                                                  shallow multiple nods
63         .hhh ↓to::: (1.5) to espress myself.
       s                         throws hands out, double nod
64 Ther:   yeah.
       t   shifts posture
```

At the beginning of this extract, Sofia launches into a story about going to a party with her husband. Almost immediately, her talk becomes overlaid with a wobbly voice, which displays some distress (~this pa:rty.~). At lines 08–15, her story turns into a deep and extremely formulated criticism of the husband (he was~ .hhh serious … com-com-<pletely>; so:: (.) fo:rmal,; lacked (0.5) a sponta::neity (.) so much.). She then, lines 17–21, expressed a realization that the husband is perhaps as unhappy as she is in the marriage. But afterwards, lines 22–28, she attributes his negative qualities more to his persistent and unchanging character (he was ↑ALways li-that). In lines 29–33, the therapist produces a formulation that orients to the husband's unhappiness in the marriage (maybe this is really ↑bringing him do:wn too.) rather than him having any enduring negative attributes. But rather than engaging with the therapist's gist formulation – for example, through an agreement followed by further reflection of the marriage and its effects through disagreement followed by an account – Sofia ignores the formulation and continues with her story. In lines 34 and 35, she prefaces her turn with "**I me:an**", thus signalling that she will most likely expand on her own story rather than engage with the therapist's talk. From lines 35 to 52, Sofia draws a comparison between her niece's relationship with her own. From her observation that her niece and husband "were having such a good time", she then begins to draw a negative conclusion in regard to her own relationship, but does not finish (an I:] loo:k (.) at .hhh u::hm my husband and I,). The therapist, in line 54, produces what appears as a designedly incomplete utterance (DIU) (Koshik, 2002) in which she focuses on how Sofia might have felt upon coming to this realization (yeah? and you just fee:::l,), leaving it to Sofia to fill in the missing piece of affect. But again, Sofia does not engage with the therapist's words and instead, in line 55, she produces overlapping speech that completes where she had left off; that is, in looking at her niece and husband, she sees that she is not able to enjoy herself. Sofia's responses of taking her own track and not responding to the therapist convey a disengagement from a cooperative conversation in which speakers orient to and build upon each other's actions. By not taking the therapist's contributions into account, Sofia's story verges more toward a monologue rather than a dialogue.

## 8.5 Building Opposition

Opposition is realized when clients move *against* the therapist (Eubanks et al., 2015 use the term *confrontation*). From my CA-informed interactional perspective, although the characterization of "moving against" seems well-grounded in terms of social actions such as opposition or overt conflict, the idea that the object of opposition is *the therapist* seems to limit opposition to those episodes in which the therapist is verbally attacked in some way; that is, only when there is complaint or criticism (or an implication thereof) directed at the therapist. Thus, within Eubanks et al.'s (2015) alliance rupture-resolution model, disagreement or rejection per se, when done collaboratively and not with the intention to injure the therapist, does not necessarily act to "move against." This, however, requires the analyst to make decisions regarding clients' intentions, which runs contrary to the CA/Ethnomethodological principle that talk or conduct does not provide a clear window into the speakers' "mind" (Coulter, 1979). Moreover, research has shown that disagreement, even if it is done in a so-called "cooperative" way or is mitigated in strength, has the potential to be face-threatening and to place some degree of stress on social relations (Brown & Levinson, 1987; Heritage, 1984; Muntigl & Turnbull, 1998). Thus, in this chapter, rather than make opposition dependent on what the speaker has intended, I will link it to argumentative or conflict-bound acts irrespective of whether they involve blame, criticism, complaints and so on – see especially Goodwin (1990) for actions that *build opposition*. Thus, opposition will involve responsive actions that do not conform to the constraints of the initiating action by *overtly* and *actively* opposing or challenging these constraints (Clayman & Heritage, 2002; Stivers, 2005b).

Two general kinds of opposition will be examined. The first involves oppositional moves such as rejection and disagreement. The second relates to more antagonistic forms (or *aggravated* opposition, Goodwin, 1990) – more in line with Eubanks et al. (2015) – that involve blame or criticism.

### *8.5.1 Oppositional Moves*

Opposition is displayed in two general ways. The first involves a conflict of views that is expressed through *disagreement*. In these contexts, the participants tend to compete over epistemic rights and access and entitlements to experience. These kinds of conflict sequences tend to often occur when understandings are being negotiated and when epistemics is a prime issue. The second occurs when proposals to engage in tasks are outright *rejected.* In these cases, *deontics* or who has rights to decide on what to do, when and why (Stevanovic & Svennevig, 2015), are at issue.

*Disagreement* In Extract 8.7, I show how disaffiliation is built up around a conflict of views between the therapist and client (part of this conversation has already been examined under Extract 2.24, Chapter 2). At the core of these interactions is a disalignment in which therapist and client are pursuing different agendas that become realized in opposing action plans – that is, the oppositional client would make her disagreement of the therapist's view explicit and would articulate a clear contrasting view. In this conversation, the therapist attempts to explore how the client's staying in her relationship creates restrictions for her and the client repeatedly resists that trajectory by claiming to have options (i.e., she is not trapped).

**Extract 8.7:** 304.07(2)

01 Sofia: it is difficult. (.) ↑yuh. it is.
s *double nod.* *wipes eyes*
02 (0.8)
03 Sofia: .snih I-just the only s(h)ing ~that I am tryin to do
04 (1.1)
05 Sofia ((swallowing)) is to cope. at [this time.]~
06 Ther: [ri::ght. ]
t *double nod*
07 (0.3)
08 Ther: °ri:ght?°
09 Sofia: ((blows nose)) it's not fortunately is not gonna have to be
10 for a ↑long time. °.snih .snih°
11 (0.4)
12 Ther: uh huh.
13 Sofia: but uh:m.
s *wipes eyes, looks at T*
14 (1.6)
15 Sofia: but that's the only s(h)ing that I can do.
16 (0.4)
17 Sofia: [right] now.
18 Ther: [.hhh ]
19 (0.3)
20 Ther: right I mean i=feels like you're really trapped °right now
21 right?°
22 (1.3)
23 Ther: [in trapped] in having [to cope]
24 Sofia: [uh::m ] [**↑NN::** ] **no not trapped to to to::.**
25 .h °.snih°
26 (2.5)
27 Sofia: **n:ot tra:pped like I-I wouldn't say no. (.) look Sofia**
s *takes tissue*
28 **you don't have any other choices?**
29 (0.2)

30 Ther: yeah,
31 Sofia: so.
32 (1.4)
s *sweeps hands out*
33 Ther: .hhh [cause y-]
34 Sofia: **[you are ] dead. no.**
s *smiles.* *shakes head*
t *smiles*
35 (0.3)
36 Ther: mm::.
37 Sofia: **not trapped to that degree:.**
t *double nod, smiling*
38 Ther: su::[re. okay.]
39 Sofia: [o:ka:y? ]
t *multiple nods→*
40 (0.8)
t -->
41 Sofia: **no.=**
42 Ther: =meaning in [that if you wanted to] get out that you could?
43 Sofia: [(in that meaning,) ]
44 (0.3)
45 Ther: °is that what you're sayin?°
46 (1.8)
47 Sofia: **not if I wanted to get out=if I cou:ld n:↑o::.**
48 (0.5)
49 Sofia: .SHIH is=jus that while the option is not here ↓now.
50 (0.5)
t *nod*
51 Sofia: but the option will be there. soon.
52 (0.5)
53 Ther: right.
54 Sofia: is l[i:ke ]
55 Ther: [°uh huh,°]
56 (2.3)
57 Sofia: uh::m.
58 (1.0)
59 Sofia: putting myself in suspense.
60 (0.7)
t *nod*
61 Ther: °y:eah.°
62 (0.3)
63 Ther: .hhh and yet it seems very difficult for you to put yourself
t *fast multiple nods, smiles*
64 in suspense. .hhh
65 Ther: you know I mean it's not as if you just put yourself on
66 ho:ld, .hhh a::nd (0.2) you've resolved okay in this: X time
67 [I'm gonna leave]
68 Sofia: [°hm::? ° ]
69 Ther: =an until then I'm just gonna hold it togeth'r.=.hhh
70 becau-and I im↑agine that-that the difficulty of holding
71 yourself in suspense is that you're not getting what you nee:d.
t *shakes head, throws palms out at S*
72 Ther: .hhh
73 Sofia: ↑oh no.

| | | |
|---|---|---|
| | *s* | *looks at tissue, shakes head* |
| 74 | | (0.4) |
| 75 | Sofia: | [no- .hhh] |
| 76 | Ther: | [on a ] daily basis right. |
| | *t* | *shallow nod* |
| 77 | | (0.7) |
| 78 | Sofia: | **ahhhxx** |
| | *s* | *smiles, looks down* |
| 79 | | (0.6) |
| 80 | Sofia: | **hm. .hhh an even- even- even. (0.6) .SHIH if I::somes(h)in** |
| 81 | | **estremely estrange (0.3) estremely estrange ha:ppen.** |
| | *s* | *looks up. widens eyes. shallow nod, looks, points at T* |
| 82 | | ( 1.1 ) |
| | *t* | *shallow nod* |
| 83 | Sofia: | ((lip smack)) during the la:st uh:: .SHIH I would say:: |
| | *t* | *rests hand on cheek* |
| 84 | | (1.5) |
| 85 | Sofia: | two weeks. |
| 86 | | (0.6) |
| 87 | Sofia: | no two weeks no one week. this las week. |
| 88 | Ther: | mm hm,= |
| 89 | Sofia: | =.hhh uh:::m. |
| 90 | | (1.9) |
| 91 | Sofia: | my husband- estarted (2.0) behaving (0.5) in a ve:ry (0.3) |
| 92 | | weird (.) way. I mean I haven't known him |
| 93 | | (0.5) |
| | *s* | *tilts head, looks at T* |
| | *t* | *smiles* |
| 94 | Sofia: | acting li-that. |

Sofia begins this extract by talking about the troubles she faces in the relationship, saying that it is difficult and that she is just trying to cope (lines 01–10). She also evinces many features of distress and crying during this time (Hepburn, 2004), such as wobbly voice, sniffing, blowing nose, wiping eyes and swallowing hard. She then states that her troubles will not continue indefinitely (fortunately is not gonna have to be for a ↑long time) but then concedes, in lines 15–17, that her "having to cope" is what she must do at the present time. The therapist, in lines 20–23, draws an implication from Sofia's talk by stating that this "having to cope" leads her to feel trapped. Sofia, beginning in line 24, forcefully disagrees with the therapy in overlap ([↑NN::] no not trapped) and later provides an account, claiming that she has other choices (line 28) and that she is not "dead" (you are dead. no.). Sofia then emphasizes that she is "not trapped to that **degree**:." before ending her turn with a "no." in line 41, which may be working toward a consensus of views – see Chapter 7. The therapist then seeks clarification, lines 42–45, by asking if Sofia could get out of the relationship if she wanted. After a long pause, line 46, Sofia again provides explicit disagreement (`not if I wanted to get out=if I cou:ld n:↑o::.`) and then re-states that, even if she does not have that option now, she will have it soon (lines 49–57). Then, in line 59, she closes by alluding to the potential anxiety that results from being in this situation (`putting myself in suspense.`). In response, the therapist first nods and then provides "quiet" acknowledgement (°**`y:eah.`**°). Then, in line 63, she launches into a disagreement in which she questions Sofia's ability to maintain this form of tension (`and yet it seems very difficult for you to put yourself in suspense.`). Following this, lines 65–69, the therapist performs a self-repair by explaining what she means; that is, putting oneself in this kind of suspense or "on hold" would require much effort and would not be a painless endeavour. During this time, Sofia mainly remains stolid, producing only a minimal request for clarification in line 68 (`°hm::? °`). It is then in line 70 that the therapist changes her track somewhat, easing up on disagreement, and instead focuses on the high costs involved when Sofia holds herself in suspense, perhaps with the aim of securing agreement from the client (Sacks, 1987): "`you're not getting what you nee:d.`". In line 73, Sofia does produce strong agreement to the claim that she would be relinquishing her needs (`↑oh no.`), but rather than engage with this dilemma that was just topicalized, she then lets out a heavy sign while smiling (ahhhxx). When she resumes her turn in line 80, it becomes clearer that she is moving to shift the topic and launch into a story about her husband's "bizarre" behaviour (`somes(h)in estremely estrange (0.3) estremely estrange ha:ppen.`). With this move, Sofia clearly resists the therapist's offer to explore the difficulty in being in suspense, in favour of initiating a complaint story that targets her husband.

*Refusals* Overt opposition may also be displayed when clients directly refuse a therapist's proposal with an unadorned "no," as illustrated in Extract 8.8. Prior to this extract, the client Paula had been discussing her relationship with her mother, stating that her mother had controlled many components of Paula's life (e.g., having to be home right after school) and that her parents had discouraged her from pursuing various goals.

**Extract 8.8:** 312_9

```
01 Paula:  a::nd (0.5) le-I-I wanted to get into:: (0.3) like
02         something arts related.
03         (1.1)
04 Paula:  an:d like it + shust g(h).hh (0.4)
05         it wasn't even acknowledged.
        p    smiles->+ gaze to T/forward->
        t  leans face on finger-> nods
06         (1.5)
```

```
07 Paula:  and then like the only:, s:thing: like I
08         (1.5)
09 Paula:  and since I didn't know like what (.) else to do and so I decided
10         like to ke- continue school and even that,
11         (0.9)
12 Paula:  like >when it didn't turn o:ut=like when I:< (.) had all these
13         problems like (0.5) with thuh: (.) vis- vith the teachers,
14         like (0.3)
15 Paula:  with the other students with the subject matter it was well .hhh
16         you know like you ↑wanted to do this: you know [now   ]
17 Ther:                                                  [°hm.°]
        t                                                 nod
18 Paula:  it doesn't work.
19 Ther:   °m:m,°
        t  nod
20         (1.0)
21 Paula:  li-i- jus: like absolutely no::: support.
22         °mm hm°
        t  small nod
23         (0.4)
24 Paula:  at a:ll.
25         (0.8)
26 Ther:   .tch ye'know? you've talked? before about your father and on
        t  shifts posture, gaze up, interlocks fingers,
        p       bites lip, gaze to T->
27         some- .hh quite a lotta the feelings you s:: you(d) (.)
        p                    very small, rapid nods
28         mentioned toda:y, and things you [struggle] with se[em to]
29 Paula:                                   [mm.      ]          [mm,  ]
30 Ther:   go ba:ck tuh .hh to that relationship.
31         en I was thinking, .h (.) it might be good (0.3) <to go back>
        t                        gaze upward                   gaze to P
32         to working the way we once did (.)+ a few weeks ago with
        p                                    + smiles->
33         (.) .hh (.) bringing your father into the room,
        t  extends hand, smiles
34         (0.7)
        t  smiles
35 Ther:   ju-would that feel comfortable to try that again? I?
36         (0.4)
37 Paula:  no:         [hhih heheheheh] [.Hh h        ]
38 Ther:               [hh::          ] [no, because,]
        p  turns head. broadens smile, tilts head, finger to cheek->
        t                raises chin, smiles->
39 Paula:  .hhh
        p  gaze forward and to T->
40         (1.3)
        p  smiles->+
41 Paula:  Hhhx
42         (2.2)
43 Paula:  °.tch°
44         (4.3)
```

```
         t  smile->, rubs interlocking fingers->
         p  gaze downward, finger on cheek->
45  Paula:  O:h because I'm gi:s so:: I'm jus-I-I'm so: (.) angry about (.)
46          all these things because I realize .hhh
47          that it affects me so much no:w,
48          (0.7)
49  Paula:  >like<
50          (2.7)
51  Paula:  I-I really <don't kno:w like what he:> (1.9)
52          what he ↑wa:nted from me:. like .h
            .
            .
            .
53  Ther:   .hh so what's the feeling if we (0.8) try en work with him he:re.
         t                       waves hand, palm out
54          is it almost like .hh (.) it's gunna hurt too mu:ch?
55          or there's no use even to bring him in in kind of an
56          imaginary way, it feels futi:le? .hh
57          (0.3)
58  Ther:   or is it a self protec[tion thing like] I don't=
59  Paula:                        [ehhhih °hih°   ]
         t                          waves hand, palm out, walling motion
         p                       smiles, gaze to T/down
60  Paula:  =it's probably a c(h)ombin(h)ation of th(h)i(h)ngs.
         t  nods, smiles, brings hand to mouth->
         p  laughing, gaze to T, fingers extended
61  Ther:   °combination.°
62          (0.6)
63  Ther:   .h ↑well en maybe that's important to understand even that
64          because .hh (0.6) even to bring him in he:re feels,
65          (0.3)
66  Ther:   what threatenin:g? o:r?
67          (2.0)
68  Paula:  uh:mhh
69          (3.3)
         p  closes eyes for duration of silence
70  Paula:  tch
71          (0.5)
72  Paula:  oh I guess li-I'm ju:st (0.2) no:t.
73          (1.4)
74  Paula:  re-maybe next time but right nigh (.) e-right now I'm just
         p  shrugs shoulders
75          not ready like to (0.2) to really fa:ce it?
76  Ther:   =h:m,
77          (0.6)
78  Paula:  like it's::
79          (1.1)
80  Paula:  [just::   ]
81  Ther:   [it was so] powerful=
82  Paula:  =very up↑setting. .hh ↑well(hih)ye:ah,
```

```
         t   nods              sits back in chair
         p                tilts head, gaze up, smiles->
83 Ther:     =>°mm hm.°<
84           (2.0)
85 Paula:    eh-eh-eh (.) also becaus:e (0.4) Hhhx
86           (3.3)
         p   during pause P gaze upwards over T's head
         t   gaze at P
87 Paula:    .hh well beca:use of all this
88           (5.8)
         p   during pause P gaze upwards over T's head, excessive blinking
         t   gaze @ P
89 Paula:    I have (0.3) always (.) avoided
90           (3.7)
91 Paula:    my father … ((enters into storying about her father))
```

At the beginning of this extract, Paula recounts an episode in which she did not receive any acknowledgement from her parents for beginning her studies in an arts-related field. She then tells of her problems with her teachers and fellow students, lines 12–15, and that it turned out badly. Paula then presents the parents, via direct quoted speech, as articulating a negative (vindictive), affective stance in which they undermine her scholarly ambitions: "`you know like you ↑wanted to do this: you know now it doesn't work`". These kinds of stance displays tend to warrant an affiliative response from the recipient and perhaps even empathy, showing, for example, how the parents' cruel acts have been understood. But instead, the therapist's response contains merely a minimal acknowledgement (°`m:m,`° `+ a nod`). In this context of minimal affiliation, Paula then, in line 21, develops her stance further by strongly emphasizing the parents' lack of support through extreme case descriptors such as "`absolutely`" and "`no:::`". Even in this context, however, the therapist refrains from offering more affiliation than minimal acknowledgement, which presumably leads Paula to continue developing her affective stance of "extreme uncaring parents" as offering her no support "`at a:ll.`" (line 24). But then in line 26, instead of engaging with Paula's report of her parents' cruelty toward her, the therapist initiates a topic shift. Her turn is prefaced with "`ye'know?`" and "`you've talked? before about`", which signals that what she is about to say will deviate from Paula's immediately prior talk – or at least will not directly connect with it. The therapist continues by topicalizing Paula's struggling relationship with her father (lines 26–30). She then uses this as a "lead in" to propose a different activity, chair work, in order for Paula to directly confront the father (lines 31–33). The proposal is made with some contingency, "`I was thinking, .h`" and "`it might be good`", and the therapist produces a few affiliative smiles toward the end of the turn, which may be working to gain an affiliative return smile from the client (Bänninger-Huber, 1992).

Paula, however, does not respond and nor does she offer a return smile and thus might be signalling a possible impending rejection. Faced with a possible disaffiliative scenario (i.e., a lack of agreement to engage in chair work), the therapist, in line 35, produces a subsequent version of the proposal (Davidson, 1984), one that, because it more directly seeks confirmation, is more highly response relevant (Stivers & Rossano, 2010). The therapist's reference to the client's degree of "comfort" may also be orienting to the lack of affiliation displayed by the client thus far "ju-would that feel comfortable to try that again?". Following a brief pause, Paula refuses (no:) and then quickly laughs while smiling. The therapist, in line 38, returns Paula's smile, repeats the "no" and then seeks an account from Paula that explains or justifies her refusal. What follows are a number of interactional features that convey Paula's distress at being asked to confront her father: silences, hesitation, inbreath, sighing, smiling (lines 39–44). Following these disaffiliative features, Paula provides an account and the talk turns toward the father and the difficulty that Paula has in facing him in the chair at this moment in time. The proposal's eventual rejection may be explained for varying reason. First, the proposal format lacked a clear orientation to contingency and to the client's greater entitlement to give assent. Second, and perhaps more important, is that it did not display an elaborately articulated description or reformulation of the client's trouble with the father. Following from this, the proposal resulted from a topic shift that was produced without offering the client adequate affiliation in relation to her complaints about her parents' uncaring attitude. Thus, it would seem that the therapist may not have invested in enough affiliative work beforehand, in order to properly ease the client into engaging into this new activity, one that is fraught with distress and anxiety over having to confront the father.

A few minutes later in the conversation, lines 53 onwards, the therapist returns the discussion back toward the potential reasons why Paula may not want to engage in chair work. These reasons are couched in terms of the client's feelings and how they may be working to resist confronting her father at the present time: "it's gunna hurt too mu:ch?"; "there's no use even to bring him in in kind of an imaginary way/it feels futi:le?"; and "a self protection thing". Thus, by confirming one of these choices, Paula could affiliate with the therapist and, if willing, proceed to explore what is holding her back and, if resolved, proceed with chair work. Instead, Paula remains equivocal by suggesting that it could be a combination of reasons (line 60). The laugh particles may not only reflect her hesitation but also her anxiety at confronting the father now (a c(h)ombin(h)ation of th(h)i(h)ngs). The therapist then echoes the client talk through partial repetition "°combination.°" (Ferrara, 1994), but after a brief silence in which Paula does not resume her turn, the therapist resumes exploration of why Paula cannot directly engage with her father (lines 63–66). One main reason given for Paula's hesitancy is that it would be too threatening for her. But after the therapist trails off her turn with a turn-final "or," inviting the client to confirm or provide a different reason, Paula again displays a reluctance to respond. This reluctance, as evidenced through silences, closing her eyes in possible contemplation, an extended "`uh:mhh`", precedes her answer, which accounts for her not being able to do chair work (lines 72–80). First she postpones her confrontation with her dad to a later time (`re- maybe next time`) and then she accounts for her non-compliance by claiming not to be "ready" (`right now I'm just not ready like to (0.2) to really fa:ce it?`). Toward the end of the extract, Paula then launches into a story about her father, showing perhaps that storytelling is at this time a less threatening form of engagement than meeting him directly in the empty chair.

### *8.5.2 Criticizing*

In some cases, oppositional conduct can run much deeper than disagreeing with the therapist's perspective or rejecting the proposed task. Most commonly, these forms of disaffiliation verge on being antagonistic/aggravated and are highly critical of the therapy and how it is being conducted. Three different forms of client criticism will be reviewed in this section: criticizing therapist's understanding, criticizing the (effectiveness of) therapy and criticizing the roles (that client and therapist are required to assume) in therapy.

*Criticizing Therapist's Understanding* Extract 8.9 involves the client Eve, who had displayed increasing distress during the beginning of the session while reporting on memories and experiences of her deceased brother. During this phase of interaction, the therapist would often display her understanding of Eve's distress by responding to the "content" of her talk, that is, by orienting to what the client was saying in her reporting of distress rather than her in the moment emotional display of upset. But when the therapist began to push further in exploring Eve's reported upset, Eve would tend to reject and criticize the therapist's course of action (see Muntigl, 2020 for a more extended analysis of how the therapist manages Eve's distress in different sequences over the beginning of the session).

**Extract 8.9:** 020.15; Muntigl (2020)

```
01    Eve:   ~UHm, (2.1) °.snih° (3.3) ((lip smack)) .hhh <I: had no
02           idea ho:w,> *.hhh HX::.* (0.4) °hm.° (0.6) ho::w, (2.2)
          e            *heaving shoulders and chest*
03           deep my feelings we:re about that whole thing. (.) an I
04           had no: idea, .hhh ho:w, (0.9) pro↑foundly. (2.1) it
05           affected the course of my li:fe.~
06           +(          0.3        )
```

```
        t   +slow shallow nod→
07   Ther:  mm h:m[::,]+
        t   ---------->+
08    Eve:  ~[an so] I >was just< like, (0.3) cruising o:n.~
09          (1.5)
10    Eve:  *.hhh HX::.*
        e   *heaving shoulders and chest*
11          (1.2)
12    Eve:  *e- you know sort of:, (0.4) scra:mbling,*
        e   *circles fingers forward ----------------->*
13          (       3.2        )
        e   slows down fingers
14          but like treading wa:ter.
15          (1.3)
16    Eve:  °a:n uh,° (0.3) [I just-]
17   Ther:                  [so <yo]u:: hadn't really fully:>
18          appreciated how much impact his *death °had had on you.°
        t                         shallow nod
        e                                        *multiple nods-->
19          (0.3)
        e   -->
20   Ther:  °an you were kind of-° * (  0.4  ) tryin to carry on blithely
        e   ---------------------->* wipes eye
21          an, (       1.9          )hadn't stopped to realize
        e      shallow multiple nods
22          maybe there's a hole *in your ship or-*
        e                       *shallow double nod*
23          (        7.6         )
        e   shallow multiple nods
24    Eve:  °.hhh° hx:::.
25          (3.5)
26    Eve:  ((lip smack)) yea:h. =
        e                 rubs eyes
27   Ther:  = °so his death was very significant for you:.°
28          (          1.8           )
        e   runs hands through hair
29    Eve:  °.snih°
        e   clasps hands behind head
30          (1.0)
31    Eve:  hx::.
32          (0.8)
33   Ther:  somehow it <s::ounds> perhaps as if, (2.2) you're
34          saying you didn't s:top enough to kinda- (1.5) process
35          it, an (.) integrate *it °an-° (0.4)* change course?
        e                         *drops arms to lap, looks away*
36          (0.3)
37    Eve:  well. n:- no I never ha:ve. (.) but, =
38   Ther:  = mm hm:[:,]
39    Eve:          [I ] mean-
40          (0.4)
41   Ther:  °does that° sound important?
        e      looks at T
42          (1.6)
        e   looks away
```

43 Ther: [to do:?]
44 Eve: [hx:. ]
45 (2.1)
46 Eve: **↑gee when you put it like °tha:t.°**
e *mocking tone*
47 (0.8)
48 Eve: uhm.
49 (1.1)
50 Ther: >°d'you feel I'm twisting your arm,°<
51 (0.4)
52 Eve: pardon?
53 Ther: >°d'you feel I'm twisting your arm,°<
54 (0.6)
55 Eve: **hehheh hehheh heh .hhh .hhh .hh n(h)o it's just so:**
56 **O:bvious what you're saying. that of course it's tru:e.**
57 .hhh uhm.
58 (0.8)
59 Ther: °°but=chu may not want to.°°
60 (0.7)
61 Ther: °°doesn't°° matter >whether it's< true° °°or not.°°
62 (0.7)
63 Eve: ((lip smack)) °ooh I don't know.° .hh *.hhh HX:::.*
e **heaving shoulders and chest**
64 (3.5)
65 Eve: like it- it n- (0.3)*~I mean the thing is is is* that,~
e *choked voice* **rubs hand over eyes**
66 (2.4)
67 Eve: °.snih°
68 (2.9)
69 Eve: ~(y'know),~

At the beginning of this extract, Eve reports on the significance her brother's death had on her (lines 01–16). The therapist responds to the client's reported distress by formulating the gist of the client's message, in a way that subtly transforms yet stays close to her wording. For example, the client's "I: had no idea" becomes rephrased as "you:: hadn't really fully:> appreciated" and "I >was just< like, (0.3) cruising o:n" as "you were kind of-° (0.4) tryin to carry on blithely". Further, the therapist's metaphorical expression "maybe there's a hole in your ship" (line 22) offers a relevant extension in meaning to the client's use of "scrambling" and "treading water," for it also implies vulnerability; that is, a hole may cause a ship to sink. It should be noted that the client conveys affiliation along many points of the therapist's turn and afterwards. Eve consistently nods during and immediately subsequent to the formulation and verbalizes agreement in line 26 (see Muntigl et al., 2012; Stivers, 2008).

It is at this point, however, where the conversation proceeds to get off-track. Starting from line 27, the therapist initiates a shift in frame in which she begins to move away from the client's initial revelation and the ways in which her life had been affected into an activity that focuses on the implications of the client's talk (°so his death was very significant for you:.°). Further, the client withholds her confirmation from line 28, which may be conveying implicit disaffiliation or even that she is having a hard time grasping the impact that her brother's death had on her life. In line 33 onwards, the therapist continues to draw implications, but prefaces her turn with the epistemic markers "it <s::ounds>", "somehow" and "perhaps". In this context, where the client has not displayed explicit affiliation in her prior turn, the therapist seems to be orienting to this ascription as being something delicate to do. The therapist's formulation explicitly points out the possible consequences of not having "fully appreciated" or "realized" the impact that the brother's death had on her; that is, Eve may have taken more time to reflect on these events (process it, an (.) integrate it) and to take a more agentive role in her life (change course). This more interpretive move by the therapist may be seen by the client as no longer fully endorsing her original stance and that may explain why, in line 37, Eve starts her turn by reluctantly agreeing with the therapist (well. n:- no I never ha:ve.) and then produces a disagreement token "but." The therapist then takes another turn (line 41) that explicitly seeks confirmation from the client (°does that° sound important?), but rather than offer her endorsement, the client continues to disaffiliate by turning away (line 42) and by producing an exasperated outbreath that overlaps with the therapist's turn continuation (to do:?).

Explicit disaffiliation occurs in line 46 when the client underscores the "obviousness" of the answer, while simultaneously mocking the therapist (↑gee when you put it like °tha:t.°). It is here that the client's dilemma in reference to the *problem of experience* becomes apparent (Heritage, 2011): she is being confronted with an expert's view and (rational) understanding that this perspective on her is correct, which, at the same time, does not orient to her in-the-moment experience of feeling devastated, vulnerable and exposed. Thus, the "mocking tone" would be indexing the client's reluctance to get in touch with her feelings, but she *is* admitting that the therapist has made a point. Furthermore, Eve's derision is doing additional emotional work; for example, by mocking the therapist, Eve seems to be conveying her annoyance with what the therapist has said and, by implication, that she may be displeased or angry with the therapist.

After withholding from taking up a turn at talk and thus allowing the client to continue and account for her disaffiliative response (lines 47–49), the therapist then orients to the interactional trouble by suggesting a possible reason for the client's displeasure (>°d'you feel I'm twisting your arm,°<); that is, the client may feel that the therapist's interpretation was made too forcefully and is perhaps not in step with the client's own perspective. The therapist's response also orients to who has primary rights to control the direction of the interaction, termed *deontic status* (Stevanovic and Peräkylä, 2014), suggesting that the therapist may have overstepped her bounds. Following a brief *other-initiated repair* sequence in lines 52–53 (Schegloff et al., 1977), the client first denies the therapist's reason and then provides an account that criticizes the therapist's prior intervention as being incongruous and inappropriate and challenges its relevance (`it's just so: O:bvious what you're saying. that of course it's tru:e.`). There may also be an implication of a breach in the therapist's genuineness or authenticity (Rogers, 1957); that is, in stating the "obvious," the therapist may be running the risk of appearing as lacking an adequate professional commitment and as simply supplying formulaic expressions as a response to the client's troubles – see also Chapter 4. This criticism conveys an affective stance of continued anger or annoyance at the therapist's response.

Subsequently, the therapist does further work in order to re-establish affiliation, agreement and a shared perspective on the prior interactional trouble. In line 59, the therapist's utterance (`°°but=chu may not want to.°°`) displays her understanding of the client's prior disaffiliative action of line 37; that is, although the client may have realized that she could have more deeply reflected on and dealt with the brother's death, she has no desire to do so. But following "no response" and thus "no confirmation" from the client in line 60, the therapist then provides another opportunity to engage the client by orienting to the implication in the client's prior turn that the therapist's interpretation is not relevant (`°°doesn't°° matter >whether it's< true° °°or not.°°`). But even this attempt fails to garner an affiliative response. Rather, the client first makes a claim of no knowledge (`°ooh I don't know.°`), which seems to simply dismiss and frustrate the therapist's line of action (Drew, 1992; Hutchby, 2002), then produces a prolonged sigh and finally proceeds to return to the topic of the brother.

*Criticizing the Therapy* Client criticisms may also target the therapy more generally. In these cases, dissatisfaction is voiced toward the (lack of) accomplishments made in therapy and, thus, the benefits of engaging in therapeutic work are questioned. Criticism of the therapy may be seen in Extract 8.10, again with the client Eve but taken from an earlier session – this conversation was also examined as Extract 4.1 in Chapter 4.

**Extract 8.10:** Evelyn Case 020.02(01)

```
Ther:   °so how's it been.°
        (0.7)
Eve:    mm? (.) °I:? I- (.) I.° I found. I:, (1.1) after the
        last session I was ↑re:ally like frustrated an:,(0.4)
        disappointed and I didn't know what to do with it.
        (0.3)
Ther:   ye:s?
Eve:    a:nd, I sort of- (1.3) I felt like I'd, (1.4) touch
```

```
          on alotta things an then just walked away from the:m
          a:nd,
Ther:     mm h[m:,]
Eve:          [and] it didn't really have any shape and didn't
          really (.) do anything? an [didn't-       ]
Ther:                                [so you seem ] very
          dissatisfi:ed?
Eve:      ↑yea:h.
          (0.4)
Eve:      yeah.
          (0.4)
Eve:      a:n- (.) km(hh). ((clears throat))
          (0.5)
Eve:      [    I'm in a-         ]
Ther:     [(you thought it had)] been too scattered
          someho[:w? or (maybe like)      >all over]=the map.<
Eve:            [yea:h. it was way- (.) like >I w-<]
          (0.5)
Eve:      [   yea:h.     ] >an when I< [(          ) I was a:ngry]
Ther:     [((coughs))   ]              [      ((coughs))]
Eve:      when I left, just cause it was so,
          (0.3)
Eve:      frustrating and so:,
Ther:     so did ↓you [feel] very frustrat[e:d, a:nd,]
Eve:                  [°hm.°]             [ye:a:h.   ]
          (0.3)
Eve:      yeah. an- (.) .h like, (0.3) uh- just (0.3)
          o:ne futile dead end after another.
```

In line 01, the therapist utters a *wh*-question that generally targets Eve's feelings and experiences (°so how's it been.°). In response, lines 03–13, Eve launches into a complaint about the last therapy session, claiming that she "was ↑re:ally like frustrated an:,(0.4) disappointed and … didn't know what to do with it." and that the therapy itself "didn't really have any shape and didn't really (.) do anything?". The therapist, in lines 14–15, produces an epistemically downgraded formulation that succinctly summarizes how Eve feels (so you seem very dissatisfi:ed?). Eve strongly confirms this view in lines 16 and 18 but, as Eve does not immediately expand or elaborate on her acknowledging actions, the therapist provides another formulation that addresses Eve's criticism of what happened in the last therapy (it had) been too scattered … >all over]=the map.<). Eve again provides confirmation, line 25, and then expands her turn by stating how she felt after leaving the session (I was a:ngry; it was so,(0.3) frustrating). The therapist affiliates using a summary formulation of Eve's feelings, line 32, which yields client confirmation and Eve re-iterating how she found the last session futile.

*Criticizing the Roles in Therapy* Another dimension of client criticism involves the expectations during therapy and the requirements or constraints placed upon each person's mode of conduct; for example, therapists have certain "roles" in which they use talk in certain ways and clients may thus be confronted with unexpected or "atypical" responses to what they normally receive in everyday contexts. Thus, criticism may take the form of not knowing what to expect from one's interlocutor and also being "forced" into a discursive role in which one must deviate from what one normally does and is comfortable with. This form of criticism is shown in Extract 8.11, which occurs very soon after Extract 8.10. To summarize, Eve had just been criticizing the past session, stating that it made her angry and that it seemed futile. In this extract, Eve begins to state more explicitly what had bothered her.

**Extract 8.11:** Evelyn Case 020.02(01)

```
01   Eve:   and I'm also not used to being, (0.5) like you said last time,
02          >it's like< ↑I: have tuh set the agenda.
03          (.)
04   Eve:   and I'm not ↑used to tha:t,
05   Ther:  mm [hm::.    ]
06   Eve:      [ya know ] I'm used to talking .hhh y:- y'know being
         t  deep nod
07          more responsive. f:i- figuring out what-
         t                            double nod---------->
08          (.)
09   Ther:  what the other person wanted.
10   Eve:   yeah. yeah. that's right. eh a:lso (.) y'know figuring out
11          what the situation is asking of you (.) an then .hh
12          ↑doing it.
13   Ther:  mm hm::.
14   Eve:   an then, (0.4) when you just went [mm hm:::.]
15   Ther:                                    [hh hh h   ]
         e                                    places closed hand under
                                              chin to parody therapist
         t                                       laughter
16          (0.4)
17   Eve:   .hh an I went >bla bla bla bla bla bla bla bla bla bla bla<
         e                 places hand to mouth rapidly moving fingers
18          an I just didn't know what to ↑do.
19          (0.5)
20   Eve:   an: I'm used to- (0.4) also if I sa:y: .hh y'know well
21          it was kinda a crazy week= an that was interesting cuz I was
22          thinking about that= I'm used to people going
23          .HHH (.) OH tha:t's interesting?
         e             leans forward towards T and tilts head to side
```

In lines 01–04, Eve complains about the expectation that she must "`set the agenda.`" and that she is not accustomed to that. Afterwards, lines 06–07, she states what she is in the habit of doing, which is being "`more responsive`". Toward the end of line 07, Eve takes another turn constructional unit (TCU) (Sacks et al., 1974), but does not complete her message, thus creating an environment for an *anticipatory completion* (Lerner, 1992). The therapist, in line

09, then completes the turn (what the other person wanted.), which not only displays understanding of what Eve is attempting to say, but also offers affiliation with her predicament. Eve, in lines 10–12, first provides upgraded confirmation (yeah. yeah. that's right.) and then slightly expands or reworks her and the therapist's co-completed turn into "figuring out what the situation is asking of you (.) an then .hh ↑doing it.". In other words, she is accustomed to trying to understand what somebody else had said and then working with (i.e., responding to) that. In line 13, the therapist provides acknowledgement (mm hm::.), which is then followed by Eve emphasizing the difficulty in being able to do this in therapy. She begins with a statement that has a double meaning: "an then, (0.4) when you just went mm hm:::.". What Eve is referring to here is, first, how the therapist tended to respond in the last session and, second, how she had just responded in line 14. During this time, Eve also parodies the therapist by placing her closed hand under her chin, which then solicits laughter from the therapist (line 15). After a brief pause, Eve continues by satirizing her own conduct (an I went >bla bla bla bla bla bla bla bla bla bla bla<) while placing her hand to her mouth and rapidly moving her fingers. Her portrayal of a typical sequential context, in which she rambles on during which the therapist provides only minimal acknowledgement, leaves her feeling uncertain and unable to move forward (line 18). Following no response from the therapist, line 19, Eve continues her turn by providing another example of what she normally expects from others in everyday conversation, but does not receive from the therapist.

## 8.6 Conclusions

Psychotherapy research tends to view *problems of collaboration* through the lens of what many have termed *resistance* or *alliance ruptures*. Eubank et al.'s (2015) classification of *moving away* vs. *moving against* provides a generalized framework for identifying strategies in which a lack of collaboration becomes manifest. Although this framework provides a useful starting point for examining *what* might count as a collaboration break, there is much less focus on *how* these breaks are negotiated from one interactional moment to the next. Using CA, I was able to show how extended disaffiliation may be accomplished through interaction in these two stylistically distinct ways of opposing and withdrawing. The focus has been on specific sequential contexts such as formulation, question and proposal sequences and was limited to disaffiliative episodes spanning over a series of turns and sometimes even continuing for over several minutes – it should be noted that ruptures are sometimes analyzed between sessions or within phases of treatment (see Safran et al., 2011), but this was not considered here. In CA, resistance (as an interactional category) has been examined with respect to the dimensions of passive/active (Stivers, 2005b) or covert/overt (Clayman & Heritage, 2002), which imply degree of strength or explicitness of the action performed. By contrast, the terms *opposition/withdrawal* reference speakers' degree of engagement to (inter)act in terms of movement toward or away from each other: for example, by not responding, delaying a response or weakly acknowledging, speakers display a reluctance or hesitation to engage with the prior speaker's action. An explicit disagreement or criticism will convey a strong counter position and, depending on the manner in which the action is expressed, could implicate emotions such as anger and frustration. This kind of conceptualization seems to offer some advantages because they bear direct relevance to the relationship; that is, withdrawing may generate implications of social distance, of not wanting to connect, whereas opposition may instead convey aggression and as not particularly caring about the other's face.

Unlike Chapter 7, the focus here was to examine *clients*' repeated and extended acts of non-collaboration (with respect to therapists' prior actions), rather than the discursive strategies used by therapists to get themselves re-affiliated with clients. Most extracts spanned over numerous turns, which suggests that once opposition/withdrawal gets underway, it becomes difficult to change the interactional trajectory toward a more collaborative, affiliative one. For example, withdrawal – as may be expressed through withholding from responding, weak acknowledgement, reluctance and so on – often deepened over the course of talk and maintained a degree of *distance* between therapist and client (see Extracts 8.1–8.4). Certain extracts involving opposition through disagreement and refusals, on the other hand, illustrated how the bulk of interactional work became focused on the *account* for why the client could not agree or comply (see Extracts 8.7–8.8). Although these conflictive moments in talk could provide opportunities in doing relevant therapeutic work – that is, why does the client find it difficult to engage in talk about her feelings toward her relationship with her husband (Extract 8.7) or find it difficult to confront her father in an *empty chair task*? (Extract 8.8) – this aim was not realized. Criticism, a more aggressive form of opposition because it more directly attacks other's face, requires that the therapist address clients' grievances and, therefore, also seemed to pose a relevant challenge (Extracts 8.9–8.11). The person-centred practices used by the therapists in these extracts likely played a part in influencing the trajectory of how these *non-collaborative* instances were managed. A deeper understanding of the therapist's influence would require a targeted investigation of these practices along with a comparison of how other, non-person-centred therapists, might tackle these kinds of disaffiliative episodes differently.

# 9 Final Reflections

## 9.1 Overview

The aim of this chapter is not to provide a summary of the topics thus far addressed, but rather to offer a few final and further reflections on some of the issues – affiliation, disaffiliation and relationships – that have been central to this book. I will also return to a topic that was introduced in Chapter 1, but was mostly not dealt with in the other chapters: language/interaction and depression.

## 9.2 The Therapeutic Relationship Revisited

In Chapter 1, I argued that the psychotherapy relationship is commonly viewed as a *working relationship* or alliance that is largely influenced by institutional aims that form a part of this institutional practice (Horvath et al., 2011). As in many helping professions (e.g., doctor–patient, lawyer–client, social worker–client, clergy–parishioner), the relationship is deemed to be shaped through talk that pertains to a person's troubles and that is directed at providing some form of help. An adherence and collaboration on goals and tasks, alongside the formation of an emotional "bond," will be some of the more important relationship elements (Bordin, 1994). Thus, relationships formed during the therapy encounter will be of a different quality than the social relationships described by Dunbar (2018), which are mainly characterized through *friendship* and the degree of intimacy between persons.[1] It is because of the institutional, task/goal focus of psychotherapy that terms such as *intimate*, *close* or *distant* will most likely not capture all the nuances of the relationship. But even so, clients and therapists can and do achieve intimate moments during therapy and, therefore, certain generic social relationship elements may be common to working relationships as well. It may be that, as is generally the case in

[1] An alternative view is given by Rogers (1957, p. 101), who claims that "It is *not* stated that psychotherapy is a special kind of relationship, different in kind from all others which occur in everyday life. … Thus the therapeutic relationship is seen as a heightening of the constructive qualities which often exist in part in other relationships, and an extension through time of qualities which in other relationships tend at best to be momentary."

institutional talk (Drew & Heritage, 1992; Levinson, 1992), the therapy relationship is more restricted and regulated than everyday social relationships. Further, these restrictions may be explained through the goal-directed aspect and also the asymmetrical role relations of therapy (see Drew & Heritage, 1992). These relationship aspects – social, asymmetry, intimacy – are briefly explored under the following headings:

1. Working vs. Social Relationships.
2. Distance through Asymmetry.
3. Accomplishing Intimacy.

### *9.2.1 Working vs. Social Relationships*

The categorization of *working* relationship, very much highlights the *instrumental* or *goal*-oriented aspect of what is going on in the therapy room; that is, clients and therapists convene to get a certain job done and the implication may be that there is not much space for other, non-instrumental and more "social" kinds of conversations. Some psychotherapy researchers such as Gelso and Carter (1985), however, argue for a multifaceted view of relationships. Drawing from Greenson (1967), they argue that the relationship consists of three separate, yet interrelated, components: the working alliance; the transference ("unreal") relationship and the *real* relationship. Thus, alongside the preceding working aspect, therapists and clients are relating with respect to 1) clients' displaced and conflicted feelings, behaviours, attitudes from past relations onto the therapist (i.e., *transference*) and 2) feelings, perceptions, attitudes that clients and therapists have toward each other, emerging within the two-way therapy dialogue (the *real* relationship).

Gelso and Carter's (1985) tripartite view of relations serves to recognize that people do build feelings for one another, even if the main portion of talk is focused on getting something done. What is less clear in their conceptualization, however, is how these elements are kept separate from each other; for example, why should *task-based* talk not also have a *social* component that enables persons to accomplish a certain degree of intimacy? The view that different relationships are enacted during therapy also runs into certain analytic snags when adopting a conversation analytic (CA) perspective. This is because analysts should be able to demonstrate through an examination of participants' interactions that these different relationship types emerge through their talk and are consequential for that talk (Schegloff, 1992).

Another approach, taking CA again as a starting point, would be to posit that relationship work, whether it is more *task* oriented or *socially* oriented, is accomplished within the sequence (Schegloff, 2007). Thus, the *sequence organization* of therapeutic interaction is seen as providing opportunities for both attending to the tight collaboration of getting therapeutic business underway and to creating or maintaining *closeness*. These sequential, relationship building, opportunities can be illustrated for all sequence types. I will provide a "typical" storytelling sequence, shown in Table 9.1, to serve as an example. Clients' troubles tellings provide an empathic opportunity with which the recipient (i.e., the therapist) may respond via a formulation. In this second position, the therapist moves talk in a therapeutically relevant direction by demonstrating an understanding of the client's troubles, thus orienting to the *working* relationship. The formulation, however, also displays emotional support and thus accomplishes increased closeness between the speakers. By displaying "I understand you" – see Chapter 4 on empathy – the therapist is therefore also attending to the *social* relationship.

This illustration of a basic, 2-part, conversational sequence shows that so-called therapeutic projects – accomplished through formulations of troubles or proposals to engage in tasks (i.e., chairwork) and so on – are tightly interwoven with social-affiliative concerns. But, given the institutional properties of psychotherapy, there will be constraints placed on the interaction, especially from a friendship/intimacy viewpoint. One form of constraint concerns the asymmetrical relations constituted through therapist–client talk. Constraints may, however, be counter-balanced by opportunities in certain sequential positions, such as the third turn in sequence (Peräkylä, 2011, 2019). These two aspects, constraints and possibilities in achieving intimacy, are addressed in the sections below.

### *9.2.2 Distance through Asymmetry*

Some differences between psychotherapy and everyday talk, from a relationship building perspective, were discussed in Chapter 1. By and large, psychotherapy does not involve sequential enactments of enduring relationships marked by closeness or intimacy (see Pomerantz & Mandelbaum, 2005 and Enfield, 2006 for everyday talk). This is because there is an apparent asymmetry at work that is so commonly found in institutional talk (Drew & Heritage, 1992); that is, therapeutic activities are primarily focused on the *client's* experience and, therefore, therapeutic talk will generally not turn toward the therapist's experience or to the therapist's and client's shared experiences. Farber

Table 9.1 *2-part troubles-telling sequence*

| Position | Speaker | Action | Implications |
|---|---|---|---|
| 1 | Client | Storytelling/ Troubles telling | Empathic opportunity |
| 2 | Therapist | Formulation (Empathy) | a. Steers talk in a therapeutically relevant directions<br>b. Demonstrates emotional support/closeness |

(2006), however, has argued that therapist actions revealing information about her- or himself, so-called *therapist self-disclosures*, can form a beneficial part of therapy. For example, they may work at "strengthening the alliance, normalizing the patient's experience, and providing the patient with alternative ways of thinking" (Farber, 2006, p. 139). Farber identifies two types of therapist self-disclosures: *factual* and *self-involving* (or immediacy). Whereas the former refers generally to information about the therapist, the latter pertains to therapist responses in which therapists connect their own emotions/experiences to those of the client (cf. *second stories*, Sacks, 1995b). The benefits, however, also come with potential negative consequences, thus placing therapists in a dilemma of whether or not to use them. For example, self-disclosures may appear self-gratifying, shift the focus away from the client onto the therapist, blur the therapist–client role relationship, and so on (Hill & Knox, 2002). Although Farber (2006) claims that relational approaches to therapy (e.g., client centred) are more open to using self-disclosures during treatment because of the general ethos of being engaged, empathic and genuine toward clients, Hill and Knox (2002) have found that they are used very rarely, comprising only 1–13% of verbal interventions. The dilemmas or potential negative consequences listed earlier may offer strong reasons for their infrequent use or avoidance in actual practice. Throughout the chapters in this book, it was shown how therapists would generally engage with clients in ways that were not self-disclosing or self-involving. Therapists would not, for example, respond to client narratives with second stories (Sacks, 1995b) and they would tend not to reveal their own emotive reactions to clients' distress through sympathy. Therapists seemed to prefer to maintain some *emotional distance* by not *sharing* in the clients' troubles. Instead, close engagement with clients was achieved by displaying an appropriate understanding of what they are experiencing.

These observations pertaining to therapist–client interactions made throughout have been limited to the person-centred management of (dis)affiliation, mainly in emotion-focused, and more seldom in client-centred, treatments. Other psychotherapeutic treatment modalities come with different theoretical orientations and practices for engaging with clients and so it is difficult to make any direct claims about how these findings or analyses of interactional phenomena will pertain to these other treatment domains.

### 9.2.3 *Accomplishing Intimacy*

So far, I have argued that person-centred therapists maintain some degree of relationship distance with their clients throughout therapy. This is because they tend not to self-disclose in sequential positions that follow client troubles tellings and also because their responses tend to be lower on the affiliation scale than what is generally seen in talk between friends. In comparison with how intimates might respond to troubles telling events – for example, best friends responding with response cries ("Oh my God!"), upgraded negative assessments ("how could that bastard do that to you!") and the like – therapist responses tend to echo/mirror or formulate what clients have said, thus focusing on understanding client experience rather than sharing in their emotions or comforting them in times of distress. This does not mean that therapists and clients do not create *moments of intimacy*. Strong affiliative moments or episodes do commonly occur but these seem to be much more *context-specific*. In other words, therapists and clients can and do enact closeness and intimacy within commonly occurring interactional sequences such as troubles tellings. In Table 9.2, I have added two more sequential slots to illustrate how intimacy is interactionally accomplished.

Peräkylä (2011) has argued that the third position in sequence is crucial for doing therapeutic work; for example, in interpretation sequences following client responses, therapists can, in third position, intensify the emotional valence of client descriptions or reveal hidden or additional layers of clients' experiences. More recently, Peräkylä (2019) has argued that third positions are potential sites of *relationship transformation*. Returning to Table 9.2, third position is an opportunity for clients to ratify the therapist's display of emotional support and this, in turn, provides an opportunity for the therapist to further strengthen the mounting affiliative connection between client and therapist. Thus, when clients report their emotional experiences and/or distress to therapists, followed by the therapist's display of interest and affiliation with the client's emotional experience, this may lead to upgraded displays of agreement and non-vocal *synchronous* conduct – see especially Chapters 3 to 5. Both prosodic and non-vocal resources such as nodding and smiling have been shown to be highly effective in building affiliation and closeness in therapy encounters (Bänninger-Huber, 1992; Fitzgerald & Leudar, 2010; Weiste & Peräkylä, 2014). Thus, affiliative (and mutually affiliating) responses would appear to be *the* major resource with which therapists can maintain a productive and

Table 9.2 *4-part troubles-telling sequence*

| Position | Speaker | Action | Implications |
|---|---|---|---|
| 1 | Client | Storytelling/Troubles telling | Empathic opportunity |
| 2 | Therapist | Formulation (empathy) | a. Steers talk in a therapeutically relevant directions<br>b. Demonstrates emotional support/closeness |
| 3 | Client | Feedback (affiliation) | Ratifies support/closeness |
| 4 | Therapist | Return affiliation | Further strengthens affiliation |

supportive relationship with clients. At the very least, these sequences performed in psychotherapy can achieve *moments* of intimacy or closeness, also termed *empathic moments* (Heritage, 2011), and these accomplishments of demonstrated shared understanding (i.e., empathy) are integral in securing productive working relationships and beneficial outcomes for clients (Elliott et al., 2011). Yet because there is a limited shared history between clients and therapists, these moments of intimacy, however strongly affiliative they may be, are likely to remain transient and are unlikely to lead into an ongoing form of closeness that extends beyond the walls of the psychotherapist's office.[2]

## 9.3 Disaffiliation: Some Pros and Cons

It is generally agreed that affiliation in general, and therapist affiliative responses in particular, has positive effects. Can disaffiliation also be seen positively? Before answering, it is worthwhile considering that although therapeutic conversations may often proceed in a cooperative and affiliative fashion, stresses or ruptures in the alliance (goals, tasks, bonds), in which "the patient struggles with these problems [self defeating propensities] with the therapist," are inevitable within therapy (Bordin, 1994, p. 18). Looking also to Bänninger-Huber and Widmer's (1999) conceptualization of what they term the *balance hypothesis*, see also Chapter 3, relationship strains are part and parcel of productive therapeutic work: on the one hand, the therapist's job is to sometimes challenge the client's self-defeating propensities, which may result in momentary relationship tension; on the other hand, therapists simultaneously aim to provide a secure relationship in order to create an environment in which challenging therapeutic work may be done. Thus, whereas challenging the client may be seen as disaffiliative, this can be balanced off, even if only partially, by demonstrations of affiliation, such as smiling or minimal agreements (Bänninger-Huber, 1992).

### *9.3.1 Working toward a Balance: Affiliation vs. Challenge*

To return to the original question posed in the preceding paragraph, disaffiliation can have a positive aspect, as long as it is performed to further therapeutic work and is done in a secure environment with some accompanying affiliation. Some of the reasons for viewing disaffiliation in a positive light are as follows. As already suggested by Bänninger-Huber and Widmer (1999), disaffiliation via challenging is important for tackling clients' troubles head-on. If therapists only agreed with clients or only minimally re-formulated their descriptions

[2] The assumption made here is that therapists and clients do not strike up a relationship outside of the office or have a prior relationship before coming into therapy. This, of course, would be a different matter.

of personal experience – see Chapter 4 on empathy – it might be difficult for clients to actually move beyond their present experiences. Moreover, rupture-repair studies suggest that episodes of disaffiliation over the course of treatment may be more beneficial for outcome and that a direct exploration of (client) disaffiliation is thought to be a productive line of inquiry as it encourages engagement and participation from the client (Aspland et al., 2008; Safran & Muran, 1996). Chapter 7 focused specifically on these kinds of re-affiliative practices: how clients would disagree (and thus disaffiliate) with therapist formulations and how therapists would regain affiliation with clients by using a range of vocal and non-vocal (e.g., nodding) resources. These sequences also unfolded in a person- or client-centred manner (Rogers, 1951), with therapists retreating from own position and supporting the client's alternative one.

Overall, it was rare for these person-centred therapists to directly challenge clients and there seemed to be a preference to rework client experiences through formulations, thus remaining fairly close to clients' actual descriptions of experience. Thus, the balance hypothesis, as it may pertain to these data that were examined, seems to be tipped in the favour of offering security and affiliation over challenging clients with alternative, contrasting (perhaps uncomfortable) descriptions of their experiences. Other therapy approaches would most probably reveal different interactional patterns but this would need to be investigated from a similar CA perspective.

### *9.3.2 Deepening Disaffiliation*

Although many examples analyzed in this book could be seen as facilitating client engagement, in terms of negotiating the troubles telling and what it means, other examples were less convincing. For example, the client Sofia would often remain "combative" over the course of many sequences and would often take her own track, ignoring the therapist's displays of understanding. Kristina, on the other hand, would often withdraw, thereby repeatedly resisting the invitation to engage with the therapist's formulation – see extracts in Chapter 8. The danger, therefore, is that disaffiliation may deepen as therapy continues, leading to less client engagement and fewer episodes in which shared understanding and support is achieved. Watson and Greenberg (2000) have suggested a number of corrective steps that experiential-oriented therapists can take to deal with disaffiliation or ruptures: understanding/acknowledging clients' feelings; appropriately and selectively self-disclosing aspects of personal history or revealing concern for the client's well-being; implementing a task intervention such as chair work that focuses on the client's feelings; or using metacommunication to explain the techniques and goals of therapy. The challenge for CA in exploring extended disaffiliation is to analyze much larger chunks of talk, involving parts of sessions or even multiple sessions. By broadening the scope of inquiry in this way, more insight could be gained in how various disaffiliative and affiliative episodes, at different points in time, might be meaningfully connected (see also Voutilainen et al., 2011). This line of inquiry has been advocated by Peräkylä (2019) as an important future direction of research and awaits further CA study.

Disaffiliation can be viewed in terms of cost/benefit over time. In the short-term, disaffiliation momentarily places the relationship at risk. Immediate repair may come at little "relational cost" and may, if an empathic moment is achieved (Heritage, 2011), even strengthen the relationship; that is, as long as the therapist has accumulated sufficient relational *credit* to draw on from previous encounters, she or he may raise matters that produce anxiety (withdrawal) by the client, without necessarily risking further ruptures in the alliance. But in the long-term, extended disaffiliation may take a larger toll on the relationship. However, if disaffiliation eventually results in gaining important therapeutic results and in pushing therapeutic goals forward while safeguarding the relationship, the benefit seems clear.

### *9.3.3 Overcoming Challenges to Strengthen Intimacy and Security*

Another perspective on how disaffiliation is deemed to be important originates from the Mount Zion Group in San Francisco (Gazzillo et al., 2019; Horowitz et al., 1975). In their proposed model of psychotherapeutic development, clients will present the therapist with various forms of tests or interpersonal challenges in the form of disaffiliative acts, such as disagreeing or being angry with the therapist, to gauge the degree of safety on hand (Horowitz et al., 1975). Thus, if therapists are able to "pass the test" by dealing effectively with clients' disagreement or anger, clients will feel secure enough to disclose previously avoided distressing experiences. This kind of interactional dynamic may be seen in some of the extracts in Chapter 8. For example, client reluctance to engage in chair work may be due to the clients' apprehension concerning the therapist's ability/expertise to keep them safe during a task in which they must deal with potentially overwhelming emotions in the moment (Watson & Greenberg, 2000). Therapists would sometimes attempt to manage the client's anxiety by reassuring the client that they will not be directly confronting the "real" person and that they will be guided through the activity. Client disaffiliation, accompanied by heightened emotional displays involving anger and sadness, was also seen in Chapter 8 with the client Eve. When the therapist formulated certain implications arising from the client's reported experience, Eve responded with severe criticism, implying that the therapist's understanding of the client's grief was incorrect and unfitting (i.e., too rational). Eve's repeated displays of intense upset may have also generated inferences that she is apprehensive about disclosing more and allowing the therapist to engage more deeply with her experiences. Initially, the therapist did not successfully engage with Eve's talk and was not seen as having provided "suitable" empathy. Instead, the therapist's response was taken as lacking genuineness and authenticity (Rogers, 1957), reverting merely to formulaic expressions that provide "rational understandings." Later on, after the therapist seemed to repeatedly fail at "passing the test" of being able to offer the client enough security to go further, the therapist topicalized a rupture in the alliance or the growing strains being placed on the therapeutic relationship (see Muntigl, 2020). In sum, intimacy may engender disclosure of carefully guarded issues involving anxiety, shame and so on. This in turn increases intimacy between the participants. If the therapist in some way mismanages the client's displays of upset or troubles (e.g., by under/overreacting, being judgemental) this cycle of building intimacy can break down. CA is able to track such cyclical developments, showing the locations where disaffiliation occurs and where it is repaired (or not).

## 9.4 Language, Interaction and Depression

Peräkylä (2019, p. 276) has identified the following topic as an important future direction for interactional research on psychotherapy: *exploring aspects of interaction that are tied to particular disorders*. According to Peräkylä, CA research has so far focused almost exclusively on generic therapeutic or client practices, while being indifferent to the kind of psychological or diagnostic label that clients undergoing treatment might have. Since Peräkylä's paper, however, one study on initial couple therapy consultations has attempted to make links between certain interactional practices occurring in these sessions and the partners' diagnosed narcissistic problems (Janusz et al., 2021). One of the main findings of this study was that the partners would attempt to control the conversation in various ways (e.g., topical development, sequential position of utterances). It was then claimed these kinds of practices were intrinsically tied to narcissistic features (see also Peräkylä, 2015). Given the "achievement"-oriented ethos of CA researchers, there is a strong appeal in viewing "disorders" as something observable, as opposed to private, that is detectable from interactional practices and how persons with, say depression or something else, would present themselves in various life situations (on *presentation of self* see Goffman, 1959). The challenge, as Janusz et al. (2021, p. 12) have put it in regard to narcissism, is "how statements about the interactional realm (controlling behaviours, interactional risks) can be linked to statements about the internal realm (personality related dispositions, perceptions of the risks for the self, narcissism)." Some reflections on this matter with an eye toward depression are given in the next sections.

### *9.4.1 Language Markers*

Clinical depression is considered to be a mental disorder and is commonly diagnosed via psychological assessments that draw from self-reported symptoms, measures and scales (e.g., DSM-5, BDI-II). For making an assessment of depression, no specific attention is given to language practices; for example, what people say and how they say it. Some linguistic investigations have been attempting to address this issue, by focusing on the linguistic constructions of utterances, looking for lexico-grammatical and phonological patterns that are linked to depression or depressive symptoms listed in the *Diagnostic and Statistical Manual of Mental Disorders* (see, for example, Fine, 2008). Here, clausal constructions such as "I feel sad" and "I have no energy" or utterances with a "flat" intonation will be viewed as candidate markers for a depressed mood. Although this focus on linguistics is a move in a production direction, certain limitations remain. For example, there seems to be an implication here that the language of depressed persons – or persons with any form of psychological disorder for that matter – is a mere epiphenomenon of a pathology and that the disorder will percolate through features of talk regardless of the situation, who the addressees are, and so on. One of the difficulties with this method for identifying depressive language is determining whether utterances such as "I feel sad/unhappy" are "typical" or appropriate for the given circumstances or whether they are instead conveying a form of psychological distress or an altered, "pathological" self-image. There is also a danger of circular reasoning: depressed people will use "depressive language" and, in turn, "depressive language" will provide evidence for a depressed state.

The work of Angus and colleagues (Angus, 2012; Angus & Greenberg, 2011) has been developing this research in valuable ways. In their work, language markers for depression are examined with respect to specific client activities such as narratives – see also Chapters 1 and 5. Thus, client language is not only tied to an activity that has a certain purpose (i.e., telling personal stories to do things) but it also makes it easier to collect instances and examine whether certain language features consistently appear. Despite these gains, however, this research still does not properly address whether clients said what they did because they are depressed or because the language they used served to *perform some other kind of interactional work* that is not necessarily linked to "being clinically depressed." Thus, a further step in interactional research on depression is to ask what kind of talk and conduct would index depression as opposed to attending to other interactional matters (i.e., doing emotion stance work that may be viewed as appropriate or "typical" for the sequential context, see Sorjonen & Peräkylä, 2012, or aligning with a different self-image in Goffman's sense). One way to tackle this important issue would be to compare how non-depressed vs. depressed speakers perform certain activities. Returning to narratives, one could contrast troubles tellings (Jefferson, 1988) in these two different groups. For clients with depression, let me first briefly summarize the findings of Chapter 5. It was shown that clients with clinical depression undergoing emotion-focused therapy (EFT) would tell stories to complain about a significant other's transgressions in regular ways that appear different from everyday troubles tellings. Depressed clients, for example, tended to position themselves in specific ways with regard to the troubling event. First, there was a tendency for clients not to disclose the emotional impact of being subjected to another's transgressions at that moment in time (i.e., they did not specifically mention that they became sad, angry, disappointed). Second, clients often expressed a lack of agency, as not directly challenging the transgressor (or indeed as avoiding any conflict) implicating not only that they have no control over what happened but that they cannot take action to change the course of events. Third, clients would display their understanding of the misconduct perpetrated against them as one of surprise, shock, or incredulity. These client emotional stances suggest that they are at a loss to explain or comprehend the motives of the other or the general circumstances of the event. While these interactional features could be linked to depression, it is important to consider whether everyday complaint stories would be accomplished differently. Indeed, research suggests that, in everyday complaints about others' misconduct, tellers tend to voice their indignation at the moral offence (Drew, 1998; Günthner, 1997), which seems different from the clinically depressed clients undergoing EFT shown in this book. A more systematic comparison between complaint stories among depressed and non-depressed individuals would be needed, however, to gain a clearer picture of the differences in how such stories may be constructed and whether it can be claimed convincingly that certain interactional features are "depression relevant."

### *9.4.2 Interactional Patterns*

One could argue that the focus on "language use in context" (e.g., psychotherapy research on *narratives*) shown earlier also comes with additional limitations. For example, it does not take *interaction* properly into account. To whom are the persons with depression speaking and does the addressee make a difference? When clients narrate their troubles, they are designing their talk for a recipient, the psychotherapist, in a therapist's office. How will this form of *recipient design* (Sacks et al., 1974) influence clients' use of language? Thus, to appropriately classify someone's talk or conduct as typical/atypical or orderly/disorderly, not only must the use of expressions in different contexts – for example, "self-critical" utterances or displays of inability such as "I'm helpless" – be examined and compared, but also, as Sanders (2012) has argued, the interactional properties of talk and conduct should be considered. One of the sequential properties of conversation, he argues, is predicated on *choice*. The CA concept of *preference organization*, for example, allows for a choice between (at least two general) meaningful alternatives for responding (Sacks, 1995b). For example, recipients generally respond to assessments (e.g., "that was a *great movie*!") in two ways: via an immediately produced upgraded assessment ("it was *totally awesome*!") or by a delayed downgraded assessment such as "it was *pretty good*" (Pomerantz, 1984). Sanders' point, drawing from Goffman's work on face, is that our choices will always convey a certain *representation of self* whether this choice was made intentionally or not. He goes on to argue that representations of self "that seem to be intended because they are in the actor's self-interest are evidence of his or her competence and … that ones that seem unintentional because they are not in the actor's self-interest are evidence of a performance lapse, or more broadly, deficiencies of competence" (Sanders, 2012, p. 31). How might this relate to persons with depression more generally and psychotherapy with depressed persons more specifically? To give an example, speakers in everyday life who do not respond with emotional stances of joy when it might be appropriate to do so or do not convey indignation or agency during complaint storytellings involving another's moral misconduct may suggest a performance lapse (e.g., tired, distracted) or generate inferences about the person's mood, suggesting a deeper and more persistent deficiency. There is also the question of how the other speakers present would then, in turn, respond to these altered representations of self and possibly make the person accountable, for example, as drawing attention to the person's possible depressed mood ("you seem sad") or even becoming indignant ("what's been wrong with you lately!"). Whatever the response, the point is more that, for understanding how depression is accomplished or co-constructed, it becomes necessary to examine how recipients may be playing a part in its achievement. Emotion-focused therapists are trained to be attuned to what they term client *markers* or *micromarkers* (Elliott et al., 2004; Greenberg et al., 1993; Greenberg & Watson, 2006), which "are in-session behaviors that signal that the client is ready to work on a particular problem, or task" (Elliott & Greenberg, 2007, p. 246). Not surprisingly, emotion-focused therapists will listen to clients' descriptions of experience in a targeted fashion, not in order to form diagnoses but to perform emotion-focused work. What is relevant is that therapists' responses, be they non-vocal (e.g., nods or smiles strategically placed in a sequence) or verbalized (e.g., as formulations, repetitions, collaborative completions), will in some way shape how clients are describing their troubles.

Analyzing the talk and conduct of a clinical population, such as clinically depressed persons, is certainly a useful starting point for understanding the unique discursive practices they generally make use of in social life. CA studies on clinically depressed clients undergoing psychotherapy have been increasing over the years (McVittie et al., 2020; Muntigl, 2016, 2020; [Muntigl et al., 2013, 2020b; Muntigl & Horvath, 2014b). What is being gained is a view of how depressed persons interact in this specific institutional context and how clinically depressed clients tell stories to complain, do self-criticism and engage with or oppose therapist interventions. In order to understand how depressed persons and not just "clients" engage in and accomplish social life in more broader terms, however, the scope of the analysis will need to be expanded to include additional and more everyday contexts that they are participating in.

To conclude, the focus of this book has been on (dis)affiliation and, more generally, how clients and therapists may work pro-socially on the one hand (e.g., through agreement, confirmation or some form of supportive action), or, on the other hand, by opposing/resisting prior actions through some form of disaffiliative conduct (e.g., disagreeing, criticizing, withdrawing, disengaging). The examination of psychotherapy as an ongoing sequential accomplishment has shown how clients and therapists negotiate "being in agreement or disagreement" from one speaker turn to the next during various activities such as storytelling and chair work. It has shown how the psychotherapeutic relationship, one of the most important variables deemed responsible for ensuring good therapeutic outcomes, is enacted through a wide array of interactional resources. Thus, by going analytically "deeper" into the micro-interactional landscape of psychotherapy talk, we come to a better understanding of how certain therapeutic interventions may be working effectively and how clients and therapists are able to forge a productive working relationship in which to move forward.

# References


Adelman, M. B., Parks, M. R., & Albrecht, T. L. (1987). Beyond close relationships: Support in weak ties. In T. L. Albrecht & M. B. Adelman (Eds.), *Communicating social support* (pp. 126–147). Sage.

American Psychiatric Association. (2013). *Diagnostic and statistical manual of mental disorders: DSM-5* (Vol. 5). American Psychiatric Association.

Anderson, H., & Goolishian, H. A. (1988). Human systems as linguistic systems: Preliminary and evolving ideas about the implications for clinical theory. *Family Process*, *27*(4), 371–393.

Angus, L. (2012). Toward an integrative understanding of narrative and emotion processes in emotion-focused therapy of depression: Implications for theory, research and practice. *Psychotherapy Research*, *22*(4), 367–380. https://doi.org/10.1080/10503307.2012.683988

Angus, L. E., & Greenberg, L. S. (2011). *Working with narrative in emotion-focused therapy: Changing stories, healing lives*. American Psychological Association. https://doi.org/10.1037/12325-000

Angus, L. E., & McLeod, J. (2004). Toward an integrative framework for understanding the role of narrative in the psychotherapy process. In L. E. Angus & J. McLeod (Eds.), *The handbook of narrative and psychotherapy: Practice, theory, and research* (pp. 367–374). Sage.

Angus, L., Goldman, R., & Mergenthaler, E. (2008). Introduction. One case, multiple measures: An intensive case-analytic approach to understanding client change processes in evidence-based, emotion-focused therapy of depression. *Psychotherapy Research*, *18*(6), 629–633.

Angus, L., Lewin, J., Boritz, T., Bryntwick, E., Carpenter, N., Watson-Gaze, J., & Greenberg, L. (2012). Narrative processes coding system: A dialectical constructivist approach to assessing client change processes in emotion-focused therapy of depression. *Research in Psychotherapy: Psychopathology, Process and Outcome*, *15*(2), 54–61.

Antaki, C. (2008). Formulations in psychotherapy. In A. Peräkylä, C. Antaki, S. Vehviläinen, & I. Leudar (Eds.), *Conversation analysis and psychotherapy* (pp. 26–42). Cambridge University Press. https://doi.org/10.1017/CBO9780511490002.003

Antaki, C., Barnes, R., & Leudar, I. (2005). Diagnostic formulations in psychotherapy. *Discourse Studies*, *7*(6), 627–647. https://doi.org/10.1177/1461445605055420

Antaki, C., Richardson, E., Stokoe, E., & Willott, S. (2015). Dealing with the distress of people with intellectual disabilities reporting sexual assault and rape. *Discourse Studies*, *17*(4), 415–432. https://doi.org/10.1177/1461445615578962

Arkowitz, H. (2002). Toward an integrative perspective on resistance to change. *Journal of Clinical Psychology*, *58*(2), 219–227.

Aspland, H., Llewelyn, S., Hardy, G. E., Barkham, M., & Stiles, W. (2008). Alliance ruptures and rupture resolution in cognitive–behavior therapy: A preliminary task analysis. *Psychotherapy Research*, *18*(6), 699–710. https://doi.org/10.1080/10503300802291463

Atkinson, J. M., & Drew, P. (1979). *Order in court: The organisation of verbal interaction in judicial settings*. Macmillan.

Atkinson, J. M., & Heritage, J. (Eds.). (1984). *Structures of social action: Studies in conversation analysis*. Cambridge University Press.

Bachelor, A. (1988). How clients perceive therapist empathy: A content analysis of "received" empathy. *Psychotherapy: Theory, Research, Practice, Training*, *25*(2), 227–240. https://doi.org/10.1037/h0085337

Bänninger-Huber, E. (1992). Prototypical affective microsequences in psychotherapeutic interaction. *Psychotherapy Research*, *2*(4), 291–306. https://doi.org/10.1080/10503309212331333044

Bänninger-Huber, E., & Widmer, C. (1999). Affective relationship patterns and psychotherapeutic change. *Psychotherapy Research*, *9*(1), 74–87. https://doi.org/10.1080/10503309912331332601

Barrett-Lennard, G. T. (1981). The empathy cycle: Refinement of a nuclear concept. *Journal of Counseling Psychology*, *28*(2), 91–100.

Bavelas, J. B., Coates, L., & Johnson, T. (2000). Listeners as co-narrators. *Journal of Personality and Social Psychology*, *79*(6), 941–952. https://doi.org/10.1037/0022-3514.79.6.941

Beach, W. A., & Dixson, C. N. (2001). Revealing moments: Formulating understandings of adverse experiences in a health appraisal interview. *Social Science & Medicine*, *52*(1), 25–44.

Beck, A. T., & Alford, B. A. (2009). *Depression: Causes and treatment* (2nd ed.). University of Pennsylvania Press.

Bercelli, F., Rossano, F., & Viaro, M. (2008). Clients' responses to therapists' reinterpretations. In A. Peräkylä, C. Antaki, S. Vehviläinen, & I. Leudar (Eds.), *Conversation analysis and psychotherapy* (pp. 43–61). Cambridge University Press. https://doi.org/10.1017/CBO9780511490002.004

Besnier, N. (1993). Reported speech and affect on Nukulaelae atoll. In J. H. Hill & J. T. Irvine (Eds.), *Responsibility and evidence in oral discourse* (pp. 161–181). Cambridge University Press.

Beutler, L. E., Harwood, T. M., Michelson, A., Song, X., & Holman, J. (2011). Resistance/reactance level. In J. C. Norcross (Ed.), *Psychotherapy relationships that work: Evidence-based responsiveness* (2nd ed., pp. 261–278). Oxford University Press.

Beutler, L. E., Moleiro, C., & Talebi, H. (2002). Resistance in psychotherapy: What conclusions are supported by research. *Journal of Clinical Psychology*, *58*(2), 207–217.

Biber, D., & Finegan, E. (1989). Styles of stance in English: Lexical and grammatical marking of evidentiality and affect. *Text – Interdisciplinary Journal for the Study of Discourse*, *9*(1). https://doi.org/10.1515/text.1.1989.9.1.93

Billig, M. (1999). *Freudian repression: Conversation creating the unconscious*. Cambridge University Press.

Bilmes, J. (1991). Toward a theory of argument in conversation: The preference for disagreement. In F. van Eemeren, R. Grootendorst, J. Blair, & C. Willard (Eds.), *Proceedings of the second international conference on argumentation* (Vol. 1, pp. 462–469). International Centre for the Study of Argumentation Amsterdam, Sicsat.

Blatt, S. J. (1974). Levels of object representation in anaclitic and introjective depression. *The Psychoanalytic Study of the Child, 29*(1), 107–157. https://doi.org/10.1080/00797308.1974.11822616

Blatt, S. J. (1995). The destructiveness of perfectionism. *American Psychologist,* 50(12), 1003–1020.

Blatt, S. J. (2004). Two types of depression. In *Experiences of depression: Theoretical, clinical, and research perspectives* (pp. 15–52). American Psychological Association. https://doi.org/10.1037/10749-001

Bordin, E. S. (1979). The generalizability of the psychoanalytic concept of the working alliance. *Psychotherapy: Theory, Research & Practice, 16*(3), 252–260. https://doi.org/10.1037/h0085885

Bordin, E. S. (1994). Theory and research on the therapeutic working alliance: New directions. In A. O. Horvath & L. S. Greenberg (Eds.), *The working alliance: Theory, research, and practice* (pp. 13–37). John Wiley & Sons.

Boyd, E., & Heritage, J. (2006). Taking the history: Questioning during comprehensive history-taking. In J. Heritage & D. W. Maynard (Eds.), *Communication in medical care: Interaction between primary care physicians and patients* (pp. 151–184). Cambridge University Press.

Brown, P., & Levinson, S. C. (1987). *Politeness: Some universals in language usage.* Cambridge University Press.

Brown, R., & Gilman, A. (1960). The pronouns of power and solidarity. In T. A. Sebeok (Ed.), *Style in language* (pp. 253–276). MIT Press.

Bruner, J. (1986). *Actual minds, possible worlds.* Harvard University Press.

Buttny, R. (1993). *Social accountability in communication.* Sage.

Cardoso, C., Pinto, D., & Ribeiro, E. (2020). Therapist's actions after therapeutic collaboration breaks: A single case study. *Psychotherapy Research, 30*(4), 447–461. https://doi.org/10.1080/10503307.2019.1633483

Cekaite, A., & Kvist Holm, M. (2017). The comforting touch: Tactile intimacy and talk in managing children's distress. *Research on Language and Social Interaction, 50*(2), 109–127. https://doi.org/10.1080/08351813.2017.1301293

Clarke, K. M., & Greenberg, L. S. (1986). Differential effects of the Gestalt two-chair intervention and problem solving in resolving decisional conflict. *Journal of Counseling Psychology, 33*(1), 11.

Clayman, S. E. (2001). Answers and evasions. *Language in Society, 30*, 403–442.

Clayman, S., & Heritage, J. (2002). *The news interview: Journalists and public figures on the air.* Cambridge University Press.

Clayman, S. E., & Heritage, J. (2014). Benefactors and beneficiaries: Benefactive status and stance in the management of offers and requests. In P. Drew & E. Couper-Kuhlen (Eds.), *Requesting in social interaction* (pp. 55–86). John Benjamins .

Clift, R., & Holt, E. (2007). Introduction. In E. Holt & R. Clift (Eds.), *Reporting talk: Reported speech in interaction* (pp. 1–15). Cambridge University Press.

Coates, J. (1996). *Woman talk. Conversation between women friends.* Blackwell.

Conley, J. M., & O'Barr, W. M. (1990). Rules versus relationships in small claims disputes. In A. Grimshaw (Ed.), *Conflict talk: Sociolinguistic investigations of arguments in conversations* (pp. 178–196). Cambridge University Press.

Conway, M. A., & Pleydell-Pearce, C. W. (2000). The construction of autobiographical memories in the self-memory system. *Psychological Review*, *107*(2), 261–288.

Coulter, J. (1979). *The social construction of mind: Studies in ethnomethodology and linguistic philosophy*. MacMillan Press.

Couper-Kuhlen, E. (2012). Exploring affiliation in the reception of conversational complaint stories. In A. Perakyla & M.-L. Sorjonen (Eds.), *Emotion in interaction* (pp. 113–146). Oxford University Press.

Couper-Kuhlen, E. (2014). What does grammar tell us about action? *Pragmatics*, *24*(3), 623–647. https://doi.org/10.1075/prag.24.3.08cou

Craven, A., & Potter, J. (2010). Directives: Entitlement and contingency in action. *Discourse Studies*, *12*(4), 419–442. https://doi.org/10.1177/1461445610370126

Curl, T. S., & Drew, P. (2008). Contingency and action: A comparison of two forms of requesting. *Research on Language & Social Interaction*, *41*(2), 129–153. https://doi.org/10.1080/08351810802028613

Cushman, P. (1995). *Constructing the self, constructing America: A cultural history of psychotherapy*. Perseus Publishing.

Davidson, J. (1984). Subsequent versions of invitations, offers, requests, and proposals dealing with potential or actual rejection. In J. M. Atkinson & J. Heritage (Eds.), *Structures of social action: Studies in Conversation Analysis* (pp. 102–128). Cambridge University Press. https://ci.nii.ac.jp/naid/10026328339/

De Fina, A., & Georgakopoulou, A. (2012). *Analyzing narrative: Discourse and sociolinguistic perspectives*. Cambridge University Press.

De Stefani, E. (2021). Embodied responses to questions-in-progress: Silent nods as affirmative answers. *Discourse Processes*, *58*(4), 353–371.

Deppermann, A. (2008). *Gespräche analysieren. Eine Einführung* (4. Auflage). VS Verlag für Sozialwissenschaften.

Dersley, I., & Wootton, A. (2000). Complaint sequences within antagonistic argument. *Research on Language and Social Interaction*, *33*(4), 375–406.

Drake, V. (2015). Indexing uncertainty: The case of turn-final *or*. *Research on Language and Social Interaction*, *48*(3), 301–318. https://doi.org/10.1080/08351813.2015.1058606

Drew, P. (1992). Contested evidence in courtroom cross-examination: The case of a trial for rape. In P. Drew & J. Heritage (Eds.), *Talk at work: Interaction in institutional settings* (pp. 470–520). Cambridge University Press.

Drew, P. (1998). Complaints about transgressions and misconduct. *Research on Language and Social Interaction*, *31*(3–4), 295–325. https://doi.org/10.1080/08351813.1998.9683595

Drew, P., & Couper-Kuhlen, E. (2014). Requesting – from speech act to recruitment. In P. Drew & E. Couper-Kuhlen (Eds.), *Requesting in social interaction* (pp. 1–34). John Benjamins.

Drew, P., & Heritage, J. (1992). Analyzing talk at work: An introduction. In P. Drew & J. Heritage (Eds.), *Talk at work: Interaction in institutional settings* (pp. 3–65). Cambridge University Press.

Drew, P., & Walker, T. (2009). Going too far: Complaining, escalating and disaffiliation. *Journal of Pragmatics*, *41*(12), 2400–2414.

Drummond, K., & Hopper, R. (1993). Back channels revisited: Acknowledgment tokens and speakership incipiency. *Research on Language and Social Interaction*, *26*(2), 157–177.

Duan, C., & Hill, C. E. (1996). The current state of empathy research. *Journal of Counseling Psychology*, *43*(3), 261–274.

Dunbar, R. I. M. (2018). The anatomy of friendship. *Trends in Cognitive Sciences*, *22*(1), 32–51. https://doi.org/10.1016/j.tics.2017.10.004

Edwards, D. (1997). Structure and function in the analysis of everyday narratives. *Journal of Narrative and Life History*, *7*(1–4), 139–146.

Ehrlich, S., & Sidnell, J. (2006). "I think that's not an assumption you ought to make": Challenging presuppositions in inquiry testimony. *Language in Society*, *35*(05), 655–676. https://doi.org/10.1017/S0047404506060313

Eisenberg, N., & Fabes, R. A. (1990). Empathy: Conceptualization, measurement, and relation to prosocial behavior. *Motivation and Emotion*, *14*(2), 131–149. https://doi.org/10.1007/BF00991640

Ekberg, K., & LeCouteur, A. (2015). Clients' resistance to therapists' proposals: Managing epistemic and deontic status. *Journal of Pragmatics*, *90*, 12–25. https://doi.org/10.1016/j.pragma.2015.10.004

Elliott, R., & Greenberg, L. S. (2007). The essence of process-experiential/emotion-focused therapy. *American Journal of Psychotherapy*, *61*(3), 241–254.

Elliott, R., Bohart, A. C., Larson, D., Muntigl, P., & Smoliak, O. (forthcoming). Empathic reflection. In C. E. Hill & J. C. Norcross (Eds.), *Psychotherapy methods and skills that work*. Oxford University Press.

Elliott, R., Bohart, A. C., Watson, J. C., & Greenberg, L. S. (2011). Empathy. In J. C. Norcross (Ed.), *Psychotherapy Relationships that Work: Evidence-based Responsiveness* (pp. 132–152). Oxford University Press.

Elliott, R., Bohart, A. C., Watson, J. C., & Murphy, D. (2018). Therapist empathy and client outcome: An updated meta-analysis. *Psychotherapy*, *55*(4), 399–410. https://doi.org/10.1037/pst0000175

Elliott, R., Slatick, E., & Urman, M. (2000). "So the fear is like a thing … ": A significant empathic exploration event in process – experiential therapy for PTSD. In J. Marques-Teixeira & S. Antunes (Eds.), *Client-centered and experiential psychotherapy* (pp. 179–204). Vale & Vale.

Elliott, R., Watson, J. C., Goldman, R. N., & Greenberg, L. S. (2004). *Learning emotion-focused therapy: The process-experiential approach to change*. American Psychological Association.

Ellison, J. A., Greenberg, L. S., Goldman, R. N., & Angus, L. (2009). Maintenance of gains following experiential therapies for depression. *Journal of Consulting and Clinical Psychology*, *77*(1), 103–112.

Enfield, N. J. (2006). Social consequences of common ground. In N. J. Enfield & S. C. Levinson (Eds.), *Roots of human sociality: Culture, Cognition and Interaction* (pp. 399–430). Berg Publishers.

Enfield, N. J. (2009). Relationship thinking and human pragmatics. *Journal of Pragmatics*, *41*(1), 60–78. https://doi.org/10.1016/j.pragma.2008.09.007

Enfield, N. J. (2017). Elements of agency. In N. J. Enfield & P. Kockelman (Eds.), *Distributed agency* (pp. 3–8). Oxford University Press.

Engle, D., & Holiman, M. (2002). A gestalt-experiential perspective on resistance. *Journal of Clinical Psychology*, *58*(2), 175–183.

Eron, J. B., & Lund, T. W. (1993). How problems evolve and dissolve: Integrating narrative and strategic concepts. *Family Process*, *32*(3), 291–309.

Eubanks, C. F., Muran, J. C., & Safran, J. D. (2015). *Rupture resolution rating system (3rs): Manual*. https://doi.org/10.13140/2.1.1666.8488

Eubanks, C. F., Muran, J. C., & Safran, J. D. (2018). Alliance rupture repair: A meta-analysis. *Psychotherapy*, *55*(4), 508–519. https://doi.org/10.1037/pst0000185

Farber, B. A. (2006). *Self-disclosure in psychotherapy*. Guilford Press.

Farber, B. A., & Doolin, E. M. (2011). Positive regard and affirmation. In J. C. Norcross (Ed.), *Psychotherapy relationships that work: Evidence-based responsiveness* (pp. 168–186). Oxford University Press.

Ferrara, K. W. (1994). *Therapeutic ways with words*. Oxford University Press.

Fine, J. (2006). *Language in psychiatry: A handbook of clinical practice*. Equinox.

Fitzgerald, P., & Leudar, I. (2010). On active listening in person-centred, solution-focused psychotherapy. *Journal of Pragmatics*, *42*(12), 3188–3198. https://doi.org/10.1016/j.pragma.2010.07.007

Ford, J., Hepburn, A., & Parry, R. (2019). What do displays of empathy do in palliative care consultations? *Discourse Studies*, *21*(1), 22–37. https://doi.org/10.1177/1461445618814030

Fox, B. A., & Thompson, S. A. (2010). Responses to *Wh*-questions in English conversation. *Research on Language & Social Interaction*, *43*(2), 133–156. https://doi.org/10.1080/08351811003751680

Frankel, R. M. (2009). Empathy research: A complex challenge. *Patient Education and Counseling*, *75*(1), 1–2. https://doi.org/10.1016/j.pec.2009.02.008

Freud, S. (1999a). *Die Traumdeutung [The interpretation of dreams]*. Fischer Taschenbuch Verlag. First published Wien: Deuticke, 1900.

Freud, S. (1999b). *Studien über Hysterie [Selected papers on hysteria and other psychoneuroses]*. Fischer Taschenbuch Verlag. First published Wien: Deuticke, 1895.

Gaik, F. (1992). Radio talk-show therapy and the pragmatics of possible worlds. In A. Duranti & C. Goodwin (Eds.), *Rethinking context: Language as an interactive phenomenon* (pp. 271–289). Cambridge University Press.

Gardner, R. (2001). *When listeners talk*. John Benjamins.

Gazzillo, F., Genova, F., Fedeli, F., Curtis, J. T., Silberschatz, G., Bush, M., & Dazzi, N. (2019). Patients' unconscious testing activity in psychotherapy: A theoretical and empirical overview. *Psychoanalytic Psychology*, *36*(2), 173–183. https://doi.org/10.1037/pap0000227

Geller, S. M., & Greenberg, L. S. (2002). Therapeutic presence: Therapists' experience of presence in the psychotherapy encounter. *Person-Centered & Experiential Psychotherapies*, *1*(1–2), 71–86.

Gelso, C. J., & Carter, J. A. (1985). The relationship in counseling and psychotherapy: Components, consequences, and theoretical antecedents. *The Counseling Psychologist*, *13*(2), 155–243. https://doi.org/10.1177/0011000085132001

Gergen, K. (1985). The social constructionist movement in modern psychology. *American Psychologist*, *40*(3), 266–275.

Gerhardt, J., & Beyerle, S. (1997). What if Socrates had been a woman?: The therapist's use of acknowledgment tokens (mm-hm, yeah, sure, right …) as a nonreflective means of intersubjective involvement. *Contemporary Psychoanalysis*, *33*(3), 367–410. https://doi.org/10.1080/00107530.1997.10746995

Glenn, P. (2003). *Laughter in interaction* (Vol. 18). Cambridge University Press.

Goffman, E. (1959). *The presentation of self in everyday life*. Anchor Books.

Goffman, E. (1963). *Behavior in public places: Notes on the social organization of gatherings*. Simon & Schuster.

Goffman, E. (1967). *Interaction ritual: Essays on face-to-face interaction*. Pantheon Books.

Goffman, E. (1971). *Relations in public: Microstudies of the social order*. Basic Books.

Goffman, E. (1981). *Forms of talk*. University of Pennsylvania Press.

Goldman, R. N., Greenberg, L. S., & Angus, L. (2006). The effects of adding emotion-focused interventions to the client-centered relationship conditions in the treatment of depression. *Psychotherapy Research, 16*(5), 537–549. https://doi.org/10.1080/10503300600589456

Goodman, G., & Esterly, G. (1988). *The talk book: The intimate science of communicating in close relationships*. Rodale Press.

Goodwin, C. (1986). Between and within: Alternative sequential treatments of continuers and assessments. *Human Studies, 9*(2–3), 205–217. https://doi.org/10.1007/BF00148127

Goodwin, C. (1987). *Forgetfulness as an interactive resource. Social Psychology Quarterly, 50*(2), 115–130.

Goodwin, C. (1996). Transparent vision. In E. Ochs, E. A. Schegloff, & S. A. Thompson (Eds.), *Interaction and grammar* (pp. 370–404). Cambridge University Press.

Goodwin, C. (2007). Participation, stance and affect in the organization of activities. *Discourse & Society, 18*(1), 53–73. https://doi.org/10.1177/0957926507069457

Goodwin, C., & Goodwin, M. H. (1987). Concurrent operations on talk: Notes on the interactive organization of assessments. *IPrA Papers in Pragmatics, 1*(1), 1–54. https://doi.org/10.1075/iprapip.1.1.01goo

Goodwin, C., & Goodwin, M. H. (1990). Interstitial argument. In A. Grimshaw (Ed.), *Conflict talk: Sociolinguistic investigations of arguments in conversations* (pp. 85–117). Cambridge University Press.

Goodwin, C., & Harness Goodwin, M. (2004). Participation. In A. Duranti (Ed.), *A companion to linguistic anthropology* (pp. 222–244). John Wiley & Sons. http://ebookcentral.proquest.com/lib/utoronto/detail.action?docID=214140

Goodwin, M. H. (1990). *He-said-she-said: Talk as social organization among black children*. Indiana University Press.

Granovetter, M. (1983). The strength of weak ties: A network theory revisited. *Sociological Theory, 1*, 201–233. https://doi.org/10.2307/202051

Greenberg, L. S. (1979). Resolving splits: Use of the two chair technique. *Psychotherapy: Theory, Research & Practice, 16*(3), 316–324. https://doi.org/10.1037/h0085895

Greenberg, L. S. (1989). A demonstration with Dr. Leslie Greenberg/Integrative psychotherapy – A six-part series, Part 5. Psychological & Education Films.

Greenberg, L. S. (2002). *Emotion-focused therapy: Coaching clients to work through their feelings*. American Psychological Association. https://doi.org/10.1037/14692-000

Greenberg, L. S. (2004). Emotion-focused therapy. *Clinical Psychology & Psychotherapy, 11*(1), 3–16.

Greenberg, L. S. (2010). Emotion-focused therapy: A clinical synthesis. *FOCUS, 8*(1), 32–42. https://doi.org/10.1176/foc.8.1.foc32

Greenberg, L. S. (2014). The therapeutic relationship in emotion-focused therapy. *Psychotherapy, 51*(3), 350–357.

Greenberg, L. S., & Higgins, H. M. (1980). Effects of two-chair dialogue and focusing on conflict resolution. *Journal of Counseling Psychology, 27*(3), 221–224. https://doi.org/10.1037/0022-0167.27.3.221

Greenberg, L. S., Rice, L. N., & Elliott, R. (1993). *Facilitating emotional change: The moment-by-moment process*. Guilford Press.

Greenberg, L., & Watson, J. (1998). Experiential therapy of depression: Differential effects of client-centered relationship conditions and process experiential interventions. *Psychotherapy Research, 8*(2), 210–224. https://doi.org/10.1080/10503309812331332317

Greenberg, L. S., & Watson, J. C. (2006). *Emotion-focused therapy for depression*. American Psychological Association. https://doi.org/10.1037/11286-000

Greenson, R. R. (1967). *The technique and practice of psychoanalysis* (Vol. I). International Universities Press.

Günthner, S. (1997). Complaint stories. Constructing emotional reciprocity among women. In H. Kotthoff & R. Wodak (Eds.), *Communicating gender in context* (Vol. 42, pp. 179–218). John Benjamins.

Günthner, S. (1999). Polyphony and the "layering of voices" in reported dialogues: An analysis of the use of prosodic devices in everyday reported speech. *Journal of Pragmatics, 31*(5), 685–708. https://doi.org/10.1016/S0378-2166(98)00093-9

Guxholli, A., Voutilainen, L., & Peräkylä, A. (2021). Safeguarding the therapeutic alliance: Managing disaffiliation in the course of work with psychotherapeutic projects. *Frontiers in Psychology*, 11, 596972. https://doi.org/10.3389/fpsyg.2020.596972

Haakana, M. (2001). Laughter as a patient's resource: Dealing with delicate aspects of medical interaction. *Text – Interdisciplinary Journal for the Study of Discourse, 21*(1–2). https://doi.org/10.1515/text.1.21.1-2.187

Hak, T., & de Boer, F. (1996). Formulations in first encounters. *Journal of Pragmatics, 25*(1), 83–99. https://doi.org/10.1016/0378-2166(94)00076-7

Halliday, M. A. K. (1994). *An introduction to functional grammar* (2nd ed.). Arnold.

Hayano, K. (2013). Question design in conversation. In J. Sidnell & T. Stivers (Eds.), *The handbook of conversation analysis* (pp. 395–414). Wiley-Blackwell.

Heinemann, T. (2006). "Will you or can't you?": Displaying entitlement in interrogative requests. *Journal of Pragmatics, 38*(7), 1081–1104. https://doi.org/10.1016/j.pragma.2005.09.013

Hepburn, A. (2004). Crying: Notes on description, transcription, and interaction. *Research on Language and Social Interaction, 37*(3), 251–290. https://doi.org/10.1207/s15327973rlsi3703_1

Hepburn, A., & Bolden, G. B. (2013). The conversation analytic approach to transcription. In J. Sidnell & T. Stivers (Eds.), *The handbook of conversation analysis* (pp. 57–76). John Wiley & Sons. https://doi.org/10.1002/9781118325001.ch4

Hepburn, A., & Potter, J. (2007). Crying receipts: Time, empathy, and institutional practice. *Research on Language and Social Interaction, 40*(1), 89–116. https://doi.org/10.1080/08351810701331299

Hepburn, A., & Potter, J. (2012). Crying and crying responses. In A. Perakyla & M.-L. Sorjonen (Eds.), *Emotion in interaction* (pp. 195–211). Oxford University Press. www.oxfordscholarship.com/view/10.1093/acprof:oso/9780199730735.001.0001/acprof-9780199730735-chapter-9

Heritage, J. (1984). *Garfinkel and ethnomethodology*. Polity Press.

Heritage, J. (2002). Oh-prefaced responses to assessments: A method of modifying agreement/disagreement. In C. Ford, B. A. Fox, & S. A. Thompson (Eds.), *The language of turn and sequence* (pp. 196–224). Oxford University Press.

Heritage, J. (2005). *Cognition in discourse*. In H. te Molder & J. Potter (Eds.), *Conversation and cognition* (pp. 184–202). Cambridge University Press.

Heritage, J. (2010). Questioning in medicine. In A. F. Freed & S. Ehrlich (Eds.), *"Why do you ask?": The function of questions in institutional discourse* (pp. 42–68). Oxford University Press.

Heritage, J. (2011). Territories of knowledge, territories of experience: Empathic moments in interaction. In T. Stivers, L. Mondada, & J. Steensig (Eds.), *The morality of knowledge in conversation* (pp. 159–183). Cambridge University Press. https://doi.org/10.1017/CBO9780511921674.008

Heritage, J. (2012). The epistemic engine: Sequence organization and territories of knowledge. *Research on Language and Social Interaction*, *45*(1), 30–52. https://doi.org/10.1080/08351813.2012.646685

Heritage, J., & Raymond, G. (2005). The terms of agreement: Indexing epistemic authority and subordination in talk-in interaction. *Social Psychology Quarterly*, *68*(1), 15–38.

Heritage, J., & Sefi, S. (1992). Dilemmas of advice: Aspects of the delivery and reception of advice in interactions between health visitors and first-time mothers. In P. Drew & J. Heritage (Eds.), *Talk at work: Interaction in institutional settings* (pp. 359–417). Cambridge University Press.

Heritage, J., & Watson, D. R. (1979). Formulations as conversational objects. In G. Psathas (Ed.), *Everyday language: Studies in ethnomethodology* (pp. 123–162). Irvington Publishers.

Hill, C. E. (1978). Development of a counselor verbal response category system. *Journal of Counseling Psychology*, *25*(5), 461–468.

Hill, C. E. (2020). *Helping skills: Facilitating, exploration, insight, and action* (5th ed.). American Psychological Association.

Hill, C. E., & Knox, S. (2002). Self-disclosure. In J. C. Norcross (Ed.), *Psychotherapy relationships that work: Therapist contributions and responsiveness to patients* (pp. 255–265). Oxford University Press.

Hill, R. A., & Dunbar, R. I. M. (2003). Social network size in humans. *Human Nature*, *14*(1), 53–72. https://doi.org/10.1007/s12110-003-1016-y

Hoey, E. M. (2014). Sighing in interaction: Somatic, semiotic, and social. *Research on Language and Social Interaction*, *47*(2), 175–200. https://doi.org/10.1080/08351813.2014.900229

Holt, E. (2000). Reporting and reacting: Concurrent responses to reported speech. *Research on Language & Social Interaction*, *33*(4), 425–454. https://doi.org/10.1207/S15327973RLSI3304_04

Horwitz, A. V. (2011). Creating an age of depression: The social construction and consequences of the major depression diagnosis. *Society and Mental Health*, 1(1), 41–54.

Horowitz, L. M., Sampson, H., Siegelman, E. Y., Wolfson, A., & Weiss, J. (1975). On the identification of warded-off mental contents: An empirical and methodological contribution. *Journal of Abnormal Psychology*, *84*(5), 545–558. http://dx.doi.org/10.1037/h0077139

Horvath, A. O. (2006). The alliance in context: Accomplishments, challenges, and future directions. *Psychotherapy: Theory, Research, Practice, Training*, *43*(3), 258–263. https://doi.org/10.1037/0033-3204.43.3.258
Horvath, A. O., & Bedi, R. P. (2002). The alliance. In J. C. Norcross (Ed.), *Psychotherapy relationships that work: Therapist contributions and responsiveness to patients* (pp. 37–69). Oxford University Press.
Horvath, A. O., & Symonds, B. D. (1991). Relation between working alliance and outcome in psychotherapy: A meta-analysis. *Journal of Counseling Psychology*, *38*(2), 139.
Horvath, A. O., Re, A. C. D., Flückiger, C., & Symonds, D. (2011). Alliance in individual psychotherapy. In J. C. Norcross (Ed.), *Psychotherapy relationships that work: Evidence-based responsiveness* (2nd ed., pp. 25–69). Oxford University Press. https://doi.org/10.1093/acprof:oso/9780199737208.003.0002
Hutchby, I. (2002). Resisting the incitement to talk in child counselling: Aspects of the utterance "I don't know." *Discourse Studies*, *4*(2), 147–168. https://doi.org/10.1177/14614456020040020201
Hutchby, I. (2005). "Active listening": Formulations and the elicitation of feelings-talk in child counselling. *Research on Language and Social Interaction*, *38*(3), 303–329. https://doi.org/10.1207/s15327973rlsi3803_4
Hutchby, I. (2007). *The discourse of child counselling*. John Benjamins.
Jaffe, A. (2009). Introduction: The sociolinguistics of stance. In A. Jaffe (Ed.), *Stance: Sociolinguistic perspectives* (pp. 3–28). Oxford University Press.
Janusz, B., Bergmann, J. R., Matusiak, F., & Peräkylä, A. (2021). Practices of claiming control and independence in couple therapy with narcissism. *Frontiers in Psychology*, *11*, 596842. https://doi.org/10.3389/fpsyg.2020.596842
Jefferson, G. (1978). Sequential aspects of storytelling in conversation. In J. Schenkein (Ed.), *Studies in the organization of conversational interaction* (pp. 219–248). Academic Press.
Jefferson, G. (1984). Notes on a systematic deployment of the acknowledgement tokens "yeah" and "mmhm". *Papers in Linguistics*, *17*(2), 197–216.
Jefferson, G. (1986). Notes on "latency" in overlap onset. *Human Studies*, *9*(2–3), 153–183.
Jefferson, G. (1988). *On the sequential organization of troubles-talk in ordinary conversation. Social Problems*, *35*(4), 418–441.
Jefferson, G. (1990). List construction as a task and resource. In G. Psathas (Ed.), *Studies in ethnomethodology and conversation analysis* (pp. 63–92). University Press of America.
Jefferson, G. (1993). Caveat speaker: Preliminary notes on recipient topic-shift implicature. *Research on Language and Social Interaction*, *26*(1), 1–30.
Jefferson, G., & Lee, J. (1980). *On the sequential organization of troubles-talk in ordinary conversation*. (End of grant report to the (British) Social Science Research Council on the analysis of conversations in which "troubles" and "anxieties" are expressed.)
Kendon, A. (1990). *Conducting interaction: Patterns of behavior in focused encounters* (Vol. 7). Cambridge University Press.
Kendon, A. (2004). *Gesture: Visible action as utterance*. Cambridge University Press.
Kim, H. (2002). The form and function of next-turn repetition in English conversation. *Language Research*, 38(1), 51–81.

Kita, S., & Ide, S. (2007). Nodding, aizuchi, and final particles in Japanese conversation: How conversation reflects the ideology of communication and social relationships. *Journal of Pragmatics*, *39*(7), 1242–1254. https://doi.org/10.1016/j.pragma.2007.02.009

Kolden, G. G., Klein, M. H., Wang, C.-C., & Austin, S. B. (2011). Congruence/genuineness. In J. C. Norcross (Ed.), *Psychotherapy relationships that work: Evidence-based responsiveness* (pp. 187–202). Oxford University Press.

Kondratyuk, N., & Peräkylä, A. (2011). Therapeutic work with the present moment: A comparative conversation analysis of existential and cognitive therapies. *Psychotherapy Research*, *21*(3), 316–330. https://doi.org/10.1080/10503307.2011.570934

Koshik, I. (2002). A conversation analytic study of yes/no questions which convey reversed polarity assertions. *Journal of Pragmatics*, *34*(12), 1851–1877. https://doi.org/10.1016/S0378-2166(02)00057-7

Kotthoff, H. (1993). Disagreement and concession in disputes: On the context sensitivity of preference structures. *Language in Society*, *22*(2), 193–216.

Kupetz, M. (2014). Empathy displays as interactional achievements – Multimodal and sequential aspects. *Journal of Pragmatics*, *61*, 4–34. https://doi.org/10.1016/j.pragma.2013.11.006

Kuroshima, S., & Iwata, N. (2016). On displaying empathy: Dilemma, category, and experience. *Research on Language and Social Interaction*, *49*(2), 92–110. https://doi.org/10.1080/08351813.2016.1164395

Labov, W. (1972). *Language in the inner city: Studies in the Black English vernacular*. University of Pennsylvania Press.

Labov, W., & Fanshel, D. (1977). *Therapeutic discourse: Psychotherapy as conversation*. Academic Press.

Labov, W., & Waletzky, J. (1967). Narrative analysis: Oral narratives of personal experience. In J. Helm (Ed.), *Essays on the verbal and visual arts* (pp. 12–44). University of Washington Press.

Landmark, A. M. D., Gulbrandsen, P., & Svennevig, J. (2015). Whose decision? Negotiating epistemic and deontic rights in medical treatment decisions. *Journal of Pragmatics*, *78*, 54–69. https://doi.org/10.1016/j.pragma.2014.11.007

Lerner, G. H. (1989). Notes on overlap management in conversation: The case of delayed completion. *Western Journal of Speech Communication*, *53*(2), 167–177. https://doi.org/10.1080/10570318909374298

Lerner, G. H. (1991). On the syntax of sentences-in-progress. *Language in Society*, *20*, 441–458.

Lerner, G. H. (1992). Assisted storytelling: Deploying shared knowledge as a practical matter. *Qualitative Sociology*, 15(3), 247–271.

Lerner, G. H. (1996). On the "semi-permeable" character of grammatical units in conversation: Conditional entry into turn space of another speaker. In E. Ochs, E. A. Schegloff, & S. A. Thompson (Eds.), *Interaction and grammar* (pp. 238–276). Cambridge University Press.

Lerner, G. H. (2004). Collaborative turn sequences. In G. H. Lerner (Ed.), *Conversation analysis: Studies from the first generation* (Vol. 125, pp. 225–256). John Benjamins.

Leudar, I., Antaki, C., & Barnes, R. (2006). When psychotherapists disclose personal information about themselves to clients. *Communication & Medicine*, *3*(1), 27–41.

Levinson, S. C. (1983). *Pragmatics*. Cambridge University Press.

Levinson, S. C. (1992). Activity types and language. In P. Drew & J. Heritage (Eds.), *Talk at work: Interaction in institutional settings* (pp. 66–100). Cambridge University Press.

Lietaer, G. (1993). Authenticity, congruence and transparency. In D. Brazier (Ed.), *Beyond Carl Rogers* (pp. 17–46). Constable and Company.

Lindström, A., & Sorjonen, M.-L. (2013). Affiliation in conversation. In J. Sidnell & T. Stivers (Eds.), *The handbook of conversation analysis* (pp. 350–369). Wiley-Blackwell.

Mackay, B. (2011). *Two-you work: How to work with the self in conflict* (2nd ed.). Write Room Press.

MacMartin, C. (2008). Resisting optimistic questions in narrative and solution-focused therapies. In A. Perakyla, C. Antaki, S. Vehviläinen, & I. Leudar (Eds.), *Conversation analysis and psychotherapy* (pp. 80–99). Cambridge University Press.

Malinowski, B. (1923). The problem of meaning in primitive languages. In C. K. Ogden & I. A. Richards (Eds.), *The meaning of meaning* (pp. 296–336). Harcourt, Brace and World.

Mandelbaum, J. (1989). Interpersonal activities in conversational storytelling. *Western Journal of Speech Communication, 53*(2), 114–126. https://doi.org/10.1080/10570318909374295

Mandelbaum, J. (2003). Interactive methods for constructing relationships. In P. Glenn, C. D. Lebaron, & J. Mandelbaum (Eds.), *Studies in language and social interaction: In honor of Robert Hopper* (pp. 207–219). Lawrence Erlbaum.

Mandelbaum, J. (2013). Storytelling in conversation. In J. Sidnell & T. Stivers (Eds.), *The handbook of conversation analysis* (pp. 492–507). Wiley-Blackwell.

Maynard, D. W. (2003). *Bad news, good news: Conversational order in everyday talk and clinical settings*. University of Chicago Press.

McLeod, J. (1997). *Narrative and psychotherapy*. Sage.

McLeod, J. (1999). A narrative social constructionist approach to therapeutic empathy. *Counselling Psychology Quarterly, 12*(4), 377–394. https://doi.org/10.1080/09515079908254107

McNamee, S., & Gergen, K. J. (Eds.). (1992). *Therapy as social construction* (pp. xi, 220). Sage.

McVittie, C., Craig, S., & Temple, M. (2020). A conversation analysis of communicative changes in a time-limited psychotherapy group for mothers with post-natal depression. *Psychotherapy Research, 30*(8), 1048–1060.

Mondada, L. (2018). Multiple temporalities of language and body in interaction: Challenges for transcribing multimodality. *Research on Language and Social Interaction, 51*(1), 85–106. https://doi.org/10.1080/08351813.2018.1413878

Muntigl, P. (2004). *Narrative counselling: Social and linguistic processes of change* (Vol. 11). John Benjamins.

Muntigl, P. (2016). Storytelling, depression, and psychotherapy. In M. O'Reilly & J. N. Lester (Eds.), *The Palgrave handbook of adult mental health* (pp. 577–596). Palgrave Macmillan.

Muntigl, P. (2020). Managing distress over time in psychotherapy: Guiding the client in and through intense emotional work. *Frontiers in Psychology, 10*, 3052. https://doi.org/10.3389/fpsyg.2019.03052

Muntigl, P., & Choi, K. T. (2010). Not remembering as a practical epistemic resource in couples therapy. *Discourse Studies, 12*(3), 331–356. https://doi.org/10.1177/1461445609358516

Muntigl, P., Chubak, L., & Angus, L. (2017). Entering chair work in psychotherapy: An interactional structure for getting emotion-focused talk underway. *Journal of Pragmatics*, *117*, 168–189. https://doi.org/10.1016/j.pragma.2017.06.016

Muntigl, P., & Horvath, A. (2005). Language, psychotherapy and client change: An interdisciplinary perspective. In R. Wodak & P. Chilton (Eds.), *A new agenda for (Critical) Discourse Analysis* (pp. 213–239). John Benjamins.

Muntigl, P., & Horvath, A. O. (2014a). "I can see some sadness in your eyes": When experiential therapists notice a client's affectual display. *Research on Language and Social Interaction*, *47*(2), 89–108. https://doi.org/10.1080/08351813.2014.900212

Muntigl, P., & Horvath, A. O. (2014b). The therapeutic relationship in action: How therapists and clients co-manage relational disaffiliation. *Psychotherapy Research*, *24*(3), 327–345. https://doi.org/10.1080/10503307.2013.807525

Muntigl, P., Horvath, A. O., Bänninger-Huber, E., & Angus, L. (2020a). Responding to self-criticism in psychotherapy. *Psychotherapy Research*, *30*(6), 800–814. https://doi.org/10.1080/10503307.2019.1686191

Muntigl, P., Horvath, A. O., Chubak, L., & Angus, L. (2020b). Getting to "yes": overcoming client reluctance to engage in chair work. *Frontiers in Psychology*, *11*, 582856. https://doi.org/10.3389/fpsyg.2020.582856

Muntigl, P., Knight, N., & Watkins, A. (2012). Working to keep aligned in psychotherapy: Using nods as a dialogic resource to display affiliation. *Language and Dialogue*, *2*(1), 9–27. https://doi.org/10.1075/ld.2.1.01mun

Muntigl, P., Knight, N., & Watkins, A. (2014). Empathic practices in client-centred psychotherapies: Displaying understanding and affiliation with clients. In E.-M. Graf, M. Sator, & T. Spranz-Fogasy (Eds.), *Pragmatics & beyond new series* (Vol. 252, pp. 33–57). John Benjamins. https://doi.org/10.1075/pbns.252.03mun

Muntigl, P., Knight, N., Watkins, A., Horvath, A. O., & Angus, L. (2013). Active retreating: Person-centered practices to repair disaffiliation in therapy. *Journal of Pragmatics*, *53*, 1–20. https://doi.org/10.1016/j.pragma.2013.03.019

Muntigl, P., & Turnbull, W. (1998). Conversational structure and facework in arguing. *Journal of Pragmatics*, *29*(3), 225–256. https://doi.org/10.1016/S0378-2166(97)00048-9

Muntigl, P., & Zabala, L. H. (2008). Expandable responses: How clients get prompted to say more during psychotherapy. *Research on Language & Social Interaction*, *41*(2), 187–226. https://doi.org/10.1080/08351810802028738

Newman, C. F. (2002). A cognitive perspective on resistance in psychotherapy. *Journal of Clinical Psychology*, *58*(2), 165–174.

Norcross, J. C. (2002). *Psychotherapy relationships that work: Therapist contributions and responsiveness to patients*. Oxford University Press.

Norcross, J. C. (Ed.). (2011). *Psychotherapy relationships that work: Evidence-based responsiveness* (2nd ed.). Oxford University Press.

Norcross, J. C., & Lambert, M. J. (2018). Psychotherapy relationships that work III. *Psychotherapy*, *55*(4), 303–315. https://doi.org/10.1037/pst0000193

O'Donnell, K. (1990). Difference and dominance: How labor and management talk conflict. In A. Grimshaw (Ed.), *Conflict talk: Sociolinguistic investigations of arguments in conversations* (pp. 210–240). Cambridge University Press.

Oloff, F. (2018). Revisiting delayed completions: The retrospective management of co-participant action. In A. Deppermann & J. Streeck (Eds.), *Pragmatics & beyond new series* (Vol. 293, pp. 123–160). John Benjamins. https://doi.org/10.1075/pbns.293.04olo

Pain, J. (2009). *Not just talking: Conversational analysis, Harvey Sacks' gift to psychotherapy*. Karnac.

Paivio, S., & Pascual-Leone, A. (2010). *Emotion-focused therapy for complex trauma: An integrative approach. 2010* (Vol. 4). American Psychological Association.

Pawelczyk, J. (2011). *Talk as therapy: Psychotherapy in a linguistic perspective* (Vol. 7). Walter de Gruyter.

Pennebaker, J. W., & Seagal, J. D. (1999). Forming a story: The health benefits of narrative. *Journal of Clinical Psychology, 55*, 1243–1254.

Peräkylä, A. (2004). Making links in psychoanalytic interpretations: A conversation analytical perspective. *Psychotherapy Research, 14*(3), 289–307. https://doi.org/10.1093/ptr/kph026

Peräkylä, A. (2005). Patients' responses to interpretations: A dialogue between conversation analysis and psychoanalytic theory. *Communication & Medicine, 2*(2), 163–176.

Peräkylä, A. (2011). After interpretation: Third-position utterances in psychoanalysis. *Research on Language and Social Interaction, 44*(3), 288–316.

Peräkylä, A. (2015). From narcissism to face work: Two views on the self in social interaction. *American Journal of Sociology, 121*(2), 445–474. https://doi.org/10.1086/682282

Peräkylä, A. (2019). Conversation analysis and psychotherapy: Identifying transformative sequences. *Research on Language and Social Interaction, 52*(3), 257–280.

Peräkylä, A., & Silverman, D. (1991). Owning experience: Describing the experience of other persons. *Text-Interdisciplinary Journal for the Study of Discourse, 11*(3), 441–480.

Peräkylä, A., Antaki, C., Vehviläinen, S., & Leudar, I. (Eds.). (2008). *Conversation analysis and psychotherapy*. Cambridge University Press. http://myaccess.library.utoronto.ca/login?url=https://doi.org/10.1017/CBO9780511490002

Perls, F. (1973). *The Gestalt approach & eye witness to therapy*. Science & Behavior Books.

Perls, F., Hefferline, G., & Goodman, P. (1951). *Gestalt therapy: Excitement and growth in the human personality*. Souvenir Press.

Pomerantz, A. (1980). Telling my side: "Limited access" as a "fishing" device. *Sociological Inquiry, 50*(3–4), 186–198. https://doi.org/10.1111/j.1475-682X.1980.tb00020.x

Pomerantz, A. (1984). Agreeing and disagreeing with assessments: Some features of preferred/dispreferred turn shaped. In J. M. Atkinson & J. Heritage (Eds.), *Structures of social action: Studies in conversation analysis* (pp. 57–101). Cambridge University Press.

Pomerantz, A. (1986). Extreme case formulations: A way of legitimizing claims. *Human Studies, 9*(2), 219–229.

Pomerantz, A., & Heritage, J. (2013). Preference. In *The handbook of conversation analysis* (pp. 210–228). John Wiley & Sons. https://doi.org/10.1002/9781118325001.ch11

Pomerantz, A., & Mandelbaum, J. (2005). Conversation analytic approaches to the relevance and uses of relationship categories in interaction. In K. Fitch & R. Sanders (Eds.), *Handbook of language and social interaction* (pp. 149–171). Lawrence Erlbaum.

Pos, A. E., & Greenberg, L. S. (2007). Emotion-focused therapy: The transforming power of affect. *Journal of Contemporary Psychotherapy, 37*(1), 25–31. https://doi.org/10.1007/s10879-006-9031-z

Pos, A. E., & Greenberg, L. S. (2012). Organizing awareness and increasing emotion regulation: Revising chair work in emotion-focused therapy for borderline personality disorder. *Journal of Personality Disorders*, 26(1), 84–107.

Pudlinski, C. (2005). Doing empathy and sympathy: Caring responses to troubles tellings on a peer support line. *Discourse Studies*, *7*(3), 267–288. https://doi.org/10.1177/1461445605052177

Quirk, R., Greenbaum, S., Leech, G., & Svartvik, J. (1985). *A comprehensive grammar of the English language*. Longman.

Rae, J. (2008). Lexical substitution as a therapeutic resource. In A. Perakyla, C. Antaki, S. Vehviläinen, & I. Leudar (Eds.), *Conversation analysis and psychotherapy* (pp. 62–79). Cambridge University Press.

Raymond, G. (2003). Grammar and social organization: Yes/no interrogatives and the structure of responding. *American Sociological Review*, *68*(6), 939. https://doi.org/10.2307/1519752

Rennie, D. L. (1998). *Person-centred counselling: An experiential approach*. Sage.

Rogers, C. R. (1951). *Client centered therapy*. Constable.

Rogers, C. R. (1957). The necessary and sufficient conditions of therapeutic personality change. *Journal of Consulting Psychology*, *21*(2), 95–103. https://doi.org/10.1037/h0045357

Rossi, G. (2012). Bilateral and unilateral requests: The use of imperatives and *Mi X?* Interrogatives in Italian. *Discourse Processes*, *49*(5), 426–458. https://doi.org/10.1080/0163853X.2012.684136

Roth, A. L. (2002). Social epistemology in broadcast news interviews. *Language in Society*, *31*(3), 355–381. https://doi.org/10.1017/S0047404502020262

Ruusuvuori, J. (2005). "Empathy" and "sympathy" in action: Attending to patients' troubles in Finnish homeopathic and general practice consultations. *Social Psychology Quarterly*, *68*(3), 204–222. https://doi.org/10.1177/019027250506800302

Ruusuvuori, J., & Peräkylä, A. (2009). Facial and verbal expressions in assessing stories and topics. *Research on Language & Social Interaction*, *42*(4), 377–394. https://doi.org/10.1080/08351810903296499

Sacks, H. (1973). *Schegloff lectures XV: min 45:10–47:25*. QISCA: The International Society for Conversation Analysis. www.conversationanalysis.org/schegloff-video-lectures/

Sacks, H. (1974). An analysis of the course of a joke's telling in conversation. In R. Bauman & J. Sherzer (Eds.), *Explorations in the ethnography of speaking* (pp. 337–353). Cambridge University Press.

Sacks, H. (1987). On the preferences for agreement and contiguity in sequences in conversation. In G. Button & J. R. E. Lee (Eds.), *Talk and social organisation* (pp. 54–69). Multilingual Matters.

Sacks, H. (1995a). *Lectures on conversation* (vol. 1, G. Jefferson, Ed.). Wiley-Blackwell.

Sacks, H. (1995b). *Lectures on conversation* (vol. 2, G. Jefferson, Ed.). Wiley-Blackwell.

Sacks, H., Schegloff, E. A., & Jefferson, G. (1974). A simplest systematics for the organization of turn-taking for conversation. *Language*, *50*(4), 696. https://doi.org/10.2307/412243

Safran, J. D., & Muran, J. C. (1996). The resolution of ruptures in the therapeutic alliance. *Journal of Consulting and Clinical Psychology*, *64*(3), 447–458.

Safran, J. D., & Muran, J. C. (2006). Has the concept of the therapeutic alliance outlived its usefulness? *Psychotherapy: Theory, Research, Practice, Training*, *43*(3), 286.

Safran, J. D., Muran, J. C., & Eubanks-Carter, C. (2011a). Repairing alliance ruptures. In J. C. Norcross (Ed.), *Psychotherapy relationships that work: Evidence-based responsiveness* (2nd ed., pp. 224–238). Oxford University Press.

Safran, J. D., Muran, J. C., & Eubanks-Carter, C. (2011b). Repairing alliance ruptures. *Psychotherapy*, *48*(1), 80–87. https://doi.org/10.1037/a0022140

Safran, J. D., Muran, J. C., Samstag, L. W., & Stevens, C. (2001). Repairing alliance ruptures. *Psychotherapy: Theory, Research, Practice, Training*, *38*(4), 406–412.

Sanders, R. (2012). The representation of self through the dialogic properties of talk and conduct. *Language and Dialogue*, *2*(1), 28–40. https://doi.org/10.1075/ld.2.1.02san

Scarvaglieri, C. (2020). First Encounters in Psychotherapy: Relationship-Building and the Pursuit of Institutional Goals. *Frontiers in Psychology*, 11, 585038. https://doi .org/10.3389/fpsyg.2020.585038

Schegloff, E. A. (1968). Sequencing in conversational openings. *American Anthropologist*, *70*(6), 1075–1095.

Schegloff, E. A. (1982). Discourse as an interactional achievement: Some uses of "uh huh" and other things that come between sentences. In D. Tannen (Ed.), *Georgetown University Round Table on Languages and Linguistics (GURT) 1981: Analyzing discourse: Text and talk* (Vol. 71, pp. 71–93). Georgetown University Press.

Schegloff, E. A. (1987). Between macro and micro: Contexts and other connections. In J. Alexander, R. Giesen, R. Munch, & N. Smelser (Eds.), *The micro-macro link* (pp. 207–234). University of California Press.

Schegloff, E. A. (1988). Goffman and the analysis of conversation. In P. Drew & A. Wootton (Eds.), *Erving Goffman: Exploring the interaction order* (pp. 89–135). Northeastern University Press.

Schegloff, E. A. (1992). On talk and its institutional occasions. In P. Drew & J. Heritage (Eds.), *Talk at work: Interaction in institutional settings* (Vol. 101, pp. 101–134). Cambridge University Press.

Schegloff, E. A. (1997a). "Narrative analysis" thirty years later. *Journal of Narrative and Life History*, *7*(1–4), 97–106.

Schegloff, E. A. (1997b). Whose text? Whose context? *Discourse & Society*, *8*(2), 165–187.

Schegloff, E. A. (2000). On granularity. *Annual Review of Sociology*, *26*(1), 715–720. https://doi.org/10.1146/annurev.soc.26.1.715

Schegloff, E. A. (2007). *Sequence organization in interaction: A primer in conversation analysis*. Cambridge University Press.

Schegloff, E. A., & Lerner, G. H. (2009). Beginning to respond: Well-prefaced responses to *Wh*-questions. *Research on Language and Social Interaction*, *42*(2), 91–115. https://doi.org/10.1080/08351810902864511

Schegloff, E. A., & Sacks, H. (1973). Opening up Closings. *Semiotica*, *8*(4). https://doi .org/10.1515/semi.1973.8.4.289

Schegloff, E. A., Jefferson, G., & Sacks, H. (1977). The preference for self-correction in the organization of repair in conversation. *Language*, *53*(2), 361–382. https://doi .org/10.1353/lan.1977.0041

Schiffrin, D. (1981). Tense variation in narrative. *Language*, *57*(1), 45–62.

Schiffrin, D. (1984). Jewish argument as sociability. *Language in Society*, *13*(03), 311. https://doi.org/10.1017/S0047404500010526

Sharrock, W. (1974). On owning knowledge. In R. Turner (Ed.), *Ethnomethodology* (pp. 45–53). Penguin.

Shaw, C., Hepburn, A., & Potter, J. (2013). Having the last laugh: On post-completion laughter particles. In P. Glenn & E. Holt (Eds.), *Studies of laughter in interaction* (pp. 91–106). Bloomsbury Academic.

Shotter, J. (1993). *Conversational realities: Constructing life through language* (Vol. 11). Sage.

Sidnell, J. (2006). Coordinating gesture, talk, and gaze in reenactments. *Research on Language & Social Interaction*, *39*(4), 377–409. https://doi.org/10.1207/s15327973rlsi3904_2

Sidnell, J. (2010). *Conversation analysis: An introduction*. Wiley-Blackwell.

Sidnell, J., & Stivers, T. (Eds.). (2013). *The handbook of conversation analysis*. Wiley-Blackwell. http://myaccess.library.utoronto.ca/login?url=http://books.scholarsportal.info/uri/ebooks/ebooks2/wiley/2013-01-21/1/9781118325001

Silverman, D. (1997). *Discourses of counselling: HIV counselling as social interaction*. Sage.

Smith, K. (2014). Mental health: A world of depression. *Nature*, 515(7526), article 7526. https://doi.org/10.1038/515180a.

Smoliak, O., MacMartin, C., Hepburn, A., Le Couteur, A., Elliott, R., & Quinn-Nilas, C. (2021). Authority in therapeutic interaction: A conversation analytic study. *Journal of Marital and Family Therapy*, jmft.12471. https://doi.org/10.1111/jmft.12471

Sorjonen, M.-L., & Peräkylä, A. (2012). Introduction. In A. Perakyla & M.-L. Sorjonen (Eds.), *Emotion in interaction* (pp. 3–15). Oxford University Press.

Sorjonen, M.-L., Raevaara, L. A., & Couper-Kuhlen, E. (2017). Imperative turns at talk: An introduction. In M.-L. Sorjonen, L. A. Raevaara, & E. Couper-Kuhlen (Eds.), *Imperative turns at talk: The design of directives in action* (pp. 1–24). John Benjamins.

Stevanovic, M., & Peräkylä, A. (2014). Three orders in the organization of human action: On the interface between knowledge, power, and emotion in interaction and social relations. *Language in Society*, *43*(2), 185–207. https://doi.org/10.1017/S0047404514000037

Stevanovic, M., & Svennevig, J. (2015). Introduction: Epistemics and deontics in conversational directives. *Journal of Pragmatics*, *78*, 1–6. https://doi.org/10.1016/j.pragma.2015.01.008

Stiles, W. B. (1992). *Describing talk: A taxonomy of verbal response modes*. Sage.

Stiles, W. B., & Horvath, A. O. (2017). Appropriate responsiveness as a contribution to therapist effects. In L. G. Castonguay, & C. E. Hills (Eds.), *How and why are some therapists better than others?: Understanding therapist effects* (pp. 71–84). American Psychological Association. https://doi.org/10.1037/0000034-005

Stiles, W. B., Glick, M. J., Osatuke, K., Hardy, G. E., Shapiro, D. A., Agnew-Davies, R., Rees, A., & Barkham, M. (2004). Patterns of alliance development and the rupture-repair hypothesis: Are productive relationships U-shaped or V-shaped? *Journal of Counseling Psychology*, *51*(1), 81–92. https://doi.org/10.1037/0022-0167.51.1.81

Stivers, T. (2005a). Modified repeats: One method for asserting primary rights from second position. *Research on Language and Social Interaction*, *38*(2), 131–158.

Stivers, T. (2005b). Parent resistance to physicians' treatment recommendations: One resource for initiating a negotiation of the treatment decision. *Health Communication, 18*(1), 41–74. https://doi.org/10.1207/s15327027hc1801_3

Stivers, T. (2008). Stance, alignment, and affiliation during storytelling: When nodding is a token of affiliation. *Research on Language and Social Interaction, 41*(1), 31–57. https://doi.org/10.1080/08351810701691123

Stivers, T. (2010). An overview of the question–response system in American English conversation. *Journal of Pragmatics, 42*(10), 2772–2781. https://doi.org/10.1016/j.pragma.2010.04.011

Stivers, T. (2011). Morality and question design: "Of course" as contesting a presupposition of askability. In T. Stivers, L. Mondada, & J. Steensig (Eds.), *The morality of knowledge in conversation* (Vol. 29, pp. 82–106). Cambridge University Press.

Stivers, T., & Hayashi, M. (2010). Transformative answers: One way to resist a question's constraints. *Language in Society, 39*(1), 1–25. https://doi.org/10.1017/S0047404509990637

Stivers, T., & Robinson, J. D. (2006). A preference for progressivity in interaction. *Language in Society, 35*(03), 367–392. https://doi.org/10.1017/S0047404506060179

Stivers, T., & Rossano, F. (2010). Mobilizing response. *Research on Language and Social Interaction, 43*(1), 3–31.

Stivers, T., Mondada, L., & Steensig. (2011). Knowledge, morality and affiliation in social interaction. In T. Stivers, J. Steensig, & L. Mondada (Eds.), *The morality of knowledge in conversation* (pp. 3–24). Cambridge University Press.

Strong, T., & Smoliak, O. (2018). Introduction to discursive research and discursive therapies. In O. Smoliak & T. Strong (Eds.), *Therapy as Discourse: Practice and research* (pp. 1–18). Palgrave Macmillan.

Suchman, A. L., Markakis, K., Beckman, H. B., & Frankel, R. (1997). A model of empathic communication in the medical interview. *Jama, 277*(8), 678–682.

Sutherland, O., Peräkylä, A., & Elliott, R. (2014). Conversation analysis of the two-chair self-soothing task in emotion-focused therapy. *Psychotherapy Research, 24*(6), 738–751. https://doi.org/10.1080/10503307.2014.885146

Tannen, D. (1986). Introducing constructed dialogue in Greek and American conversational and literary narrative. In F. Coulmas (Ed.), *Direct and indirect speech* (Vol. 31, pp. 311–332). Mouton de Gruyter.

Tannen, D. (2007). *Talking voices: Repetition, dialogue, and imagery in conversational discourse* (Vol. 26). Cambridge University Press.

Tannen, D. (1994). The relativity of linguistic strategies: Rethinking power and solidarity in gender and dominance. In *Gender and Discourse* (pp. 19–52). Oxford University Press. https://doi.org/10.1007/978-1-349-92299-4_12

Vehviläinen, S. (2003). Preparing and delivering interpretations in psychoanalytic interaction. *Text & Talk, 23*(4), 573–606.

Vehviläinen, S. (2008). Identifying and managing resistance in psychoanalytic interaction. In A. Peräkylä, C. Antaki, S. Vehviläinen, & I. Leudar (Eds.), *Conversation analysis and psychotherapy* (pp. 120–138). Cambridge University Press. http://myaccess.library.utoronto.ca/login?url=https://doi.org/10.1017/CBO9780511490002

Vehviläinen, S., Peräkylä, A., Antaki, C., & Leudar, I. (2008). A review of conversational practices in psychotherapy. In A. Perakyla, C. Antaki, S. Vehviläinen, & I. Leudar (Eds.), *Conversation analysis and psychotherapy* (pp. 188–197). Cambridge University Press.

Voutilainen, L., Peräkylä, A., & Ruusuvuori, J. (2011). Therapeutic change in interaction: Conversation analysis of a transforming sequence. *Psychotherapy Research*, *21*(3), 348–365.

Vranjes, J., Bot, H., Feyaerts, K., & Brône, G. (2019). Affiliation in interpreter-mediated therapeutic talk: On the relationship between gaze and head nods. *Interpreting. International Journal of Research and Practice in Interpreting*, *21*(2), 220–244. https://doi.org/10.1075/intp.00028.vra

Wagner-Moore, L. (2004). Gestalt therapy: Past, present, theory, and research. *Psychotherapy: Theory, Research, Practice, Training*, *41*(2), 180–189.

Watson, J. C., & Greenberg, L. S. (2000). Alliance ruptures and repairs in experiential therapy. *Journal of Clinical Psychology*, *56*(2), 175–186. https://doi.org/10.1002/(SICI)1097-4679(200002)56:2<175::AID-JCLP4>3.0.CO;2-5

Watzlawick, B., Beavin, J., & Jackson, D. D. (1967). *Pragmatics of human communication*. W. W. Norton.

Watzlawick, P., Weakland, J. H., & Fisch, R. (1974). *Change: Principles of problem formation and problem resolution*. W. W. Norton.

Weiste, E. (2015). Describing therapeutic projects across sequences: Balancing between supportive and disagreeing interventions. *Journal of Pragmatics*, *80*, 22–43. https://doi.org/10.1016/j.pragma.2015.02.001

Weiste, E., & Peräkylä, A. (2013). A comparative conversation analytic study of formulations in psychoanalysis and cognitive psychotherapy. *Research on Language and Social Interaction*, *46*(4), 299–321. https://doi.org/10.1080/08351813.2013.839093

Weiste, E., & Peräkylä, A. (2014). Prosody and empathic communication in psychotherapy interaction. *Psychotherapy Research*, *24*(6), 687–701. https://doi.org/10.1080/10503307.2013.879619

Weiste, E., Voutilainen, L., & Peräkylä, A. (2016). Epistemic asymmetries in psychotherapy interaction: Therapists' practices for displaying access to clients' inner experiences. *Sociology of Health & Illness*, *38*(4), 645–661. https://doi.org/10.1111/1467-9566.12384

Whalen, M. R., & Zimmerman, D. H. (1990). Describing trouble: Practical epistemology in citizen calls to the police. *Language in Society*, *19*(4), 465–492.

White, M., & Epston, D. (1990). *Narrative means to therapeutic ends*. W. W. Norton. http://www.amazon.ca/exec/obidos/redirect?tag=citeulike09-20&path=ASIN/0393700984

Williams, J. M. G., & Scott, J. (1988). Autobiographical memory in depression. *Psychological Medicine*, *18*(3), 689–695. https://doi.org/10.1017/S0033291700008370

Williams, J. M. G., Barnhofer, T., Crane, C., Herman, D., Raes, F., Watkins, E., & Dalgleish, T. (2007). Autobiographical memory specificity and emotional disorder. *Psychological Bulletin*, *133*(1), 122–148. https://doi.org/10.1037/0033-2909.133.1.122

Wiseman, H., & Tishby, O. (2015). *The therapeutic relationship: Innovative investigations*. Routledge.

Wootton, A. J. (2012). Distress in adult-child interaction. In A. Perakyla & M.-L. Sorjonen (Eds.), *Emotion in interaction*. Oxford University Press. https://doi.org/10.1093/acprof:oso/9780199730735.001.0001

World Health Organization. (2017). *Depression and other common mental disorders: Global health estimates*. Global Health Estimates.

Wright, K. B., Rains, S., & Banas, J. (2010). Weak-tie support network preference and perceived life stress among participants in health-related, computer-mediated support groups. *Journal of Computer-Mediated Communication, 15*(4), 606–624. https://doi.org/10.1111/j.1083-6101.2009.01505.x

Wynn, R., & Wynn, M. (2006). Empathy as an interactionally achieved phenomenon in psychotherapy. *Journal of Pragmatics, 38*(9), 1385–1397. https://doi.org/10.1016/j.pragma.2005.09.008

Yablonsky, L. (1976). *Psychodrama: Resolving emotional problems through role-playing*. Basic Books.

# Index

Printed in the USA
CPSIA information can be obtained
at www.ICGtesting.com
LVHW021520111123
763669LV00006B/106

9 781107 098428